The European Challenges Post-1992

The European Challenges Post-1992

Shaping Factors, Shaping Actors

Edited by
Alexis Jacquemin and David Wright

Preface by
Jacques Delors

Edward Elgar

Published by

Edward Elgar Publishing Limited
Gower House
Croft Road
Aldershot
Hants GU11 3HR
England

Edward Elgar Publishing Company
Old Post Road
Brookfield
Vermont 05036
USA

A CIP catalogue record for this book
is available from the British Library

ISBN 1 85278 829 1
      1 85278 830 5 (paperback)

Printed in Great Britain at the University Press, Cambridge

Contents

**PART II: TWELVE NATIONAL INSTITUTES
OF THE EUROPEAN COMMUNITY
REFLECT ON THE LONG TERM**

Preface

by Jacques Delors
President of the Commission of the European Communities

This study of the factors that will shape tomorrow's world is the antithesis of an in-house analysis conducted in a vacuum. It represents the culmination of an extensive information-gathering exercise and listening to many outside views. Twelve national think-tanks and an impressive number of businesses were involved. Publication of the study is a logical step even though - or perhaps precisely because - its findings may come as a surprise.

It is interesting that think-tanks and businesses alike emphasize the necessity of social consensus, the quality of public services and a strong sense of belonging. The search for competitiveness has lost none of its validity but is seen in a different light:

-       It is no longer measured solely in terms of the performance of firms but increasingly by yardsticks such as the standard of education systems, the quality of the social dialogue, the consistency of industrial relations systems and the scale of infrastructure provision.
-       It is seen as acceptable only in combination with other imperatives, with social cohesion and respect for cultural diversity heading the list.

Think-tanks and businesses may share the same approach but they draw different conclusions as to the role the Community is expected to play. And this is one reason why this study is so interesting.

The business world faces fierce competition on a daily basis, therefore it would like the Community to be slightly less political - because that is divisive - and more practical, concentrating on vital projects such as implementation of the single market, rapid construction of trans-European networks, increased cooperation on research, and improved training for the workforce.

The think-tanks, by contrast, attach more importance to other tasks, emphasizing the need for coherency and leadership at Community level. As they see it, the arguments in favour of the Community developing a political vision of its own include the complexity and interplay of tasks 'in the common interest', the demarcation between policy areas calling for competition and those in which cooperation is more appropriate, and the need for a European model of society to serve as a point of reference.

The difficulty for the Community will be to reconcile these expectations, each valid in its own way.

A first point is that, as we enter 1993, the Community is actively considering a package of practical measures consistent with the pragmatic approach requested by the business community.

But I would add that in the troubled times that this 'Shaping Factors' study leads us to expect, there is a real danger that pragmatism without vision could plunge us into confusion and inconsistency. Today's difficulties are not entirely unrelated to the lack of visibility of the various players and to the need for strong institutions capable of providing the necessary impluse to reduce uncertainty and adapt strategies.

What is also cruelly lacking today is the ability to generate new visions. Because there is no vision, tension and wariness are rife, putting a real brake on economic activity. In the 1990s, we have more to fear from deficient levels of cooperation, political will and imagination than from any other form of scarcity.

Foreword

by Jean-Claude Morel
Director General of the Cellule de Prospective, Commission of the European Communities

The European Community and its Member States have always needed a common vision in order to progress. A vision able to raise their collective sights above the daily routine and able to mobilize their energies. A vision founded on common interest and shared ambition. Since the introduction of the 1992 Internal Market programme it is not exaggerating to say that the entire concept of the European Community, what it is and what it may become has changed profoundly. We find ourselves in a short period of history where, concomitantly, we have witnessed the collapse of the Berlin Wall, the reorientation of the rest of Europe towards the EC and at the same time the EC transforming itself, its own structures, its functions and its objectives. Managing such changes is neither easy, nor frictionless. But to succeed it is necessary, more than ever, to scrutinize the future, to identify the main shaping factors and shaping actors who will govern the dynamics of change, and to explore the possible strategic responses.

It is in this spirit that A. Jacquemin and D. Wright have conducted the present research project on behalf of the Cellule de Prospective. The Cellule is a small task-force of the European Commission attached to the President, Jacques Delors, whose mission is to research and produce new ideas on the medium- and long-term prospects for European integration.

This book is the collective effort of many people. Besides the contributions of several Directorates General, especially II, III and XIII, we are particularly indebted to: Vice-president Pandolfi, P. Lamy, E. Landaburu, A. Mayhew, A. Sapir and P. Buigues. The support of DG.XXIII and its Director General H. von Moltke is especially acknowledged. The Cellule de Prospective has collaborated closely and fruitfully on this project with McKinsey & Co., in particular with D. Meen, D. Turcq, K. Hladik, G. Zocco and D. Coutu, and we are grateful for their contributions. We were also delighted with the efforts made by the National Institutes, whose research work constitutes a major pillar of this book. Several members of the Cellule de Prospective have also played an important role in this exercise, notably J. Vignon, P. Löser and F. Fonseca. Finally, acknowledgements would not be complete without recognition of the role played by two secretaries, M. Berges-Martinez and S. McDonnell, whose patience and skilled secretarial work overcame manuscripts that might be politely described as fully reflecting European diversity.

Introduction

THE PROJECT AND THE METHODS USED

The objective of this book is to help identify a set of *shaping factors* that will illuminate the long-term prospects for the European Community and its Member States. We also aim to highlight the expectations and intentions of central actors who, through their policies and strategies, can exert at least some influence on the future. Our hope is that our main contribution will be to open a debate on a number of issues of fundamental concern to the European Community, namely the challenges of the post-1992 period, viewed perhaps from new angles and supported by new research. As a prospective work it is both ambitious and subject to varying degrees of uncertainty and risk.

What are these shaping factors that we are trying to identify? No formal definition is attempted but broadly speaking, they are the long-run structural factors, be they socio-economic, socio-political or cultural, that are, *de facto*, influencing our European futures. They are unlikely to be of a short-term nature, will-of-the-wisp or *hewing factors*. However, they could be sudden external shocks or brutal ruptures in previous trends.

This book adopts a multidisciplinary, qualitative approach which we feel is the best way to throw light on the aspirations and preoccupations aroused by the future of the Community. Unlike the Cecchini Report (*The Cost of Non-Europe*),[1] which concentrates on the internal economic dimension and proceeds from a set of theoretical analyses and empirical estimates, this study centres on socio-political and cultural concerns and the systemic interplay between them and economic phenomena. Moreover, it is not based on formalized material. Although it uses quantitative indicators, it mainly relies on an extensive body of expert

---

1   P. Cecchini, with M. Catinat and A. Jacquemin, *The European Challenge* (Wildwood House, 1988); M. Emerson et al., *The Economics of 1992* (Oxford University Press, 1988).

opinion which combines conjecture with scientifically sound propositions.[2]

The approach chosen seeks to sidestep the trap of a deterministic vision of behaviour conditioned by a set of structural factors. The role of *shaping actors* is seen as vital. In the dynamic process of change, conceived as an evolutionary historical process allowing scope for retroaction and space for unpredictable shocks, both the public and the private sectors will endeavour to adapt to structural constraints as fully as possible. However at various stages in the time-span they can also influence their environment and its development; they themselves can become *environment makers* as opposed to *environment takers*. Therefore, the rhythm of change - and the process of change itself - are open to influence by the leading actors.[3]

This study concentrates on three types of *actors*, namely major European firms, the European Commission and, to a lesser extent, some of the sensitivities and concerns of the Member States of the Community. Structurally, two main pillars provide the substance and empirical evidence for the project. A schematic description of the study is set out in Figure 1.

---

2 It is similar in this respect to the Delphi technique launched by the Rand Corporation in 1950. See J. Helmer, *Looking Forward* (Sage Publications, 1983).

3 In the field of industrial economics, this approach has prompted dynamic analysis making it possible to model intertemporal changes in market structures through business strategies. See A. Jacquemin, *The New Industrial Organization* (Oxford and MIT Press, 1987).

Figure 1   EC Shaping Factors in the post-1992 period

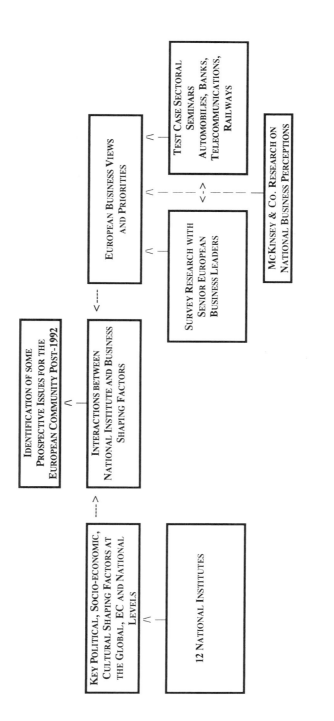

PILLAR I

The first of these research pillars Consists of a trans-European network connecting twelve National Institutes selected by the Forward Studies Unit (one from each of the Member States of the Community), specializing in medium- and long-term prospective analysis. Each Institute was requested to provide a comprehensive forward-looking overview of the main socio-economic, socio-political and socio-cultural shaping factors that will govern the future and reflect the specific sensitivities of their respective countries. A comparative reading of these twelve contributions, bringing various points of convergence and divergence to the fore, highlights not only the richness of European society but also draws the reader into the major intellectual debates about European society and Europe's future.

Given that the spatial context has its importance and that any research and analysis team is bound to be influenced by its cultural and institutional surroundings, all the Institutes selected sought external contributions within their own countries, notably from the two sides of industry to enrich their own analyses. We also asked them to point out where there are major areas of disagreement. A number of features of the general approach deserve specific attention.

First of all, the Forward Studies Unit merely acted as a facilitator and gave the Institutes no precise indications as to the priorities or issues they should address. The Institutes were also asked to work in isolation. Once all the reports were received the Forward Studies Unit set up a meeting between the twelve Institutes to discuss the results. A final Conference on the results was organized on 16 and 17 July 1992 and was largely devoted to establishing a synthesis of the main results and a programme of future work. The President of the European Commission, Jacques Delors, participated in the proceedings.

A second feature of the approach adopted was that the National Institutes were requested to categorize their shaping factors into four broad bands (not necessarily mutually exclusive), namely:

-       World-scale factors as opposed to more specifically national
        factors.
-       Socio-economic factors as opposed to cultural and political factors.
-       Factors on which a consensus was possible, and those surrounded
        by controversy.
-       Factors having a direct or indirect influence on business strategies.

Behind these slightly arbitrary distinctions lies a series of issues and balances, not all of them immediately obvious. For example, the distinction between global and local factors reflects the notion that the social area necessarily expands or contracts at will, depending on the point under consideration. Given the growing importance of the principle of subsidiarity within the Community, the question of the spatial context in which the challenges associated with individual factors are to be examined arises repeatedly. So, removal of the *Iron Curtain* shielding the countries of Eastern Europe has had an obvious impact on global equilibria but it presents an even greater challenge for neighbouring countries. Again, environmental issues are of local, European and global concern at one and the same time. And the sense of responsibility will be all the greater as issues are handled closer and closer to the citizen.

It is likewise true that the time-scale will vary from one factor to another. It would be pointless to examine monetary matters in relation to the year 2010, whereas this would be a perfectly valid horizon for demographic trends and ageing of the population. And any consideration of possible scenarios for 2010 will sometimes entail other horizons, some nearer, some more distant. On the other hand a short-term phenomenon such as a business recession can cloud the longer-term horizon simply because of the uncertainties, *white noise* and even the bias it generates.

The distinction between economic, social, cultural and political issues raises the additional question of the extent to which these shaping factors are - or are not - exogenous. While it is never easy to intervene to influence the underlying patterns of demographic evolution or nationalistic sentiments, there is more room for manoeuvre with the pace of innovation or the process of regional decentralization. This is the crux of the dynamic interaction between a set of structural factors and the strategic response of those with public and private sector responsibility who can change the environment to their advantage through a loop effect. The difficulty lies, of course, in distinguishing between what can be changed and what cannot.

It is also vital to bear in mind that the analysis of shaping factors is not designed to assess their combined effect in terms of a simple addition but in terms of interplay, which can generate convergence, contradiction and tacit or explicit arbitration. The Institutes were also asked to take this interplay into account. An illustration of it is the emergence of a conflict between two trends - the mutual recognition of diversity and the growing pressure of globalization which favours homogeneity. Can a balance be established between cosmopolitanism and parochialism? Does the irreversible pattern of globalization, coupled with the increased mobility of capital, people and ideas, mean that a European model of society in the future is quite illusory?

A second, related, example concerns the interdependence of competition between firms and competition between national socio-economic systems. Business competitiveness is not only a function of the firm's resources but increasingly of the relative efficiency of government policies, of institutional structures, and of social and cultural values.

In this sense, it is possible to identify several models of capitalism influenced by different combinations of shaping factors - the Reaganomic model, based on self-reliance, mobility and short-term financial gain; the Japanese model, based on a mixture of collective behaviour patterns, consensus and long-termism;[4] and what Michel Albert terms the *Rhine* model based on economic performance and social solidarity.[5]

A decision to opt for one or the other will determine not only the education and training system, the quality of public infrastructure and the sense of collective responsibility, but also the level of social marginalization, the rate of unemployment and the degree of social protection. But will there be arbitration, will there be hegemony, or will we see the emergence of hybrid systems, incorporating elements from each model?

This brings us to the sequence of the analysis.

The first stage is to identify the principal shaping factors that are most likely to determine the general dynamic of world, European and national trends.

The second stage, at which the actors are identified, raises two questions. In terms of incentives, what are the triggering mechanisms that will create awareness of the new patterns of the future? These could range from the brutal shock delivered by forces at work in a globalized market, restrained until flashpoint was reached, to the completely unpredictable, or to strategic far-sightedness fostered by forward analysis.

Once awareness has been achieved, how will actors in the public and private sectors respond to the new situation: will they remain passive and simply adapt, or will they actively seek to impose their will, shaping the

---

4   There are those who refer more broadly to an Asian model inspired by Confucianism: subordination of individual rights to group cohesion; priority to economic development over human rights, trade union independence and press freedom; authoritarian, paternalistic government systems. Given the enormous variety of cultural and historical patterns around the Western Pacific Rim, it is most unlikely that a uniform system of values will emerge there.

5   M. Albert, *Capitalisme contre Capitalisme* (Seuil, 1991).

shaping factors after the event? The National Institutes were asked to pay particular attention to the role of firms and the European Community authorities in this respect.

PILLAR II

The second pillar of our study consists of a series of business surveys conducted in collaboration with McKinsey & Co., Management Consultants.

The business world has substantially anticipated the needs of the single market with a series of restructuring operations, mergers and cooperation agreements. By refocusing their basic activities and broadening their geographical outlook, firms are gradually transforming the potential gains of the single market into actual gains. But the European venture in the wake of Maastricht extends far beyond the purely economic dimension.

So, given the impact that shaping factors can have on Europe and the world, an effort was made to establish to what extent these leading actors in the single market have their own vision and priorities. Research therefore concentrated on the expectations and options of firms. What, we asked, does the business world perceive as its *European* priorities in the post-1992 period?

Three research techniques were used:

- Four seminars brought together representatives of the Commission's Directorates General, the Forward Studies Unit and McKinsey & Co. experts and considered the futures of the automobile industry, the railways, banking and telecommunications services as examples.
- Seminars and interviews conducted by McKinsey & Co. experts highlighted attitudes among industrialists in the various countries under study.
- Meetings with a broad cross-section of 30 Chairmen and/or senior executives of European firms in different sectors of the economy, most of them members of the European Round Table, led to direct dialogue with some of the leading protagonists in the European single market.

The objective of this approach was to secure two types of input. In the first instance, the business world was asked quite openly to express its aspirations and priorities for post-1992 Europe. Then, a series of general themes, reflecting a summary of some of the major shaping factors identified by the Institutes were used to prompt firms to describe their own vision of the future.

The results of the business surveys and interviews were examined at the July conference and compared to the National Institutes' results (see Chapters 3 and 4).

Lastly, the role of the Community itself as an actor has been considered. In many fields the Community is no longer merely an *environment taker* but an *environment maker* too. In this context the Commission is expected to develop and apply the broad thrust contained in the principle of subsidiarity, and at the same time preserve its role as the driving force behind the new Europe. A key question put to the National Institutes and the business world was: how can pragmatism and vision be reconciled?

Given the limits of the study, there was no possibility of providing a full answer to these questions. Our main, less ambitious objective is to set out the findings, favouring the descriptive rather than the prescriptive. For the first time, information on major factors and priority themes have been supplied by a trans-European network of Institutes which, from their national vantage points, scrutinized Europe and the world at the dawn of the twenty-first century, concurrently making us more aware of the roots and sensitivities of their own countries. These views are contrasted and compared in the study with the information supplied by captains of industry who have to tango with both short-term commercial constraints and longer-term strategic goals.

The fact remains that representativeness, both in terms of National Institutes and major firms, is less than complete. Further research will be needed. Our study is therefore an interim rather than a final report.

STRUCTURE OF THE BOOK

Part I concentrates on the factors shaping the European Community. Chapter 1 situates briefly this research in the historical and intellectual context of European prospective work. It covers both a retrospective glance at previous European prospective studies as well as some recently published new European scenarios. Chapter 2 contains a synthesis of the global and national shaping factors as identified by the National Institutes, whilst Chapter 3 contains the second pillar of the research, namely the views of Europe's business community on post-1992 European integration. Chapter 3 has been drafted by McKinsey & Co. in collaboration with the editors.

Chapter 4 contains the comparisons, convergences and divergences between the National Institute results and business priorities. Is there any common ground? Why and how do the results differ? These are some of the issues taken up and explored.

Chapter 5 concentrates on the implications for the European Union. As 1992 ends, the Community, with all the turbulence it has faced surrounding the ratification of the Maastricht Treaty, needs more than ever to orient towards new objectives and new horizons and determine what might be the European Community's value added in the 1990s. We offer some preliminary thoughts.

Part II contains in sequence the national shaping factors' sections of the twelve National Institutes' reports. Here the reader can determine for herself or himself some of the different post-1992 national perceptions and priorities that these distinguished European intellectuals have determined as future long-run structural issues of strategic importance for their own countries and for Europe.

The editors of this book both work for the Commission of the European Communities. They wish to make it clear that the views and analysis contained in this book do not, in any way, engage the Commission.

PART I

The Future of Difference:
Factors Shaping the European Community

1. The Basis for a Post-1992 European Prospective Study

INTRODUCTION

Before presenting the empirical results of our research work, we feel it is important to situate this project in the historical context of European prospective thinking.

In recent years, traditional planning procedures have been abandoned in the Western countries that used them, and the collapse of Communism has destroyed the concept of historical determinism.

The future, it appears, is no longer predetermined; the range of options and futures, once again, are wide open.

Simultaneously, it has become increasingly evident that the main problems facing our societies are structural in nature, consequently requiring medium- to long-term analysis and perspectives.

If we are to take up the challenges of the decades ahead, we must ascend to the crow's nest, to borrow the metaphor used by Futuribles International[1] and be constantly on the look-out for the economic, technological, social, cultural and political elements that will condition tomorrow's world.

Without claiming to determine the course of future events, those in positions of influence in the public and private sectors need to be able to identify the main underlying currents which are already guiding their choices and strategies.

---

[1]   See the monthly review *Futuribles*.

Little wonder, therefore, that there has been a proliferation of individual and collective attempts to get to grips with these questions. Many eyes are scanning our future, including those of A. Toffler,[2] H. Kahn,[3] J.Naisbitt,[4] MITI,[5] the Club of Rome[6] and the Anglo-Dutch Shell Group[7] among others. Growing affirmation of the European dimension has also prompted a substantial volume of conceptual work and writing on the future of Europe, both by the Commission of the European Communities[8] and a number of research centres.[9]

The methodologies for such studies vary widely, ranging from general qualitative discussions to the construction of computerized data storage and retrieval systems for some long-term studies,[10] and the elaboration of detailed scenarios from econometric modelling exercises.[11]

J. Lesourne has pointed out[12] that eclecticism must be the order of the day since every approach has its limitations and futurology, like any other technique, will make advances if it absorbs improvements from whatever source - from basic research to empirical experience.

In Europe, then, and throughout the world, the outlook for the twenty-first century is being scrutinized so as to identify the *underlying patterns*, the *megatrends*, the *shaping factors* that are at work and to situate the *shaping actors* in an environment that is, to some extent at least, malleable and open to influence.

---

2   *The Third Wave* (Random House, 1980).

3   *The Coming Boom: Economic, Political and Social* (Hutchinson, 1983).

4   *Megatrends: Ten New Directions Transforming our Lives* (Warner Books, 1982).

5   See for example MITI, *International Trade and Industrial Policy in the 1990s: toward creating human values in the global age*, Tokyo, 1991. See also the research made by the National Institute for Research Advancement (NIRA), a foundation created by the MITI, especially its *Agenda for Japan in the 1990s, NIRA Research Output*, 1988.

6   Cf. the new report by A. King and B. Schneider, *Question de survie* (Calman-Lévy, 1991), which stresses development policy.

7   See for example P. Wack, 'Scenarios: uncharted waters ahead', *Harvard Business Review*, September 1985.

8   Cf. the impressive studies by the Monitor and Fast teams directed by R. Petrella.

9   Cf. M. Godet and J. Lesourne, *La fin des habitudes* (Seghers, 1986) or W. Weidenfeld and J. Janning, *Europe in Tomorrow's World* (Bertelsman Stiftung, Gütersloh, 1991).

10   The OECD recently set up a major data-bank covering published and unpublished studies on the long-term future that could be useful to member governments as policy-making aids.

11   An example is *Economie Mondiale 1910-2000: l'impératif de croissance*, report by the Centre d'Etudes Prospectives et d'Informations Internationales (CEPII) (Economica, 1992).

12   In *Plaidoyer pour une recherche en prospective* (Futuribles, November 1989).

UNDERLYING PATTERNS, DISCONTINUITY, CHANCE AND DETERMINISM

Foreseeing the unforeseeable is, of all exercises, the least likely to generate unanimity.

Recently, in a meeting to prepare a world political summit, the participants undertook a brainstorming session in which they were asked to identify the unexpected events that might take place in the next ten years. Each was allowed to nominate three shocks. The wide variance of the perceptions of this small sample is as illuminating as the subjects raised. The issues nominated were:

	NUMBER OF VOTES
Weakness of Democracies in Combining Collective Action with Individual Freedom	2
Disintegration of the USSR	2
Siberia-China-India Conflict	1
North Africa	1
Demotivation of Young People	1
Environment	1
Regional Conflicts due to Poverty and Extremes of Rich and Poor	1
Political Difficulty due to the Appearance of more and more Specific Groups	1
Nuclear Proliferation	1
Decline in Family Values	1
Influence of Islam in Western Societies	1
Ideological Conflict between the West and Asia around Different roles of the Rights of Man	1
Trade Conflicts	1
Flabbiness of Democracies after Decline of Communism	1
Drugs	1
Ageing of the Population	1
Water Shortages	1
Terrorism	1
Financial Risks linked to US/Japan Financial Systems	1

The main result is that there have been only two issues where there has been any overlap at all!

But, as B. Cazes showed us[13], close study of the literature of futurology reveals that this diversity of opinion is more apparent than real. It is even possible to pinpoint a few major factors that crop up repeatedly - the

---

[13]   B. Cazes, *Histoire des futurs*, Seghers, 1986.

environment, technological change, world economic growth, the geo-political context, changing values, employment and labour, and the role of government.

To illustrate this point, it is firstly worth devoting a few paragraphs to a retrospective of two past prospective exercises, *Megatrends* (an American exercise) and *Facing the Future* (an OECD exercise); secondly some recent European scenarios for the world's economic evolution up to the year 2000 and beyond are presented.

The first *Megatrends* report, written in 1982, is based on a method called *content analysis*, i.e. an analysis of the content of local newspapers in the United States. It covers more than 2 million local articles about local events in the cities and towns of the United States over a twelve-year period.[14]

On this basis, ten major transformations taking place in American society have been identified. According to the author, J. Naisbitt:

(i)   We have shifted from an industrial society to one based on the creation and distribution of information.

(ii)   We are moving in the dual directions of high-tech/high-touch, matching each new technology with a compensatory human response.

(iii)   No longer do we have the luxury of operating within an isolated, self-sufficient, national economic system; we now must acknowledge that we are part of a global economy. We have begun to let go of the idea that the United States is and must remain the world's industrial leader as we move on to other tasks.

(iv)   We are restructuring from a society run by short-term considerations and rewards in favour of dealing with things in much longer-term time-frames.

(v)   In cities and states, in small organizations and subdivisions, we have rediscovered the ability to act innovatively and to achieve results - from the bottom up.

---

[14]   The news-reporting process is described as *forced choice in a closed system*. Indeed, given that the amount of space devoted to news in a newspaper does not change significantly over time, something must be omitted when something new is introduced. In keeping track of the preoccupations that are added and the ones that are given up, it is argued that it is possible to measure the changing *share of the market* that competing societal concerns command and to see what the new US society looks like. See J. Naisbitt, *Megatrends*, Warner Books Edition, 1982. The most recent edition is *Megratrends 2000: Ten New Directions for the 1990s*, Avon Books, New York, 1990.

(vi)   We are shifting from institutional help to more self-reliance in all aspects of our lives.

(vii)   We are discovering that the framework of representative democracy has become obsolete in an era of instantaneously shared information.

(viii)   We are giving up our dependence on hierarchical structures in favour of informal networks. This will be especially important to the business community.

(ix)   More Americans are living in the South and West, leaving behind the old industrial cities of the North.

(x)   From a narrow either/or society with a limited range of personal choices, we are exploding into a free-wheeling multiple-option society.

This general enumeration includes the main factors already mentioned - technological change, the global dimension of the economy, changes in the political system, and new values, but two aspects, mentioned below, merit particular attention.

Firstly, a number of expectations have not been met. One example is the view that 'American businesses appear to have discovered the advantage of the long-term approach and have developed the capacity to change the direction of a business as the world changes'. Secondly, a number of trends observed in the United States in 1982 are of particular interest to European society. A case in point is the view that, whether the issue is energy, politics, community self-help or entrepreneurship, the new creed is one of self-reliance and local initiative. 'In this new era of geographic diversity and decentralization, the conformity of mass society is a thing of the past.'

The Interfutures report,[15] commissioned by the OECD Council in 1975, takes a harder look at the future development of advanced industrial societies in conjunction with that of the developing world. Its main thrust is economic, but political and social considerations are not ignored. The first part is devoted to growth. Taking its cue from the Club of Rome report, it investigates the limits to growth, using statistical projections to examine demographic trends and the prospects for food, energy and commodity supplies and the physical environment. Its conclusions are reasonably optimistic, stating that 'the economic growth of the countries of the world taken as a whole can continue during the next half century without encountering long-term physical limits'.

---

[15]   *Facing the Future* (Paris, 1979).

But it goes on to warn that growth will be affected by relations between man and the ecosphere, by economic and social constraints and by social and political challenges. After exploring a variety of scenarios, it focuses on four key issues:

(i)   Changing energy patterns.
(ii)   The attempt by governments of industrialized countries to devise new policies to match the new context.
(iii)   Joint efforts to develop the Third World.
(iv)   New forms of international cooperation.

Several other aspects of this OECD study, which is still remarkably topical, deserve a special mention.

For example, the general outlook for the European Community was perceived as far from rosy:

> With problems of unemployment, inflation and industrial redeployment, low growth will affect the EEC countries differently because of the great differences in structure and social divisions. Their structural adaptability is likely to be low, especially if account is taken of national and regional features, conflicts between the decision-making processes at the national and Community levels, and the ageing population of all the countries and particularly of the most prosperous country, the Federal Republic of Germany. In these circumstances there can hardly be any other strategy than to take the narrow path in search of a consolidated internal common market, keep open frontiers insofar as the resulting adjustments are acceptable to all partners, develop relations with the Third World, and improve decision-making procedures within the present or enlarged Community. (p. 400).[16]

By contrast, a much brighter view was taken of the outlook for the USSR and Eastern Europe:

> Even if these countries' trade with the OECD area and the Third World remains limited, it will reach a level where they will have a considerable influence in world industrial competition. Allowing

---

[16]   J. Lesourne, project director, himself gave an assessment of the project six years later, suggesting that its major weakness was that it had under-estimated Europe's handicaps and over-estimated those facing the United States (*Le Figaro*, 7/8 December 1985).

for the economic prospects of the OECD area, the Third World and China, the USSR's share of world income may reach its peak around the end of the century. (p. 400).[17]

New Long-Term Scenarios

Recently new alternative scenarios for the future world's economic evolution have been built up, using sophisticated econometric models.

A valuable example are the results of the 'four world scenarios for the period 1990-2015 devised by the Dutch Central Planning Office'.[18] These results can be expressed in the form of a continuum, extending from the worst-case scenario to the most favourable. These scenarios have been summarized in the French report on Shaping Factors and we follow below their presentation.

The *global crisis* scenario is caused by a persistent decline in the competitive position of Europe and the United States faced with a Japan which firmly believes that its structural surpluses are entirely due to its superior economic performance. The developed world gradually splits up into hostile protectionist blocs. A *systemic crisis*, linked for example to serious world food shortages, triggers a prolonged economic recession.

The two median scenarios concern situations where one of the two major partners in the Triad - the US or the EC - changes its ways sufficiently to rediscover a pattern of high growth, whereas the other does not. According to the 'new global configuration' scenario, the United States would benefit from the economic opportunities offered by the Asia-Pacific region, with Europe lagging behind; the *European revival* scenario on the other hand, naturally envisages the reverse.

At the other extreme, the *balanced growth* scenario envisages a benevolent process whereby a widespread commitment to doing away with as many rigid and archaic elements as possible in each member of the Triad creates a general climate of prosperity. This in turn fosters a greater degree of international cooperation, so that reconciling relatively rapid growth in the advanced nations with the more backward countries' need to catch up and respect for the environment is no longer just a pipe dream.

On a world scale, the differences in growth between worst-case and best-case scenarios may appear fairly modest (3.75% compared with

---

[17] In a similar way, the possible collapse of the Soviet Union is not mentioned by P. Kennedy in *The Rise and Fall of the Great Powers* (Random House, 1987).

[18] André de Jong, *Scanning the future*, Centraal Planbureau, 5 September 1991.

2.25%). However, if we take account of demographic growth over the period in question, we notice that in the most favourable scenario the growth in GDP per capita would be 2.25%, compared with 0.15% in the worst-case version - i.e. 'the figure would double in thirty years in the first example, and in nearly a hundred years in the second'. Furthermore, the distribution of the results per major region, and in particular in the *rest of the world* column (not detailed in this table) reveals that *Africa* would be particularly sensitive to contrasts between scenarios, since in the most favourable scenario its GDP per capita would *grow* at an annual rate of 1.8%, and *decline* by 0.8% in the global-crisis scenario.

Table 1.1   Global economic results for the various world scenarios, 1990-2015

REGION								
Scenarios[19]	NA	WE	JAP	DAE	CE	SU	ROW	WORLD
GDP Growth (%/Year)							(Index) 1990 = 100	
BALANCED GROWTH	3	3.25	3	7	3.25	2.25	4.5	3.75 (244)
GLOBAL SHIFT	3.5	1.75	4.25	7.25	1.5	-0.25	3.75	3.25 (230)
EUROPE	1.75	2.75	3.75	6.25	4.25	3	3.75	3 (212)
GLOBAL CRISIS	1.75	1.75	3	5	1	0.75	2.5	2.25 (174)
(%/Year)								
POPULATION	0.75	0.25	0.25	1.25	0.25	0.50	1.75	1.50

Sources: 'Scanning the Future', Central Plan Bureau, the Netherlands.

The other scenarios mooted (Cambridge Econometrics, Nomura, the Japanese Economic Planning Agency) mostly opt for an average hypothetical figure of around 3% annual growth for the world economy. The developing countries and the industrialized countries would experience roughly this level of growth (less in the case of the United States, more in the case of Japan). The growth curve for Central and Eastern Europe and the OPEC countries would be significantly lower, while that of the newly industrialized Asian nations would be double the average. In all of these tendential scenarios, global integration continues slowly.

In another exercise made by the Centre for Exploratory Studies and

---

[19]   NA: North America - WE: Western Europe - JAP: Japan - DAE: Dynamic Asian Economies - CE: Central Europe - SU: CIS - ROW: Rest of the World.

International Information,[20] the speed at which Eastern and Southern countries become integrated into the world economic systems was taken into account. The Centre has simulated the course of the world economy between now and the year 2000 according to two scenarios, one of which is 'tendential' and the other 'integrative'. *According to the former*, Western economies experience mediocre growth: 2.5% per annum, with 2.3% in the United States, 2.4% in the EC and 3.3% in Japan. The result for the world economy as a whole is approximately 3.1% annual growth per year.

According to the *favourable scenario*, the acceleration in growth and economic integration is achieved through increased funding for the East and South, representing 1% of the OECD's GNP by the year 2000, and through the gradual opening up of Western markets. Initiatives aimed at the East are optimistically expected to give the best return over this period. As a result, annual world growth will be 0.7% higher over the period 1992-2000, with significantly greater increases occurring in certain peripheral regions. The annual growth of the world economy, according to this optimum scenario, thus works out at 3.8%, but this presupposes 'joint, responsible management of the world economy by the industrialized countries', mainly in order to generate additional funding. The main parameters for the two scenarios are shown in the Table 1.2.

On this basis, as A. Brender[21] observes, speculating about how the international division of labour is likely to change between now and the year 2010 is extremely hazardous. In order to clarify our thoughts however, we should perhaps try to draw a *reference image*, based on what we know of the economic aspects.

This image is based on an observation: by the year 2010, demographic conditions in the Western countries (Europe, North America) will be markedly different from those in the *South*. By 2010, the working population in the former will be on the decline in relative, and in many cases, absolute terms, whereas in the latter, the reverse will be true. The result will be a high degree of potential complementarity in financial and commercial matters, which from 2000 onwards and in the first few decades of the next century would mean a more rapid increase in large-scale capital flows from the West to the South. The South could thus create a large number of new jobs and at the same time, increase labour productivity. The capital flows necessary for the South could be supplied

---

20 CEPII: *World Economy 1990-2000: The growth imperative*, CEPII report, compiled in cooperation with the Mimosa team from the OFCE, Paris, Economica, 1992.
21 Previous Director of the CEPII, to whom these comments belong.

by some of the savings of the ageing, highly productive North thereby helping the South to develop a skilled workforce and establish political stability. In order for this to happen however, these countries would have to have won market shares from the North and to have develop substantial export capabilities. The international division of labour between North and South would thus appear to be closely linked to the development of a sort of *international division of retirement*, leading manufacturing industries, especially those with a high labour input, to relocate to the South.

The situation in Eastern Europe differs from that of most southern countries in so far as they have much lower population growth and more sophisticated specialization potential, particularly in capital-intensive industries such as mechanical engineering and intermediate industries. It is quite likely that by around the year 2010, some of these countries, after following the example of the South and accumulating current account deficits in the early years of the twenty-first century, will have managed to redress their trade balance and even produce surpluses.

While this reference image is highly consistent with economic theory, it does presuppose major progress in terms of world economic integration, on both the commercial and financial fronts. Such progress is certainly possible (it would more or less echo the situation at the beginning of the century) but it is based on the assumption that the next twenty years or so will see a fairly radical change in political relations between the regions concerned. And it is here that we could see major deviations between now and 2010 from the reference image outlined above.

The integration-disintegration debate thus rears its head once again: either societies will be increasingly capable of cooperating and fitting into vast entities, right up to world level, or social and international disintegration will be punctuated by conflicts and wars. Supra national integration can only be based on national integration, which is itself dependent on the integration of communities of private individuals; conversely, minority conflicts can break up entire nations - be they large or small - and spread to an international level.

Are there any other Models on which to Draw?

Is standardization from above-major rift, or integration-disintegration the only way of looking at the long-term future of the international system? In order to try and imagine the conditions under which some alternative polarity might emerge, we need to imagine a different form of universalism from that which underlies the current model.

Many of those who believe in Islam will undoubtedly be tempted to make this the new reference point for the course of history. As we see it however, the chances of this happening are slim, unless Islam moves quickly to bring itself into line with the rest of the modern world, in terms of scientific and technological development and democracy.

Table 1.2   World growth and current account balances

	TENDENTIAL SCENARIO		INTEGRATION SCENARIO	
	Growth in GDP 2000/1991	**Current Balances 2000 in Billions of $ (as % of GDP)**	**Growth in GDP 2000/1991**	**Current Balances 2000 in Billions of $ (as $ of GDP)**
United States	2.3	-166 (-1.8)	2.8	-251 (-2.4)
Japan	3.3	91 (1.2)	3.9	204 (2.3)
West Germany	2.3	93 (3.5)	2.7	156 (5.4)
Reunified Germany	3.1	85 (2.8)	3.5	152 (4.6)
France	2.5	-27 (-1.4)	3.1	-10 (-0.5)
Italy	2.8	-35 (-1.9)	3.4	-36 (-1.8)
UK	2.2	-47 (-3)	2.3	-52 (-3.2)
Other EC Countries	2.6	23 (1.2)	3.5	71 (3.3)
Other European Countries	2.7	60 (3.9)	3.4	106 (6.1)
Other OECD Countries	2.5	-75 (-5.4)	3.1	-80 (-5.1)
Latin America	3.6	-28 (-1.1)	4.7	-86 (-2.8)
Arab World	4.0	44 (2)	4.5	50 (2)
Black Africa	3.3	-10 (-1.8)	4.3	-48 (-7.8)
Newly Industrialized Asian Countries	6.9	3 (0.2)	7.6	23 (1.4)
Rest of Asia	6.0	-40 (-0.8)	6.5	-73 (-1.2)
Eastern Europe	1.5	-40 (-0.6)	2.9	-170 (-2.3)
EC	2.7	0 (0.0)	3.3	126 (1.1)
EC Excluding East Germany	2.4	8 (0.1)	3.0	130 (1.2)
OECD Excluding East Germany	2.6	-82 (-0.3)	3.1	109 (0.3)
World	3.1	-159 (-0.3)	3.8	-199 (-0.4)

Source: CEPII-OFCE, MIMOSA Model.

The emergence of a new power base around the Sino-Japanese region, with 'the former providing capital and technology and the latter manpower'[22] seems more plausible in the long run. So will we end up with a future Eastern Empire, initially close to its Western twin, but later intent on outliving the latter and carrying its founding principles higher and further? Such a shift would in any case occur long after 2010. There is no reason however, why some form of regional or other integration should not begin within the next twenty years, significantly altering the geopolitical context.

Finally, should we completely discard one last hypothesis which is not predicated on the emergence of certain inexorable mechanisms, but assumes instead that current trends will become stabilized, through fear of triggering forces beyond our control and through mutual preservation of the existing balance of power - the weaker players having as their main advantage the ability to create major uncertainties? This would be the *stationary hypothesis*, with developments occurring more or less around the present context and with the gap narrowing between East and West but persisting between North and South. The main drawback with this hypothesis however, is the fact that it is increasingly resented and less and less accepted.

Perilous Exploration of an Unknown Future

All the former exercises have been carried out with extensive resources and undeniable expertise. They bring important insights and supply important materials to the intellectual and political debates. Their eventual errors do not suppress their added-value. They show just how perilous the exploration of an unknown future can be. Several phenomena are worth mentioning in this context. To begin with, one and the same factor may be perceived in terms of different preoccupations over the years. It took time, for example, for environmental problems to be perceived in terms of the biosphere as a whole and the interplay between economic growth and the natural environment to be treated in terms of *sustainable growth*. Then again, a shaping factor will be completely misread occasionally. To give an illustration from demographics, J.C. Chesnais[23] reminds us that five years after the trend went into reverse, President Nixon was still worried about the effects of the

---

22   P. Lellouche, *Le nouveau monde*, Grasset, 1991.
23   J.C. Chesnais, *Prévision et Project*, Le Débat, 1981.

baby-boom. The Presidential Commission he appointed to investigate the question reported its findings in 1972 and firmly supporting a halt in population growth. The upshot was that 10 million couples opted for sterilization.

Natural resources (e.g. estimates of oil and gas reserves) and technological change are other areas where errors abound. Computers provide an eloquent example: before 1950 the view was that there was no commercial demand for this kind of machine.[24]

The most recent - and most striking - example of an unexpected brutal changes lies in the European venture itself. At the very time when the Community was preparing to celebrate the magical 1992 date with the birth of the single market, the collapse of the Berlin Wall[25] and Communism in general was engendering a new Europe, with vastly more at stake than a large market. Less than three years earlier M. Gorbachev wrote: 'Let me say quite plainly that all these statements about the revival of German unity are far from being Realpolitik. And what there will be in a hundred years is for history to decide'.

It must not be forgotten therefore that the path to the future will not always follow a simple pattern: trends go into reverse, are broken, or split into sub-trends, and linear extrapolation of straight lines or curves is a singularly hazardous exercise.

Historical studies bear this out. F. Braudel, for instance, in his monumental study *Civilisation Matérielle, Economie et Capitalisme*, shows how the capitalist system is founded on a multiplicity of possibilities for influencing the economic game and the rules according to which it is played.

> Privilege of a small number, capitalism really belongs to people like Bardi, J. Coeur, to J. Fugger, J. Law or Necker. These actors have been capable of generating far reaching changes in entire sectors of the European economy. They transformed trade into profit, upset the established order. They created anomalies and turbulence.[26]

In the same spirit, K. Popper has argued that mankind's history is irreversible, non-linear, and discontinuous and that it consists of

24   See S.Schnaars, *Megamistakes, Forecasting and the Myth of Rapid Technological Change* (New York: The Free Press, 1989).

25   M. Gorbachev, *Perestroika, New Thinking for our Country and the World* (New York: Harper and Row, 1987).

26   F. Braudel, *Civilisation Matérielle, Economie et Capitalisme* (Paris: A. Colin, 1979).

acceleration and deceleration. The course of this history is profoundly influenced by the growth of human knowledge itself. 'This knowledge is not simply an instrument in the fight for survival; it is driven by an internal logic continually urging it to develop further.'[27]

Discontinuities are presumably the fruit of a combination of factors, driven by a variety of predictable and random phenomena, as well as by deliberate strategies.

The question has been reformulated by scientific work of recent years on the dynamics of change; chaos theory has emerged as a result. This theory shows that a simple relationship that is deterministic but non-linear can yield an extremely complex time path.[28] Intertemporal behaviour can acquire an appearance of disturbance by random shocks and can undergo violent, abrupt qualitative changes either with the passage of time or with small changes in the values of the parameters.[29]

Then, distinguishing deterministic dynamics from dynamics primarily governed by stochastic elements becomes quite difficult. Furthermore, where chaos occurs forecasting becomes extremely difficult, and this provides strong caveats for both the analyst and the policy designer.

It is not surprising, therefore, that forward studies have always resisted the temptation to prophesy. The more modest objective is to identify factors impacting on the future and explore possible outcomes. Seen in this light, the future is not assumed to be fixed - it is open, it is multifaceted and it is influenceable.

---

27 K. Popper, *The Poverty of Historicism*, Harper & Row, New York, 1957.

28 Let us underline that, contrary to the common usage of the word, chaos in this context describes the behaviour of a variable over time which appears to follow no apparent pattern but in fact is completely deterministic, that is, each value of the variable over time can be predicted exactly.

29 For economic applications, see W. Baumol and J. Benhabib, 'Chaos: significance, mechanism, and economic applications'. *Journal of Economic Perspectives*, No. 1, Winter 1989. The classic illustration is the so-called *butterfly's wing phenomenon* according to which a butterfly fortuitously flapping its wings in Hong Kong can cause tornadoes in Oklahoma if weather is controlled by chaotic relationships!

2. The National Institutes' Global and National Shaping Factors: Convergences and Divergences

SECTION 1: THE GLOBAL FACTORS

Introduction

The global factors identified by the National Institutes are an opening gambit, the first domino in the shaping factors exercise. At a critical moment in the development of the European Community, they offer an empirical survey, a catalogue of some of the major issues and factors perceived to be important by a kaleidoscope of Europeans looking forward to the horizon of 2010. We can be quite sure that some of these issues will shape all of our outcomes.

Whilst these analyses no doubt reflect an intellectual *mainstream* perception of possible futures viewed from the binoculars of each of our Member States looking outside the frontiers of the Community, they also incorporate a quotient of the preoccupations, psyche and demands of the diversity of people and opinion that make up the sum of the European Community.

This sample of results is not exclusive, not always breathtaking in its originality, nor of course complete. It is also true that to a certain degree there may be some correlation or even bias as the global shaping factors that are raised by the national experts may dovetail with the specific knowledge and specialization of the chosen authors and their Institutes. Conversely, some ideas may have transferred from one Institute to another during the first meeting of Contractors, reducing the variance between the reports. What is more, the factors that are not suggested as major global issues may be as interesting as those that are raised. Likewise, the convergences between the National Institutes could be as interesting as the divergences.

17

It is also important to remember that these global factors are European perceptions. They will differ, perhaps profoundly, from these of our major trading partners, or those that might be identified by the poorer countries in the world or by the former Communist States. There are no *rights* and *wrongs* in prospective analyses, but rather opinions of experts, conjectures and best estimates. What we have is an *historical point estimate* of our future, a future which is becoming increasingly complex to interpret and predict. There are no projections about possible exogenous *shocks* or a quantification of the major risks and uncertainties, desirable though this would be. But some Institutes have made a major effort to look at alternative scenarios, particularly concerning the futures for the European Community itself.

Socio-Political Global Shaping Factors

The socio-political global shaping factors underlined by the National Institutes cover several dimensions: the European Community, Europe from the Atlantic to the Urals, the North-South, the world as a whole. They reflect a double preoccupation: firstly those linked with geographical proximity or more generally "propinquity" reflecting close ties of interest arising out of territorial, cultural and historical affiliations[1]

The European Community is seen as a major global shaping factor or *environment maker* but not by all Institutes. The propensity among the larger countries (two of whom have permanent seats on the UN Security Council and four who are in the G7 Group) is significantly lower. Conversely Belgium, Portugal, Ireland, the Netherlands and Greece, in other words the smaller Member States, strongly see the EC itself as a factor in the global shaping factors context. The strongest statement can be found in the Netherlands report: 'The European Community's integration is the major driving force in the years to come'. The subpoints most frequently mentioned here are the future architecture of the Community, the depth of its own integration and the pace and geographical spread of enlargement. The Greek paper summarizes an interesting view that the unification of Europe will depend on the clash of political fission (former USSR/East Europe) and political fusion (the Community itself) and that the two major parameters for the Community to develop are its security role and the economic and monetary component

---

[1]   It is worth recalling that the Havana Charter contained provisions with respect to preferential agreements among parties that are either *contiguous* or belong to the same *economic region.*

of the European union. These issues are taken up in more detail in Chapter 5.

There is unanimity among the National Institutes that the decline of Soviet Communism and the evolution of Eastern European countries, Russia and the other CIS States will be a major shaping factor in the time span we have chosen. The UK report states that: 'whatever the troubles of the Former Soviet bloc over the next two decades, there will neither be the capability, nor the motive to mount a military threat to the West'. Whilst there is agreement on this factor, the implications appear less clear. Few Institutes speak of a peace dividend although *defence restructuring* is mentioned by the Institutes emanating from Europe's major military powers. The Institutes are also cautious about their predictions on the *Eastern* European revolution, accepting nevertheless that if it fails or ethnic conflicts continue to erupt, then the Community can expect a very large increase in the flow of Eastern European immigrants. A connected issue, and one strongly raised by at least five Institutes, including Germany, are the new potential splinter security threats, such as the safety of Eastern European and former Soviet nuclear power stations and, more serious, the dangers of nuclear proliferation, sourced from the ex-Soviet nuclear stockpile. Apart from the nuclear dangers, there are few mentions of other major security threats. International terrorism or organized crime are not, apparently, seen as major threats. Drugs proliferation or an impending energy/oil crisis are not mentioned at all. Ten years ago they surely would have been.

Several Institutes raise the issue of the long-run costs of reconstruction in Eastern Europe, the amounts of capital required, and the need for the Community to open markets and offer more trade and economic opportunities as well as technical aid programmes. But apart from Germany and to a lesser extent France, few touched on the delicate question of the future of East-West Europe's division of labour - certain to be an issue if Czechoslovakian or Polish labour costs are 1/10 or less than the average in the EC. The French report comfortably deals with developments in the East within the parameters of its dual scenario approach (a world moving towards *Universalism* or *Vers un nouveau grand schisme*). In other words, will the East be able to accept, not only economically, but also culturally and politically the move towards neo-liberalism and globalization of markets driven by greater transparency and information - or will it stumble and fall into new political divides?

A marked emphasis is also placed on underdevelopment and future North/South relations. A majority mention the fact that 80% of the world's resources being consumed by 20% of its people is an unsustainable equation, and the source of increasing tension in the future. Only one Institute mentions that some middle-income developing countries might at last be turning the economic corner. Views that the pressure on resources is leading to water shortage, desertification, food demand exceeding supply and therefore an expansion of hunger/deprivation are promulgated by the UK and BRD. Overall there is general pessimism on the North/South outlook. For France, the unequal distribution of income between North and South is the overarching and first factor mentioned at the beginning of their report and there is a clear implication that unless long-run progress is made, demographically, economically and ideologically (e.g. a detente in anti-Western propaganda), the scenario of *le grand schisme*, alternatively described as *l'universalisme tronqué*, becomes more likely.

This leads to the worrying question of expanding immigration pressure on the Community from the South and East and in particular from the Southern Mediterranean Basin, where the population is set to double in the next 20 years (i.e. plus around 200 million more people). Immigration towards the Community could be triggered by combinations of underdevelopment, declining water resources, poor agricultural possibilities, high unemployment and uncontrollable urban sprawl. The reports do not speculate about whether intolerable tensions will erupt, but the perception that the pressure will exist clearly flows from a horizontal reading of the texts. The most optimistic comments on this issue are that some of the migratory pressure from some countries could possibly be alleviated by an improvement in the oil price (DK), and a flow of immigrants may be required in the Community to replace the Community's own ageing workforce and relieve pressure on the Member States' social security systems (Ellas, Belgium).

Concerning the world dimension, several Institutes (notably France, Portugal, Belgium and Spain), analyse the complexity of political globalism.

Most convergence can be found on the prospective theme of *structures of Government* - in other words global subsidiarity - from the United Nations at the top to the local authority or below at the bottom. In other words, how are we, global citizens, going to manage our affairs in the future? Supranationally, through regional arrangements, nationally, and at local level - how will power flow (upwards and downwards); can the Bretton Woods Institutions be reformed? And how can we accommodate growing numbers of minority groups who want a share of political power is another central theme to emerge. More specifically, the Spanish text asks whether globalism and corporatism will result in a decline in solidarity, between the rich and poor, between young and old, between the centre and the periphery - driven by weak economic growth, the spread and acceptance of ultra-liberal ideology, the prevalence of privacy over social life and, perhaps most importantly, the weakening of the historical planks of social democracy (raised also by the Netherlands, Denmark and France).

In the context of substantial philosophical differences among the major industrialized countries, the French paper poses this question differently by analysing the role of world institutions in general and whether they are able to overcome some of the previous problems. Like others, the paper says the climate is favouring spatial and sectoral integration, with business networks acting as important motors. Indeed, integration and cooperation are essential for containing cross-cultural and cross-economic tensions and for reducing market uncertainty. But there are also disintegration scenarios and the need particularly 'for a transparent articulation of institutional space'. These forces could result in UN/regional agencies defined even further by objective, the possible institutionalization of the TRIAD (plus Russia eventually) with overall success being dependent on the priority accorded to dealing with the North/South cleavage.

Historico-Cultural Global Factors

The historico-cultural factors tabled by the National Institutes yield less transparent messages; there is more of a *pot-pourri* and a greater variance around the mean.

The issues of diversity, identity and regulation were recurrent themes, but ambiguously expressed. Whilst there are doubts on European identity concepts (less so for the elites suggests Portugal) several ask whither post-nationalism? Nationalism appears still a strong prospective variable - especially for the UK, BRD, and, quintessentially, for France. In fact, the future of relations between the European Union and the nations which make up the present EC are not taken for granted. Each nation has its own reasons for being tempted to pursue a process of globalization alone, mixed with a strong attachment to its own national politico-cultural identity.

In addition, differences in terms of past history, power and wealth could lead each, sometimes for opposite reasons, to curb the common enthusiasm and future of Europe as a whole. One only has to look at

France[2] where there is a permanent talk of the risk of domination by a unified Germany, or, elsewhere, France's ambition to become the brain of Europe, or the UK's purported preference for *going it alone....*

According to the Spanish paper, this diversity in the EC spills into the global context by the deep, long-standing historico-cultural relations that Germany has with Eastern Europe, the UK with the US, Canada and Australasia and Spain with Latin America. The Portuguese paper proffers hierarchies and segmentation against the more preferable social cohesion as one prospective trade-off, multiracial melting pots or multiculturalism against the ugly alternative as another, with social exclusion lurking as a menace threatening the fragile societal consensus.

The question of prospective cultural convergence is raised by the British, French, Portuguese, German and Belgian papers as one of the possible prices for globalism, neo-liberalism or internationalism.[3] Globalism appears as a double-edged sword for the future. It will allow Europe to make the most of what is perhaps its most highly prized asset: its wealth of cultural diversity, based on a common heritage, and which gives it its unique capacity for listening, discussing and moving forward. Although *European culture*, such as it existed as an independent reality up to the middle of this century has now lost some of its uniqueness by spreading throughout the world, the variety of opinion which it represents still makes an invaluable contribution to world diversity. One cannot conceive of a European identity which is not made up of diversity, juxtapositions of singularities, crossing and boundaries... Globalization is a new sphere of experience for these singularities. What's more, European cultural identity is fundamentally based on its relationship to *the other*: conflicting or competitive, the notion of otherness permeates the conditions governing identity.

But as a powerful factor in encouraging greater convergence in matters of education, qualifications, ecology, technology transfer and closer links

---

2   The first three French motivations for a <u>no</u>-vote to the ratification of the Maastricht Treaty were: losing France's sovereignty (58%), the Brussels' technocracy (57%), fear of Germany (41%).

3   For F. Fukuyama, 'cultural relativism (a European invention) has seemed plausible to our century...But if, over time, more and more societies with diverse cultures and histories exhibit similar long-term patterns of development; if there is a continuing convergence in the types of institutions governing most advanced societies; and if the homogenization of mankind continues as a result of economic development, then the idea of relativism may seem much stranger than it does now...Mankind will come to seem like a long wagon train strung out along a road...The apparent differences in the situations of the wagons will not be seen as reflecting permanent and necessary differences between the people riding in the wagons, but simply a product of their different positions along the road...' in The end of history and the last man, Penguin Books, 1992, p.p. 338-339.

between different cultures, globalism is just as likely to reinforce *comparative frustrations* both outside and within Europe. These are sources of conflict to which the European Union would be particularly vulnerable because of its openness and the persistent instability in its peripheral areas.

More specifically, the perceptive Danish analysis of a possible transition from *traditionalism* to *modern values* contains the likelihood of greater female participation rates, smaller family sizes and greater consumption of international goods. But the paper says 'change is gradual and clashes between tradition and nationalism, cultural homogeneity and tight family ties with new internationalism can be expected'.

Another interesting side issue is: Could post-industrialism in the Western world lead to less materialism? Both Belgium and Spain strongly emphasize the possible decline in societal solidarity as individualism increases and *competitivity, profitability and flexibility* become ends in themselves.

How can and will the public interest be defended in a corporatist world, constrained by budget discipline and changing values, asks the Greek paper?

The key cultural shaping factor could then be a triplet, not musical, but education-training-information (France) to which technology might be added. Without assimilation (i.e. education) and adaptation (openness to diversity), says the French text, the cultural fault-lines may not be able to be managed and repaired especially if economic growth is low and unemployment rates stubbornly high.

Global Socio-Economic Shaping Factors

One of the strongest convergent views in the socio-economic field is that the next decade and beyond will be characterized by (rapidly) increasing global competition. Driving this trend are technological change and ease of technology transfer, the concentration and transnationalism of business aided by faster information flows and improved international transport links. The mobility of the factors of production is a further cumulative reason with some Institutes also mentioning the likelihood of reduced trade barriers and cultural convergence as contributory elements. But globalism, as the previous sections show is not limited to pure economics and business. Growing international interdependence, e.g. in the environmental and research areas, is forcing more horizontal political cooperation. Likewise, Denmark foresees expanding cooperation between the social partners confronted with the fierceness of international competition.   The Dutch report sees the corollary of interdependence being policy competition between the Member States.   Policy competition in this context means governments competing against each other to improve their relative competitiveness thanks to the quality of their *immobile factors* (infrastructure, presence of efficient local suppliers, favourable unit labour costs), which attract foreign direct investments.   It is worth noting that no-one mentioned policy competition between trading blocks.

Concerning the macroeconomic context, the perspectives offered are not rosy. There are almost no signs in the National Institutes reports of an expectation of a decade of fast economic growth. A few Institutes (BRD, Luxembourg, UK) seem to hint at a 2-2.5% average economic growth rate, but without conviction.   The Danish paper, for example, tilts towards predicting modest economic growth (i.e. more 1970-90 average rates than 1950-70) with high real interest rates one major factor and economic uncertainty another, the latter driven by increasing global complexity.

The Greek paper looks at the positives and the negatives on economic growth. Negatives slowing economic growth prospects will be the fiscal imbalances of the US, BRD, the low saving rates in the OECD region, increasing investment demands (East Europe, Middle East reconstruction, and possibly for LDC development) driving up the cost of capital. Likewise, persistent North/South disequilibria will act as a drag on growth. But on the brighter side, world economic policy-making is, say the Greek Institute, more mature, the dangers of protectionism are better understood, the filtration of liberal economics into the Third World rapid. Furthermore, capital and commodity markets are more organized, and OPEC currently weak.

Among the Institutes, there are few residing in the camp expecting a major increase in world economic tension in the next decade or so. However, the structural disequilibria in the world economy, e.g. the US double deficits, Japan's growing export surplus and world debt, are not expected to be resolved rapidly.

In spite of the growing demands on the world's capital markets, capital shortage does not feature as a major socio-economic global factor, even though many Institutes feel the upward pressure on real interest rates will continue to be significant. The danger of a decline in world savings gets a mention by Spain and as for Europe, the Belgian paper talks of the need to reduce public sector dissaving. There is also a fear that developments in

Eastern Europe will drain capital away from Europe's peripheral countries and regions.

One of the striking features in our analysis of this section is that the weaker economies in Europe (Spain, Ireland, Portugal, Greece) all mention that *changes in the organization and distribution of labour* will be a significant shaping factor. This is barely mentioned by the other Institutes. Spain says a post-modern 1990's new labour market entrant will have to modify his training and specialization as many as three times during his working life, a radical change from the characteristics of the post-war labour markets. Ireland puts more emphasis on the patterns of production and location, with the growing role of foreign direct investment flows deciding the international division of labour.

This leads to the crucial European problem: the high rates of persistent unemployment. As has been previously mentioned, many Institutes link high unemployment levels with social exclusion and dualism, with the Danish text adding criminalism and authoritarian populism on top. The Portuguese paper feels unemployment will not be solved by technology change, whilst the Danish text states that increasing world-wide competition will tend to cause greater concentration of business and therefore perhaps a higher proliferation of pockets of structural unemployment with low growth scenarios, which is an Irish fear as well.

There is also a broad-based consensus among the Institutes that education and training will be important shaping factor components of successful economies in the 1990s and beyond, as well as a long-term response to some forms of unemployment. The French paper says endogenous human capital will be a crucial component of growth whether it be R&D policy and practice, education or demographic change. The education-training-information triplet could transform economic activity in the decades ahead they suggest. Likewise, technology and the ability to absorb technological change feature strongly across the board, with much emphasis placed on the growing ease of technology and diffusion, the information networks and the speed of information flows as a means of generating greater economic flexibility in a growing interdependent world.

Trade policy is mentioned frequently by the Institutes as a major global shaping factor. The UK paper argues that the speed of liberal market economics will drive trade policy to reduce trade barriers, whilst Ireland, understandably, places much more emphasis on the effects of the liberalization of agricultural trade (but at what speed?), and the pressure to fundamentally restructure the Community's CAP. The Netherlands sees this issue in terms of international policy competition, but Greece is more cautious on the outcome of whether we will see more trade blocks and protectionism or greater liberalism. Regional integration arrangements can lead to important trade diversion effects if external trade policies are not open. There is barely a passing reference, except in the BRD analysis, to the spread of trade barrier dismantlement in a growing number of LDCs. Again, one is left with a feeling of the expectation of change towards *greater trade liberalization, but at a slow pace*, not surprising, it has to be said, where ending the Uruguay Round has proven to be so difficult.

The questioning of the future role and financing of the public sector has already been mentioned. This is a strong factor for Spain, the Netherlands and Belgium in particular. The Spanish report talks of a schism between the financing and provision of the public sector and the perception of its inability to solve market failures plus the general public's increasing critical analysis of its role.

The Portuguese analysis detects a concentration of economic and financial power in the hands of new players (especially the multinationals) who are taking on the role of strategic planning with the political powers. The events in the weeks before and after the French Referendum in retrospect might have persuaded our National Institutes to add the currency speculators and foreign exchange dealers to this list!

The Belgian paper fits into the same slipstream: we are in an era of *public sector reform* driven to a large extent by European Community political agreements on EMU/EPU which include the pressure to reduce public sector deficits, deregulation, reductions in fiscal receipts for international policy competition reasons. What then is the corollary for the social contract and social welfare? Who is going to pay for health, pensions, education and social protection? How is it possible to avoid the collapse of the social system through a less costly and more efficient forms of organization?

In the global context, environment, energy and demography are also mentioned as shaping factors. Post-Rio is the world likely to take on a new sustainable development paradigm? There are few signs that the Institutes think so. *The environment* is a shaping factor indeed, but *not yet* perceived as *a driver*, policy motivator or a source of long-run competitive advantage. The Danish paper says the public are becoming more aware of the costs of the environment and therefore there is more opposition building up against radical change. More emphasis will be placed on socio-economic responses in the future. Greece warns of the dangers of trade-environment protectionism, and France that ecology could be a constraint on economic growth. But the UK Institute flags the major global environmental threats strongly.

Energy issues are mentioned more in the context of environment, and the need to pursue robust demand side energy saving reductions (e.g. Belgium, France) rather than on the problems of supply. The 1970s' and early 1980s' preoccupations of the world running out of energy or facing rapidly increasing energy prices seem to be judged much less important today.

Demographic movements and migratory pressures are, as previously mentioned, considered as major socio-economic shaping factors. Markets will change (more leisure, more health demands, less saving, etc.); there will be pressures and tensions in local labour markets and public health budgets can expect to increase in relative terms as Europe's active population ages and the old become even older. Population increases in the South will, *ceteris paribus*, require very high rates of economic growth just to maintain average per capita income, so the relative income differential between North and South may not be able to be reduced (France). Therefore, for many more in the South, migration will become the most attractive card they have to play.

We return, therefore, volte-face, to the North/South issue again. Can the maintenance of the levels of North/South income disequilibria be sustained in the next two decades? Will the failure of the OECD countries to transfer modest amounts of their income (e.g. the unfulfilled 0.7% GDP commitment), technology, management and hope be a major shaping factor in the years ahead? Or as the Greek paper says, do we face a choice between Third World goods or Third World immigrants?

SECTION 2: NATIONAL SHAPING FACTORS

Introduction

A horizontal reading of the National Institutes' reports concerning the national shaping factors of relevance for the future of their societies, businesses, and citizens might be expected, given the spectral diversity that makes up their individual countries, to yield interesting insights, complementarities and divergences, different methodologies and sensitivities, different expectations and different implications for the European Community and/or the European Union.

Indeed it does.

Each document, to varying degrees, provides a chink of light, a clarification of where each country sees its strengths, its weaknesses, its future strategy, its desired or even plotted direction for the European Community. But it is a complex jigsaw, complicated by the interweaving of often subtle socio-political, cultural and economic factors which are themselves alone difficult to interpret. Interactively even more so. Is this complexity a function of the moment, the political and economic uncertainty we all face, the unravelling of post-war power structures, a transition from narrow nationalism to a new era of mutual common interests, a crisis in democratic systems or the empirical logic of exploding information flows and information systems? How certain (or unsure) are the views and prospective themes we are dealing with? Where will be wrong, or right? Is it even sensible to try to separate the wood from the trees and risk by distillation and filtration oversimplification, banality, even flippancy?

The risk is worth taking - if only to stimulate discussion, disagreement and further reflection. Indeed, we could argue that not to take a horizontal cut at this material is itself a failure of logic, because the world, its elements, actors, powers and businesses are horizontally and spatially linked, like it or not. The difficulty is to find the drivers, the puppeteer who pulls the strings or the deterministic creative forces.

A most striking feature of the national shaping factors taken together is *the major role played by the social and the economic factors, a role where the two types of factors are closely intertwined.*

Ireland say early on in its report that 'the major Irish concern is with a set of interlinked economic problems encompassing unemployment, poverty, emigration, Ireland's relative prosperity within the Community, high taxation'.

The British reading also contains more *socio-economics* than socio-cultural or political emphasis, with particular stress placed on technology and globalization, the maturity of the UK economy, and some biting analysis of socio-economic developments in the UK in recent years.

Similarly, in the Belgian and Danish reports there is a heavy emphasis placed on the conditions and perspectives of the key competitivity variables, and on their links with the role of the public sector and the Welfare State in the future.

The focus of the Greek text is economic reconstruction and how to regain a position in the mainstream economic fold. Spain places much emphasis on the future international competitivity of the Spanish economy and the efficiency of its public sector. The Dutch *leitmotif* is that policy efficiency, i.e. the policy competition between nations to attract technology, capital and labour, is the crucial factor. Luxembourg perhaps fits into this approach as well.

The integrated and comprehensive Portuguese paper contains much analysis of the impact on Portugal of the Community's EMU convergence criteria, with competitivity a worrying variable.

The Italian reading, an original but different approach from the others, flags two central socio-economic concerns that have strong socio-cultural and political *raison d'être*, namely the uncontrolled growth of public spending and a plethora of *imbalances* causing sub-optimal pareto welfare results impacting on many aspects of Italian life.

These approaches are not unique, but rally a core of main issues that will be listed below. The French paper contains more socio-cultural insights with interesting analyses of the possible direction and orientation of segments of French society. Furthermore, in the French paper there are passages, an exception rather than the rule, on whither the Nation State, where are the flash points and the future division of powers possible between France as a Nation and the Community, debates of course that surfaced during the Maastricht Referendum.

Finally, the German report suggests that the next 10 to 15 years will be a time of rather unideological, pragmatic policy-making, with a likely price to be paid for it, i.e. the political resistance against the bribing of special interest groups may be reduced and the call for budgetary discipline may weaken.

Main Socio-Economic Factors

International Competition

There is unanimous agreement that all the Twelve face increased economic competition in the future. This competitive pressure, which may accelerate, is derived from both inside the Community, via the construction and functioning of the single market, from the Triad, the emerging NICs and, eventually, segments of industrial goods from East Europe, hand in hand with GATT trade liberalization. Likewise, all national reports, but to a lesser extent the German one, put strong emphasis on a number of factors that will determine the outcome for the Community. These are:

(i)   *Our relative technological position,* innovatory capacity, scientific and technical creativity with particular stress on electronics, biotechnology and new materials, with policy prescriptions extending as far as product marketing.

(ii)   *Research expenditure* which is considered by all Institutes as being too low in Europe against our main competitors.

(iii) *Inadequate training* and supply of technically qualified personnel, and the skills supply in general together with an inadapted education system.

(iv)   *Insufficient infrastructure* requiring major public (and/or) private investments in the future.

(v)   *In the smaller countries* or less advanced economies, problems of economies of scale, international experience and access to patient capital at the right price.

Consensus Among the Social Partners

Given the uncertainties and the risks created by an increasing international competition, the construction of a consensus among social partners is more crucial than ever.

But there are some major differences of view, not just about the existence today of differing relations among the social partners, but also on whether and how they may become shaping factors in the future.

For the Netherlands, Belgium, Denmark, Germany and Luxembourg consensus formulation at the bi- or tri-partite levels has been largely successful and an essential stimulus for economic success in the past. Stress is placed on the maintenance of this factor as being a crucial competitive vector in the future. This is not to suggest that neo-liberal forces will not place these systems under pressure, nor that more decentralization could (or indeed should) result from increased globalization, or that the pricing of wages should be more in line with local productivity change.

In the remaining countries matters are more heterogeneous. In Ireland, there is a perception of the importance of social consensus, but the jury is out on whether a social consensus mechanism can succeed. Portugal is in the same camp. In the UK, it is argued that there has been virtually no dialogue at all between the Government, employers and trade unions for 15 years and the present Government has recently voted to scrap the only remaining and occasionally used vehicle for such a dialogue, namely the National Economic Development Council. In Greece, the private sector dialogue is developing, but the public sector social partners' relationship might be expected to remain difficult as the public sector is reined in. Spain reports the strong trade union tradition of political struggle, a lack of experience in negotiation, and strong leverage in the public sector. Relations are not good and could remain so under the pressure of the Community's convergence criteria.

France, as well, has difficulties in this area and declares itself ill-equipped for dialogue and consultation in the twenty-first century as does Italy, faced with trade union splintering and militancy as economic reformism takes hold.

Socio-Economic Dualism

One central characteristic of European countries is the value given to social equality and solidarity. In America a stronger weight is given to freedom. In spite of growing doubts created by ethnicity and a new class-consciousness,[4] the belief is still that individuals are rewarded according to their individual efforts and merits. As shown in the following table, public opinion in European countries considers on the contrary that equality is a major value and is not automatically obtained through market forces: it is part of the government's responsibility.

Table 2.1

Which is more important: equality or freedom?			Is it government's responsibility to reduce income differences?	
% choosing	Equality	Freedom	%	Yes
United States	20	72	Italy	81
Britain	23	69	Hungary	77
France	32	54	Holland	64
Italy	45	43	Britain	63
West Germany	39	37	West Germany	56
Spain	39	36	United States	28
Source: Gallup International Research Institute, 1987-88 quoted in The Economist, Sept. 5th 1992.				

In the European Community's Member States, there is a growing feeling that as we enter a world where only the skilled and well educated will

---

4   For a stimulating analysis, see M. Kaus, *The end of equality*, Basicbooks, 1992.

make a decent living, the gap between the very rich and the very poor is going to keep growing.

Even in countries where the social dialogue works well, the danger of a *dual society* is becoming a central problem. Many National Institutes report the proliferation and dangers of a burgeoning excluded and deprived social category in Europe, linked in part, but not entirely, to high levels of long-term unemployment and unfavourable tax and benefit systems. We read from the Irish paper of 'a set of residual classes stranded in the cause of industrial development, especially farmers on marginal holdings and labourers without skills', without an exit.

From Italy, '19% are living below the poverty line, of which around 1 million live in real misery'. With close to 3 million out of work, the UK reports that many are caught in the poverty trap, with income inequalities in the UK exacerbated by the widening gap between higher and lower earnings, social benefits frozen in real terms since 1979 and tax cuts favouring higher incomes under successive Governments. Like Italy, around 20% of UK adults are below national average income. The UK paper warns starkly:

> there is a danger that this growing underclass will be subject to increasing hardship and deprivation, with a permanence extending to further generations and that this will lead to increasing bitterness and alienation from the rest of the Community including a withdrawal from involvement in democratic political processes.

Even Denmark says that the long-term unemployed are beginning to form a distinct subculture of *outcasts*. Politically to the left, with some aggressive traits.

Social exclusion is mentioned elsewhere, perhaps with less ferocity, and it is a major and worrying European shaping factor even more so as European employment prospects are uncertain and as the role of the family (an additional or unique social insurance mechanism) also appears to be on the decline (see below). Dualism in the labour market can also take another form (see France, Spain) between those who are permanently employed and those temporary employees who tend to take the brunt of changes in the labour market. Dualism is the offshoot and inflexibility in the labour market a side-effect.

Demographic Trends

Europe is ageing. Not all parts, not at the same speed, nor with the same effects on the labour market but the overall trend is crystal clear. What are the dynamic implications of this ... *revolution grise* ... or an ...*end of career* ... boom. As stated by the Belgian report,

> demographic trends may have an impact on social and employment policy, particularly in the framework of dialogue between the two sides of industry, the freedom of movement of workers and migration policy, equal opportunities for men and women, etc.

More specifically, several important factors are at play:

(i)   In the longer term, particularly post-2000, the dependency rates spiral rapidly upwards thereby increasing, substantially, the financing costs of public welfare systems, pensions, health etc. ... The German paper says 'the welfare state is in trouble...'. The Netherlands agrees unless major changes are made.

(ii)   The number of very old (>80 years) is expected to increase very markedly, having a disproportionate effect on health budgets.

(iii)   There is a perceived need, particularly strong in some countries, to increase participation rates in the economy to pay for the required welfare schemes (e.g. the Netherlands in particular).

(iv)   That major labour shortages are not likely in the short-term with the present levels of unemployment in Europe, but may develop towards the end of the century if the economic situation is healthy. This clearly depends on a range of factors such as females participation rates. There appears to be an implication that widespread immigration may not be needed to fill these labour market gaps in the near term (i.e. to 2000), except perhaps in Luxembourg where immigrants and *frontaliers* make up a large proportion of the workforce.

(v)   In certain countries, the demographic outcome is particularly uncertain. In particular in Portugal there is no consensus on the overall balance (immigration $> <$ emigration) taking into account the 600,000 Portuguese nationals who still reside in her former African colonies. Greece cannot predict its demographic path given the present situation in the Balkans with a quarter of a million or more refugees already within Greek frontiers and the many ethnic Greeks living in the CIS States. Ireland will witness an increase of inflows to its labour market in the 1990s greater than past or present rates of job creation, so emigration will be expected to continue at the high rates of the 1980s.

Industrial Policy and the Role of the Public Sector

The trend towards the globalization of trade and competition, the necessity of being competitive to maintain a high standard of living and to fight unemployment and to safeguard the social consensus require some forms of voluntarist policy that creates a supportive environment for industry. This could be the bacillus of a new form of industrial policy. What do the Institutes say on this?

The French report, as might be expected, makes a strong appeal in favour, listing some of the above contents. The British report puts particular emphasis on R&D expenditure, the training and skills deficit and the promotion and adoption of high technology. In the German paper we read:

> As international competition strengthens, traditional BRD liberalism may come under pressure ... with more emphasis on trade related investment measures and international competition rules. ... The front line against industrial policy (in BRD) may be weakening, spurred by a growing belief that BRD is behind Japan and US in some key strategic areas ....

The Danish paper says industrial policy has never been important in the past, but there is now an important shift in thinking on education, training, and ways to stimulate domestic R&D in the competitivity race. Italy speaks of uncontrolled proliferation of agents and attitudes, the *open door* to public expenditure which has led to inefficiency and the lack of collective vision, strategy and application plus the inability to innovate or create added-value.

However, there are elements that find less consensus, one of them being competition policy. The German script warns starkly that competition policy has to be effective against subsidies, there being a role for the EC to provide the public good of *openness of markets*. France however, appeals for competition policy being sited in the new globalized market framework and part of industrial policy.

A specific aspect of this topic is the future role of the public sector. Most reports list this issue but in a variety of different ways with different nuances. For example, there is the challenge of liberalism and public sector market opening (e.g. tenders), growing financial difficulties with the ageing of Europe and the increasing per capita costs of health care, the pressure of the EMU convergence criteria, or the need to radically trim the fat to release capital for investments in the private sector.

Likewise, much emphasis is placed on redirecting public expenditure away from transfer mechanisms to capital and particularly infrastructural investment (a view which would not be entirely accepted by the *cohesion* countries). Both the role and the efficiency of the public sector are questioned along with the merits of privatization as a strategy, and the level of fiscal consciousness (low in Spain, Greece and Italy).

In Spain, the objective of public sector efficiency can be agreed on, but not the remedy among the social partners. In Luxembourg, an efficient public policy and consensus on it is seen as a crucial method of attracting foreign capital, and finding the balance between specialization, minimizing risk and maximizing yield. Denmark has 60% of its GDP covered by the public sector, and questions whether this is sustainable (even if unduly supported and ingrained in the social consensus) in the long run under the competitive whip of its trading partners. The Dutch paper talks of rebalancing public expenditure to reduce social security costs in order to increase public investments, to meet the convergence criteria and encourage higher participation rates in the labour market. It also speaks of shifting the system to provide social subsistence in the future or a *trampoline* and not a *hammock*, recognizing, nevertheless that more than 70% of Dutch citizens support the present system, which is still qualified as an overall *economic asset*.

The Italian text says the uncontrolled *open door* growth of the State's public spending has to come to an end - and provides a range of interesting insights as to why this has come about. Effectively it is the private sector, its *market dialectic* that controls the public sector but this will be increasingly challenged as the Italian welfare system comes under the twin pincers of an ageing population, rising life expectancy, and a desperate need to fund the pensions scheme.

The German text also says the sizeable fiscal burden of German unification will be a major shaping factor for the next ten years. Consolidating public finances will be a major theme with permanently higher deficits (required for transfers to the East) not being monetized by the Central Bank, implying a period of high real interest rates. Current transfer mechanisms to the East, they say, are unsustainable, and will lead to a dual economy in the East, with unemployment rates of 20% or more. We could have the Saar/Ruhr restructuring revisited in the 1990s in the East.

For Greece, with a 60% GDP share under public control economic convergence will require *drastic* changes in the public sector. First of all to reduce it, secondly to make it efficient, and thirdly to redirect expenditure to repair vital infrastructural deficits. Depoliticizing the public sector is considered an additional necessary condition. Greece's social security is also under a major threat, with an efficient tax gathering system another urgent requirement. But reducing the *psychological dependency* on the State will be the most difficult of all.

The UK may have one of the most efficient public sectors, but it too faces a number of key public financing variables going in the wrong direction in the medium-term.

Finally, this problem is strongly raised in the Belgian paper where it is stated that the public sector is increasingly contested, whether it be regulations, finance, the share of budgets between the regions, the Maastricht conditions, financing health and the future *pensions shock* (by 2010) or even providing the cash for traditional State functions (e.g. R&D, infrastructure).

The Community Itself

Throughout the National Institutes' reports, the Community itself appears as a major national shaping factor in the socio-economic sphere.   The main spheres quoted concern:

-       The competitive effects of the SEM.
-       The convergence criteria of EMU.
-       Cohesion policies.
-       Social Charter (to a lesser extent).
-       Agriculture.
-       Environment.

This role is much more emphasized by the smaller countries and those whose economies are behind the EC average, than by the larger ones.

For both Portugal and Greece the cohesion principles are perceived as essential for economic convergence and industrial and agricultural restructuring, building up competitive infrastructure and so on.

Spain emphasizes the major sacrifices that will have to be made. The stakes are very high: 'Achieving convergence for the third phase of EMU is without doubt the biggest challenge facing Spanish society at the moment'. Achieving it will put Spain in the group of the most advanced EC countries and justify the costs and benefits of belonging to such a group. The consequences of failure? Unleashing anti-EC forces, anarchistic tendencies and possibly losing a major dynamizing factor in social and economic change in Spain for many years. The most important part of Spain's modernization is membership of the EC.

The Netherlands sees the Community as laying down the determinant policy competition framework, whereas for Ireland, apart from agriculture, the Community cohesion issue is the vital one and one which needs new perspectives, a new strategic approach and new measurements beyond spatial equity to take into account social issues and progress.

Italy pleads for new criteria, whereas European integration along with the environment and social policy are listed among the major factors for the BRD. Apart from the BRD's well-known reserves on EMU, the paper warns that, contrary to the aspirations of some, the EC must make it clear that the adjustment problems of some countries will not be alienated by regional fiscal transfers to help with wage rigidities otherwise BRD support for the Community and EMU will weaken further.

The UK sees the Community's long-run shaping role mainly through the EMU/SEM mechanisms.

France has detailed comment on the major socio-economic shaping role of the EC on EMU / SEM / industrial and technology policy / trade / agriculture / energy / competition / defence although less in the social and primary education spheres.

There is further discussion of the European Community dimension in Chapter 5.

Main Socio-Cultural Factors

Declining or Changing Role of the European Family

Most Institutes report that the place of the family in society is in steady decline most spectacularly in the North; there is a boost of individualism, new social priorities, a decline of *collectivism*. Many reasons are given - including increased female participation in the workforces, low birth-rates, social stress and the very rapid rise in the rates of divorce noted and expected to continue.

Greece points out that if such social values weaken - and the family can no longer play its nuclear role as the income maximizer - the State will have to provide additional social and intergenerational insurance. Portugal is more optimistic, saying that the Portuguese are still expected to maintain a preference for the family, although personal achievement is a highly valued social ethic, but not, apparently, in contradiction with social participation and formulas for collective criteria. The Irish family situation, leaving aside the problems of social exclusion, is exacerbated by the high emigration rates that are expected to continue. Overall the family position is weakening. The Dutch analysis suggests individualization is on the rise, with less family solidarity. Sports clubs, friends and outside groups among others are playing the role of substitutes.

These trends are noted in France as well, where women have enjoyed a huge change of status in recent decades, but 'social cultural modernism is only just beginning to be debated' in France. Alongside a decline in traditional symbolic institutions, France also sees some importance in the vertical expansion of families as Europe ages. More generally, the current evolution is compatible with the fact that new forms of familial organization emerge leading to new types of solidarity, especially in the Northern countries and in the young generation. These models are characterized by unofficial cohabitation, a high degree of autonomy and mobility, but also a requirement of equity between partners and a sense of responsibility that goes beyond the narrow circle of the institutional family.

National Versus European Identity

There are few Institutes which believe in the significance or likelihood of *a European identity* as a shaping factor although some place great emphasis on this issue as a *sine qua non* for real European integration. National identity is more frequently listed as important and sensitive in the larger countries (UK, BRD, France) and in Denmark.

The French text says French identity remains strongest at the lowest levels of the social structure and it postulates, prospectively, one of two possible outcomes - either that many old values and traditions will become obsolete and disappear or, for a hallowed number of subjects and traditions, they will be safeguarded at all costs. The French describe this as the antagonism of two forces - social weightlessness versus French symbolism.

The BRD sees the importance of Germany being at the cross-roads of multiculturalism, new Western values, Eastern (but not Southern) immigrants, but also underlines that the collapse of East European Communism will reinforce German identity and could lead to a renewed nationalism.

The management of heterogeneity is flagged by the Netherlands. But if National identity is not perceived as a central shaping factor, the Dutch approach is increasingly influenced by fears of the bigger Member States calling the European tune in Community cooperation as well as intergovernmentally.

Luxembourg reports that national identity will remain a sensitive issue, notably in the context of its high foreigner population and in future voting in local elections, a Maastricht Treaty provision. Conversely, Portugal sees the next decade as a period of moving Portuguese society from *closeness* to *openness*. The Spanish paper contains an interesting section on *Europeanness*. Spain is among the most pro-EC countries in Europe, because during the dictatorship the Community was associated with democratic liberties, tolerance, social and economic development. But the acceptance of the idea of Europeanness loses sight of the short-term sacrifices and disciplines required that could, if too deep, erode this *appartenance*.

Concerning European identity, there is little discussion in the reports. But two insights seem central:

(i)   Identity can only be found in relation to something else.
(ii)   The European *public good* is not evident, explained or defined or, as the Irish paper says, 'centrality of political discourse is lost as we concentrate on the centrality of the National interests, which encompass less and less the real interests in European society'. The absence of values leaves the field to ethnic and other ideologies.

The French paper is surely right when it says that the 'existence of the powerful welfare state is central to the European social model ...' and it is, as we have seen, precisely this model that is under a barrage of criticism and questioning. The European model is prospectively under more threat by the questioning of this internal consensus on which the Welfare State was founded, particularly if the model fails to adapt to the far-reaching demographic changes underway. The thrusts of globalization, competitivity, internationalism and mono-liberal philosophies are additional external arrows to deflect. Here a key role could be played by education. According to France, 'interaction and exchanges between National education systems would be warmly greeted by younger generations to translate the differences of cultures, languages and countries among themselves ....'

Overall, the National Institutes appear to consider that, through such interactions, convergent visions of a common destiny could emerge. What makes a nation state is its common history, culture and traditions. But it has to be recognized that our Common *European* memory is especially of divisions and war. The European Community has as its destiny to create itself from the future. This is not a future that entails becoming a super-state but rather a *meta-nation state*, which will be able to coexist with other nations and which will express a pluralist identity that we might call *unitas multiplex*.

Regionalism Versus Centralism

In the national shaping factors context, there is not a universal view of whether this range of issues will become a central theme. Is a rise in regionalism likely in Europe? Might it be the logical consequence of subsidiarity and political reform? The evidence is mixed. For the smaller countries, the substance is mentioned but without great vigour. Denmark notes that its *H* road/bridge infrastructure projects will integrate both North and South Denmark and its East-West axis with its neighbours. Ireland says that there is no consensus on whether to devolve more power to the local authorities, but the crucial geo-European issue is Ireland's place at the Community table. Luxembourg, as a sovereign state, foresees that it has advantages over being purely a regional entity, by having more flexibility, instruments and especially the sovereignty to decide on the logistics. Although Catalan and Basque nationalism are strong current political factors in Spain, they do not emerge as major prospective issues in the Spanish paper, given that the autonomous regions have already inherited 80% of the former centralist powers of the dictatorship era. In Belgium, the Federal State retains only three major powers, monetary policy, social security and security. The State has already become a bipolar and centrifugal federal state, and in the future further fiscal powers could drift towards the regional governments.

The Italian position is interesting. They predict that a general shaping factor will be a return to the *territorial dimension*, centred on the local/regional space in parallel with the international/global dimension which will entail strengthening our identity, our needs and own social responses. Indeed, *territorialization* seems a major consequence of European integration, creating not necessarily new institutional spaces, but transnational and transregional subsystems that could form and constitute *l'Europe des régions* and horizontal Community integration. The idea continues that Europe cannot be a homogeneous group of Northern rich countries. Real integration requires integrating the rich and poor, the North and the South. It is surprising how rapidly some of the Community's Regions are linking up and creating joint projects together. France also mentions the importance of integrating Europe's territories, its network of towns and regions as a means of developing European citizenship. The French paper mentions the notion of transport *mesh* concepts rather than star-shaped constellations as one of many policy ideas for linking Europe's territories more widely.

France also lists two other great prospective spatial challenges to rural/urban life, namely:

(i)   Controlling the natural areas eaten away by urbanization and infrastructure.

(ii)   Set-aside policies devastating the rural areas.

Today 80% of French citizens live on 20% of its land (compared to a 50:50 ration in 1900). The costs of this equation are expensive (a loss of 7.5 million working hours/day in Paris due to congestion). Worse still, the cost of providing services to the nomadic rural regions is becoming impossible. Hence the Community involvement is striking and shaping.

The devolution debates in the UK (Scotland, Wales, Northern Ireland) have taken a place on the back burner after the 1992 election, but feeling is nevertheless running quite high that the centralism of London needs to change in the medium-term - indeed, the subsidiarity principle needs to be fully applied throughout all layers of government.

Immigration

The possibility of large-scale East-West and South-North migration is a growing concern for most EC countries.

There are some indications about the quantitative importance of this phenomenon. Taking flows from Southern to Northern Europe as a whole, around 3% of the population of the South moved North during 1950-70. In recent years, the Southern members of the EC have experienced relatively little continuing emigration.

This arguably because of their membership of the EC, which not only relieves factor market pressures by encouraging goods trade, but also lends credibility to their political and economic reform processes.[5]

Concerning migration from Central and East European countries (CEEC), a recent report by the Centre for Economic Policy Research concludes that even current income disparities seem unlikely to generate flows in excess of 5% of the CEEC population (5.7 million people) over twenty years; such an inflow is about 1.5% of the population of the EC plus EFTA.[6] However, migration could increase in response to severe political disruptions and the immigrants would not be evenly spread through the EC, so difficulties could arise for particular countries and regions.

Nearly all Institutes mention these immigration pressures, whether they be from the South or East, building up on the Community. Some are more pessimistic than others about the prospects for controlling them, all seem to orient towards the need for a Community solution.

Spain in the front line in the South, says North Africa will be the most destabilizing area of all in Spain's international relations, possibly leading to crisis and difficult to solve diplomatically. The BRD is likely to take the brunt of East-West movements of people, Italy and Greece from the South-East, although the flow of East Europeans towards the Community so far has been much below expectation. The BRD is therefore moving from a *de facto* to a *de jure* immigration country. Xenophobic reactions exist, but they could remain localized. Trade liberalization is the best policy weapon to encourage potential migrants in their country to stay, the BRD says. Portugal is unsure of the direction of the possible flows but a large stock of Portuguese passport holders are in her former African colonies. Greece's traditional tolerance towards races of all creed and colour might be put to the test in the 1990s, whereas the UK, perhaps feels (wrongly?) that its major flow of immigrants is over even though the number of asylum seekers from the poorer countries is increasing. Denmark reports that the fear of more foreigners and refugees getting into Denmark (i.e. the lack of common borders) was called *the hidden agenda* of the Maastricht referendum because expressions referring to ethnicity

5   CEPR, *Is Bigger Better?* The Economics of EC Enlargement, Annual Report, London, 1992.
6   Op. cit., p 86 to 88.

are taboo - therefore the *no* vote was used as an acceptable way of expressing this fear.

The Netherlands reports that the number of immigrants in the country is relatively lower than in Belgium, France and the BRD but they already face high unemployment and low participation rates. The management of this heterogeneity is therefore a major challenge. Italy describes its situation as *a real emergency* of which demographics are only one indicator. In fact there are many different types of economic immigrants requiring different types of solution: they have different motivations, raising entirely new cultural problems and requiring new thinking on the rights of citizenship, diversity and the right of equality. Indeed the Welfare State has to be revisited in a multicultural way.

France says this factor is a manifestation of a central problem affecting all post-modern societies namely, the coexistence of two conflicting trends: on one side, the gradual uniformity of lifestyles on the other the division of society into three states - a central constellation, a superclass, and a poorly educated *underclass*, the young, unskilled and immigrants.

A crucial and central factor is whether the Community can remain open to multiculturalism and, if it has to change, at what speed can it change. Can Europe's highly prized asset - its cultural diversity - buffeted by globalization and multiplicative, exponentially growing information flows be accommodating and receptive to multiculturalism as well?

The German paper sums up the situation quite well. Germany, it says, needs to become a bit less Swedish and a bit more American in its sociological structure. *Can (European) cosmopolitanism develop, pari passu, with the influx of ideas and the inflow of people?*

Socio-Political Factors at the National Level

Mondialization Versus Eurocentrism

A striking and contrasting feature of the National Institutes' reports is the degree of external emphasis they put in the socio-political dimension.

The BRD report could be described as Eurocentric, with Central and East Europe German unification and the Community's own integration as central themes. Conversely, France centres its report on *l'universalisme et le globalisme*. The UK text takes a global view, whilst indicating that the privileged UK-US relationship is not of the same dimension than in the past. Of course Europe and the Community are important, *because there is no alternative.*

Whilst for the smaller countries, in general, there is much greater emphasis on Eurocentrism (the Netherlands, Ireland, Luxembourg, Portugal, Spain) and for Italy as well.

There are additional interesting comments from Germany, Portugal, Denmark and Greece. For Germany, the collapse of the East has redefined and made clearer German foreign policy interests. Whatever the outcome it will defend its Eastern *bias* interests more stoutly, in Brussels and elsewhere in the future. But it will not be able to escape from increased international responsibilities even if it wanted to in the medium-term.

Denmark looks at the issues of Nordic and Baltic solidarity, in the context of enlargement. It concludes that inter-Nordic relations are not identical; they all want free access but for different kinds of products, and therefore close Nordic cooperation to influence the economics of the EC is unlikely.

In Portugal there is an ongoing debate of the merits pitching the historical Atlanticists versus the Europeans. The latter are in the ascendancy of course, but the door is not shut tight, and Atlantic revivalism could be rekindled if convergence and economic cohesion fail, in Portuguese terms, to deliver the goods.

Greece lists both the Balkans and Turkey and the Mediterranean as major foreign policy shaping factors, which, *ceteris paribus*, will, given the instability and historical suspicions, require Greece to maintain its large defence spending. There will be no peace dividend for Athens. If the European Community (the most important multilateral institution in the area) fails in the region to provide the security premium required, Greece will have to turn to the US for guarantees.

Globalism however spills over into other policy areas considered as important shaping factors of the future, namely reforming agricultural policies and for dealing with global environmental threats. This is mentioned by most Institutes, but with less vigour than might have been some two or three years ago. Here there is a general recognition of Community competence and relevance.

Political Decision-Making Processes

A general aspect is the feeling that there is a crisis of the Nation State and a necessity to improve the dialogue between the citizens and the politicians. However, as might be expected, there are some very different national perspectives.

For the BRD, a medium-term (15 years) period of unideological pragmatism is to be expected in domestic policy-making. This is partly due to the fusing together and convergence of the Eastern and Western poles of the main political parties. Both will move to the centre ground and may be more vulnerable or open to the pressure of lobbies. A period of more critical scrutiny of the Community, its decision-making procedures and democratic processes will become the order of the day, with German reservations on EMU likely to remain very strong, and even intensified as EMU deadlines approach.

For Portugal, there is a certain bipartisanship on economic matters, even political disinterest, but the social costs of modernization are a future potential flashpoint. The critical Greek political battle centres not on the need to find much greater efficiency in the public sector but on the equality versus efficiency trade-off, where there are crucial differences likely to remain among the parties.

For the UK, major decision-making changes are not likely after the results of the last election. Federalism will still mean devolving power to Brussels and the Community, and not a rebalancing of political sovereignty through all levels of decision-making.

The centrifugal Belgian political process has resulted in no national political parties being left, with no less than four political parties required to form a government at the national level. Is such a growing heterogeneity in political systems indicative of the future or will the homogenous *Nation State* model (privatizing the law of the market, competitivity, productivity, flexibility...) persevere at the European level?

It might be suspected that much more has been learnt about the Danish political system after the 1992 referendum than probably at any time in its Community history. Denmark will still maintain its *broad political agreements approach* to political decision-taking based on consensus forming, harmony and societal acceptance even though the political parties are losing members, and more voters are shifting their votes. Danish voters will probably still opt for a right-wing economic policy, a social democratic redistributive policy and a *green* environment policy that does not hurt Danish competitiveness. The stress on egalitarianism, anti-elitism and economic liberalism might be a type of post-modernism that could spread.

The French paper subjects its own political system and the European Community's to close analysis. The paper states the importance and need for political change and modernization - a *fundamental review of the political system*, which has already begun, but which like most French symbols, is destined to change. The crisis of the Nation State is at odds with individualism and modern consumer concepts of public goods. Local governments are beginning to take over where the Nation State has failed to assume its role: dealing with poverty, unemployment, cities, or helping businesses to compete and innovate or within the wider multilateral spheres (the domain of higher law or ecological planetary rights). France's attitudes to the European Community are still shaped by the view that the European integration is a means for increasing its market size, reinforcing its international influence, allaying Europe dominated by Germany. *La France par l'Europe!* France has idealized political Europe into an enlarged version of France, but only now is it beginning to understand the disparities and difficulties involved.

3. Views of the Business Community on Post-1992 Integration in Europe

Diane Coutu, Karen Hladik, David Meen and Dominique Turcq*

INTRODUCTION

Despite the controversy over the future of Europe that has erupted around the Maastricht Treaty, corporations in most instances take the perspective that an 'integrated' Europe is highly desirable and worthy of a vigorous, concerted effort. Although this support for a more integrated Europe does not translate into full acceptance of all the social and political changes outlined in Maastricht, the European business community is nonetheless looking to the future with an ambitious set of priorities that would push economic integration even further than the single market did. Rather than articulate a new theme or grand vision, however, most corporations are adopting a concrete approach to European integration that focuses on leveraging a few targeted project areas. This pragmatism is conditioned not only by the day-to-day realities of running a business, but by business leaders' extensive experience in 'major change'. Seasoned by their own successes and failures in change management over the last few decades, top executives and industry leaders warn that launching a major new vision before the gains of the single market are consolidated could very well jeopardize future market integration in Europe.

There is also profound agreement and support in the business community for a specifically European form of capitalism - for example, for investing greater resources in the 'social safety net' than either the Americans or the Japanese do. But a major preoccupation of businessmen as they look forward over the next five to ten years is the prospect of a very considerable loss of jobs - several hundred thousand in the automotive sector alone - with all the implications this would have on social stability and the economic sustainability of 'Eurocapitalism'. In

*   McKinsey & Co, Eurocenter.

this regard, it is interesting to note that although much of the business community perceives the competitive gap with the Japanese actually to have widened in the last year or so, there are as yet few calls for greater protectionism in Europe. On the other hand, senior corporate executives and industry leaders express anxious concern that the basic groundwork of rules and regulations governing further economic integration be structured with as much clarity and fairness as possible in order to allow them to meet the challenges arising from Japan and other non-European competitors. Here, the relationship between business and governmental authorities is seen as critical, particularly in the way new regulations are created and administered, and in the approach deemed necessary for establishing an effective government-industry dialogue.

This dialogue is particularly important given the different perspectives of the Commission and the business community towards the single market. When European businessmen talk about a single market, they are generally thinking about an 'integrated' market. The distinction goes deeper than words. The single market mainly involves removing tangible barriers that inhibit the free movement of people, goods, services and capital. An integrated market would go even further - it would, for example, break down intangible barriers, such as nationally-based economic and technical preferences.

These are just a few of the very clear messages that have emerged from the joint research conducted by the European Commission and McKinsey & Company[1] on how the European business community perceives post-1992 integration issues (namely, the 'second pillar' of the broader study discussed in the introduction to this book). With striking emphasis and consensus, European businessmen told us that implementation of the single market is their top priority and the *sine qua non* for creating the right conditions for Europe to become further integrated and more globally competitive in the future. Although this message is remarkably homogenous across Europe and industries, there are also a number of issues that could split the business community. These potentially divisive issues will be treated at the end of this chapter.

---

[1]   The core team consisted of Alexis Jacquemin, David Wright and Paul Löser from the EC Commission's Cellule de Prospective and David Meen, Dominique Turcq, Karen Hladik, Giuseppe Zocco and Diane Coutu from McKinsey & Co. This chapter reflects the findings of our work together, but does not necessarily reflect the views either of the Commission or of McKinsey & Co. Final responsibility for all opinions expressed in this chapter lies solely with the authors.

SECTION 1: BACKGROUND OF THE PROJECT

Methodology Used

The objective of the joint Commission-McKinsey project was to cover a suitably representative sample of large European corporations, taking into account such factors as number of employees, contribution to GNP, and geography. Our aim was to adopt a methodology that would allow an open and unbiased exchange of ideas on business concerns and priorities in order to identify the full range of issues and questions actually confronting European corporations today. To stimulate business leaders to articulate their own aspirations and priorities for post-1992 Europe, we presented them with five broad themes that more or less summarized the major shaping factors that were identified by the National Institutes[2] in other research conducted by the Commission. Although these themes were refined and altered over time, generally speaking they were: (i) implementation of the single market; (ii) mobilization of human resources and management of the social contract; (iii) environment and sustainable growth; (iv) risk management in the highly uncertain post-1992 period; and, (v) development of a uniquely European model of society, based on harnessing the benefits of diversity. To ensure as frank and uncensored a discussion as possible, all participants were guaranteed confidentiality.

As described in greater detail in the introduction to this book, a threefold approach was adopted to meet our objectives. First, we held intense sector-oriented workshops involving between 15 to 20 top European Commission officials and McKinsey consultants in each of four critical European sectors: automotive, banking, telecommunication services, and transportation (chiefly railway). Second, we interviewed more than 30 top executives of leading corporations and industry associations, most of them members of the European Round Table of Industrialists. Thirdly, we conducted an extensive survey of some 100 McKinsey partners and industry experts who have jointly served more than 50% of the Fortune 500 European companies in the last decade. In addition, we initiated informal discussions with business clients and with colleagues in leading European business schools.

Since most of the corporations we looked at were large, well-established European companies, it is important to keep in mind that the perceptions

---

[2]   These National Institutes are the economic research institutes of the various Member States. The Cellule de Prospective researched their understanding of post-1992 integration issues in another part of this study. See Chapter 2 for a summary of this perspective.

presented here may differ from those of small- and medium-sized enterprises (SMEs). Similarly, while most European countries were well covered through the series of interviews and workshops, a few national viewpoints (e.g. Greece, Ireland, and some members of the European Free Trade Association) were underrepresented, given, in part, the predominance of SMEs in these economies.

Nevertheless, during the nine-month project, more than 300 people were interviewed in eleven EC and EFTA countries. The findings reported here are necessarily subjective, reflecting the preoccupations of the various participants we interviewed. However, by systematically testing the reaction of this influential cross-section of the European business community to alternative scenarios for post-1992 integration, some indication emerged of the thinking of one of the major shaping actors on the European stage. It must be underscored, though, that in researching the priorities of this subset of the European business community, we focused on those areas that most directly affect the functioning of organizations and, hence, are most relevant for public authorities in their interaction with industry. Other issues that invariably surfaced in our discussions and interviews, such as demographic shifts, immigration, nuclear proliferation, North-South tensions, and enlargement, are covered in greater depth by the National Institutes. Given this focus, the rest of this chapter details some of the specific comments and suggestions that are being voiced by the European business community today.

The Competitive Gap: *The* Shaping Factor

Businessmen look at the European integration process not as macroeconomists or socioeconomists, but as people involved in productive activities leading to income and value creation in society. Thus, they tend not to analyse key macroeconomic social issues related to the way that created wealth is redistributed. Still, it has been an interesting finding of our research that businessmen generally accept and support, without significant national differences, the continuation of a distinctly 'social' model of capitalism in Europe, such as the one described by Michel Albert.[3] Albert has compared the various capitalist systems by contrasting the North American model, founded on individualism, with the so-called 'Rhine' model, which he describes as a

---

[3]   Michel Albert, op. cit. See also Herbert A. Henzler, 'The New Era of Eurocapitalism', *Harvard Business Review*, July-August 1992.

'market social economy', where social health is a major objective and economic health a major tool. The European model of capitalism is based on this Rhine model, with national specificities. In articulating their belief that Europe needs to maintain its own version of the social contract, executives raised and agreed with many of the points made by Albert.

At the same time, however, European business leaders frankly fear increased social costs in a future of slower growth and heightened competition, and they deride the inefficiencies arising in the distribution of wealth - for example, inefficient management of health-care systems - since these can interfere with their ability to create wealth and jobs. The comment of a French industry leader was characteristic: 'Reducing public sector inefficiencies could be the next step in the progression of the single market. Europe needs to make better use of its taxes in terms of better public service.'

Unlike Europe's other shaping actors, moreover, the businessmen represented in our study focused primarily on what future integration means for corporate competitiveness. Regardless of nationality or industry, their single greatest preoccupation turns out to be how to achieve a sustainable competitive position in global markets. As one industry leader put it: 'The Community institutions often think in political terms, while we're concerned with competitiveness first, competitiveness second, and competitiveness third'. This sentiment is almost universally shared by the senior executives and experts we interviewed. Thus, when these leading protagonists in the drive towards the single market were asked what future vision for Europe could energize corporations, the common thread running through all of their responses was that business would be excited by anything that could allow European companies to build a new competitive advantage - particularly versus the US and Japan. Not surprisingly, then, these corporations evaluate the impact of the integration process chiefly in terms of the tangible benefits it brings (e.g. lower costs or improved market opportunities) *vis-à-vis* competitors both within and outside of Europe.

Is this stress on competitiveness any stronger than it was ten years ago? We believe it is. Paradoxically, while the single market was itself a response to increased global competition, it has also created unprecedented competitive pressures for many European corporations by forcing them into a difficult transition period. And while the Single Market Act made it easier for corporations to enter new markets, it also made the behaviour and actions of both traditional and new competitors - to say nothing of national and supranational authorities - more unpredictable than ever before.   Under these new conditions of uncertainty, corporations tend to emphasize bottom-line pragmatism and are highly sensitive to their competitive position *vis-à-vis* other companies in the industry.

It would be misleading, however, to assume that European businessmen's stress on competitiveness derives simply, or even primarily, from their wanting to achieve or maintain leadership in a given industry. While a number of company chairmen and industry leaders in our interviews and workshops talked about the challenges of staying in the forefront of technology, product design, or low-cost manufacturing, a significant number of them expressed serious concern with 'catching up'. Indeed, some European top business leaders perceive themselves to be at a considerable disadvantage compared to Japanese and American competitors, and they look to an integrated European market as the primary means of avoiding further deterioration of their position. As one senior business leader emphasized: 'We're not even at the point where we can begin thinking about competitive advantage. First we need to think about catching up'.

The Focus on Global Markets

Significantly, this focus on a sustainable competitive advantage is not limited to markets in Europe but extends to global markets as well. The global dimension of business concerns is, of course, a natural follow-on to the issues of competitiveness.   Executives and industry leaders repeatedly drive home the message that in many European industries, the key competitive challenge comes from the Far East and the US, and not from other European players. One German business leader, for example, explained that 'for many German industries, the competitive "benchmarking" standards are being set by Japanese companies and not European ones'.   In this context, it is important to underscore that corporations do not take a pan-European view of external competitors but have a very individual perspective, based on their own position within a particular industry. This caveat aside, it is inconceivable for many, if not most, European corporations to consider future economic developments in Europe without taking a hard look at what impact these can have on their position versus specific external competitors.

Inevitably, then, post-1992 directions and possible integration initiatives, including specific priority areas for economic development, are also assessed on the basis of the competitive impact they would have on

Europe's long-term position in world-wide markets. Indeed, many corporate executives feel that the logical next step beyond 1992 has to be one with a strong global role for Europe. As the chairman of one of Europe's leading corporations put it: 'Brussels now needs to worry more about what will make Europe competitive at a global level rather than just looking at its own internal market structure'. As they look to the future, moreover, business executives and industry experts almost without exception insist that Japanese competitiveness is a major factor that cannot be ignored if Europe hopes to have a global role in the future.

But competitiveness is not the only reason behind this increased emphasis on a global view. The expansion of international trade, the globalization of financial markets, as well as the global nature of many of today's most pressing problems (e.g. environment, North-South tensions, population) have already forced corporations to think beyond Europe. Businessmen are well aware that the major problems facing society can no longer be considered as relatively neutral exogenous factors because of the huge impact these social, political and economic issues have on their business activities, on global competitors, on free trade and, ultimately, on overall social stability. As the European Round Table of Industrialists summed up with respect to integrating Eastern Europe into the Western economic system: 'Can we afford to bring [them] in? Wrong question - the fact is that we cannot afford to leave them out'.

Long-Term Vision and the Practical Implementation of Change

European businessmen are united in commending the Commission for the single market project and the vision it represents; they strongly endorse the push - and direction - it gave to European integration. As one top executive expressed the general tenor: 'The 1992 programme was a real stroke of genius'. Given this overriding sentiment, and the genuine concern with the global competitiveness of European industry, the general managers and presidents of some of Europe's largest corporations have immersed themselves in the 'nuts and bolts' activity of implementing the 1992 programme. Indeed, throughout our interviews and discussions, interviewees often seemed more eager to discuss the remaining bottlenecks that are now slowing down the implementation process than they were to discuss a new energizing vision for Europe. As one British general manager put it: 'The Community has a lot to digest - even without Maastricht. This might not be the right moment to launch another crusade'.

Remarks such as these reflect the unease that many corporations feel about supporting any new long-term vision before the single market is itself fully implemented and the benefits of it achieved. As a senior chemical industry leader in Germany explained:

> It's not hard at all to have a grandiose vision of world excellence in biotechnology. The problem is that it all starts with being able to conduct sophisticated R&D programs today. The Americans and the Japanese can do it, but we can't. The obstacles here are numerous and cause extraordinary delays at a time when speed is the most vital element of the race. No matter how lofty our aspirations may be for the future, that future starts today. We need a solution to the problems we're wrestling with *here and now*, if we're to become the market leaders of tomorrow.

This same message was echoed not only in debates about R&D policy and choices, but in virtually all discussions of issues relating to the removal of barriers that are still preventing corporations from reaping the full benefits of the single market.

This emphasis on the 'future starting today' derives in part from the fact that in contrast to Europe's other shaping actors, the business community is almost uniquely forced by the economic realities of the free market to reconcile the vision of a single market with immediate strategic and operational choices. For some corporations, this difficult art of balancing long-term prospects and short-term performance can even be dramatic: caught as they are in the throes of an intense competitiveness crisis, their overriding concern is one of basic survival. These players do not find the benefits of a more distant 'endgame' to be particularly relevant; their first priority is to regain competitiveness and to be around long enough to benefit from the single market. This was stated very bluntly in the automotive industry, for example.

We believe, however, that there is another reason why the European business community has generally reacted to post-1992 integration by focusing on the 'here and now'. Their thoughts on how best to proceed in the European integration process are inevitably coloured by their own major change efforts, which has convinced them that implementation is the real challenge. Indeed, corporate experience has increasingly suggested that major change is an evolutionary process that requires continuous monitoring, adjustment and intermediate steps in order to realize the long-term change vision. For this reason, the philosophy of corporations looking to post-1992 integration is, as we shall see, one of pragmatic, consensus-building, energizing projects.

SECTION 2: THE CHANGE PROCESS AND THE SINGLE MARKET

There is no question that there has been much concrete progress in the march towards a single market in Europe. Over 90% of the measures for eliminating borders have already been approved by the Community institutions, and 75% have been transposed into the national law of the Member States.[4] Nonetheless, the widely-shared perception in the business community today is that there is still important work to be done to capture the full potential of the single market. Consensus among senior executives and industry leaders is that the Community now finds itself somewhere in the middle of the implementation phase: the movement of people, goods, services and capital has been eased, but there is still a long way to go before the single market can be considered anything like a *fait accompli*. The message from the European business community to public authorities is forceful and clear: full implementation of the internal market is an absolute priority.

For business itself, 'full' implementation has involved a significant transition process, but the majority of large European corporations is already well along in making major adjustments to the 1992 programme. They are revamping their organizations, operations and strategies in order to be in a position to be able to take advantage of the benefits of a single market. Thus, many of the senior executives we interviewed cited new initiatives they had launched to increase their companies' competitive advantage - for example, through new market development strategies now feasible because of the 1992 directives. And whether or not they are currently in a position to capitalize on them, industry leaders virtually all agree that lower costs are now more easily achievable by low-wage country sourcing, consolidation of manufacturing facilities, and brand / product standardization.

However, implementation is a very uneven process. Bottlenecks and setbacks are to be expected - even anticipated - in any major change effort, and this is even more true of the European integration process, given the scope and ambition of the change vision. From a corporate

---

[4]   See the 'Seventh Report of the Commission to the Council and the European Parliament Concerning the Implementation of the White Paper on Completion of the Internal Market', 3 September 1992.

point of view, there are a number of factors complicating the integration process, among them: differences in firms' competitive starting positions and in the pace in which corporations and national environments are adapting to the single market; corporations' difficulties in evaluating new game rules and in translating expectations into reality; persistent old barriers and the emergence of new barriers and uncertainties. Together, these elements conspire to slow down the integration process. They also give the impression, at times, that corporations are hesitant to push forward the single market - a seeming paradox, given the business community's insistence that European integration is the essential first step for long-term competitiveness in global markets.

In this context, it cannot be stated often or emphatically enough that *all* implementation efforts run up against such complications. Indeed, these change 'blockers' were so hotly debated in our interviews and survey - and their impact on the implementation of the single market is so critical - that they need to be addressed here in some detail before we highlight the proposals that are being put forward by the business community itself.

Differences in pace of change. Even among corporations deeply immersed in their transition process, the speed with which they are moving forward differs considerably. Companies that are not yet competitive and have difficult transition periods ahead are relatively cautious. They worry that a too-quickly implemented competitive environment will develop, in which 'the poor get poorer and the rich get richer'. Executives and industry leaders from Italy and Spain were vocal on this front, and more extensive coverage of small- and medium-sized enterprises in this project would only have strengthened the point. By contrast, a group of forerunners has emerged that is now impatient with the roadblocks that still remain or have newly emerged to hinder pan-European competitiveness. Many UK companies, for example, perceive that privatization and deregulation policies in the UK have already forced them to undertake the adjustment process, which has left them in a far stronger position to adapt to the liberalization of the European market. Many of these companies now take the view that other countries cannot postpone this process much longer, painful though it may be. Clearly, the tension between companies that are just beginning the transition process and those whose major adjustment period is behind them could easily intensify in the future.

Differences in the speed of national compliance. Discussions with the business community clearly revealed that the different speeds at which national governments are moving to transform 1992 directives into reality

- i.e. removing existing barriers - poses another formidable obstacle to fully implementing the single market. In banking, for example, deregulation has not taken place to the same extent everywhere in the Community. Regulatory constraints still vary widely across countries, and a single market for financial institutions has been seriously hindered and delayed. The reasons for these delays are numerous and well known, but it was not within the scope of this project to prove or disprove them. However, the growing divergence among Member States is sufficiently disconcerting for the European Round Table of Industrialists to have called attention to it in their 1992 position paper:

> We attach the utmost priority to completing the Single Market, implementing what has been agreed and carrying out the long list of supporting policies. This message is particularly addressed to *national governments,* which often seem blissfully unaware of the true cost of disagreement (emphasis added).

Interestingly, the business community sees the Commission as having a major role to play in this area by 'coaching' national governments to implement what has already been decided. The reason businessmen would welcome such intervention is clear: the risk of fragmenting the implementation process is obviously very high if the speed at which Member States comply with Community directives diverges too greatly.

Difficulties in understanding the new rules of the game. Corporations trying to adjust to the single market are sometimes trapped in a Heraclitean reality: they are changing to adapt to a new environment, only to find that the environment itself is in a constant state of flux and change. The ensuing confusion threatens to demotivate even the most pan-European executive. In a number of areas, for example, corporations now find themselves subject to different - and sometimes conflicting - national and European Community rules. In advertising and pharmaceutical distribution, two cases that are often mentioned, there are often two sets of relevant legislation. The core issue for corporations caught in this sometimes surrealistic web of complexity is whether they should proceed with adjustments to the single market in the hope that these obstacles will be removed or, given the costs involved, delay further adjustments until the future direction is made clear.

Difficulties in realizing expected benefits; some unexpected costs. Another factor complicating the implementation process is the difficulty some companies are experiencing in their attempts to realize the benefits they expected from the single market. For example, economies of scale have been elusive in certain industries. Thus, top executives in retail banking say that additional scale economies from centralized automation and account management have been lower than they originally expected (despite the fact that the Cecchini report had anticipated only modest-scale economies in banking to begin with). Similarly, in automobile production, the benefits of mass production need to be balanced against new market demands for flexibility and customization.   Post-merger and post-acquisition integration is yet another area that has turned out to be more technically difficult than originally anticipated. The 1992 momentum has also slowed in some quarters as various corporations learn that the real costs and risks involved in the integration process are higher than they initially expected.

This discrepancy between initial expectations and actual experience is characteristic of all change processes, and the transition to the single market is no exception. And while realigning expectations with reality can be difficult and costly, the real risk is that enthusiasm can wane. This is especially true for weak companies, but not only them since the general managers of even the most robust European corporations could become cynical   about   the   link   between   the   single   market   and   global competitiveness. This is due, in large part, to their growing perception that Japanese and American competitors may be in a position to reap the benefits from the single market more quickly than the Europeans can. Given the characteristics of their home markets, Japanese and American corporations have considerable experience and skill in competing in large, integrated markets. The concern expressed by even the strongest European corporations is that if they cannot safely integrate because of new obstacles and uncertainties, then the initial beneficiaries in post-1992 Europe could very well not be the Europeans. As one senior executive said with exasperation: 'The Americans and Japanese may become more European than we are!'.

Persistence of old barriers.   Given the inescapable resistance and 'backsliding' in major change efforts, it is not surprising that some barriers have proved to be stubbornly resistant to the integration process and continue to distort competition in Europe. While important progress has already been made on all of these fronts, businessmen most frequently mention standards, state subsidies and public procurement as the barriers they perceive to be the slowest to come down. Standards, particularly harmonized standards in many high-tech industries, illustrate very nicely some of the areas that still need special attention: for example, computer software, telecommunication equipment and service protocols, and R&D rules in biotechnology. It is important to note, however, that positions taken by various players can be quite extreme, depending on whether they are on the user or on the provider side. Users of telecommunication equipment and services deplore the slow speed at which pan-European systems are established, but equipment and service providers in each country do not see why they should give up the standards or systems they have created.

The business community is taking the perspective that since national and supranational authorities are a major initiator - and supervisor - of the change effort, they must closely monitor the removal of such barriers or run the risk of European integration becoming a sham. As one industry leader put it: 'The Commission still has its work cut out in ensuring that the tough decisions get made'. The call for partnership with European authorities is unmistakable here.

Emergence of new barriers. All major change efforts generate unanticipated new barriers in formerly unnoticed fields. Environment, where multiple new restrictions on the movement of goods have appeared, is the most frequently cited area where new barriers are beginning to have an impact on business operations. In the simplest form, the environment now functions as a barrier because of the different regulations for packaging products that have appeared in the various Member States. For example, plastic wrappings are allowed in the UK, but not in Germany. More subtle examples of how the environment can be used to exclude *de facto* non-national competitors include new regulations governing recycling systems, plant safety, and the transport of dangerous material.

But businessmen are generally less concerned with the existence of new environmental regulations *per se* than they are with their timing (when will they come into effect?), consistency (single market or fragmented markets?) and with the decision process itself (how well do rule makers understand the issues at hand?). Any business in an industry potentially affected by future environmental regulations needs to be setting its own guideposts now. For this reason, most of the corporations we interviewed insist that a gradual sequencing of new environmental regulations and restrictions over the next ten years is critical. Cooperation and consultation between industry and all relevant public authorities is also seen as absolutely essential.

Emergence of new uncertainties. Predictably, new uncertainties have developed during the implementation process, most notably doubts about the European Monetary Union (EMU). Business is generally sceptical about the EMU timetable; moreover, the EMU's short- and medium-term benefits are not immediately obvious to the business community. This explains, in large part, why businessmen have been more reserved in their reaction to the EMU than anticipated. Their equivocation is underscored by the widespread consensus - at least until September 1992 - that the European Monetary System (EMS) and the freedom of capital movement have already brought about many of the important benefits that might otherwise have been linked with the EMU (e.g. exchange rate stability and access to capital). As one general manager said: 'The EMS has given us sufficient exchange rate stability in Europe; we don't need anything more. The real concern is the fluctuation between European currencies, the dollar and the yen'. This statement was reinforced, although from another angle, by another senior executive: 'We know how to manage exchange rates in a superior way compared with our competitors. An EMU would only water down this advantage'.

These two remarks, very representative of business thinking at the time this project was conducted - that is, before the September 1992 turmoil in the EMS - reflect a period when the stability of the EMS was taken for granted. Later interviews confirmed that the September crisis has already altered this perception significantly. The feeling seems to be growing that implementation of the EMU should perhaps be speeded up given that it could be a useful tool for ensuring long-term exchange rate stability. Nobody knows for sure. But this much is certain: there is widespread agreement among the business community that an unreliable EMS would create unacceptable uncertainty in decision-making (e.g. investment in production) because executives would not know whether their decisions entailed a considerable exchange rate risk. This uncertainty is particularly unacceptable in a 'single' market and only underscores the need for further integration. Notwithstanding this fact, however, support for the EMU remains conditional. Even among those businessmen who perceive the EMU to be a useful step towards an integrated market, there is some fear that implementation may create some economic and social disturbance throughout the Community - for instance, deflationary effects due to convergence.

To sum up, what all these bottlenecks and obstacles mean in everyday business is that corporations could easily become reluctant to take further steps towards future integration. Cross-border reorganizations, for example, can appear less attractive to pursue lest actions taken now prove unworkable later due to new national barriers. Several illustrations emerged in discussions. Senior managers are now asking themselves whether product management really should become pan-European and replace country management. And whether manufacturing should be concentrated and specialized on a pan-European dimension. Or, if this is the right time to transform logistics into a pan-European system. (In theory, logistics is clearly more efficient if managed at the pan-European level, but also extremely costly and difficult to change.) Managers do not like to take unnecessary risks in such fundamental decisions, and some firms have already adopted a 'wait-and-see' approach. Obviously, if more companies were to strike this cautious posture, European integration would be threatened.

Moving Forward to Regain the 1992 Momentum

What is to be done? One conclusion of our research is that the European business community has clearly evolved its own proposals for moving forward economic development in Europe over the next ten years. With some variations on the theme, their message is that public authorities should set the right conditions to 'help corporations help themselves'. In this respect, both senior executives and industry experts say that the basic groundwork of rules and regulations governing future integration must be structured with as much clarity and fairness as possible in order for them to be able to compete effectively. As one business leader commented, 'We are ready to fight, but we would like some assurance that it will be a fair battle ahead'. Here, the interaction between business and public authorities is seen as critical, particularly with regard to the ways in which regulations are drafted and administered, and in the development of a constructive dialogue with industry.

Greater Clarity

While acknowledging that the various European authorities are beginning to address some of the issues surrounding clarity, businessmen emphasize the need to proceed as fast as possible in this area to avoid the many false turns that can derail the change process. The concerns they articulate can be grouped into three basic categories: (a) laws that do not yet exist, either because treaty objectives still have not been translated into practical directives or because the issues themselves have not yet been taken up in treaties at the European level; (b) laws that are too ambiguous in their application; and (c) confusion about who the relevant decision-maker is.

Most of the remarks on this subject centred around the lack of clarity in what businessmen perceive to be confusing gaps in the regulatory framework. One of the chief targets is tax law. A number of senior executives commented on the ambiguity in the current tax legislation of the various Member States. An industry leader in the Netherlands, for example, noted that unclear tax treatment had wreaked havoc in a number of situations where new investment had been planned. As he explained: 'Tax laws can be so ambiguous that businesses may genuinely not know how they will be taxed in the future (in the different countries in which they operate)'.

The way in which rules and regulations are sometimes communicated also evokes strong feelings in discussions of clarity. All too often, a breakdown in communication can occur in the way that the directions set at the political/administrative level are translated into tangible implications for business. Recent environmental legislation was frequently cited as a prime example. As one industry expert remarked: 'There are more than 60 different definitions of sustainable development!' Agreed another: 'The feeling is that [the public authorities] just can't make up their minds, and in some areas, such as packaging covenants, trust is breaking down'. While recognizing that perfect transparency is impossible, the business community would like to see the practical significance of political visions made more explicit - as was the case for the single market. As a French business leader explained:

> [Whatever new vision the Community chooses], the energizing potential will always be higher if they put a real effort into communicating the microeconomic benefits to the business community. When the communication is focused too much on macroeconomic goals and objectives, corporations and citizens themselves do not see the immediate implications.

Because our interviews and survey were conducted during the debates over the Maastricht Treaty, however, it is possible that interviewees overemphasized this point. European businessmen generally believe that, in stark contrast to the 1992 programme, the microeconomic implications of Maastricht have not yet been made very concrete.

Another series of issues involving clarity revolves around who the relevant decision-makers are. Are they the national authorities? Or the European Community institutions? Are they some unclear combination of both? In other words, European corporations sometimes feel trapped in the 'pull' between national and EC authorities, and current merger control regulations are often singled out as a particularly good example of the problem. As one business leader pointed out, 'There is a real problem in knowing which merger control rules apply - local or European'. Even at the European level, however, there is often considerable confusion about which Directorates General are involved in the decision-making process. One company chairman, for example, noted that his company's dialogue with the Commission was generally quite good: 'But the problem is that there are too many chapels [within the Commission]. We need more of a 'one-stop shop'. The more general observation to emerge from the telecommunication services workshop is that 'relationships and boundaries between national authorities and the EC need to be clearer in order to ensure that the environment for change is optimized at a European rather than at a national level'. The clear consensus is that multiple layers of unnecessary decision-making must be avoided, be it in industrial policy or mergers. In this respect, the business community is apprehensive that enlargement, without due consideration of the implications on the decision-making process, might only create further delays and obscurities.

Consistency

Closely related to the issue of clarity is the conviction that rules and regulations need to be much more consistent across the different Member States. Banking executives and experts, for example, stress that deregulation has not taken place everywhere to the same extent, leading to intricate hurdles in attempts to coordinate pan-European expansion. Moreover, regulatory constraints still vary widely from country to country. In the area of labour mobility, to take another example, the business community pinpointed a broad range of inconsistencies, such as pension recognition or diploma equivalence.

The issue of consistency was particularly vivid in discussions with transportation industry representatives and experts. In railways, for example, it is increasingly clear that there will emerge across Europe fundamentally different national approaches to infrastructure management - both in terms of organizational structures and of processes for securing access for service providers. While this is not *de facto* a problem, it will seriously limit the potential for low-cost pan-European goods flows if prospective competitive rail service providers cannot be assured of comparable performance standards along the entire route. The argument was made during one workshop that:

International freight offerings will be broken or made on the industry's ability to ensure provision of the right capacity at the right prices across multiple railways. If railway companies and their authorities adopt fundamentally different approaches to infrastructure management, then some sophisticated means of coordination must be found to ensure reasonable consistency in track access ground rules.

Finally, most European business leaders cited the extremely time-consuming administrative burden of dealing with the many complex and confusing differences across countries as a hindrance to pan-European expansion.

Fairness

Fairness is a third area in which the business community is asking for some cooperation from public authorities as it sets its strategic objectives for the years ahead. When they speak of fairness, businessmen generally mean that they are seeking a competitive situation where one player is not subject to more restrictive rules and regulations than other players are. The question of fairness comes up frequently in discussions of new environmental regulations, for example. As one industry leader in the transport sector summed up:

> At the end of the day, the regulators should take into account two things. First, greater environmental restrictions will mean higher costs, disadvantaging some industries more than others. Secondly, within a given industry, all competitors should have to face the same rules and regulations. At least it should be a fair battle.

Given these new environmental restrictions, fairness emerges as a central concern in discussions of imports into Europe. The European business community is particularly sensitive to 'environmental dumping' from non-EC countries. It fears that countries with lower environmental standards can, for example, produce products at lower manufacturing costs in their home country, import them into Europe, and sell them at a substantial competitive advantage *vis-à-vis* local European manufacturers. As a number of interviewees emphasized, the issue requires a global solution to ensure fairness not only within Europe, but world-wide.

Trade reciprocity - namely, fair and mutual market access, particularly in Japan - was also mentioned on numerous occasions, most notably by executives and experts in industries where this is an immediate issue (e.g. automotive and consumer goods).

Finally, it should be noted that the subjective nature of many of the remarks made in the discussions on fairness strongly underline the need for extensive communication among all the parties involved. It became very clear in our interviews that companies often approach the fairness issue from a particular country and/or industry perspective. The following comment from an industry leader in Italy highlights the point: 'The concept of fairness should be taken into account during the implementation phase. The role of the Commission should be to manage this transition in a fair way, not just in favour of the strongest countries'. Whether this perception is accurate or not, a two-way dialogue is clearly needed to address the issues head on. The danger is that concerns about fairness could easily escalate into major disagreements, thereby stimulating further resistance to implementation of the single market and to future European integration. The business community, therefore, sees a vital role for European authorities to play as facilitator.

Dialogue

There is a broad consensus that the dialogue between industry and the Commission could be strengthened and improved in several ways. Today's dialogue is felt to be a weakness of the European socio-economic system, and a source of competitive disadvantage *vis-à-vis* non-European competitors. In the US and Japan, the economic dialogue between business and public authorities is organized in a highly sophisticated way - although very differently in the two countries. In the US, the dialogue centres primarily around economic, and less on social, issues, and it is structured around the efforts of professional pressure groups and lobbyists. This is not the place to discuss the particular strengths or weaknesses of the US system; the point is that it ensures direct and frequent contacts between the private and the public sectors, with a substantial exchange of information and viewpoints on specific proposals. By contrast, in Japan the administration-industry dialogue is socio-economic and is structured around intricate working groups, organized on a sector level, where opinions are readily exchanged. This almost always involves difficult and lengthy discussions until a mutually acceptable consensus is reached. Although the process is very time consuming, once decisions are reached they can be easily implemented. While neither system could be applied in its entirety in Europe, the European business community would welcome any approach that permits more up-front, *ex ante* dialogue.

For such a dialogue to succeed, however, the Commission needs a better understanding of business issues. A persistent undercurrent running through all our discussions on competitiveness was business leaders' concern that perhaps too many decisions affecting the future competitiveness of European industries are being made by public authorities who, because of too little input from the business community, sometimes have a poor understanding of the issues faced by corporations in their struggle to be more globally competitive.

The business community enumerated a number of practical ways for improving this dialogue, and made some observations about the functioning of the Commission and its interaction with national authorities and industry. Although they did not put forward any specific recommendations, the following questions were frequently raised:

(i)   How can the Commission and industry organize a satisfactory dialogue for addressing 'horizontal' (i.e., interdisciplinary) issues? This is particularly important when issues concern several Directorates General simultaneously and require consistency in analysis and strict coordination of the decision-making process. Key examples of areas where such horizontal action is deemed essential include industrial and competition policy, environment and energy, and relations with Japan.

(ii)   Can the Commission, through a concentrated dialogue, modify and redirect its skills from an earlier, primary emphasis on the drafting of rules to the kind of implementation and monitoring that is needed now? This point is critical, since business attention is sharply focused on the implementation period.

(iii) How can the Commission best act as a facilitator to ensure that the necessary information is disseminated in such a way as to improve the dialogue and accelerate the decision-making process? In railway industry discussions, for example, one suggestion was that the Commission 'make explicit [the cost-benefit analyses] at the pan-European political level [of] the trade-offs being made implicitly at the national level today (i.e., congestion versus cost versus employment versus subsidization)'. Furthermore, it was proposed that the Commission go even one step further and 'underpin hypotheses such as these with credible scoping numbers to utilise in political and industry debates'.

For their part, businessmen say that they need to organize themselves better to become a more credible and articulate partner. Readily acknowledging that they have not been sufficiently proactive in the past - for example, that they have tended to react only after a directive has been issued - the business community generally believes that it must work with the Commission in a more coordinated and focused way. As one senior industry leader put it: 'The Commission should be able to look to industry to come up with solutions'. A key topic for discussion between the Commission and industry could, for example, be the question of which initiatives are better managed by public sponsorship and which by private initiative and capital. This notion of 'double subsidiarity', although never expressed in precisely these terms, often surfaced as a major point of interest for the business community.

Integrated versus Single Market

An effective, two-way dialogue between industry and public authorities is especially needed given the nuances in the way that the Commission and the business community understand the single market. As noted earlier, when businessmen speak of the single market, they generally think in terms of an 'integrated' market and the additional opportunities this would permit. The distinction between the two is important to understand since it informs much of the thinking of the European business community today.

A single market removes the barriers to the movement of people, goods, services and capital. It gives access to certain freedoms that did not exist before and, as such, is a necessary precondition for further integration. For management, the key benefits of a single market revolve around tapping previously blocked market opportunities and achieving scale economies by consolidating some functions at the European level. An integrated market, on the other hand, goes even further in that it opens up new competitive possibilities by bringing an end to nationally-based preferences. It is in these additional possibilities - sometimes called 'positive' freedoms because they involve more than the mere removal of 'negative' national restrictions - that European corporations see the greatest potential for future gains. The reason is clear: an integrated market would enable corporations to realize important efficiency and effectiveness benefits with respect to the size of the European economy.

It would also dramatically contribute to increasing the competitive potential of European industry.

One simple, but illustrative, example that businessmen repeatedly cite involves the construction of trans-European linkages. In an integrated market, the decision of what technology to use to develop a fast-speed train system would be made purely on a rational basis, without national preferences playing a role. It would also be financed by consistent funding systems, and constructed according to a coherent time-frame so that, for instance, the British, French, Belgian and German segments of the London-Paris-Brussels-Düsseldorf network would all be ready at the same time.

A second example concerns the efficiency gains that would come from successfully coordinating all functions across the corporate business system. For many of the corporations represented in this project, an integrated market essentially means a market where they can more readily put in place the most efficient configuration of activities. In other words, the suppliers a firm selects, the markets it serves, and the way its own internal operations are structured would all be decided according to criteria in which national considerations are no longer paramount. Thus, in an integrated market, the location of manufacturing, research, logistics, and financial functions for a German corporation could be Spain, Germany, the Netherlands and the UK, respectively, if each of these locations presented the best rationale for that specific function.

An integrated market, then, basically means one in which corporations have less constraint - actual and self-imposed - in their decisions than they do even in a single market. Along these lines, businessmen often raised the analogy with the US and the Japanese markets. The situation in Europe will always be more complex, of course, and the choices will be less clear-cut. This is especially so since Europe's 'natural' barriers - e.g. language, taste and traditions - must be respected; Europe will continue for a long time to be characterized by regions that require different approaches. It is for this reason that projects promoting pan-European infrastructure, R&D cooperation, more - and better - linkages among educational institutions are particularly energizing to the business community. Together, such projects would help to break down the intangible barriers to an integrated market. Moreover, European citizens are likely to have much less emotional resistance to a pan-European train network or to an international cellular tele-communication system than to a single monetary unit. Once systems such as these are in place, European integration is secure. There is no going back.

SECTION 3: FOCUSED PROJECTS - STEPPING STONES TO AN INTEGRATED MARKET

Since the task of European economic integration remains formidable, the business community generally believes that a focused-project approach could bring the most substantial and motivating results. Once again, it is their experience in major change efforts that has convinced most of the senior executives we interviewed that the implementation process is best managed by targeting a few critical areas, where resources and efforts can then be concentrated. In the context of European integration, targeted projects are widely perceived to be the necessary stepping stones both for capitalizing on the opportunities created by the single market and for moving forward to capture the greater potential benefits of an integrated market. The influential president of a major European company summarized the concept simply and powerfully by calling these projects the 'fields which, if left unexploited, could 'fragilize' the existing accomplishments [of European integration]'. Other industry leaders added that a focused-project approach also creates a dynamic that energizes organizations, thereby helping to overcome the resistance that has developed to the change vision during the implementation process. Hence, business leaders seem to agree that the time to launch a project-based effort is *now*, precisely because of the new barriers and uncertainties that have emerged to slow down the 1992 momentum.

There are several such projects that the business community would be ready to support in the move towards an integrated market. What follows is an overview of the four projects that were mentioned most frequently and forcefully by business and industry leaders. One should keep in mind, however, that they are only an indication of the direction of change in which business leaders would like to see the Community move, and not detailed proposals.

Infrastructure Improvement and Integration

By 'infrastructure', businessmen primarily mean 'hard' infrastructure, such as roads, railways, energy and telecommunication systems. But there is also 'soft' infrastructure that they consider important; for instance, air traffic control, telecommunication services, and information technology networks.

There is virtually unanimous agreement by businessmen in all countries and industries that infrastructure is a key building block of an integrated market. Indeed, the lack of physical infrastructure has already impeded development and investment in certain areas of the Community. As the chairman of one of Europe's largest manufacturing corporations insisted, 'Good infrastructure is vital for maximizing the internal market gains for all Member States'. In many ways, an improved and integrated infrastructure is also the logical 'next step' in moving beyond the single market in that it helps consolidate and even accelerate the benefits of the 1992 programme. Now that many of the barriers to the movement of people, goods, services and capital have been removed, the business community wants to take advantage of the opportunities that have been created and to speed up some of the infrastructure operations that have changed so slowly in the past. As a British industry expert commented: 'The focus [of Community efforts] could shift from removing barriers, as in the 1992 concept, to proactively creating infrastructure and networks to foster the benefits of faster and deeper integration in Europe'.

The railway industry is a good example of how inefficiencies due to a lack of pan-European integration carry over into higher costs throughout the economy. In rail freight operations, for example, open wagon-load systems, which account for as much as 50-75% of freight revenues and an even higher percentage of employment in Europe, operate with enormous inefficiencies. Marshalling yard operations drive costs well beyond truck competition and create large shortfalls in customer service, e.g. the lack of consistency, lateness and lost shipments.

As our discussions with industry leaders revealed, however, the solutions in the railway industry are not seen to lie in increased subsidies or regulatory involvement, but in fundamental business system changes. In many instances, this could take the form of point-to-point destination trains, with dedicated assets, which avoid marshalling yards altogether. Industry experts say that this would be even more efficient if such economic entities could be put into place without regard for borders. In general, these comments reflect two of the refrains sounded over and over again among the large, functionally-complex, infrastructure industries. First, change *can* happen, but it requires multiple stages, perhaps even pilot projects to energize it. Second, all infrastructure industries are a complex mix of competitive and non-competitive elements. The greatest progress can be made by creating the conditions whereby progressively more and more of the competitive elements are disentangled and allowed to manage themselves. If cross-subsidization must exist, it should at least be transparent.

These kinds of inefficiencies became apparent throughout our sector discussions. In telecommunication services, for example, specific object-ives that are being targeted include reductions in the cost of calls and improvements in service levels. Although the methodology of our study focussed more on railways and telecom services, comments made during the interviews suggest that these remarks could be extended to most hard and soft infrastructure sectors, including sectors like energy.

Efficiency and competitiveness improvements, moreover, are often linked to finding the right blend of private initiative and public intervention. It was generally felt that public initiatives would be better left to, and managed by, private capital, wherever possible without damaging the public service dimension. A typical comment along these lines was that:

> The EC should focus on removing barriers in areas that are potentially attractive to private investors and consider public investment only in areas that cannot be better served by the private sector, but which are essential for the economic and social development of the Community.

A specific role for the Commission as facilitator would be to help Member States harmonize their operational organizations. Businessmen often cited the pressing need for better interconnections between different national systems. As one senior executive put it:

> In European infrastructure, the competence is national, but the dimension is supranational. Consider the paradox of the TGV (trains à grande vitesse), which works nationally but not yet internationally, and whose key function should be to link European capitals. Or the discrepancies in making long-distance phone calls. The distance may be the same, but the prices aren't if one is a domestic call and the other is cross-border.

Businessmen also see infrastructure as one way that the Community could cement integration and gain credibility fairly easily.

Finally, the business community mentioned the link between infrastructure and the competitive advantage of harnessing diversity. For many businessmen, Europe's diverse range of backgrounds, cultures, and skills is seen as a unique asset - and a contrast to the melting-pot concept in the United States or the relative homogeneity of Japanese culture. Infrastructure improvement is seen as one important way of making a 'virtue' out of reality: it encourages diversity while, at the same time, ensures the critical linkages that would allow rapid movement and cross-fertilization of people, ideas, and information.

Technology and Greater Innovation

Very succinctly, corporations need a large enough market and a large enough expected share of that market to justify the high fixed costs of technological innovation. In this respect, the single market was hailed as a crucial boost for European R&D. Many of the proposals now being put forward by the business community deal with pushing this process even further, with more harmonized standards and more open public procurement policies for high-technology products. Moreover, given that the scope of high-technology industries is beyond the European market, business leaders say that the crucial next step is the 'internationalization' of R&D and projects that can help European corporations access global markets. But faced with the significant lead that Japanese and American corporations have in many high-tech industries, there is also the closely-related question of which sectors can provide realistic opportunities for technological leadership. Europe's weak position in the information technology industry is of particular concern, especially in the light of Japan's dominant position in such areas as semiconductor machinery (i.e. the machine tools required to produce the key elements of microelectronics, including microprocessors).

In terms of reducing R&D costs, the perception that more and broader technological alliances are also badly needed is very widespread throughout the business community. In electronics, for example, the necessary investments are far beyond what most European companies can afford. Thus, there is a very strong feeling that cooperative projects could spread much further along the spectrum from generic and precompetitive R&D to market application projects, as is reflected in the following comment by the managing director of an Italian corporation:

> Technology is the number one issue for long-term survival. A European-wide policy is necessary in R&D, especially one that supports more joint ventures and other integrated R&D efforts. It is possible that the EC has been too prudent in defining the limits of precompetitive R&D.

This argument explains why another key area that could energize the business community is that of technology and innovation. The business community would enthusiastically support a strong, technology-driven project aimed at helping Europe catch up, as well as projects that could stimulate and diffuse innovation. This is especially true of R&D projects in biotechnology and information technology. As one corporate chairman said:

> Europe will not become more competitive in the Triad by spending vast amounts of money on sugar, milk, or cereals. Europe has to compete better in the more advanced areas, particularly in biotechnology and electronics.

Technology-oriented projects are also widely discussed as a basis for creating a long-term sustainable competitive advantage for European businesses. As noted earlier, the business community is intensely preoccupied by the competitive position of European industry 10 to 15 years down the line. In the automotive industry, for example, even discussions of short-term survival strategies eventually circled back to the reality that long-term revitalization of the industry depends heavily on vital technological capabilities that are being developed today. Some of the issues raised in these automotive discussions provide a good illustration of the kinds of technological questions that European industry leaders and executives are generally asking themselves, namely:

(i)   Can EC manufacturers leverage current superior technological capabilities (such as driveability and safety) to become more competitive?

(ii)   Will European automotive producers continue to improve productivity in R&D by shorter design cycles and less expensive developments? The design time for a new Japanese automobile model is now about three years compared to an average of about four-to-five years for European manufacturers (an improvement from seven years just a few years ago).

(iii) How aggressively do EC automobile manufacturers need to invest in basic new car technologies, e.g. electric cars, zero-emission vehicles, new material applications?

(iv)   Should Europe be thinking in even broader technological terms and moving towards new 'holistic' transportation systems - i.e. a systematic approach to transportation that would take into account variables such as the integration of different transportation modes, urban planning, the environment and energy consumption.   If this approach is taken, what is the link between these new 'leap-frog' technologies and European manufacturers' competitive advantage *vis-à-vis* other global competitors?

Beyond the broad acceptance of a technological objective, however, there is no overall agreement in the business community as to what specific projects the Community should pursue.   The discussion of which race is worth running was inconclusive, and the methodology used in this project did not permit further investigation in this area.

Economic Development in Eastern Europe

The third area that the business community deems worthy of a Community project involves Eastern Europe.   As one senior executive said: 'Eastern European development could be an energizing theme of the first order'.   There is real consensus that Western Europe should be an economic anchor point for Eastern European countries (and for North African countries as well, but to a lesser degree).   There is also a pervasive sense of urgency here because of the political uncertainty in Eastern Europe and the enormous economic and social gains or losses that are at stake for its Western neighbours.   As one industry expert commented:

> Eastern Europe is an extremely high visibility issue.   Whether the EC does something or not, every major Western corporation has been looking at the threats and opportunities there.   In a sense, this is the 'new frontier'.

When it comes to practical, economic involvement in Eastern Europe, businessmen often use the terminology of a 'Marshall Plan' - meaning a programme that would require a major joint effort between public authorities and corporations.   The European Round Table of Industrialists heartily endorses such an initiative: '[What we need is] coordination of help to the East within an overall framework instead of by bilateral deals, so as to make the best use of limited resources, and covering trade as well as aid'.   However, most Western business leaders also believe that building managerial capability in Eastern Europe should be an even greater priority than funding alone.   In this context, 'management capability' means basic management techniques such as accounting, logistics, distribution, and quality control - i.e. very basic skills that can have an immediate positive effect on corporations in those countries and on their ability to survive the current transition period.

Education, Vocational and Language Training

The last major area where businessmen express interest in a Community-organized project is in the field of education, vocational and language training. There is a strong feeling that basic education and lifelong training and retraining are fundamental to Europe's future economic well-being, although there is not always unanimous agreement on where this responsibility should lie.

Businessmen mention both the long-term impact of improving the basic educational structure of primary and secondary school systems and the medium-term objectives linked to vocational training programmes. In discussions with UK business leaders, for example, basic education is one of the few areas where more, rather than less, involvement by regulatory authorities is considered worthwhile. To quote from this debate, 'one 'interventionist' policy that [British] businessmen could support is setting minimum standards in education and training'. The idea of minimum standards was echoed in a number of other countries, with technical skills, scientific and mathematical training, and languages being the areas most frequently cited.

But the debate on corporate involvement in educational issues revolved mostly around the growing importance of lifelong training needs. Here, the majority of executives that we talked with acknowledged that the pressure is increasing for employees to update their knowledge base (e.g. computer skills) and to retain at least some degree of flexibility with regard to what industries or types of jobs they could work in. This is already beginning to have a direct impact on corporations' competitiveness, as is reflected in the following comment:

> Corporations are waking up to the adverse effects on competitiveness and profitability that comes from the problem of finding good people and training them. The fact that customers are also demanding improved service levels only exacerbates the problem, by raising the level of training needed.

The business community also focused strongly on the link between education and mobility. Programmes that foster international cross-fertilization by facilitating and encouraging the exchange of students, academics, and employees across Europe were deemed a top priority. As one company president stated: 'It is important to get educational systems to improve their pan-European networking. There should be more networking like the student exchanges that took place in the early 1950s'.

In this context, business leaders also stressed the importance of better and more numerous links between European industry and universities. The encouragement of freedom of movement for researchers and scientists is considered essential, particularly for long-term technological excellence. Once again, feelings run strong that programmes already initiated by the Commission in this area are a real step in the right direction. Indeed, businessmen would be encouraged if the Community were to go even further. As one German business leader suggested: 'In order to get their degrees, researchers and engineers should be required to spend one year in another country'.

Overall, most of the corporations that participated in this study are willing to play a far greater role in helping to meet the training needs of the Community. This is entirely in keeping with the position taken by the European Round Table of Industrialists: 'The systematic provision of training and life-long retraining is essential, and cannot remain purely a matter of national and regional concern'.

CONCLUSION

While the project-based approach suggested above may be far from visionary, its pragmatism could energize the business community, as well as generate the credibility needed if the Community is to move forward with integration in Europe. The benefits to be derived from proceeding in this way should not be underestimated. Although different in scope and nature than the 1992 programme, the focused projects that businessmen are now targeting could nonetheless help crystallize the constructive, creative and participatory energies of the Community. Such an approach would not only speed up implementation of the single market, and facilitate the move to an integrated market, but it could also foster a new sense of community at a time when the road ahead for Europe is not as obvious as it once was.

At the risk of some oversimplification, we have tried to summarize in this chapter the most prominent thoughts and reflections of an important part of the European business community with regard to some factors that are shaping the long-term prospects of Europe. In reality, there is no unanimity, and there is no simple solution. 'The European business community' is itself more of a concept than a fact. Moreover, as we discuss in the coda to this report, there are a number of issues over which the sundry executives and industry leaders participating in our project expressed strong differences of opinion. Nonetheless, this exercise has shown that even in the midst of great diversity, it is possible to identify some energizing guidelines that generate a consensus. The challenge now is to begin a dialogue that will enable the Community to move forward.

CODA: DIVISIVE ISSUES IN THE BUSINESS COMMUNITY

While the picture presented in this report reflects a high level of consensus within the European business community, there is also potential dissension among businessmen over some critical issues. As we have seen, the agreement about the need for an integrated market is strong, but divergences in opinion surface immediately in any discussion about which barriers should be removed or how the various projects should be implemented. These divergences result, in large part, from well-known disparities in the economic situation of the various players. Formerly protected national companies cannot react the same way that globally-strong companies do. And corporations that are relatively small in a pan-European or global markets - however large in their home market - cannot approach the future as do well-established multinationals. Beyond these generic categories, however, our study identified key issues on which divergences could dangerously divide the entire business community, therefore posing a real threat to European integration. This is especially so since most of the divisive issues are closely related to differences of opinion among the Member States. In this case, a split in the business community could quickly escalate into tensions within the Community itself.

(i)   *Different risks involved in corporations' transition periods.*   All European corporations are navigating two transitions: one within their own organizations and another related to the collective move towards European integration. As noted earlier, a complicating factor is that weak and strong players are approaching these transition processes differently. Specifically, weaker players are afraid of being absorbed or destroyed by the implementation of the single market. This fear is particularly acute in countries where weak players (relative to competitors in other countries) represent the bulk of the industrial base.   In this case, precautionary measures, such as permitted delays in adapting to European integration or the use of cohesion or structural funds, may be necessary.   The divisive issue is that these markets or industry sectors are claiming special attention and extra time to negotiate the change process, which is opposed in principle by strong players who counter that global competitiveness comes at a price and that the demise of some players is unavoidable.   They argue that special consideration, such as subsidies and other 'protectionist' measures run counter to the whole spirit of the single market.   The issues underlying this contention between the more and the less competitive corporations, however, cut deeper and are potentially explosive between countries.   If the single market carries the day, will production remain national or not?   If not, what are the consequences?   How can national governments deal with the ensuing employment displacement?   What are the implications of the industrial dependence that would result?   Clearly, what at first glance looks like a pure competitiveness issue has huge ramifications for governments, Member States and, indeed, the future of the Community itself.

(ii)   *Access to Corporate Control.*   Strong national differences exist about the rules governing cross-border acquisitions. The possibility of acquiring corporations varies greatly from country to country, being relatively easy, for example, in the UK and difficult in Germany.   This unequal access creates strong resentment and a sense of unfairness among certain European players.   However divisive, the issue is also extremely delicate and defies easy solutions.   First, the power to change the situation lies more with Member States than with European authorities.   Second, the status quo is related more to fundamental differences in thinking about how capitalist systems work than it does to 'simple' rules that can be easily modified.   Closely linked to the question of access to corporate control are issues like the place of institutional investors and banks in the shareholders' base of corporations and their role in managing companies; foreign ownership; cross shareholding; and special systems separating ownership and control.   There are, therefore, fundamental differences in various countries' thinking about what the best system and rules are.   These differences are particularly pronounced between, for example, Germany and the

UK, and few possibilities for convergence emerged in our interviews and survey.

(iii) *Developments in Eastern Europe.* While there is a general consensus on the need to address the issue of developments in Eastern Europe, there are strong differences of opinion about how best to do so. The obvious reason is that opening trade with the former Eastern bloc will affect corporations and Member States differently. Thus, while Eastern Europe presents a genuine opportunity for some businesses, and some countries, it poses a considerable threat for others. The price advantage of Eastern products is considerable, given that Eastern European firms have no real current capital costs and low labour costs; the only real barrier they are experiencing is capacity. Some Western industries (e.g., steel, fertilizers and aluminium) fear that they will be seriously hurt by imports.

(iv) *Implementation of the EMU.* The cost of economic convergence needed to implement the EMU could prove to be a divisive factor in the European business community. Once again, the problem is that convergence would affect the various industries and countries differently. There would be a greater impact in banking, for example, than in consumer goods. The latter already operates more or less at a pan-European level and would reap more than it loses, while the banking industry clearly stands to lose some of the benefits it currently enjoys from a multi-currency system like the commissions on foreign currency exchange. Similarly, Spain would be more affected by implementation of the EMU than Germany, since the economic convergence hurdles are greatest for countries where the gap is the largest. The possibility of explosive tensions developing between industries and countries is, obviously, very great.

(v) *Environmental and Social Issues.* Contention is rife throughout the business community over the environmental and social issues that are hovering on the horizon. Although very different in nature, both issues raise similar concerns and clashes of opinion. Can countries pursue extremely ambitious and costly objectives for improving the quality of life and still accept unfettered competition from companies in other EC Member States that either do not want - or cannot afford - to pursue these same objectives? This is more than a question of 'fairness' and deals primarily with the concept of competitive advantage. Is it acceptable to the Community that different social or environmental policy choices confer or reduce competitive advantages? Should regulations be created in such a way that minimum and maximum standards do not create a competitiveness gap? Here, again, the debate was inconclusive, but it was beyond the scope of this project to probe the issues in greater detail.

4. A Comparison of the National Institutes' Results and Business Priorities

After having identified the global and national shaping factors, and brought the convergences and divergences to light, and after an analysis of the views of the business Community on Europe post-1992, our next step is to examine the complementarities and divergences between the National Institutes' results and business expectations. Before considering the degree of compatibility in the results highlighted in Chapters 1, 2 and 3 above, it is necessary to contrast briefly the methodology used in both cases and to review the main messages.

SECTION 1: MAIN THEMES FROM NATIONAL INSTITUTE FINDINGS

The *National Institutes* were given a *carte blanche* to list the major socio-cultural, socio-economic and political prospective shaping factors for their country in the next 10-15 years. The only instruction given to them was our request for a simple classification of the shaping factors firstly into global issues, secondly into those of specifically national scope, thirdly how the global and specific factors might impact on the European Community, fourthly the implications for business strategy and finally reflections on the priorities for the European Union.

One way of putting forward the main priorities emerging from the various shaping factors identified in the twelve reports is to group them around general themes which themselves could be relevant and understandable for business. On this basis, we built up five unifying themes reflecting some of these major priorities.

Table 4.1   Europe post-1992 emerging themes

1	Making a Single Market work in a broader and a deeper Europe.	Europe can achieve greater competitiveness and growth as well as strengthen its position in the world, by fully exploiting Single Market benefits at individual and collective levels. Focus should be on: - Ensuring effective implementation of 1992 concepts and directives - Adapting European institutions and systems in a way that helps broader and deeper socio-economic integration.
2	Productive participation.	Europe can improve the economic well-being of its citizens by creating better conditions for the full enrichment and mobilization of individual and collective talents. It will be made possible if: - Economic, fiscal and social systems are more efficient and more able to avoid social exclusion - New working roles appear for existing workforce - Education-related communities and institutions pursue actively the objectives of skills' improvement and people's adaptability.
3	Leadership advantage through sustainable development.	Europe can ensure sustainable growth and build leadership on a worldwide level through promoting and enacting the responsible use of natural resources. This would require: - Enactment of new metrics - Recognition of intergenerational responsibilities - Building on technological leadership - Taking the lead on an international level to promote environmental protection.
4	Sustained growth through greater individual certainty.	Europe can achieve a sustaining level of long-term development by rebalancing the roles among governments, individuals, and collections of individuals and achieving a new social contract in which each assumes significant responsibility for the solidarity of activities. The hallmarks of new roles within the social contract would include: - Government commitments to deliver relative stability and certainty in those areas where individual control is minimal - Individuals stepping up to the responsibilities that are concomitant with increased personal control and certainty - Collectives, such as business, contributing actively to create a productive sense of affiliation for their members.
5	European diversity: a unique asset.	Make a virtue from the reality of the increasingly diverse regions and cultures that make up Europe, by further refining the skills necessary both to make flourish the positive attributes of regional and cultural identity, and to build consensus where and when required to make progress for the whole. Accomplishments should also include: - Increasing the cross-fertilization of the fruits of diverse cultures - Enhancing the forums and skills to create multilateral partnerships within the whole - Providing a new pluralist model for European democracy.

At a less general level, the National Institutes have also provided some reflections about direct implications of their findings for business activities.

Several messages closely linked to the factors presented in Chapter 2 appear. Five are underlined below.

The Globalization of Activities, the General Increase of Competitive Pressures and the Multiplication of Risks and Uncertainties

> The business community will be confronted with increased competition as a consequence of the Single Market... It will force it to revalue all existing arrangements. This regards both the various markets on which the companies operate and their internal organization (Dutch report).

> In fact, there is a whole set of factors which will widen and intensify international competition: the EC internal market, but also EC enlargement, a new GATT agreement and the opening of Eastern Europe to capitalism and trade (Irish report).

Such a more competitive environment will affect all businesses services as well as industry.

> In industry, it will be the further decline of communication and transportation costs, the emergence of low cost producers from Eastern Europe and NICs in world markets for low-tech goods, the further pressure from Japanese competitors in high-tech branches, and the completion of the Common Market especially in matters like public procurement which will siphon off a large part of the monopolistic rents still existing at present. In the market for services - notably transport, commerce, banking and insurance - which in most countries have been largely shielded off from foreign competition by restrictive legal frameworks and trade practices, the pressures will emanate from a factual deregulation which will come about if competitors from less regulated markets have distinct cost advantages. Even the public sector will face a rising tide of competition: the ongoing need for fiscal consolidation suggests privatization and contracting out on a broad front and more application of commercial principles in the core of the public domain; as far as there are rather close substitutes to products offered by public monopolies (e.g. parts of the postal services), it will become ever more difficult to keep up the traditional practice of monopoly pricing and marketing (German and also UK report).

The coming into effect of the Single European Market and the reduction in barriers to other markets will not only greatly extend the *markets* to which businesses have effective access, it will also mean that they will have wider choice in where they:

- Raise their finance.
- Site their production.
- Buy their energy, materials and components.
- Find their subcontractors and suppliers of business services.
- Locate their R&D.
- Recruit, train and post their staff.
- Show their profits and pay their taxes. (UK report).

According to the types of companies, these opportunities will be more or less exploited: there are firms which have succeeded in acquiring a solid national base and are in a position to become Europeanized; firms in the process of Europeanization already possessing a multinational organization and identity; firms which have already achieved the *status* of European champion, and which are currently in the process of globalization, at the world level.

This leads to the second aspect.

The Role of Multinationals and Foreign Direct Investment

National Institutes generally view positively foreign direct investments. Compared to exports, these investments create employment and transfer specific assets from the parent company in the form of production techniques, managerial capacity and technology. Such investment can contribute to the European restructuring process by giving it greater depth and speed and can improve European competitiveness on foreign markets to which Community subsidiaries of foreign multinationals can export.

But foreign direct investments also evoke strong sentiments, i.e. the fear of a control of the host-country's economy, compromising its sovereignty.

This ambiguity is mainly reflected in the case of some small countries such as Ireland, Greece, Luxembourg and Belgium, but also in larger ones such as Spain.

The strategic responses of Ireland to the increased internationalization of economic activities are governed by its dualistic industrial structure: the existing multinationals are predominant in electronics, electrical engineering, chemicals and pharmaceuticals, while local firms are mainly engaged in activities characterized by slow growth, low value-added and commodity products. A general view is then that Ireland has become over-dependent on foreign-owned enterprises in developing its industrial base and needs to redress the balance to achieve greater output and employment growth in the indigenous sector. This implies a need to overcome the dichotomy in the economy and to promote synergies between the two types of activities.

A similar concern appears in the Luxembourg report, where the large companies (with the exception of ARBED and CFL) are subsidiaries of multinational groups, making their decisions on the basis of variables over which the public authorities have only scant influence. The message is then that it is important to maintain the competitiveness of Luxembourg's location but, simultaneously, it is necessary to maintain a diversity of domestic activities.

As with the two preceding countries, Belgium, in spite of the numerous multinational enterprises established on its territory, is still a country of small- and medium-sized enterprises. But there is a permanent debate about the fact that a series of major Belgian enterprises have passed into foreign hands. The report's view is that 'whilst socio-political discourse is often *against*, in fact the response has rather been *for*, and this attitude totally pays off so long as our advantages as a place of siting are preserved'.

A large country like Spain appears to share some of these preoccupations about multinationals. This is because it is felt that a large volume of direct foreign investment seems to flow towards the weaker EC economies in order to profit from temporary economic advantages (e.g. lower labour costs, social security etc.) which, *ceteris paribus*, will erode over time as economic convergence accelerates. The fact that Spanish companies are of a relatively small scale and have a low level of internationalism with the virtual non-existence of multinationals, makes it impossible to penetrate certain markets and weakens the negotiating position of firms in many external markets.

Such fears are less present in countries where there is not a strong asymmetry between inward and outward foreign direct investments.

This is true even for a small country like the Netherlands, suggesting that there is not a strong correlation between the size of a country and the size of its corporations. In this country, the inward flow of foreign direct investment has in fact been smaller than the outward stream. There is a remarkable number of Dutch transnational firms in energy and manufacturing as well as in services, which enjoy a strong international position in their particular sector.

It is therefore not surprising that the general message, sustained by public policy, is one of further internationalization, mainly through external growth (mergers, take-overs, cooperative agreements), an expansion of services on EC markets and easier entry of small and medium businesses into EC and international markets.

Use of New Technologies and Training

All National Institutes underline that the effective use of new technologies will be an increasingly important requirement for competitive success, across the whole range of economic sectors. One implication is the requirement of more technically qualified people, not just in top management but at all levels. Access to know-how, exchange of skills and mobility of people, will thus be determining factors in firms' competitiveness.

According to the French report,

> the promotion of the European technological and industrial base as a condition of identification and means of enhancing the attractive power of the European area, support for the research and training networks formed by scientists and industrialists, are vital conditions for conscious commitment to a political reality whose costs might initially outweigh its benefits.

The British report (see also Greece), goes a step further by emphasizing that technologies are only of value if they not only have a practical application, but also if they are actually adopted. Various factors underlie the pace of adoption, including firms having enough people with the right expertise to use them and enough financial resources to develop the applications, and both factors are often serious constraints in smaller enterprises. A further factor is the institutional, social and technical infrastructure. As stated in the Belgian report, the economy, technological innovation and culture are interdependent and grow together. The role of education is from that point of view crucial. It is important that the secondary education system and universities prepare for the creation and assimilation of new technologies and that the system of training ensures a follow-up (permanent education). The situation has been especially worrying in Ireland, Portugal, Greece and Spain. However, their entry into the EC has strongly reduced their cultural, scientific and technological isolation and has led to an increasing inflow of students into higher education, the expansion of research workers and, to a certain extent, to more training and retraining programmes within companies. Enterprises have specific responsibilities in this domain. Japanese experience suggests that, to get the very highest standards of quality, it is necessary to enlist the active participation of everyone in the workforce. The Japanese have done this through a participative, consensual style of management, giving the workers, in exchange for their full commitment, a high level of training, a high degree of security and a reasonable share of the fruits of improvements in productivity and sales. In this perspective, European business is expected to take a greater social and financial responsibility for the workforce. 'Firms have to find a *partnership role* with the employees and the local trade union branch in order to get a better motivation and a better education of the work force'. (Danish report).

Environmental Issues

According to the National Institutes, there is every indication that environmental problems and protection will shape corporate strategies in the years to come. Present industrial growth is not *sustainable* in the future without major risks for the ecological equilibrium of the planet, and this problem will without doubt be one of the most worrying of future years, if only as a result of the population explosion in the Third World. The expected business reactions are multiple: cooperation with government in development of standards, generally cleaner production, a drive towards less polluting agriculture, growth of environmental technology...

According to the Belgian report, the protection of the environment is at the same time an ethical problem, a new field of opportunity and a restriction on competitiveness:

-    It is an ethical problem as enterprises are expected to accept more and more certain forms of internalizing the external social costs. It is in the sphere of the environment that the phenomenon has most markedly commenced. Under the pressure of major technological risks, economic feedback of catastrophes, public opinion, but also in a considered manner by the more enlightened representatives of the profession, industry is going to internalize the costs of protection of the environment.

- It is also a new field of opportunity as a policy centred around sound management of the environment creates without question a competitive advantage for enterprises. According to an OECD study, the market for goods and services linked with the environment is estimated at the present time at $54 billion. In the year 2000, for Europe, a budget of $78 billion is forecast, and the world-wide turnover for pollution clearance operations should reach $300 billion by the end of the century. It is therefore not surprising that, according to the OECD *Observer* of February 1992, enterprises finance no less than 80% of total environmental research, against 50 to 60% of total research and development costs. It should be noted that the share of environmental research in total public spending on research and development is much more modest, not exceeding in general 3% of total public research and development expenditure.

- Finally, the protection of the environment could also create restrictions on competitiveness for enterprises; such restrictions vary strongly according to the risks, the sectors, the countries concerned and the solutions adopted. Enterprises are thus led to react negatively to certain initiatives by national and European authorities, for fear of unilateral measures which could affect their competitiveness *vis-à-vis* their foreign rivals.

This leads to issues dealing with the impact of trade on the environment and vice versa. According to the German report, environmental regulation affects the endowment of countries and consequently trade. And production, exchange and consumption of tradables affect the environment at home and abroad. Although under *ideal* circumstances the case for exploiting comparative advantages calls for a differentiated environmental policy, matters are quickly getting very complex once we take into account second-best problems, associated with real world complications like *environmental dumping*, international externalities, imperfect information and the impacts on and effects of innovation. In a way, there is a prognostic value to this mess: with so much scientific uncertainty and so much practical relevance, the debate on trade and the environment will be around for a long time, and is certain to be at the heart of the post-Uruguay Round GATT agenda of the 1990s.

The Role of Industrial Policy

As Chapter 2 has shown, in most reports, the current efficiency of the public sector as a provider of public goods and services, and as a remedy for market failures, is contested.

The role of the public sector in a modern market economy facing the major challenge of global competition is strongly expected to change in significant ways in the future. As emphasized by the Spanish report, several requirements appear the light of the various national experiences of deregulation, including the need to:

- Clearly define the idea of subsidiarity in advanced late twentieth-century economies.
- Reach agreements which are socially and economically feasible with respect to the optimum level of protection that the State should provide.
- Improve the efficiency of public spending programmes, and devise alternative supply mechanisms for public goods provision.

The success or failure of these efforts are considered a major influence on the future business environment and will substantially determine the competitive positions of the EC and its members, and their attractiveness as a place to invest.

A further question is the relationship between public and private firms. In countries characterized by an important public sector, especially France and Italy, it will be necessary to clarify the roles, powers and controls of public corporations. The establishment of a sort of *code of good conduct*, which is capable of providing a common framework of action, making it easier for national behaviour patterns to converge and avoiding suspicions and conflicts, is also proposed in the French report. This would possibly enable gradual definition of the reality and the purpose of a European public sector with a global strategy in 2010.

Beyond these problems, most reports also underline the role of public policy for sustaining the market process. Economic factors and entrepreneurial function are not sufficient to promote a process of modernization of societies.

If the political component is lacking, and if there is not a direct channel from entrepreneurial efficiency to political legitimacy, these factors of change are deprived of control and political coordination... They could even have a destructive effect before their benefits are sufficient to stabilize societies around new norms and references of behaviour. (Portuguese report).

For example the Italian situation has been characterized for a long time by:

- A fragmentation of territory, with a multiplication of many micro-institutions.
- A fragmentation of participation, which has become ever more individualistic and conflictual (in the 1970s) and ineffective (in the 1980s).
- A fragmentation of the channels of representation of interests, with a huge multiplication of independent trade-union agents and of spontaneous forms of representation of all kinds. (Italian report).

It is then not surprising that from the national reports, a possible role for a *new* industrial policy (or, to use a less disputed concept, a structural policy) is emerging. It reflects a possible reconciliation in the design of future EC politics between the traditionally liberal German position and the more *étatiste* Franco-Roman standpoint on the role of state interventions. This policy, made of indirect and horizontal measures such as large investments in infrastructure, R&D promotion, support of generic technologies rather than sectors, education and human resource development, implies a broader view of government-business relations, very much in line with the EC Commission's proposals for a European industrial policy.

Such an industrial policy straddling competition and cooperation is pragmatic: the best hope for European industry lies in the competitive discipline imposed by the single market, but simultaneously there is a need for a variety of instruments which are designed to overcome market imperfections and failures; to take account of external costs and benefits which are not fully reflected in the decisions of private industry; to accelerate structural adjustment, and to make companies more competitive. (In this vein, the British report argues that Britain's problem is that its economy has become unduly *mature*.) Since the problems in Britain and some of the other weaker economies may become sufficiently serious to put at risk the stability of the European union, and since national governments will no longer have adequate powers of intervention, *it is likely that the Community itself will need to take measures, on a transitional basis, to help economies, industries and regions which have difficulty adjusting to the new conditions.*[1]

This reorientation is also a challenge for the business community and its aptitude to overcome rent-seeking strategies to the benefit of a more broader dialogue with the public authorities.

To conclude this section, it must be underlined that the National Institutes consider that, besides the shaping factors already discussed, the business environment will be changed by many others: the collapse of Soviet Communism creates important shifts from the military-defence sector to the civilian sector; increased pressure for migration will provide new supplies of cheap, young labour; the ageing population will imply fewer young adults with uncommitted incomes, more people in their fifties in jobs as well as more people in older age groups, which could lead to an increase in the demand for medical and health-care products and services; dangers of widening gaps in earnings, growing social divisions and persistent high levels of unemployment could lead to some shift from private spending on personal consumption to public spending on social services; and within personal expenditure, some shift from high-income discretionary spending to low-income spending on basics.

Overall, therefore, it is expected that the new strategic vision of the business sector for the future of European industry will include these broad economic, institutional and socio-cultural issues.

SECTION 2: THE BUSINESS EXPECTATIONS

The *business results*, as Chapter 3 describes, come from multidimensional sources (principally the Commission itself, McKinsey & Co. experts, and interviews with a sample of senior executives and company Chairmen from major European industrial companies).

The research methods used were based on a two-stage process. First, the experts and the interviewees were asked to express and discuss their major prospective issues and priorities for Europe post-1992. Then, the same people were asked to react to the themes presented in the previous section (see page 83).

Two main messages have emerged: firstly, scepticism with respect to many general shaping factors and most of the previously discussed

---

1   For various views of these topics, see EC Commission, Industrial Policy in an open and competitive environment, COM(90)556, 16/11/90; M. Bangemann, *Meeting the global challenge: establishing a successful European industrial policy,* Kogan Page, London, 1992; A. Jacquemin and J.-F. Marchipont, 'De nouveaux enjeux pour la politique industrielle de la Communauté', *Revue d'Economie Politique,* February 1992.

themes; secondly, a strong priority given to the effective implementation of the single market.

Concerning the themes, the main reactions are the following:

- As mentioned in Chapter 3, the question of an improvement of European education systems and training is quite important for the business community. However, an extension to broader social issues, including the perspective of a new social contract and participation creates the suspicion of interventionism and the fear of higher costs for business corporations. However, there is a wide measure of support for Europe's social model in the broad sense of the term.

- Potential European leadership through sustainable development is doubted. Firstly, it is not very probable that Europe could acquire such a leadership. It will be very difficult to generate a first mover advantage, given the dynamism of some Japanese and some American corporations in this domain. Furthermore, there are the added difficulties of finding the capital for huge investments required and the time lag for getting the bottom-line benefits. Secondly, businessmen fear that their external competition, mainly from Eastern Europe and Asian countries, could exercise some forms of *environment dumping* (competitors having access to the EC market despite their lower environmental standards) and force delocations. Generally speaking, many companies seem to take a reactive rather than a proactive stance towards environmental protection. Even though intentions are good, many have no policy and approach the problems unsystematically on an *ad hoc* basis.

- A search for more stability and security at the Community level is viewed with suspicion. Except for some specific problems such as nuclear proliferation, the attitude is that increased uncertainties and risks are inherent to a process of liberalization, and such a situation is superior to a system of protection for weak players. Of course, in weak countries, the positions are less clear-cut and some pleas for helping transitions are made.

- As such the positive value of European diversity is not denied but the implications appear controversial. Too much diversity could maintain segmentation while a more homogeneous market through breaking down intangible barriers may enlarge the level playing field. Let the market forces determine the appropriate level of diversity.

- But, implementing the single market is seen as the crucial issue, so much so that no new vision should be introduced before the 1992 Single Market Programme has been firmly and fully implemented. Most businessmen consider that the single market will be a reality and that it will be necessary to accept the corresponding increased competition. But, for Europe post-1992, it is more a necessity than an energizing theme, all the more because the adjustment costs are already there while some of the benefits are still expected.

Although the businessmen's responses are clearly affected by the state of the industry, the profile of the company and its external exposure, etc., the main perspective is: what can the European Community best do in the post-1992 period that will improve the chance of my company being more competitive in the future?

As illustrative of some business views, we underline some highlights of our business leader interviews below.

The Social Contract

- We do not want Euro-employees, Euro-social insurance, Euro-wage contracts since this would end up in EC-social transfer mechanisms to the benefit of the weaker countries which even might undermine their willingness to work for economic progress.
- Except for the top level, language barriers are still a serious obstacle for an exchange of personnel between a company and its European affiliates.
- We need a European model of management including basic education and vocational training.
- Clearly members joining the EC wanted to attain the highest common denominator for their social security nets and those with the highest nets do not want to be pulled down to the lowest levels. Neither approach is realistic. An optimal approach is to set minimum rules and let each system develop over time... The (European) social dialogue is unhelpful.

Sustainable Development

- The shortage of capital will make it necessary to examine further environmental projects strictly in terms of costs and benefits.

- If EC norms were binding, the more advanced countries would get frustrated about the slow pace in the EC. Hence, who would support a middle-of-the-road policy?
- Sustainable development finds no interest in our country, nor is it likely to inspire the virility of the youth who strive more for the latest consumer toy, be it a walkman or a noisy motorbike.
- Environment cannot be the new theme: industry cannot be pushed any further. There is a delicate balance to be found between restoring and renovating Europe's industrial tissue and environmental protection.

Uncertainty/Security

- Some aspects of security are important today but being a risk taker is necessary for a dynamic economy. Reducing too much uncertainty diminishes the incentives.

European Diversity

- Diversity must be combined with subsidiarity so that it could lead to the respect of differences in ways of living, at the national, regional and local levels.
- Diversity is Europe's great strength. But should we be emphasizing diversity now? Shouldn't we be talking about accessing diversity?

European Competitivity

- Reinforcing Europe's technological capacity, especially to fend off Japan, is the No. 1 issue for internal survival.
- Europe will never be economically efficient subsidizing milk and sugar rather than biotechnology and electronics research.
- We must work on new building blocks which, if they are not exploited, will render vulnerable the gains we have already made.
- We need to trigger some imaginative big *market pull* projects in Europe in the 1990s.

Miscellaneous

- The Community is in a trough, Maastricht has reawakened a number of ghosts and demons, the European and global economies are weak. We cannot remain even stationary: we must move on and create new internal dynamics.
- We must allow the Community to mature but develop, nevertheless, some strong new policies.
- We must agree on the EC's non-negotiable essentials.
- Let us be modest and digest what we have achieved.

The Single Market - a Priority

A clear priority is given by the business community to the effective implementation of the single market. For the Commission, it implies a change of emphasis, from a legislative to a management strategy. As shown in Chapter 3, the perceptions are that:

- There is still important progress to be made in actually implementing it, and the transition period is critical.
- New obstacles and uncertainties have emerged, including the temptation, in the name of subsidiarity, towards some 'renationalization' to limit transnational competition.
- Concrete projects are necessary for fully implementing an 'integrated' market.

In this context of fragility, pragmatism is a must, vision much less so. The view is that clarifying Europe's strategies around a set of concrete projects is necessary. The Community has a great deal to digest and must consolidate its results, define its essential binding, non-negotiable interests and agree on well-identified issues, before launching another crusade.

As analysed previously, several focused practical projects in certain key areas of economic development emerge from the enquiries. At the internal level, the development of trans-European infrastructure and networks, including telecommunication services as well as railways; an improved flexibility of the labour market and education systems meeting business needs; a reinforced competitivity of European technology. At the external level, a *Marshall plan* for Eastern Europe and the building up of a managerial capability with concrete results benefiting European industry; a better access to foreign markets and reciprocity at the world level.

Small- and Medium-Sized Enterprises

To conclude this section, it is important to recall that the research on how the European business community perceives post-1992 integration issues has not covered *small- and medium-sized enterprises*. A recent inquiry made by P. Löser[2] provides, however, interesting indications based on a series of interviews with British, German, French and Spanish SME associations.

Four messages are especially relevant in the light of the information coming from the large companies.

Firstly, as in the case of big business, SMEs attach the greatest importance to the completion of the internal market and they warn the Community authorities almost unanimously 'not to invent new things, first get Europe 1992 working'.

Secondly, Europe post-1992 is perceived as an opportunity *and* as a threat. On one hand, no single national government would ever have had the courage to enforce deregulation in a way Europe 1992 does, since it means challenging the vested interests of hundreds of thousands of established companies and of their employees. On the other hand, the internal market appears as a threat for European SMEs who work only in a protected local market, with little or no export experience. SME owners are strong individualists and like to remain their own boss.

> The dynamic entrepreneurial characters among them know that in order to exploit the new market opportunities rapidly they need partners and cooperative agreements. In some cases they accept them, (preferably for less than a 50% stake), but the large majority remains sceptical and attitudes are changing only slowly.

So SMEs have to rely strongly on self-financing or on credits and they complain strongly about banks being too prudent, basing their lending too strongly on securities and preferring clearly to do business with bigger companies.

Thirdly, there is scepticism towards EC R&D programmes which, in terms of total spending on R&D are 'a drop in the ocean anyway'. They benefit mostly the big companies and the money set aside for the SMEs would not be much more than 'cosmetic balancing'. The procedures to get EC finance are also too complicated, thus contributing to frustrations

---

2   P. Löser, A snapshot of European SMEs, working document, Forward Studies Unit, EC Commission, 1992.

about the Community. Scepticism also prevails towards an EC industrial policy. There is unanimity that it would benefit mostly the big companies and therefore distort competition.

Finally, SMEs argue that:

> Brussels has to become more transparent, give earlier information, develop formal procedures to include SMEs in decision-making and by doing so 'making small business more of a partner'. The goals of EC legislation have to be defined precisely, its cost and benefits have to be balanced and thought has to be continuously given about the administrative instruments to achieve them. The Commission must not do too much, respect the principle of subsidiarity, concentrate on the essentials and only establish rules that are clear and stable.

SECTION 3: THE CONTRASTS BETWEEN BUSINESS VIEWS AND THE NATIONAL INSTITUTES' RESULTS

At this stage, an expected contrast emerges when comparing the messages delivered by the National Institutes and the priorities of the business community.

The National Institutes' reports have expressed in various ways the perspectives of an ambitious European project. Through different national traditions and histories, the European Community is moving from an era of narrowly-defined and self-contained commercial bargains, to an era of potentially unlimited overlapping common interests. Project 1992 with its mythical dimension has worked and built much more than a free-trade area. It took off after 1986 when the Single European Act provided the legal basis for overcoming the principle of national vetoes that had long paralysed the Community's rule-making with the effect that policies have really changed in the domain of freedom of movement of people, goods, services and capital.

The essential role played by firms in responding to these challenges and the opportunities offered by the large internal market is well recognized. Indeed, over the last few years, the workings of the European economy have come increasingly to depend on strategies intended to anticipate the conditions of the post-1992 Single Market. In other words, the business community has been the main engine of the integration process, through its internal and external restructuring and its cross-border cooperative agreements, mergers and acquisitions.

But, if European integration has been and continues to be largely about economics, the National Institutes have shown that social, cultural and political dimensions are becoming more and more important. The Maastricht ratification debates underline this even further.

Internal and external phenomena analysed by the reports require new options and new steps. Internally, it appears that 1992 cannot be simply a policy of deregulation aimed at the gradual dismantling of the Welfare State established in post-war Western Europe: accompanying common policies based on deliberative democracy are necessary, in so far as the objectives of the proposed actions cannot be sufficiently achieved by the Member states. Even from a pure industrial competitivity view-point, there is no sustainable market mechanism without political and social regulation where the concept of *public good* is asserted.

The external pressures also lead toward a more ambitious Community. The disintegration of the rest of the continent and the liberated economies of Eastern Europe have made the need for political integration in Western Europe stronger than ever. The multiplication of regional trading arrangements and, beyond, the cultural challenges from countries such as the United States and Japan call for a Europe respected in the world. The combined size of EC countries makes them a major economic actor on the world scene, but the challenge is to be strong politically for asserting a socio-cultural identity, for promoting partnership, and for overcoming a position of being an *environment* taker in favour of one as an *environment* maker. It is important to note here that in general, European business focused on external Community issues different from those emphasized by the National Institutes. What was mainly mentioned by business and industry leaders were the globalization of financial markets, the expansion of international trade, the importance of helping Eastern Europe to develop and the growing role of Japan. But broader socio-political issues such as migration or the North-South challenge were relatively neglected.

To illustrate this, it is interesting to note that in the European Round Table of Industrialists publication entitled *Reshaping Europe*, which was released in September 1991, most, but not all, of the issues raised tend to be focused on internal Community issues. Of the major nine priorities listed, only one and a half are externally related. Likewise, in the report itself, the developing world, the Lomé Convention and the Mediterranean receive only six paragraphs. Much more emphasis is placed on a wider

Europe and in particular the development of East Europe, a result that is mirrored in our own findings.

Another issue where the National Institutes' views and those of business diverge to some extent are those concerning economic and monetary union. In general, EMU is seen in a rather positive light by the National Institutes although without underestimating the difficulties of achieving economic convergence, a single currency or an independent Central Bank. The views of business however, are more nuanced and less positive (as we have seen in Chapter 3). Some companies are unambiguously favourable believing that the foreign exchange transaction costs saved will increase company profits. Others are sceptical, doubting that such a system, given the diversity in European economies, can work. Particular caution, even veering towards hostility, was mentioned by some German interviewees. The dangers of a *two-speed* Europe were also mentioned. A third strand feel comfortable with the *status quo* on the grounds that these companies feel they have a competitive advantage over their competitors within the ring fence of the present system. We do not want to level the financial playing field, they argue, our treasury department outperforms those of our rivals!

Overall, it appears that, given its objectives, its constraints and its horizon, the business community cannot be the main engine for a major qualitative jump in the next phase of European construction which would rely on a grand political vision. On the contrary, the businessmen seem to hope that the European authorities, especially the Commission, will do the necessary minimum and leave more room for market mechanisms. In this perspective, the Commission will be recognized, not through the affirmation of ambitious new designs, but in investing in the tangible and measurable rather than the philosophic, quixotic, or even the cultural and external. In responding to concrete needs expressed by its citizens and the Member States' Governments and by demonstrating clearly that adequate answers must be found at a pan-European level, the Commission has to demonstrate the capacity to provide policy-efficient answers that respect, rigorously, the subsidiarity principle.

Should we be surprised by these conclusions? Not really. The genius of those who invented *Europe* in the 1950s (J. Monnet, R. Schuman, P. H. Spaak, K. Adenauer), was precisely to promote tangible measures of obvious mutual interest and let greater political integration follow naturally from those practical steps. This method has been explicitly expressed in the Preamble of the Treaty of Paris establishing the European Coal and Steel Community in 1951, in which it is said that the goal is:

> To create... the basis for a broader and deeper community among peoples long divided by bloody conflicts; and to lay the foundations for institutions which will give direction to a destiny hence forward shared.

But the Preamble also recognizes that:

> Europe can be built only through *practical achievements* which will first of all create real solidarity, and through the establishment of common bases for economic development (emphasis added).

Two reflections are then possible. On the one hand it is undoubtedly true that the increasing competitivity demands on Europe's business world tend to coagulate into a message of prudence; do not open up any more Pandora's Boxes; give us time to distil what is already on the table. On the other hand, these messages are less positive, less dynamic than those the Commission solicited in 1984/5, when businessmen provided the essential turbo-charge for the Single Market Programme. Their overall replies are also tinged, inevitably, by the poor economic situation.

At this stage, there is no radical choice to make. Rather it means asking how can the Commission be the architect or even the arbitrageur responding to both the direct, pragmatic requirements of European business and the long-term, ambitious challenges which emerge from the shaping factors outlined by the National Institutes and which correspond to the qualitative political and institutional jump created by the European Union. One implication is that such a difficult juggling act requires an improvement in the dialogue, organization and consultation procedures between European business and the European Commission, a subset of a wider problem of communication, transparency and its democratic structure that the European Community has to face up to in the 1990s.

5. Implications for the European Union

INTRODUCTION

In the previous chapters of this book, we have examined the empirical evidence that has been laid before us in order to determine and understand the long-term shaping factors and shaping actors that will be influential in moulding Europe's future.

In this more political chapter, we want to concentrate on the implications for European integration and the European Union, and try to contrast some of the crucial future choices for the Community.

There is no shortage of theories on the matter. In the framework of the debates on European Union, there has been a welter of proposals about the Community's future socio-political model and the main challenges for the European Institutions.

A starting point is the nature of the EC's construction with respect to the concept of the *Nation State*. Historically there have been several conceptions of a nation. In the tradition of the German romanticism and the idea of *Volksgeist* (national genius), one extreme view is that a nation is not made from the will of its members: it is the deterministic result of a set of historical, geographic, linguistic, cultural and racial conditions, which create a unique *collective soul*.[1] Conversely, there is the view that a nation cannot be identified by race or language. It is based on a community of ideas, interests, affections, memories and hopes. Linking with the message *des lumières*, E. Renan affirms:

---

[1]   In the eighteenth and nineteenth centuries, this conception has been promoted by various historians and philosophers, such as Herder, Mommsen, de Maistre, Le Bon and Barrès. J. Benda, in his famous book *La trahison des clercs*, J.J. Pauvert, Paris, 1965, shows the dangers of such a view that exacerbates the national specificities at the expense of universal values.

> A Nation is composed of solidarity made up from the feeling of
> sacrifice that one has made and sacrifices that one is disposed to
> make. It presupposes a past. Yet it is summarized in the present
> by a tangible fact: consent and the clear desire to continue
> communal life. The existence of a Nation is a daily plebiscite.[2]

In other words, human beings consciously form the community in which
they live: the community being composed of the voluntary efforts of its
members.   This view has been deepened in the recent analysis of
J. Habermas[3] who writes: 'the nation of citizens does not derive its
identity from some common ethnic and cultural properties but rather from
the praxis of citizens who actively exercise their civil rights'.

From this perspective, the possibility of a 'national' European feeling is
not to be excluded. But it would be based less on common European
historical memories of division and war, than on a feeling of common
destiny for the future. As E. Morin[4] wrote, 'the actual destiny of the
Community can look back on the European past to understand what it has
in common'.

The situation is quite different for the concept of a European state. The
EC by no means approximates to a realistic image of a modern state. It
does not rely on a unique and inalienable sovereignty, but on another
socio-political model, i.e. an elaborate set of networks, legal, political,
social and economic.   This model oscillates between inter govern-
mentalism and supra nationality.

> The European Community is an exercise in the pooling and sharing
> of sovereignty. Unlike international organizations, the European
> Community as a whole has gained some share of states'
> sovereignty... Yet national governments continue to play a
> dominant role in the decision-making process.[5]

Such a complex, emerging model, far from closing a debate, opens it
largely to the extent that it raises crucial questions for its survival, its

---

2   E. Renan, *Qu'est-ce qu'une nation?* in Oeuvres complètes, Calman-Levy, 1947.
3   J. Habermas, 'Volkssouveränität als Verfahren', in *Die Moderne - ein unvollendetes
     Projekt*, Leipzig, 1990.
4   E. Morin, *Penser l'Europe*, Gallimard, 1987.
5   See R. Keohane and S. Hoffman, 'European integration and neofunctional theory:
     Community politics and institutional change', mimeo, Florence workshop, September 1989;
     A. Winckler, *L'empire revient*, Cahiers de la Fondation Saint-Simon, 1991; W. Wallace,
     'Working backwards towards unity', in H. Wallace, W. Wallace and C. Webb, eds., *Policy
     Making in the European Community*, Wiley, 1977.

credibility and legitimacy. What are the characteristics of the institutional equilibrium that is pursued? Which is the most appropriate level of competence for exerting a given power? To whom should be attributed a given political function? How can a pluralistic and multiform model be made transparent? To what extent can an active European citizenship function in this model, given that it is at the level of nation states that the role of citizen has been institutionalized? More specifically, there are important problems such as the internal efficiency of the Community institutions, the external implications of a European Union, not simply in terms of policy but also institutionally; perhaps most crucially is the legitimacy of the decision-making process, which includes issues of representativeness, transparency and control.[6]

These difficult issues have also been discussed in the reports of the National Institutes and by the business community.

We have drawn on these sources of information. We have also added material from our final Conference at which a number of distinguished experts were invited to participate and comment on the proceedings[7] as well as the views of some of the members of the Forward Studies Unit. In this chapter we underline their main messages and at the end we attempt to draw a small number of major conclusions.

SECTION 1: THE COMMUNITY'S IDENTITY UNDER THE MICROSCOPE

The ending of the Cold War in 1989, the chance, at last for Europe to unite on the basis of common ideas, interests, democracy and the respect of human rights has unleashed an upsurge of questioning about the Community itself, its identity, its competences and its future. The Community has turned in on itself. Why is this and are these trends set to continue into the 1990s and beyond?

---

[6] For early and stimulating reflections on these topics, see P. Ludlow, 'Beyond 1992', in *European Affairs*, 1988.

[7] H. Wallace, formerly Royal Institute of International Affairs now Sussex University.
J. Lesourne, Conservatoire Nationale des Arts et Metiers, Paris.
Prof. R. Prodi, University of Bologna, Italy.
Prof. F. Scharpf, Max Planck Institut für Gesellschaftsforschung, Köln.
E. Friberg, McKinsey & Co.

The Malaise of Democracy

The first and most evident factor is the persistent and unexpectedly slow growth in the European economies with little additional wealth being created. We have the risk of playing 'a zero sum game' in the sense that a marginal increase in the income of one group or country would be made at the expense of another. This is compounded by high levels of unemployment, economic insecurity and financial turbulence. In this economic climate, further steps towards European integration have become much more difficult as the complex Maastricht ratification procedure has shown.

But some postulate that the reason for this new mood is that the ending of european communism in 1989 has fragmented Europe's common security interest, the plaster-board and cement that bound the European Community countries together. It is argued that the perceived removal of this external threat at a time of economic uncertainty has triggered this introversion, which leads to questioning the need for further and deeper European integration. However, a counter-argument would be that the former external military threat has been substituted by new threats and growing economic, social and nationalistic tensions in Eastern societies resulting in fresh conflicts between ethnic groups, contested state boundaries and dangers of mass migration to the West.

A further school points towards the pressures of globalization-monoculturalism threatening deep national, regional and local European sensitivities. Footloose capital and labour are beyond the control or understanding of most political *decideurs* and this is chipping at generational solidarity, triggering the need to match the policy competition of major competitors and catalysing the need for harmonization at a supra national level. This in turn, it is suggested, causes the 'regulation-freedom friction' with civil societies tired, angry and constrained by having less and less policy choice.

But the main arguments concern the *malaise of democracy*. It is suggested by some experts that the Community is suffering the after-shocks of such a *malaise* which is itself at the heart of the European Nation State. This is provoked by a political elite losing touch with the concerns of ordinary men and women who feel increasingly disenfranchised and unrepresented, political parties who have retreated to homogeneity and defensiveness, some electoral systems that seem deeply flawed and a rise in the demand for more local and regional democracy. As H. Wallace said 'it is the political transmission systems that have fault lines'. Without a rejuvenation of democracy in the Nation State, Europe will suffer the consequences, it is suggested. The task is especially difficult given that our societies have grown old and rich, and that a large proportion of the population seems ready to defend their 'status' more than collective and societal 'values'. This complex situation is compounded further by the horizontal interweaving of most issues, the growing power of special interest groups and generally complex political decision-making apparatus in most Member States. As a result, the political class will then be tempted to adopt conservative positions or opt for the *status quo*.

Others suggested that it is the political legitimacy of the Community that is its *Achilles' Heel*. A minority view is that the Community is a deeply flawed set of institutions, outmoded, bureaucracy and centralism run wild, and inadapted to the needs of the modern world. The Community, according to this thesis, is the author of its own troubles by being over-ambitious and power-hungry. Such views go on to suggest the need to castrate the Commission, reduce Community competences and reorient Europe towards latent intergovernmentalism in the future. According to an observer:

> All the talk about creating, in the mind of the citizens, a sense of loyalty and attachment to the EC is not worth much now, given that the new total structure will be as obscure as the Holy Roman Empire.[8]

The cause could be the 'constitutional inadequacy' of the EC, derived from the fact that the EC is neither diplomacy nor democracy since both approaches are used at the same time for reconciling interests. The EC system will never be a system of freedom, order and security until there is a real EC political system through which we could seek 'the public interest and the common interest of the Community, and not merely an aggregation of the national interests of the Member States'.[9] It is also what F. Scharpf suggests when he argues that the Community's legitimacy, derived from the Treaty of Rome, the Single Act etc., is founded on the jurisprudence of the Court, e.g. by legal interpretations some of which are 'fictional'. But this hardly constitutes political and democratic legitimacy. These views claim that the democratic deficit is at

---

[8]   P. Allott, 'How to Cross the EC Pain Barriers', *The Wall Street Journal Europe*, 5 March 1992.

[9]   P. Allott, op. cit.

the heart of the problem and therefore the legitimacy of the Community's institutions must be solidified in the 1990s.

In fact several National Institutes and experts mentioned the need for a clearer definition of the European public good upon which a deeper more democratic European Community could be based.

The most powerful European public good, the preservation of peace, freedom, security and democracy in Europe is often passed by - hopefully assumed. But European wars and conflicts this century (area-wide) have cost the lives, civilian and military, of some 74 million people including 24 million deaths alone in the former USSR. Therefore, doesn't any other European public good appear trite against this horrendous incalculable historical externality? Surely so, but for many, and not only the young generation, the European project must be justified today, not by the past but by the future.

The Danish paper suggested three criteria have been used to define the Community's activity, namely, scale economies, externalities and political homogeneity. A fourth, it was proposed, should now be added, namely, the democratic impact of Community decisions.

Indeed, prospectively, one of the difficulties of defining the European public good is, as we saw in Chapter 2, that there is proliferating disagreement over the role of public versus private goods in general (N. Tsaveas of the Greek Institute).

One helpful pointer is that it may be *clearer for the smaller Member States to define what the European public good is*. They have, *de facto*, had to share parts of their national sovereignty already and most smaller Member States feel safer, securer and more influential internationally within the Community umbrella than in an inter-governmental context, where their influence could be significantly reduced.

As we reported in Chapter 2, there is little belief in the imminence, desirable or otherwise, of a new, powerful European identity value. Some suggest it will take at least one to two generations to create it, others talk in decades. Do we have any current practical examples that could be magnified? One was mentioned - the biannual Europe versus United States, head-to-head Ryder Cup Golf competition, when there is a real and noticeable European *esprit de corps*! R. Fraisse (France) painted this issue in terms of 'appartenance' or belonging. What are our feelings of belonging to the Community, and will this change in the 1990s? Most importantly can we create additional layers of 'belonging' that preserve the tissue of European life and culture? Whatever the outcome, the preservation of Europe's diversity is seen to be crucial. As Jean-Luc Nancy writes, '...one cannot conceive of a European identity which is not made up of diversity, juxtapositions of singularities, crossings and boundaries...'.[10]

There was little mention of the concept of 'European citizenship' in our work although it is mentioned in the Maastricht Treaty. Some believe however that this is a promising avenue for creating a new sense of belonging and identity to the European Community in the future.

Subsidiarity and Architecture - Scaffolding or Excuse

In the 1987 Padoa-Schioppa report,[11] the conclusions concerning institutional issues suggested three conditions for a viable evolution of the Community system:

-   More selectivity in Community responsibilities, the feeling being that the Community's effectiveness is undermined by expectations that it contributes to an excessively wide range of policy domains.
-   More space for decentralized application of Community policies, which implies that within its main areas of responsibility, the Community should prefer techniques of policy-making that allow for decentralized implementation.
-   Stronger institutional powers in some priority domains.

These issues have been embodied in the concept of subsidiarity. Subsidiarity is like federalism in more than one sense. First of all, it is nothing more or less than ensuring that decision-making is executed at the most appropriate level of government, which is what federalism also purports to be. It is not just a technical question therefore but a major element of democracy. But secondly, subsidiarity is ambiguous, it means different things to different Europeans. R. Maldague lists three interpretations and uses:

(i)   Subsidiarity defines the border between supranational and national issues.

(ii)   Subsidiarity is portrayed as a means of arbitrage between public and market forces.

---

10   *L'Europe au-delà de sa culture*, 1992.
11   T. Padoa-Schioppa et al., *Efficiency, Stability and Equity*, Oxford University Press, 1987.

(iii)   Subsidiarity is a defensive weapon to be wielded by old-fashioned nationalists.

But as much as the European debate has centred on the respective roles of the Community and Nation States, it has largely forgotten to follow through the principle to the regional or local level, where Basques, Scots, the Welsh or people from Lombardy are also keen to discuss the subsidiarity principle.

> The fundamental problem which requires political initiatives in the EC is the achievement of an equilibrium between efficiency and unity in decision making on common matters and the recognition of not just national but regional diversity, writes S. Sanchez (Spain).

This was supported by E. Landaburu (Director General of Regional Policy in the Commission), who says 'unless power sharing from the apex to the summit and vice versa is discussed and decided then the *malaise démocratique* cannot be resolved'.

The ultimate result of this debate is difficult to forecast. Will we have to assure, as F. Scharpf suggests, that Nation States and regions maintain new 'reserved competences' if we want to find balance; in other words, have we to try to draw up a list of specific policy areas for each administrative level? Logical as this sounds, the practical difficulties are formidable. Issues today cross-cut, they are more horizontal. Reserved competences for the Community in agriculture, or trade, can spill into areas of mixed competences (e.g. environment, energy etc.). Casting competences in stone is also an inflexible approach to changing economic conditions and to shifting political agendas (a national issue can become a transnational one because of external effects, and vice versa). We should also remember that subsidiarity also means responsibility at the lower levels to carry out the decisions of superior levels of government, although this is rarely mentioned.

But could there not be other reasons for the frontal assault on the subsidiarity principle being applied at the Community level but not apparently elsewhere? Does it mask a refusal to progress further towards European integration? Does it boil down to a desire for a Community that is no more than a free-trade area? Is it camouflage for political and economic failures elsewhere? And, indeed, why are all the proposed remedies and solutions for increased transparency, accountability and economic efficiency not always applied by the propagators of those ideas themselves? Indeed, is there not a danger of the more powerful Member States of the Community increasing their relative power at the expense of the smaller ones thereby disrupting the political equilibrium of Community decision-making. At the core of the problem could lie institutional inertia - both the inelasticity of the Nation States' Institutions to change (on the grounds of national identity among others) and the need to modernize the Community's architecture, with the result that we end up with institutional incongruity and incompatibility caused, in part, by different objectives for European integration.

These problems of power sharing within the Community are reflected also in the institutional and administrative heave-ho's of the United Nations and other international bodies. Most surprising of all, and frequently and conveniently forgotten, is that the Commission has no powers except those given to it by the Member States. The architecture of the Community and of Europe has to be agreed by the Nation States of its entity. However many pillars, parts or concentric circles there are, the resultant democratic outcome enshrined in the European Community Treaties is voted, usually unanimously, by the Nation States. Who, therefore, can solve the democratic deficit in the Community? And who is responsible for it?

Without an efficiently structured Community, democratic and accountable, the enlargement of the Community will be doomed to second-best success at best, unless the Community is merely regarded as a free-trade area. Therein lies the nub. As S. Sanchez says 'What in the end do we want - an economic product or a political project?'

Solidarity and Social Europe

Other factors spill over into the debate. Firstly, the global embracing of 'neo-liberalism' appears to have weakened solidarity among the poor and the rich, among the unemployed and the overemployed, the dynamic regions at the expense of the depressed and the new sectors of the economy with only a blind eye turned towards Europe's depressed and declining industries and regions. The increasing fear of the poorer Member States of the Community is compounded by an uncertain economic situation, the difficulties over the Delors II financial package and the convergence requirements for the later stages of EMU which will force Governments to trim their public spending to fit the entry criteria. Recalling J. Monnet, Europe, some say, is no longer generous (N. Delai, Censis), and the old paymaster but also the main EC beneficiary,

Germany, has saddled itself with colossal transfer payments to the former East Germany for years to come. Who is going to pay for European solidarity, for cohesion, for Europe's collective project? If an inward-looking Europe turns in on itself, reinforcing nation statism (at the expense of shared sovereignty, the essence of the Community) then it is certain we are in serious trouble. If this is the case, then the Community will no longer itself be able to be the 'rationalizing factor' for European integration (G. Gago). We will be in a new world that we might call 'isolationist neo-nationalism', instead of 'modern neo-cosmopolitanism'. We will not be able to provide the safety ledge for holding Europe's social and political forces together (N. Delai).

Or is all this the swing of the pendulum - normalcy, routine cyclical Community politics? Such a view was suggested to us by J. Lesourne who said that historically the Community has always been a succession of building blocks, not always logical nor in the right order, and whose ultimate end is unpredictable. Each building cycle lasts around ten years. J. Lesourne insists that:

> We are not reforming the Nation State at a European level but rather embarking on a new experiment, a 21st century model, which is based on sharing sovereignty, recognizing common interests, largely preserving national identity, and attempting to increase solidarity.

This leads to an issue that has the potential of being one of the great European political themes of the 1990s.

Leaving aside the structural aspects to the social equation and the fact that 11/12 of the Community Member States Governments signed up to the Social Charter at Maastricht thereby politically endorsing its importance, there were several strong pleas that this issue must be taken more seriously.

For example, N. Delai (Censis, Rome), said 'the foundation of politics is the capacity to be recognized by people as an expression of profound needs, not just materialism'. We must, he said, work on our European asymmetric thinking especially in the social dimension.

R. Maldague (Belgium) spoke of an 'unsure social equilibrium', whilst S. Sanchez (Spain) spoke of 'Economic Europe going faster than Social Europe. If this relative gap widens, the Community project may not be viable'.

And there are signs from further afield that the social dimension of policy is beginning a renaissance. Witness the unexpected revival of Democratic Party politics in the US. Witness the Managing Director of the IMF, M. Camdessus, saying that the IMF has neglected the social dimension for too long in its structural adjustment programmes for developing countries.

Why is this issue so central? Because many perceive the uniqueness of Europe as indeed its social model - a model now buffeted (see Chapter 2) from all sides.

One interesting prospective suggestion came from Denmark. 'The Community should concentrate on those aspects of social policy not vulnerable to competition between Nations.' The distribution of wealth is subject to policy competition between Nations, but social investments (e.g. training, education) much less so.

Undoubtedly there will be strong forces lined up against this revival, even if it takes place. Ultra-liberals denounce the paralytic interventionism created by the Welfare State. Others believe the social Europe project provisions that do exist could have perverse effects on social cohesion and convergence, since harmonization drives up the relative costs for the less productive players, increasing unemployment and widening regional income differences.

Financing the Community in the 1990s - Who Pays?

Irrespective of arguments about the overall level of Community spending in the future and the share for specific spending programmes, there is much agreement that financing the European Community is going to become increasingly difficult in the 1990s and beyond.

The Institutes suggest several reasons for this:

(i)   Germany now faces years of heavy transfer payments to the East German *Länder* and there is no replacement lender of last resort.

(ii)   Most Community Governments, so far, seem intent on reducing their public sector deficits to ensure that the economic convergence criteria necessary to achieve economic and monetary union can be reached.

(iii)   Savings levels in the Community are low, and probably inadequate to lubricate overall European capital requirements, including reconstruction costs in East Europe and the CIS states.

(iv)   Strong trends are blowing in the direction of greater 'accountability' of public and Community finance, a reduction in fraud, and 'value for money' cost efficiency which will press down on Community spending plans in order to reduce the overall Community budget, or at least to make better use of it.

(v)   A Community North-South schism could open up, as the Northern Member States try to rein in Community expenditure driven by requestioning the role and efficiency of the public sector versus the poorer Southern countries who will insist on increasing 'side payments' for cohesion, harmonization, solidarity, territorial equilibrium and the discipline of the SEM and the EMU. Community burden sharing, never easy, will be even more prickly in the financial arguments of the 1990s.

The budget outcome is, according to the Greek paper, likely to be 'the minimal likely to keep the Community's cement together' which will strain the poorer countries. But the German paper warns that there should be no overburdening of tax payers to pay for social cohesion in the Community.

Whatever the balance to be found, it is not very probable that the Community will have its own tax mechanism in the medium term.

The External Agenda: an Opportunity for Cohesion?

The prospective external agenda is daunting. The Community is still viewed externally as a role model of stability, democracy and peaceful economic evolution in Europe; it has accumulated an exceptional experience in reconciling divergent interests and different historical traditions. It is therefore not surprising that it is faced with external demands for membership beyond perhaps its current institutional capacity to supply. There is probably a large degree of agreement on the need for enlargement although perhaps less on the objectives of enlargement (wider European integration or dilution of the current Community model). There are also some difficulties concerning the procedure, the mechanics and the timing. From the Commission side, it is often asked how can the Community's current institutions cope with 18 or more members? How will the Council of Ministers function? What will be the respective roles of National Parliaments and an extended European Parliament? Unanswered questions that, to date, remain in the freezer.

Whether the Commission can manage so many enlargement negotiations with its present resources and whether the Commission's vertical structure is appropriate to deal with the forthcoming complex enlargement negotiations are other concerns.

Even more difficult to forecast is how the European meccano will be pieced together to wedge the Eastern European democracies into the Community bloc but allow sufficient transitional time for these new democracies to convert and transform economically. In other words, what political and security structures can be found to provide enough adhesive to fix the direction but enough latitude for economic flexibility and transition?

Other great external challenges face the Community. One mentioned by the Kiel Institute is to manage the GATT international trading rules to prevent protectionist whiplash or beggar-my-neighbour international economic warfare; this is important for the Community because commercial policy is an exclusive Community competence under Article 113 of the Treaty of Rome. Another crucial issue is how to lift quotas imposed on non-EC countries by individual Member States so that the single market will work properly after 1992. There is also the need to reintegrate agricultural trade to the normal rules of international trade, not just to satisfy the US and the Cairns Group and low-cost ACP producers, but also to open the Community's own market to Eastern European agricultural commodities in the near term. This will require profound long-run analysis in the Community of alternative agricultural and rural models, including using set-aside land to produce alternative energy / industrial crops or for recreational and nature areas. The trade-environment problematic also faces the 1990s GATT negotiators.

The second major dimension, especially noted in the French report, is the North-South issue. Here the Community has the crucial bridging role to try to find a new social, economic and political compact with the South that draws the poorest, but democratic, countries of Africa, Asia and South America into the fold of democratic and sustainable societies. This is a role which the Community is historically suited to - a role which is unavoidable because there are elements of development cooperation which, if not resolved, will result in the Community facing an intolerable wave of pressures not least those related to mass demands to emigrate to the EC.

The third post-1992 challenge is the clutch of security issues facing the Community: protecting the Community from outside, conflict prevention and settlement in Europe, arms control and disarmament and the prosecution of Europe's security interests at the international level. Maastricht sets an opening framework for intergovernmental cooperation on foreign policy and defence which will evolve in the 1990s. But the how and when are unclear, although the need is pressing.

SECTION 2: PROJECTS, PRIORITIES AND SCENARIOS FOR THE EUROPEAN COMMUNITY

We have seen throughout this book that European business leaders are in general sceptical of a new European vision - a new son of '1992' - preferring a period of European consolidation as global and European competitive forces gather strength.

Along these lines, Chapters 3 and 4 have shown that the business community has expressed specific messages on post-1992 integration, and several of them lead to core issues for the institutional and political organization of the European Community.

What is mainly requested are a greater clarity of the rules and more convergent interpretations, an improved transparency of the Community's decision-making process and more consistency of treatment of certain cross-sectoral issues.

Some domains and policies are identified as especially concerned by these issues. One of them is the relationship between EC competition policy and industrial policy. There is a broad consensus that market competition exerts a positive influence but simultaneously that the European antitrust policy is much more developed than industrial policy. Competitiveness at the world level demands an active policy for industry, with the Commission expected to provide a strategic framework for business. 'It is not a plea for defensive protectionism, but for support allowing a more offensive attitude at the world level'. What is involved is a realistic view of the international trading environment. The danger would be an EC competition policy reflecting dry legal theory rather than market realities. Some European industrialists are even beginning to feel that the Brussels authorities are over-stepping their powers in this domain. Similar concerns are expressed about the articulation of R&D policy and industrial policy as well as trade policy and industrial policy. Improved understanding of business issues and an improved aptitude to see the external EC implications on EC initiatives are then necessary.

More generally, business expectations with respect to the Community and the Commission are clear-cut. 'The Community has to be better managed by better defining its objectives and ensure that it is consistent in the pursuit of them'. Such a conception requires several important reforms. Firstly, it implies a different pattern of behaviour within the Commission. More time must be spent on examining the effects of policy measures, rather than on favouring the proliferation of new rules, all of which could add to the total administrative burden and potentially create further rigidities. It also assumes major advances in the methodology for cost-benefit analysis, impact assessment, counter-intuitive effect diagnosis, and consultative processes to engage the economic actors whose livelihoods are at stake. 'Such a programme is compatible with both the Latin philosophy of the need for the creation of orders, and the Anglo-Saxon tradition of organic development within broad parameters.'

Secondly, this conception puts into question 'the Commission's vertical structure that is unadapted to deal with the growing horizontal dimensions of policy. We need by topic a one stop shop that can cater for all aspects of industry'.

The Commission must be strong but does not require a growing bureaucracy. On the contrary, 'the Commission must be a referee or a broker rather than a coach'. In this role, it has to improve its ability to communicate and avoid 'using opaque, Byzantine language that nobody understands'. This implies a *remarketing of Europe* and a clarification of Europe's strategies so that companies and the average European citizen can understand what is going on, who is responsible and the objectives being sought. 'Europe was conceived for the bottom up but today is being built by a technocratic top-down approach'. We need to recreate bottom-up support and show, for the European citizen as well as for the businessmen, the advantages of the Community. The political acceptance of the Community's benefits is in question. The Sutherland Report (Brussels 1992) raises a similar issue for 'The Internal Market After 1992'. Its main message is that:

> ...for too long, it has been assumed that the rules of the internal market are self-evident, lending themselves to easy application. The challenge now is to reassure the consumer and to capture the imagination of business, particularly of smaller firms, that the rules of a really frontier-free market will be applied across the Community.

Two of its recommendations are especially relevant:

-    All proposals for Community action should be based on a wide-ranging analysis of its political, social and economic impact, comparing the advantages and disadvantages of intervention and of non-intervention.   This analysis should be based on five criteria: need, effectiveness, proportionality, consistency and communication.

-    The Commission must develop a communication strategy, involving all the Community institutions, national administrations and other non-governmental organisations in a systematic and co-ordinated way. This strategy would set the key objectives and organise the resources which are available at the Community and national level.[12]

Such recommendations could improve the dialogue between Industry and the Commission, knowing that business itself has to sort out and adopt more coherent positions.

The desired dialogue is not intended to plan but to discuss together strategies.

> We must strengthen the overall strategic politico-economic dialogue in the Community, define our essential binding, non-negotiable interests, and develop a narrower and deeper approach based on manageable projects.

Such a search for finding efficient interrelationships between corporate developments and public authorities leads naturally to references to the successful Japanese experience. As we know, MITI today does not adopt interventionist policies but plays as a mechanism which ensures that all firms act on a common set of expectations, and contributes to a consensus-building process.   Undoubtedly, the Japanese socio-cultural model cannot be transposed to the European context, and its future is uncertain.   Nevertheless, the business community has expressed a major interest for a similar EC structure where there is combined cooperation, shared information and objectives... and competition!

The National Institutes express most of these concerns but as expected complement them by *a broader systemic view of the issues* facing the futures of the European Community. For example, one said:

---

12   Reacting positively to the Sutherland Report, the EC Commission has decided to adopt several measures to improve the functioning of the internal market after 1992.

Technocratic integration interests no-one - we must found Europe on a political project - we must review our capacity, legitimacy and identity to better define arguments and defend European integration.

Similarly, J. Lesourne argues that the economic dimension of the Community will not survive political rupture.   Open markets could fragment in the end as Nation State interests supersede the collective project. The Community cannot be an environment maker unless 'we can launch common, horizontal and global projects... without which solidarity will weaken... and Europe will crumble' is the essence of another message, whilst the following was put forward by a Northern National Institute:

Tradition can be counteracted by dynamism - new initiatives, tangible progress in some areas and a sense that something is happening. To keep the train moving it seems necessary to launch spectacular new initiatives which gain hold of the public's imagination.

The National Institutes Priorities for the European Community

Below is a brief summary of some of the main specific proposals put forward for post-1992 Europe by the National Institutes.

Censis (Italy) offers an holistic menu of ten prospective priorities that they regard as the essential components to ensure European Union.

The ten points are interesting, first because they are cross-sectoral, interlinked with as strong an emphasis on the social and cultural as the economic, and second because their paradoxical nature reflects the 'impossible' challenges of our European society. They are:

(i)   To integrate both the materialistic and non-materialistic factors of development.
(ii)   To integrate both the economic and social approaches to European integration.
(iii)   To integrate a European perspective coming from the 'top' and a European perspective rising from the 'bottom'.
(iv)   To integrate a 'Europe of the rich' with a 'Europe of the poor'.

(v)   To integrate the different spatial and territorial levels of the Community, to have concurrently a Europe of states, regions and functions.

(vi)   Integrating 'factors' with 'actors'. Europe is not process but people.

(vii)   To integrate the spirit of security (and fear) with a spirit of risk (and courage).

(viii) To integrate homogeneity with diversity. How to maintain European diversity with a common vision and projects for the future.

(ix)   To integrate the lungs of Europe (the West and East) with the diaphragm of Europe (the South).

(x)   To integrate the spirit of generosity and hope with the spirit of defence and caution.

These points, although described as integration by CENSIS, are in fact demonstrating the need for discontinuity, an alternative approach, broader, but deeper as well.

For Ireland, the vital Community priority is that of cohesion and a new politicized approach to it (see Chapter 2). But to attain this, the internal market programme must be established and made to work in order to create European competitive advantage because without economic strength the achievement of political union will be illusory.

Another essential condition is for the European Community to reform its institutional structure and transform itself from quasi-inter-government-alism to a political entity. ESRI (Ireland) warned:

> The national interests represented by Member States can less and less encompass the real interests in European society and hence their debate does not bring the real forces to light. The Community, its agenda and its debates cannot currently engage the allegiance of its citizens, and the absence of values for its discourse leaves the field to ethic and other ideologies.

The Dutch paper states unambiguously that the process of European integration is the major driving force in the years to come. Whilst completing the single market is a necessary condition for improved economic performance it is not sufficient. As previously mentioned, other conditions are improving European infrastructure, consolidating the social dimension with common sense, ensuring free trade inside and outside the

Community and enhanced intergovernmental technology programmes. Like many others, the Netherlands encourages a more avant-garde environment policy. Externally, strong emphasis is placed on the Community's role to avoid protectionism. But at the heart of this conception is a world in the 1990s and beyond that will be dominated by tough policy competition, where each country's policy options are restrained by Community agreements.

The rumbustious political argument in the UK on the future of Europe and the United Kingdom's full or partial participation or otherwise in the project is certain to coagulate for many years yet. A crucial issue will be the durability of the strong emphasis placed on economics and whether what the UK paper describes as Britain's mature economy will be able to withstand the onslaught of new tranches of competition - both European and global, sentiments rejoined by the Spanish paper. We read from the British text:

> Since the problems in some of the weaker economies may become sufficiently serious to put at risk the stability of the Union, and since national governments will no longer have adequate powers of intervention, it is likely that the Community itself will need to take measures, on a 'transitional' basis, to help economies, industries and regions which have difficulties adjusting to the new conditions.

On the social chapter, the UK paper states that:

> Its eventual adoption in the UK might be expected to check the trend towards a wider spread of earnings levels... and higher earnings levels at the bottom and higher social benefit levels should have a direct effect in reducing the numbers in poverty in Britain.

Two specific initiatives are tabled. First of all Community funded initiatives to stimulate the development of environmentally sustainable and competitive economies and communities. They would seek to promote experimental programmes in cities, towns and rural areas that would seek to integrate environmental concerns with local economic development strategies and maximize the scope for application of new technologies. Included would be:

(i)   Innovations in transport patterns, encouraging substitutes for private car use, tele-working/shopping etc.

(ii)   Intensive development of green forms of economic activity with the potential for job creation, such as tourism, landscape rehabilitation, forestry, use of set-aside land.

(iii)   Innovative policies for the diffusion of new energy technologies such as low energy lighting and application of new environmental technologies (pollution control, recycling etc.).

(iv)   Intensive application of information and communication techno-logies in environmental management, transport, education and training.

The approach would be to create 'learning networks' to provide a valuable 'bottom-up' input to European policy-making as sustainable economic growth patterns are sought.

The second initiative proposed by the UK paper is enhanced Europe-wide technology training. The idea would be to create leading-edge European training modules to encourage the Europe-wide application of information technology to equip people with the skills to use modern information technology. Such an initiative could provide high social returns in relation to costs in terms of improved competitiveness, employability of students, as a unifying force in Europe and as a way of setting some standards.

The Greek Institute takes a more economic approach, also highlighting the technology and training gaps, the importance of improved European infrastructure, and the necessity to reduce long-run unemployment. But it emphasizes that social cohesion will be a vital issue for the Community, because if the income differentials widen between the Northern and Southern Member States, disaffection will grow against the EC and the further steps towards European Union will falter, hence the need for substantial 'cohesion' side payments. Allowing each country to go their independent ways could increase economic, political and trade tension in Europe.

The Community is faced with a choice of 'fusion' or 'fission'. Forces acting in favour of 'fusion' are the pressing external issues, the common interests of coordinating policy, and the achievements so far. Factors swinging in the opposite direction are a resurgence of ethnic demands, 'renationalism' and decentralization demands.

The Danish text also suggests a number of priorities for the European Community in the post-1992 period precisely because '1992' is wearing out and European integration will lose momentum if there are no new clear policy initiatives.

Its first proposal, described as spectacular, is to double European Community research R&D expenditure by 1998. This is justified by a logic whose opening premise is that Europe, in the medium term, cannot generate competitive advantage from labour-intensive or commodity-based goods. On the contrary, the best chance to lead is in the education / knowledge-based sectors of the economy. There are several segments included in this initiative:

- Supporting education.
- Diffusing technology more widely.
- Encouraging SME collaboration in technology projects.
- Strengthening intellectual property rights.
- Reducing bureaucracy and improving European contract law.

According to this paper, technology in Europe has to have a more humanistic and human dimension. The second prong is to increase the global competitiveness of the EC by a 'clever industrial policy', by thoroughly searching for efficient institutional solutions and encouraging policy competition between institutional arrangements. Customers, it is argued, will seek out and demand efficient public policies.

Another important initiative could concern the encouragement of consensual patterns of management in the European company, including raising the social awareness and responsibility of employers.

A further role that the Community should carve out for itself is that of 'market maker'. The Community could work towards creating the European stock exchange, a European freight and commodity market etc. and develop the framework for the twenty-first century European company.

The German paper warns that this is no time for complacency after the completion of the internal market and the first steps for political union.

> To stand up to its historical role in the post Communist Europe as a model and a catalyst for peaceful cooperation, and as one of the major economic players in the world besides the US and Japan, the EC has to strengthen its profile not only in economic matters but also in the realm of policy issues.

The Community has to work towards creating an identity as a citizen of Europe, whilst preserving the social, cultural and political roots of the citizens in their local, regional and national environments.

Much emphasis is placed, as expected, in the financial front on the pursuit of the stability of the value of money, and therefore a guaranteed independence of the Central Bank is considered crucial for lasting economic success of the Community. Economically, the most important challenge is to steepen the rising tide of protectionism to which the Community, albeit not alone, has contributed throughout the 1980s, writes the Kiel Institute. Competition policy must be on the alert to protect the competitive process and the Community has a prime role in strengthening its surveillance of national subsidy programmes.

The Community's own assistance programmes should be transparent and non-discriminatory, harnessed to increase competitiveness. Environment is mentioned as a specific area for Community action at the transfrontier and global levels. As for social policy, a mandated rise in standards would 'unless matched by increases in productivity, lead to higher unemployment in the backward regions'. As with other Community policies, the second-round effects must be taken into account, but overall reaction in Germany to the Social Charter is nevertheless estimated as quite positive.

From an economic angle, the Belgian paper suggests that the opening of markets, demographic ageing, technological progress and environmental protection seem to be the four essential factors likely to dominate the future of the Community. These structural factors suggest a number of political priorities. At the global political level, the key issue is to complete the European Union 'in as much as this constitutes an essential element of stability, security and equilibrium'. This in turn will play a vital role concerning the economic reconstruction, political and democratic stability of the Eastern European countries, as well as reinforcing the strength of the Community in the Triad and in the role it can play with developing countries. The European Union responds well to the economic criteria, the Belgian report states, but less well to some major cultural or social concerns such as the 'flexibility-security' or 'individualism-solidarity' dilemma, or the rivalry between generations on social inequalities and the social contract.

At the level of Member States, the Belgian paper advises towards a redefinition of their role as economic operators, whilst reserving a place for the renegotiation of a new social contract.

The impressive Portuguese paper takes an exhaustive scenario approach to analysing some of the implications for the European Union. The four basic structural scenarios are:

Table 5.1   European scenarios suggested by the Portuguese Institute

SCENARIOS	CHARACTERISTICS	CONDITIONS
COORDINATED HARMONIZATION	Strategic decision-making unit with internal specializations and joint participation in formation of Community policies	Convergence Harmonization Operating networks Community institutional system
DIFFERENTIATED HARMONIZATION	Hierarchy of powers in the system of circles with a motor centre and peripheral areas which are modernized by being dragged along	Differentiated levels of development with a need to manage internal tensions within Europe
MULTIPOLAR FRAGMENTATION	Establishment of areas of influence of a traditional type with leadership for regional areas	Establishment of relations between influence blocks within Europe Return to traditional European conflicts
REGRESSIVE FRAGMENTATION	Collapse of the Community project with return to assertion of the Nation State and the attributes of traditional sovereignty	Large-scale European crisis with regressive isolation and uncoordinated policies

The discriminant factor between the four scenarios is a political one, according to the Portuguese paper.

It depends on the will of the political leaders to choose between these four structural possibilities, no other dimension of modern societies - economic, social or cultural - has the ability or organized institutions to ensure sufficient consistency in important decisions.

The Portuguese text continues that:

At successive cross-roads in the evolution of the European Community, alternative routes will always be of the same kind: to strengthen Community institutions and coordinate politically the problems of European integration and establishment of entrepreneurial networks, or to allow the problems of modernization to lead to the formation of national blocks and powers in Europe with a consequent general spread of defensive reactions of a nationalist kind and strategies of an extra-European kind.

For the Portuguese, economic factors alone cannot modernize societies. This is because without political legitimacy, these economic factors are deprived of control and coordination mechanisms... which implies that on their own they are insufficient for ordering societies. The political dimension of Europe is therefore essential.

In a significant passage in the light of the Maastricht referendum result, the French paper states that France has traditionally supported European integration for reasons that coincided with the views of all the pro-European forces, namely the desire to work towards peace and reconciliation among European peoples and to profit from the inherent advantages of a continental-sized market. But France's attitude towards the EC has also been shaped by 'the hope of reinforcing its international influence, of allaying fears of a Europe dominated by Germany and by offering the French State an *area* commensurate within its ambitions which the National framework is too small to satisfy...'. Hence, historically there was a large effort channelled into furnishing the European Community with all the attributes of a State, namely a currency, diplomacy and defence (Laurent Cohen-Tanugi in *L'Europe en danger*), leading to many French people idealizing political Europe. But the Maastricht process has woken up the political milieu that some of these assumptions are less certain that once believed and that the political methods used in the European Community do not exactly coincide with France's traditional ways. For example, whereas France's democratic tradition embodies the public interest and universal suffrage as the sole basis of political legitimacy, the European Community recognizes other measures of legitimization and democratic control, via the sharing of sovereignty and the supremacy of European judicial power. Likewise as France's traditional method of regulation is the informal negotiated agreement, the European Community, the French paper says, relies more on supervision by judges. This means that France's public elites are faced by new challenges in understanding the mechanics of European politics.

The conclusion of this analysis is an interesting one: '...in order to work, the process of European integration needs credible forms of national legitimacy...'.

Another part of the paper concludes with a second important warning shot:

> ...simplification is an essential objective for the European authorities. In other words, it is not through building up a European bureaucracy to match that of the old National States but rather through the implementation of comprehensive strategic decisions that the European economic and political player will be

seen to gain strength, with regard to the Member Staes and the rest of the world.

Finally, the key themes of a twenty-year strategy for European Union suggested by the French paper are summarized in the table below:

Table 5.2   European Union priorities suggested by the French Institute

I.   With regard to the rest of the world:
- Furthering demographic transitions.
- Restricting migration movements by encouraging joint N-S-E-W development.
- Reducing ecological imbalances.
- Organizing economic development more efficiently.
- Participation in global development of information and training.
- Cooperating in new concepts of world security.
- Encouraging the modernization of international institutions (GATT, IMF, WB, UNESCO, G7, TRIAD...).
II. With regard to the European Community's Member States:
- Giving substance to the meaning of subsidiarity.
- Spatially integrating the Member States.
- Encouraging the rapprochement of Europe's educational and training system.
- Fighting against social exclusion.
- Constructing a more homogenous European public area in terms of public administration, management, etc.
III. With regard to itself:
The crucial issues here are legibility, visibility with respect forEurope's intrinsic diversity.
- To construct institutions which combine unity and diversity.
- Encouraging Europe's population to become conscious of its common interests and of its internal solidarity, which will involve redefining Europe's Welfare State models.
- Developing a coherent European technological and industrial potential, capable of lauching its own strategies will be the driving force behind European integration.
- A rapprochement and eventual integration of Europe's educational systems.
- Development of a common security strategy.

SECTION 3: A SOCIO-ECONOMIC MODEL FOR EUROPE POST-1992

From the rich harvest of information brought by the research on shaping factors and shaping actors, it would be presumptuous to pretend to extract a single and simple message.   In any case it was not the goal of our exercise.   However it seems useful, at the end of the first part of this book, to underline that among the important convergences emerging from the study, a wide consensus has been expressed around a European model of society.   Whether they be the expectations of the Member States as expressed by the National Institutes or the preoccupations of the business community, we find a reference to core values where the dynamics of the market economy combine with the solidity of social cohesion. This vision does not draw on the old ideas of social engineering and large-scale government activism, but expresses the need for a new paradigm.

This can be made more explicit by using the famous distinction proposed by O. Hirschman[13] between two types of mechanism able to ensure the functioning of an organization or a society: Exit and Voice.

In 'Exit' social change is ensured through a decentralized and anonymous mechanism that secures victory for the most efficient. Winners are awarded with growth, and losers are obliged to disappear. Results worked out by the market are considered natural and legitimate, including international, national, regional, and personal redistribution of resources.   In 'Voice' the process of social adjustments rests on a collective consensus that establishes solidarity of existing interests and decides the general direction of change.   Consequences of change are themselves tempered by effective redistribution between winners and losers. Outcomes of market mechanisms are not automatically considered as legitimate and can be politically modified.

Each of these types leads to perverse effects in its extreme form. In the exit type, transmitted information is poor, the mechanism is brutal, and the probability of reconciliation of conflicting social interests is low. On the contrary, there is the risk of a *dual society* developing, in which a significant proportion of the population becomes peripheral and marginalized and in which the legitimacy of the *winning circle* is as much based on a strategy of domination as on initial efficiency. In the voice type, on the other hand, the concern for consensus and equitable compensation is liable to undermine the inducement to creativity, initiative, experimentation, and diversity. Defence of group interests and acquired rights easily deviates toward corporatism and protectionism. Growing and paralysing interventionism create inefficiencies, even in the social sphere.

The problem is then not to choose between Voice and Exit but to combine their virtues whilst avoiding their vices. Nor does it boil down to a radical and irreversible choice between public initiative versus private initiative, thus freezing the abilities of each; rather it should raise the issue of the difficulty of implementing mobility in respective spheres according to appropriate modalities.   For instance, deregulation of spheres mismanaged by the State is undoubtedly desirable. This, however, does not imply the return to a utopian free market but a change of regulation:

---

13   O. Hirschman, *Exit, Voice and Loyalty*, Harvard University Press, 1971.

delegation of functions, grants for public services, or transfer of assets to the private sector must be matched with institutional rules and alternative forms of social control. If the public authorities renounce the monopoly of determining social welfare, it would nevertheless remain a privileged player among the participants in the games of social and economic relations. It would take on only what is strictly necessary but it would safeguard pluralism, avoid replacement of public monopolies by private cartels, and ensure effective redistributive transfers.

As suggested in the figure below, the European project could then be the reference for the building up of such a social market economy where dialectic relations and not opposition are developed between market mechanisms and social cohesion, competition and cooperation.

But this project, related to the *Soziale Marktwirtschaft* model that the Freiburg School has promoted, is fragile. In the context of a *multi-speed Europe*, the temptation for some is to put into question not the timing for convergence toward the same objective, but the objective itself. A multiplication of opting-out clauses could be used, not simply as a device to help some countries to reduce the tensions and social costs of their difficult transition, but as a means for rejecting crucial dimensions, economic or social, of the global project. As long as divergent views persist not only about the pace at which we should proceed, but also about the direction, i.e. the desired goals of integration, the issue of who will be core EC members and who marginal players remains open.

Figure 5.1   A socio-economic model for Europe post-1992

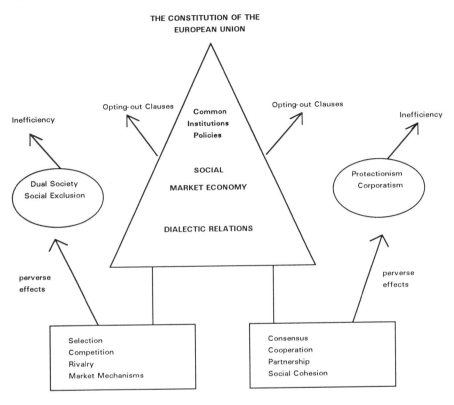

In any case, the European project cannot lead to a closed club. It must stay an open system where differentiated participations and associations are possible. This requires a pragmatic institutional evolution able to accommodate variable geometry and diversity in practice.

One precondition for such an approach will certainly be to find new consensual, non-conflictual systems of management and political dialogue that leaves dogmatism and ideology behind. Or as one National Institute succinctly puts it:

> The fundamental challenge for European managers, scholars and scientists is to devise styles of management, information systems and organization that turn democracy, humanism, and social representation into competitive advantage.

Today, in Europe, is it not correct to say that the most performant economies, the happiest societies are those that have found a degree of social consensus, a political willingness to cooperate, a desire to share responsibility and debate joint futures and strategy? The conflictual models, whether rigid and centralized management structures or ideological politics, appear to generate second division players and sub-optimal performance.

This ambitious direction will be difficult to attain. It will require the relationship between politics and the citizen to change, because the exchange of ideas will need to flow much more in both directions, bottom up from the people of Europe to top down from democratically elected political leaders. This will also require a new balance between the different levels of political decision-making. The words of the Secretary General of the United Nations Boutros Boutros-Ghali remind us:

> The time for absolute and exclusive sovereignty has passed; its theory was never matched by reality. It is the task of leaders of States today to understand this and find the balance between the needs of good internal governance and the requirements of an ever more interdependent world.

In the end, and we cannot escape this, it means clearly defining our common values, the level of our ambition and our ultimate goals, in other words, the ethical dimension of Europe.

PART II

Twelve National Institutes of the European Community Reflect on the Long Term

The National Institutes

Belgium:
Robert Maldague, former Commissaire du Plan, Brussels.

Denmark:
Institute of International Economics and Management, Copenhagen.

France:
Commissariat Général du Plan, Paris.

Germany:
The Kiel Institute of World Economics, Kiel.

Greece:
Foundation of Economic & Industrial Research, Athens.

Ireland:
The Economic and Social Research Institute, Dublin.

Italy:
Centro Studi Investimenti Sociali, Rome.

Luxembourg:
Institut Universitaire International, Luxembourg

Netherlands:
Scientific Council for Government Policy, The Hague.

Portugal:
Instituto de Prospectiva, Lisbon.

Spain:
Fundacion Empresa Publica, Madrid.

UK:
Policy Studies Institute, London.

6. Belgium: Shaping Factors*

INTRODUCTION

The General Context

Belgium can be defined as a small open economy, which is comparatively rich if it is judged by the degree of social protection which is attained and the high level of GNP/inhabitant. There is undoubted social consensus, but the mixing of two cultures makes this fact difficult to reflect institutionally, as shown by the political evolution of the last twenty years, during which time Belgium has gone from a Unitarian State to a Federal State.

The Belgian economy is open as a result of its small size, which has led it to turn naturally towards being an export-based economy. This makes it highly conscious of the development of its own productivity and its competitiveness.

Moreover, Belgium has for a long time been welcoming foreign investors, whilst on the other hand itself investing relatively little abroad. It can be said without doubt that it foreshadows in some way the Europe of the future if one judges this by the increase in the number of international mergers, take-overs and acquisitions which have been carried out on its territory with 1992 in mind. The extent of these is such that measures have been taken with a view to ensuring a greater level of transparency in the practice of take-over bids, the most striking example of which was the purchase of the largest Belgian holding company by the French group Suez. But this openness poses a question of national stability when it is realized that nearly 40% of the GNP is produced by foreign-owned enterprises. On this point, however, it will be noted that alongside the major multinationals, which are generally foreign, there appear a large number of small- and medium-sized enterprises, notably in the service sector, which ultimately ensure national stability.

---

*   R. Maldague, P. Leroux and A. Gilot.

The Belgian economy is in effect relatively service-orientated in comparison with the European average and has been so particularly since the oil crisis in 1973, a consequence of which was a drastic loss of industrial jobs.   This increased expansion of the service sector is also explained by the phenomenon of externalization: by concentrating above all on their quality products, enterprises have instigated the development of a certain number of services to enterprises.   Parallel with this, a substantial development in the non-commercial sector has also taken place within the framework of programmes designed to reduce unemployment and to cover new needs of the population.

Since 1974, Belgium's public finance situation has worsened considerably and the national debt, fortunately financed by relatively plentiful national savings, has increased to the point of exceeding GNP by a considerable margin.

Finally in spite of a GNP/inhabitant which is higher than the European average, the unemployment rate remains a problem, in particular long-term unemployment with significant regional disparities existing between the North and the South of the country.

Some Factors which are Particularly Crucial Both on an Economic and Social Level and on a Political and Cultural Level

At a first glance it would be tempting to believe that a small open economy such as Belgium's, situated in the centre of Europe, is not affected or little affected by many of the key European shaping factors raised in earlier chapters of this book, with the exception of public finances.

More careful analysis nevertheless reveals specific Belgian 'economic and social particularities' in several respects:

- Brussels' position as capital of Europe.
- The material infrastructure for transport and communications.
- Teaching, training and research.
- Production and enterprise structures.
- The debate on economic identity.
- The labour market and in particular free but regulated wage formation.
- The problems of the environment.
- And, of course, constraints on public finances.

'Belgium's particularities on the cultural and political level are both well-known and unknown.'

An endeavour will be made to group them around several major themes:

- The apparent contradiction between social consensus and *political dissent*.
- Federalism, confederalism or separatism?
- The development of major political trends.
- The future of the role of the State and of the public sector.
- The development of financial transfers between the regions and their medium- and long-term implications.

SECTION 1: THE ECONOMIC AND SOCIAL FACTORS

Brussels, Capital of Europe

Brussels is a city of one million inhabitants, and the fact that it accommodates at the present time the majority of the European Communities' departments has constituted and still constitutes *a shaping factor*.

This can be judged from the recent property speculation which has caused a considerable rise in the price of land, housing and rents which were until then relatively modest by comparison with other European capitals. Significant investments have already been made in the property market, and the hundreds of multinational headquarters which have come to set up in Belgium, for tax reasons admittedly (coordination centres) but also in order to be in the vicinity of the centres of European decision-making.

Brussels, capital of Europe, signifies not only a significant direct creation of official jobs, but also has numerous indirect implications (consultancy companies, translation services, transport, catering, cleaning, renting agencies), thus providing an additional source of income for Belgium which will contribute to consolidating its service sector characteristics.

But that also implies challenges to be overcome and not least of these are the progressive rise in rents and the risk of paralysis in the road traffic inlets to the city, coupled with the problems of pollution by noise and CO_2 affecting the inner city quality of life. Some of these problems will be studied in the sections which follow.

The Material Infrastructure for Transport and Communications

This is vital for enterprises in as much as it contributes to growth in the same way as human resources and investment.

A Highly Developed Transport Network

By developing its infrastructures, Belgium has been able to take advantage of its favourable geographical situation, which doubtless explains a part of its economic success and its selection as a decision-making centre by numerous international organizations and enterprises. The contribution of the transport sector to GNP is, moreover, one of the highest in Europe.

The road, rail, sea and river networks are very dense. The efforts made in air infrastructure during recent years with the collaboration of the private sector (BATC) should also not be forgotten. It is necessary nevertheless to note that, for imperative budgetary reasons, public investments in the 1980s were seriously reduced. At the same time, an effort towards rationalization of the public transport enterprises was undertaken which led to the loss of several thousand jobs and there has been a growing tendency to grant greater management autonomy to these enterprises. This autonomy is taking shape today (creation of Belgacom in the telecommunications sector, management contracts with the railway company (SNCB), the privatization of SABENA). In addition it should be pointed out that since the institutional reform of 1989, urban transport and infrastructure have come under the jurisdiction of the Regions; the airways, railways and telecommunications remaining under national control.

But Two Challenges have to be met: Urban Traffic Congestion and Backwardness in Telecommunications

Two problems will doubtless form the focus of attention of the public authorities during the course of the coming years: urban traffic congestion and telecommunications efficiency.

The entrances to Belgium's large cities are threatened with traffic saturation in the rush hours, with all the consequences this implies regarding pollution, waste of resources and economic inefficiency. With the aim of ensuring greater mobility, whilst at the same time protecting the environment, projects have been initiated with regard to public transport: a suburban network (of the Regional Express Network type) around Brussels and improved access to the stations. In addition, tariff policies will be implemented with a view to encouraging the use of public transport, and tax measures (in particular concerning the deductibility of car expenses) will doubtless discourage commuters from using cars.

Telecommunications only occupy a relatively modest place in GNP in Belgium, if it is compared with the European average (2.7% against 3.6% in the EC). In the sphere of telecommunications, Belgium has to make up for backwardness in some areas (connection delays, mobile phones, etc.), if it wishes to remain competitive at the European level. The recent creation of Belgacom and the Belgian Telecommunications Institute go in the direction of a greater liberalization of the telecommunications market, particularly in the sphere of value-added services.

Opportunities for Business

With the development of a 'pan-European transport system' (TGV, high-speed trains, Channel Tunnel), trading will be greatly facilitated, as will the mobility of people, which should lead to a better allocation of the factors of production.

In the sphere of 'communications', standardization of the systems as well as competition between the telecommunications enterprises should exert pressure towards a lowering of prices and improve the variety and quality of the service.

At the level of 'the production of components', opportunities doubtless exist if this is judged on the one hand by the size of the needs which arise from the position of Brussels as capital of Europe, and on the other hand by the low public investment in this sphere in recent years.

Teaching, Training, Research

In as much as there exists a positive relationship between the introduction of new technologies and the growth of productivity and in as much as innovation is the result of a cumulative process of the acquisition of knowledge, it is important that the secondary education system and universities prepare for the creation and assimilation of new technologies and that the system of training relating to this ensures a follow-up (permanent education), thus contributing to the motivation of staff.

The integration of new techniques into the production system will be even more necessary in the future as competition becomes intense and the active population diminishes, whilst needs grow as a result of the ageing population.

For enterprises, the challenge for the future will be to innovate and get new products established in the market quickly.

Some Strong Points

Teaching and training appear without doubt amongst the strengths of a small open economy such as that of Belgium which has almost no primary resources but where the number of university researchers in relation to the active population is almost the highest in Europe. Pride may be taken in having high-quality teaching on the one hand, and on the other hand a relatively productive industry, as a result mainly of foreign investors who are not indifferent to the availability and the quality of the labour force. Moreover the share of research spending in total corporate capital investments in Belgium is amongst the highest of the European Community countries.

But Also Some Weak Points

Research, teaching, professional training and employment policy depend to a very large extent on the authorities. Since the reform of the State, they have come very largely under the control of the Communities and the Regions.

In the sphere of assistance to research, it is noted that the share of internal research spending financed by the authorities is relatively modest by comparison with the European average. This admittedly stems from budgetary constraints, which have weighed heavily on the research effort since the beginning of the 1980s, but also from the relatively traditional production structure of Belgian industry and the very small share of public research funds devoted to defence.

The French community is for its part confronted at the present time with a grave crisis in secondary teaching, which stems as much from demographic problems as from the problems of financing, organization and objectives which it has to face. In the medium term, the Flemish community will face similar problems.

With regard to employment policy (see below), international comparison shows that Belgium invests less than others in the training of staff, or vocational integration and reintegration, but that it is more generous with regard to subsidies for the creation of employment. The majority of unemployed people are unqualified, but there is still a strong demand for qualified workers at all levels.

Implications for Business

Belgium's participation in European research and development programmes allows enterprises to have access to new technology (space, new materials, information technology) and to compensate to some extent for the disadvantages of small size in those spheres which demand significant financial resources.

The development of technology is exponential and ongoing discussions between the teaching profession and business are essential if supply is to better adapt to demand on the Belgian labour market.

The boundary between applied and fundamental research is becoming more and more blurred. The bases for close dialogue between industry and the universities already exist in Belgium (for example: the Industry-University Foundation, scientific zoning) and should allow the consolidation of scientific potential and distribution of the products of research.

With the progressive dematerialization of production, the significance of intangible investments (organization, training, research and development, the purchase of patents and licences) will grow. Training should increasingly be considered to be an investment rather than a cost factor.

In the future, as a consequence of the budgetary difficulties of the authorities, business will probably have to count less and less on the public financing of research.

Besides vocational training, a knowledge of languages will prove to be increasingly vital in a multicultural Europe.

The Enlargement of the Markets and the Production and Enterprise Structures

The opening of the frontiers will enlarge the horizons of enterprises, in the first place by the removal of non-tariff barriers, for the Europe of twelve, and in the second place to the countries of EFTA, with the creation of the European Economic Area, thus creating a market of nearly 400 million inhabitants. Such an enlargement will have varying effects on the areas of operation and also will affect the size of enterprises.

The Impact on Areas of Operation

In spite of having a relatively modest industrial sector, Belgium is the largest exporter in the world per inhabitant. Its foreign trade is very largely directed towards the European Community and in particular towards Germany. Its strong export propensity is owed principally to its *industry* which was strongly internationalized in the 1960s, as a result of a massive influx of foreign investment. Apart from some traditional sectors where certain restructuring has already taken place with a view to 1992, industry should not suffer too much from the opening of the frontiers, hardened as it already is to confrontation with international competition.

Belgium is, moreover, a 'country which is relatively centred upon the service sector and in this sphere may perhaps find itself confronted with the problem of opening frontiers more than others'. In fact, up to now, national regulations, together with the intangible nature of service production, have given the sector a level of protection which has sheltered it from international competition. In so far as the regulations lapse or new information technologies allow certain services to become more and more *materialized* and thus industrialized and commercialized, certain operations which have benefited until now from a kind of guaranteed income could in the future be confronted with profitability problems resulting from the pressure on prices caused by increased competition. It is doubtless to be expected that in the service sector further restructuring and growing internationalization will occur. This internationalization is already effective in the younger expanding sectors such as security services, temping agencies, cleaning agencies, estate agencies etc.

And the Size of Companies

In spite of the numerous multinational enterprises established on its territory, 'Belgium is still a country of small and medium-sized enterprises'. This can be seen in the average size of enterprises, which remains relatively small: 99% of companies employ less than 200 people whilst the remaining 1% accounts for 40% of employment; amongst the major European enterprises only a few are Belgian, contrary to that observed in other countries of a similar size.

The small- and medium-sized enterprises are a very heterogeneous group, a large number of them being found in the service sector. They are generally 'family business' which jealously guard their independence, as seen from their methods of financing capital, essentially by self-financing, and the fact that a relatively small number of small- and medium-sized companies are subsidiaries of a large company. These companies constitute in fact national economic stability, which is somewhat weakened by the strong multinationalization which began in industry and is continuing now in the service sector. More than 40% of GNP is in fact produced today by foreign companies.

These enterprises constitute a major advantage for the national economy in as much as they allow a greater flexibility of the machinery of production and a differentiation of production, but they risk, in certain cases, confronting problems of size.

Implications for Business

The availability of qualified labour, together with taxation and parafiscal taxation, will play without doubt an increasing role as a factor of localization of the large *mobile* companies seeking to become established in the new European economic area.

On the level of the small- and medium-sized enterprises, the challenge of the optimum size to be reached will have to be met sooner or later in an enlarging market, whether this is by mergers, cooperation agreements with foreign companies, or through cross-frontier investments.

The problems of succession, financing of investments, marketing and access to research are other problems which will have to be solved in the small enterprises if they wish to grow in the new European market.

New opportunities will be available certainly for high-performance small- and medium-sized enterprises, whether in industry, where new production techniques lead enterprises to concentrate their efforts on their high-quality products and thus turn to subcontracting (the *just-in-time* technique), or in the service sector through the process of expansion of the sector linked with the growing complexity of the economy (legal services, taxation services), with changes in society, with urbanization, or with the opportunity afforded by Brussels as the capital of Europe.

The Discussion on Economic Identity

The discussion is not entirely new, far from it, but it has been revived 'in public and political opinion' as a simultaneous result of:

-     The fact that several leading Belgian industrial flagship companies have passed under foreign control: OIP, Raffineries de Tirlemont, Côte d'Or, Bell Téléphone, FN, etc.
-     The recent publication of several studies on this problem, amongst them a report from the King Baudouin Foundation, which emphasizes the fact that foreign companies are now creating more than 40% of added-value in Belgium.
-     More fundamentally, the fact that whilst during the 1960s and 1970s the wave of foreign investments had created added value and employment and introduced new technologies, recent years have seen in particular the take-over of Belgian enterprises by foreign groups, often going hand in hand with employment rationalization and a feeling of loss of autonomy.

At the time of the discussions preceding the formation of the present government, the question was clearly raised.[1]   There is therefore unquestionably a debate on the psychological and political level. Where does it actually stand from the point of view of economic rationality?[2]

Why have Numerous Belgian Companies passed under Foreign Control?

The attitude of most Belgian companies, characterized by a high level of exports but a relatively low level of foreign investment, implies, in a context marked by an increase in the size of enterprises and the world-wide growth of the economy, that enterprises are becoming ever smaller, and that, in the process of acquisition, they tend to be taken over rather than buy.

Moreover, it appears from an OECD study that Belgium is the OECD country which places the least restrictions on direct investments.

The 'family nature' of the majority of companies and their reticence to take on any association with third parties means that in the end a large number of SMEs under family control find themselves in a situation where the only solution to their problems is to sell up.

'The structure of Belgium's economic fabric' consequently contains the seeds of a significant supply of companies for take-over.

---

1   M. Wathelet, *The stakes of new citizenship. Three challenges for the federal Belgian state*. Belgium is taking care to conserve its economic identity by fixing its strategic decision-making centres.

2   See particularly, 'The internationalization of decision-making centres: a threat to Belgium's prosperity', *Bulletin from the Générale de Banque*, 15 November 1991.

A significant part of Belgian industry is concentrated in traditional sectors where industrial strategy often consists of gaining market shares and limiting competition through acquisition. In this way a series of major Belgian enterprises in the food, rubber processing, construction and building materials industries, 'have passed into foreign hands'.

As far as the sectors of rapid growth are concerned, such as the chemical or the motor industry, these are largely dominated by foreign industry, in the main as a result of an active policy of attracting foreign investment during the 1950s and 1960s.

In the sector of advanced technologies (telecommunications, defence, photography, optics), on the other hand, Belgian companies have been forced, taking account of the tightness of the market, to become integrated into larger groups which offered them broader outlets and allowed them to make the necessary investments in research and development.

In the service sector, small- and medium-sized enterprises are numerous in Belgium. But on an international level they are often small. Following the example of industry, this sector is becoming more and more internationalized, because it is often necessary to become established abroad, through acquisition or otherwise, in order to offer services there. For this reason a series of companies which are large by Belgian standards, are today controlled by foreign enterprises, for example in the insurance sector.

For or Against Foreign Control?

Naturally foreign control implies foreign decision-taking on the key principles of the management of the company and is thus the subject of controversy.

But on the other hand:

- Numerous Belgian enterprises owe their survival to their integration with a foreign entity; they were not sufficiently strong with regard to finance, marketing, research and development.
- It can also be emphasized that Belgium gains advantages from the presence of numerous multinationals on its territory, for this goes hand in hand with a transfer of foreign know-how to Belgium, not only to the subsidiaries, but also through an impetus effect to local companies.
- More fundamentally, in a European economy which is more and more integrated, the operations of enterprises will be located where

the conditions are best. Is this not the aim of the *Single European Act:* to promote prosperity through the free circulation of products, goods and services, as well as of the factors of production, labour and capital?

- *To sum up,* it is noted that whilst socio-political *discourse* is often *against*, in actual fact the response has rather been *for*.   This attitude pays off so long as Belgium's advantages as a location are preserved.

The Advantages and Disadvantages of Belgium as a Business Location

The principal advantages of Belgium are:

- Its central location in Europe, as well as the dense transport networks and the growing significance of Brussels as an administrative and political centre. The decision-making centres of the EC and NATO, along with SWIFT, Euroclear and more than 1000 enterprises have set up their foreign headquarters in Belgium.
- The high productivity of the workers and their considerable linguistic abilities.
- The good social climate, with a limited number of strikes.
- The relatively low property prices.
- The attractive tax possibilities, mainly through coordination centres.
- The welcome given to foreign investors.

But problems also exist:

- The telecommunications potential and the quality of the transport infrastructure (national airport, high-speed trains) are not competitive enough at an international level.
- The tax pressure on executives must not persuade the best to emigrate.
- A better quality administration, with clearly defined jurisdiction and simplified procedures would help.
- The stability of company taxation is also important.

The Labour Market

In this sphere, Belgium differs from other countries, notably:

- With regard to its concerted and regulated wage formation process.
- Its system of indexation of wages to prices, widely used and near-automatic.
- Its system of unemployment benefit (unlimited in time).

Table 6.1 Wage formation, free but regulated wages, productivity and terms of trade in Belgium

	1960-73	1974-75	1976-79	1980-81	1982-89
Real observed wage rate (1)	+4.8	+6.5	+3.2	+2.2	+0.8
Job productivity (2)	+4.5	+1.2	+3.8	+2.4	+2.4
Terms of trade (3)	+0.3	-2.1	+0.0	-4.1	+0.8
Real neutral wage rate (4) = (2) + (3)	+4.8	-0.9	+3.8	-1.7	+3.2
Wage gap (1) - (4) = variation of the wages fraction	+0.0	+7.4	-0.6	+3.9	-2.4
Unemployment rate	+2.0	+3.4	+6.7	+8.9	+12.2

Average annual rates of growth and average level (for unemployment rate).
Source: H. Bogaert, T. de Biolley, J. Verlinden, W*ages, competitiveness and public finance in the face of the oil crises*- Planning Paper, Programme Office, March 1991.

As we progress towards EMU, income discipline will become an increasingly important element of the policy mix.

This requirement is even more exacting for Belgium, taking into account its orientation towards exporting and the weight of the traditional sectors where competitiveness is measured essentially in terms of price and costs (mainly wage costs).

Traditionally, Belgium has endeavoured to reconcile the parameters of a classic concertation economy, to which it is deeply attached, with the macroeconomic constraints which govern the overall level of demand, wages and prices, within a small sized economy which is largely open towards the outside world.

This policy has led to the conclusion of numerous interprofessional agreements, for which there have been four distinct periods:

1960 to 1975

A period during which seven interprofessional agreements were concluded which were true 'programmes of new experience' passing the benefits of growth to all the sectors of operation.

1976-1981

The deterioration in the Belgian economy's terms of trade commenced with the 'first oil crisis': productivity progressively declined and the unemployment rate grew inexorably.

During the period from 1974 to 1979 'Keynesianism continued to be applied simultaneously on a political, economic and social level'. This gave rise to the slow awareness of increasing mass poverty which constituted the negative development of the terms of trade, in a context of high indexation of wages and incomes.

With the second oil crisis, the macroeconomic crisis reached a peak, and the concertation economy model was put on hold for several years. The challenging of the mechanisms of wages and incomes indexation politically divided the main unions' and employers' organizations.

1981-1986: Authoritarian Social Restraint

For the first time in Belgian social history, an interprofessional agreement organized wage restraint: this agreement was signed on 13 February 1981 but was concluded under the threat by the Government to introduce a law which would be substituted for negotiation between the two sides of industry in the absence of agreement. In 1982 economic policy changed course: the Belgian franc was devalued; amongst the measures accompanying this, in addition to the temporary de-indexation of income, a wage freeze was to be strictly applied from February 1982 to 31 December 1986.

Since 1986: Return to Free Negotiation

After ten years without interprofessional agreements, but also after ten years of government *presence* in collective labour relations with a view to re-establishing the principal macroeconomic balance, the two sides of industry concluded, in November 1986, an agreement which restored negotiating freedom, particularly with regard to wages, to the sectors.

The concerted economy returned with negotiation but under a more decentralized and flexible system. Two other interprofessional agreements (1988 and 1990) were to punctuate the collective labour relations; these contained, notably, in addition to wage freedom:

-   The increase of minimum guaranteed average monthly income.
-   A rise in benefits to unemployed people aged over 50.
-   Specific efforts in training and employment for groups at risk.

From 1983 onwards a 'standard of competitiveness'[3] had already been imposed as a measure accompanying devaluation.

This meant explicitly that executive policy could potentially adjust income formation if there was a significant deterioration in the terms of trade.

In January 1989, a law 'safeguarding competitiveness' was passed by Parliament. Under this law, the Government was given power to intervene in macroeconomic policy to adjust the formation of production costs.

But, once again, the concerted economy was to play its role of mediation and consultation in the decision-making process.

In effect, the law conferred technical regulation of the development of competitiveness on the Central Council for the economy. This was an original aspect of law since the employers' associations and the unions were given responsibility for drawing up together and submitting to the Government and to Parliament each year, a report and an opinion on the development of the competitive position.

The criteria according to which the competitive position must be evaluated are enumerated in the law. They concern:

-   The development of export performance (market shares).
-   The development of labour costs per person employed in the private sector.
-   The development of financial costs (through changes in interest rates).
-   The development of energy costs (on the basis of changes in the prices of a certain number of energy products).

---

[3]   This standard was constructed on the bases of Belgium's relative wage costs, in comparison with its seven principal competitors.

-     The development of the structural determining factors, particularly on the basis of the gross formation of fixed capital and research and development expenditure.

These criteria are measured in relative indices in comparison with the Belgian economy's principal competitors.

Competitiveness is threatened if the first criteria (export performance) and at least one of the other assessment criteria show a deterioration.

Two specific intervention mechanisms are provided for by the law when competitiveness seems threatened. They involve both sides of industry, acting together, then with the Government; they must act within given fixed time limits.

Parliament must ascertain through a vote that competitiveness is threatened. The Government can then decide upon the protective measures appropriate to the situation. The (temporary) measures seeking to safeguard or restore competitiveness are set out in the law.

A similar procedure allows for more rapid action in the case of exceptional circumstances (e.g. events of external origin).[4]

'With this new law, the concerted economy entered into a new phase of experimentation': macroeconomic constraints mark out the system of collective labour relations from an institutional and legal point of view. The formation of wages arises from free negotiation between both sides of industry but instruments of economic policy regulate to some extent the scope of negotiation. In this respect, the recent decision (May 1990) to link explicitly the Belgian franc to the Deutschmark proceeded from the same process.

Taken overall, apart from some disagreements of a mainly technical nature, there exists quite a broad consensus on the original mechanism, combining free wage formation and macroeconomic regulation. Whilst it is evidently impossible to transpose such specific national mechanisms at a Community level, the Belgian experience may inspire European dialogue, where wage formation and collective labour relations are directly concerned.

---

4   It must be said that hitherto experience has not allowed the Government's attitude in the face of serious competitive breakdown to be really tested.

Wage Indexation

At the time of the great upset in macroeconomic balance in Belgium, the mechanism of indexation of wages and income to prices deeply divided the employers' associations and the unions.

The debate is, moreover, not closed and is revived regularly. However, the disagreement with regard to the indexation system should not be exaggerated. In fact beyond the *obligatory* speeches, there exists a certain consensus, at least tacit, on two points:

- When operating normally, the system allows both sides of industry to negotiate exclusively with regard to real wages, thereby preventing the phenomena of anticipation, pace-keeping or leap-frogging seen in other countries, with regard to the nominal part of wages.
- On the other hand, the system has to be corrected in the case of a marked and lasting deterioration in the terms of trade or heavy increases in indirect taxation.

Belgian Policies with Regard to the Unemployed

Does Belgium, which stands out from the other EC countries through its system of indexation, its system of wage formation through free but regulated negotiation, also stand out through its system of unemployment benefit (*unlimited* in time) and its so-called *active* labour market policies (in particular the direct creation of jobs reserved for those who are unemployed)?

The debate is a lively one, at least, on two points:

- What is the link between the availability of the unemployed person and his/her right to unemployment benefit over time?
- Should there be targeted *active* policies? If yes, targeted in favour of whom? How can this be effective?[5]

Unemployment Benefit

Even though it is often presented simplistically, or even caricatured, the uncommon nature of the Belgian system of unemployment benefit is real.

---

5   See particularly B. Van Der Linden, 'The structuring of Belgian policy with regard to the unemployed', *IRES Bulletin*, No. 155, November 1991.

In effect, Belgium is the only country in the EC where the duration of the allocation of unemployment benefit is without limit.   In spite of adjustment of the benefit after a year in accordance with the situation and income of the family, the financial situation with regard to the Belgian unemployed, estimated on the basis of the rate of gross replacement of the benefits (their yield in relation to former wages), becomes more and more favourable with time in comparison with neighbouring countries.[6]

Some connect this fact to the existence of a higher proportion of long-term unemployed (more than a year) in Belgium than in other countries.

Others judge that this *generosity* does not necessarily induce massive and persistent long-term unemployment. In this particular case, the absence of search for employment, even reticence with regard to any new attempt at vocational reintegration, only seems to arise subsidiarily from the rules of unemployment insurance.[7]

In other respects, more active searching and financial penalties for those *unavailable* would certainly have a favourable effect on unemployment statistics and the budget for unemployment insurance.   The effects on public finance would be, on the other hand, less positive, as a result of an increased recourse to social aid. Furthermore, the effects of such a policy are uncertain.

Active Policies

The early struggle against habitual unemployment is not limited to the development of so-called *active* policies, although they obviously play their part.   However, in the absence of rigorous evaluation, a certain confusion exists regarding the effectiveness of these policies.[8]

Taken overall, controversy remains on these two *peculiarities* of the Belgian system.

> In any event, neither a reform of unemployment insurance, nor active policies which are better targeted or better organized, would, it seems, release enterprises from their responsibilities with regard to the unemployment problem, which remains worrying in Belgium.

---

6   *Employment prospects*, OECD, 1991.
7   See B. Van Der Linden op.cit.
8   ibid.

Environmental Problems in Belgium

The problems of the environment in Belgium are evidently not fundamentally different from those of neighbouring countries and should dovetail with mainstream European policies in this area.

Belgium presents, however, certain particularities which it is worth emphasizing:

- With regard to 'the division of jurisdiction' between the National State and the Regions.
- With regard to Belgium's 'relative backwardness' regarding environmental protection, in particular if the effort made is measured in terms of budgetary spending.
- With regard to the 'convergences and divergences' having appeared in the discussion which has recently begun with regard to the EC Commission's proposal for limiting the greenhouse effect.

The Division of Jurisdiction

Since the institutional reforms of 1980 and in particular those of 1988 and 1989, the Regions have general jurisdiction with regard to the environment, and some jurisdiction with regard to environmental taxation (ecotaxes).

Despite some efforts at coordination, this situation evidently does not favour a coherent approach in the matter or the *legibility* of effort agreed upon globally.

The division of jurisdiction remains blurred, moreover, with regard to the ecotaxes.

Since regionalization, various systems of taxation or dues have been established in Flanders and Walloon, particularly with regard to waste water and solid waste. But a twofold problem remains:

- The Regions can only levy ecotaxes as long as national taxes do not already exist in the same spheres. What is more, if a national tax is instituted in a sphere which is already the object of a regional tax, this can be repealed by ordinary law.
- Moreover, if the national authority institutes an ecotax and the tax revenues are allocated to the protection of the environment, these revenues must be directed back to the Regions.

The Relative Progress Measured through Budgetary Spending

It is evident that we are concerned here with an imperfect measure and one which is particularly precarious, taking account of the lack of statistics in this sphere. In brief, one can nevertheless come to the principal conclusion that, in 1988, total public spending on the environment was perceptibly lower than that of Germany, France and the Netherlands, but that some ground seems to have been made up between 1988 and 1991.

The Discussion Regarding the Tax on CO_2 and Energy

The discussion on the Commission's proposals[9] well illustrates certain points which are particular to Belgium.

To recap, the European Commission has proposed, from 1993, to subject CO_2 emissions and the consumption of energy to taxation. Starting at $3 per barrel, this tax would then be increased by $1 per year in order to reach $10 by the year 2000, in order to stabilize the CO_2 emissions at the 1990 level.

With regard to this general objective, certain points can be emphasized which are peculiar to Belgium.

Belgium has undertaken to reduce CO_2 emissions by the year 2000 by 5%, an objective halfway between the stabilization envisaged by the Commission or other EC countries (France, Italy, the United Kingdom, for example) and a more significant reduction (Germany, the Netherlands, Denmark).

Since it is a question of a tax on CO_2 and/or energy, Belgium is particularly affected in that its production of CO_2 per inhabitant is amongst the highest in the Community (2.93 t. of CO_2 in 1989 against 2.34 as an average of the twelve),[10] and the same applies for its energy intensity. This is largely due to our industrial structures, since the contribution of Belgian industry to CO_2 emissions is by far the highest in the EC.

---

[9]   See in particular, *The first report of the National Council on the subject of climatic change*, Brussels, February 1992.

[10]   Certain scenarios of economic growth (business as usual) forecast moreover, increases in the order of 17% in CO_2 emissions between 1990 and 2000.

Convergences and Divergences with Regard to the Commission's CO_2 Proposals

The Points of Convergence

Quite a broad consensus exists around a policy strategy based on seven essential principles.

(i) The principle of precaution, by the prevention of pollution rather than adapting to the damage.

(ii) Priority to no-regrets decisions if climate developments should prove to be more favourable than the present forecasts.

(iii) Collective preparation for more significant reductions in emissions if the climatic development proves more worrying than the present forecasts.

(iv) A priori recourse to all the democratic instruments available to the authorities, including economic instruments (the opening up of a progressive reform of the tax system in order to give it an environmental dimension).

(v) Coherence between environmental and energy strategies (and especially energy saving).

(vi) Intensification of agreements, inter-disciplinary research, and interdepartmental work, in support of the decision.

(vii) And, last but not least our moral, economic and political responsibility towards present and future generations, at the time when the completion of the single market is to make the European Community the largest economic and commercial power in the world.

And the Points of Divergence

A significant divergence exists on the 'timeliness of this European tax initiative': it is said by the Belgian Enterprise Federation to be *meaningless*, in as much as the EC is only responsible for 13% of the total emissions of CO_2 and that the Commission's proposals would only cause industrial production to move location, the CO_2 emissions being simply shifted to other zones applying standards which are less strict.

Another significant divergence concerns 'the role of nuclear energy' as a substitute for fossil-fuel energy. Some are in favour of an increase in this role, others are much more reserved, or even squarely opposed to it.

A diversity of opinions exists also on 'the composition of the basis of taxation': some favour only taxing fossil-fuels (in proportion to the release of CO_2), others of taxing all non-renewable energy, including nuclear energy.

Another important debate is on the 'fiscal neutrality' budgetary option envisaged by the Commission for allocation of the revenue. This option would consist of keeping the level of the national tax burden constant by offsetting the new tax by an equivalent reduction in other fiscal or parafiscal levies. Some complain that such an option would prevent the following:

- Redistribution of this revenue in the form of aid to energy-saving equipment or other kinds of environmental defence.
- Or allocation of the revenue to the reduction of budgetary deficit.
- And/or the financing of new needs.

The Control of Public Finance

Belgium's particularities in this respect relate to:

- The issue of stabilization.
- The participants involved.
- The extent of the effort to reach agreement.
- The distribution of effort on spending and/or income.

The Issue of Stabilization

Bringing the overall deficit of all the public administrations (general government) from some 6% today to $\pm$ 3% in 1996 and reducing the national debt/GNP ratio gradually but significantly is an important issue for Belgium, both for internal and external reasons.

On the one hand, Belgium has everything to gain in joining as soon as possible those who will decide to pass to the third stage of EMU and subsequently form part of the few who will be able to attain full EMU.

On the other hand, only the halting and then the reversal of the *snowball* effect will allow it simultaneously:

- To regain progressively the margin of manoeuvre necessary to restore the *regal* functions of the State and ensure the (re)financing of the non-commercial sector.

- To prepare for the pensions crisis around the decade 2010.

The Participants Concerned

Here again, Belgium's situation is relatively specific. In effect the effort of stabilization imposed by the new draft of the Treaty henceforth covers 'three entities whose decision-making processes are at once independent and interdependent':

- The National Government.[11]
- The Regions and the Communities.
- Social Security.

They are *independent,* because the Regions and Communities have since 1989 had a considerable budgetary independence and a taxation jurisdiction which is still limited but will certainly be extended in the future. The Social Security is supplied in the main part by contributions from employers and workers (and thus administered jointly) and only subsidiarily by transfers from the National Government.

They are *interdependent,* either through taxation, since the trend in social benefits and contributions has repercussions on taxation revenue and since certain taxation revenue which is particular to the Regions and Communities competes with that of the National State or through the development of subsidies by the National Government to social security.

The Extent of the Effort to Reach Agreement and its Influence on the Development of Public Sector Expenditure

Reaching the objective of reducing the overall deficit to some 3% in 1996 would signify, as an order of magnitude, 'a new increase in public sector budget receipts'[12] of some 150 billion BF net (i.e. after deduction of all indirect effects). The margin for manoeuvre is small with regard to interest charges. In fact, it is to be feared that the alignment of the Belgian franc with the Deutschmark has exhausted its effects on the reduction of interest rates in Belgium and that more dynamic management of the national debt also has limits.

---

[11] Alone until now in being subject to the budgetary *double standard*: nil growth in primary spending and nominal deficit in no case higher than that of the preceding year.

[12] Which has already reached ± 5% of GNP today.

Distribution of Effort on Income and/or Spending

According to the choices made, it is certain in this connection that the controversy is greatest and the consequences most tangible for companies. The margin of manoeuvre can be quickly defined as follows.

With Regard to 'Primary' Expenditure[13]

First of all public expenditure (before interest charges on the national debt), which amounted to 51.5% of GDP in 1981 against 43.5% for the Europe of Seven, fell in 1991 to 39.6% against 42.8%.

A more detailed comparison, under broad headings, with the European average can supply certain indications which can only, however, be interpreted with care and qualification.

Whilst on the total level of *social benefits,* the social protection expenditure per inhabitant (in ECUs) in Belgium is amongst the lowest, the picture varies according to the sub-sectors concerned.

-     The expenditure on *old age* is not *atypical*, either in terms of level or development, or calculated on the rate of replacement. However, several developments are worrying: the spontaneous lowering of the age of retirement, the weight of *prior pensions*, the future for pensions after 2010, the medium-long-term choice between allocation and capitalization (in other words the future for extra-statutory schemes), the public sector pensions.

-     Spending on *health* is amongst the lowest in the EC, but its rapid growth (at constant prices) poses problems.

-     Spending on the *family* seems to be more generous than the average if referring to family allowances and taxation spending.

-     Public spending devoted to *unemployment* (in the wider sense of the term) is relatively high in Belgium. It is orientated more towards the guarantee of income than towards aid to employment. Moreover, the gap between the number of unemployed and the payment of unemployment benefits is relatively high in Belgium, which seems to be due in the main to the considerable spreading of

---

13   For more information, see Draft notification by the Higher Council of Finance on the structure of income and spending by the authorities in the framework of EMU. To appear shortly. It should be emphasized that this comparison deliberately only covers seven countries, i.e. not including the less developed countries of the EC (Greece, Spain, Portugal, Ireland), or the United Kingdom, taking account of its atypical system of financing social security and its relative weight.

consecutive part-time work / part-time unemployment and the significance of long-term unemployment, for which the duration of unemployment benefit provides a partial explanation (cf. above).

- 'Public aid to enterprises', although decreasing since 1981, remains amongst the highest, especially when account is taken of taxation spending.
- Spending on 'public investment and research and development' are clearly short of the European average and necessitate an effort at catching up in the medium term.
- A comparison of spending allocated to the civil service or to education is at this time difficult, in that it is unable to supply any valid information.
- Spending on the *environment* lags behind that of other countries and will also have to grow relatively in the future.

It is widely acknowledged, moreover, that spending allocated to other State functions (justice, authority) cannot be further cut back, but also that there undoubtedly exists a *saving* to be made through better administration of the civil service, public enterprises, and in military expenditure.

With Regard to Income

The future will depend principally on the development of income taxation elasticity and social security contributions[14] (without prejudice to the effect of 'tax competition' which has already been examined in general terms).

Income Elasticity

During recent years, income elasticity[15] has perceptibly diminished and fallen below one. Where is it today? In the sphere of 'social security contributions' the elasticity is around one. With regard to 'indirect taxation', development is essentially conditioned by decisions on a European level. Whilst the situation is now clear with regard to VAT, the same does not apply to excise taxes where it is a question only of minimum rate with no agreement reached on *objective* rates. Both for VAT and excise taxes, a great unknown remains: what will be the real

---

[14] See particularly the work of the Higher Council of Finance on income elasticity.

[15] Relationship between collected tax and its base, after elimination of *discretionary* measures.

possibilities for control when the opening of the internal market frontiers becomes effective?

It is however in the area of indirect taxation that a significant margin of manoeuvre exists in Belgium: the latter occupies here a lower position in relation to the European average (particularly with regard to excise taxes).

With regard to 'direct taxation', the elasticity of individual taxation which plummeted between 1985 and 1989 seems recently to have recovered spectacularly, reaching a figure of 1.2 for the last tax year. Some improvement is also observed with regard to company tax.

'Overall it can be hoped therefore that the total elasticity of fiscal and parafiscal income will again become positive.'

This recovery will be far from sufficient however to exclude new economic measures and/or new fiscal or parafiscal levies.

The Effects of 'Competitive Defiscalization'

From a detailed examination of the potential scope of tax competition,[16] it can be concluded that the risk for Belgium is now limited.

In so far as savings taxation is concerned, the essential work has been done. In so far as investment taxation is concerned, Belgium's position is not extreme, either towards the high level or the low, and in the sphere of indirect taxation, European agreements lay down (VAT) or will lay down (excise duties) the limits to tax competition.

Two major reservations exist, however.

The first relates to the 'control of financial or commercial flows':

- Effective control of transfer prices in direct taxation, failing which multinational enterprises could show their profits where taxation is the lowest.
- Control of international trade for VAT and excise duty.

The second relates to the effects regarding the extension of the reduction of withholding tax on financial assets from fixed income or share investments, with consequences which could spill over on to the balance to be maintained between I.Soc.[17] and IPP,[18] and therefore the supplanting of the financing basis for social security.

---

[16]   Draft study by the Higher Council of Finance on the structure of public authority income
        and spending in the framework of EMU, op.cit.
[17]   Corporation tax.
[18]   Tax on individuals.

'Whatever the choices made, their effect on enterprise strategy will not be insignificant', for example:

-   Through the development of *spending* (current, in capital or taxation) according to whether they allocate *para-wage* costs, investment or research and development spending, public aid, training, etc. or again *income*. E.g. the coordination centres, ('finally taxed income') with regard to I.Soc.
-   Indirect taxation and its repercussions on costs by way of indexation.
-   The fate of the ecotax, etc.
-   Reduction in savings advantages with regard to taxation on individuals.
-   By offering enterprises a new field of action through a certain commercialization of non-commercial services and other operations of the same kind.
-   Or, again, and the list is not exhaustive, by restricting enterprises from passing over to public finance certain responsibilities which are their own: sustaining the equity market (pension savings), the restructuring of *sick* sectors, the contraction of workforces (prior pensions, concurrent part-time/part unemployment, etc.).

SECTION 2: THE CULTURAL AND POLITICAL FACTORS

Social and Political Consensus

The Cultural and Political Level

Belgium finds itself at the crossroads of two cultures. This pluricultural composition gives it certain advantages (a knowledge of languages, talent for compromise) but is also the expression of ideological divisions (in ethical and economic matters) and of different political tendencies between the North and South which make political consensus difficult at a national level. Since 1980, numerous spheres of jurisdiction have been transferred by the National Government to the Communities and Regions; a certain community pacification can be expected, and, with the putting of rivalry to one side, tighter budgetary control.

Development of institutional reform interacts with economic life. Thus, in the 1980s, the financing of the restructuring of the traditional sectors, which were more widely scattered in the south of the country, without doubt accelerated the process of regionalization which got under way at the beginning of the 1970s. Today, the financing of one of the Belgian Communities, with regard to education, is blocked by difficulties. The regionalization of agriculture is demanded by the Walloon Region. That of social security by the Flemish circle, whilst both sides of industry remain in this respect strongly attached to the idea of national solidarity. Even the problem of the regionalization of the national debt is raised today.

The Social Level

Belgium is a country where levels of union membership are particularly high and the employers' associations strongly structured, and where, since the war, 'a strong tradition of social dialogue' has been established ('Declaration on productivity', Central Council of the Economy, National Employment Council, etc.). This social consensus has allowed, at best, the development of a particularly enviable system of social protection, and interprofessional agreements which have given all the sectors the benefits of economic growth. This consensus evidently experienced some cracks at the height of the crisis, but overall it has survived well. A level of consensus, at least tacit, was able to emerge at the beginning of the 1980s, on devaluation and the implementation of a certain number of accompanying measures, amongst which were the wage freeze and the temporary suspension of the linking of wages to the prices index. This allowed restoration of the economic competitiveness.

A certain flexibility was then instituted with regard to wage negotiations, which were moved progressively from the interprofessional level to the enterprise level. In 1989 moreover a law was passed to safeguard competitiveness, which gave the General Economic Council (where the unions and employers' organizations are represented) responsibility for an annual evaluation of the state of national competitiveness, and authorized the government to intervene in the case where the latter may be threatened and where the two sides could not reach agreement.[19]

Social Consensus Versus Political 'Dissent'

The preceding analysis could tend to give substance to a paradoxical, even contradictory, picture of a country characterized at once by a *strong* social

---

[19]   For further information see the section devoted to the employment market.

consensus and a *weak* political consensus.[20] This paradox merits clarification and qualification.

Firstly the contrast is less marked than it appears at first sight. Whilst it may be weak, a certain State consensus exists, or at least a feeling of national kinship, made concrete by various forms of cooperation between the State, the Communities and the Regions.[21] On the other hand, the social consensus is also prey to certain regionalist tendencies, traces of which are found in particular in the structures of the unions and the employers' associations.

There remains, nevertheless, an undeniable contrast between these two types of consensus. Some applicable factors can be put forward in this respect:

-   A historical tradition which has for a long time identified the State as *foreign*, which, conversely, has encouraged a strong decentralization towards the Communities and the Provinces.
-   The more artificial and more abstract nature of the notion of the State, compared with the more concrete content of social relationships.
-   The existence of two *peoples* and *nationalistic* tendencies on both sides.
-   More recently, disaffection on the part of the citizens with regard to the political parties which they often identify with the idea of the State, and, in the same way, a growing gulf between State and citizens.

What Scenario for the Belgium of Tomorrow: Federalism, Confederalism or Separatism?

During the course of the last 20 years, Belgium has experienced a 'profound reform of its institutions' which has changed it from a Unitarian State to a *Federal* State, composed of two main Communities: Flemish and French, and three Regions: Flanders, Walloon and Brussels-Capital. The creation of the Communities responded to Flemish requirements with regard to cultural and political autonomy, whilst the Regions, defined geographically, corresponded more with the requirements of the Walloons with regard to economic and social matters.

---

[20]   Or, if preferred, a 'State consensus'.
[21]   See in particular, A. Allen, *Belgium: A Bipolar and Centrifugal Federalism*, Brussels, November 1990.

Today, a great number of powers of jurisdiction have been granted to the Regions and the Communities. In so far as the Communities are concerned, these powers relate to cultural matters, education, personal matters, international cooperation in these areas and the use of languages in administration, for teaching and for social relations between employers and their staff. The Regions have jurisdiction, wholly or partly, for regional development, the environment, rural redevelopment and the conservation of nature, housing, water policy, the economy, energy policy, the subordinate authorities, employment policy, public works and a part of public transport.

But the reform is not wholly complete and is up against formidable problems (the direct election of assemblies, external relations, financial transfers, etc.).

The Present State of Institutional Reform in Belgium and its *Sui Generis* Characteristics[22]

Any federal system is a *sui generis* structure. It is in fact impossible to dissociate federal structures from the geographic, economic, historical and even ideological factors which form their basis. These factors are evident in Belgian federalism. It goes without saying that in a Federal State having two components, it is more difficult to find a balance between the requirements of the autonomy of the entities on the one hand, and an effective central policy on the other. This explains the Belgian institutional system - which at first glance seems very complex - based on a collection of balances.

At the time of an overall evaluation of the reform of the Belgian State, two readings are possible.

The first puts the accent on the rather negative aspects.

The complexity, which is explained in particular by the fact that the three Communities and the three Regions do not correspond with one another; the proliferation of institutions, for example in Brussels-Capital; the linguistic disagreements; the 'bipolarity and the centrifugal nature' which make any pattern of a Federal State impossible.

The following listing shows that it is also possible to see things from another standpoint: the prominent position of the international role and the capital-city role of Brussels, where any form of sub-nationality is moreover excluded: the concept of economic union and monetary union;

---

22   A. Allen, op. cit.

the solidarity, in particular from the point of view of a national social security system; the various possibilities for cooperation.

In fact, two major peculiarities stand out from these two readings:

The Bipolar Structure of the State

In spite of the division of Belgium into four linguistic regions, three Communities and three Regions, 'the Belgian problem' seems to lie in the co-existence of two main Communities, the French speaking and the Dutch speaking, on one and the same territory. At the level of national structure, the necessary guarantees of balance (legislative, executive, judicial and administrative power) will be *repeatedly* discussed and disputed.

The Centrifugal Nature of the Process

As with the bipolarity, the centrifugal tendency of the process of Belgian federalism also departs from usual federal practice, namely the search for unity by bringing together entities which were formerly sovereign. This centripetal tendency explains why most Federal Constitutions contain an explicit list of the federal powers of jurisdiction and leave the residual powers to the federated entities. Against this, Belgian *centrifugal federalism* tends rather to give a list of the powers of jurisdiction of the federated entities, while the residual power continues to come under the national authority.

What are the Prospects for the Future?

By reason of the youth of these new institutions and their incomplete nature, it is very difficult to outline scenarios for the future.

All that can be done is to attempt to extricate 'some strong tendencies', in view of past developments.

-    New jurisdictions will be further devolved to the Regions and the Communities, doubtless with an extension of their taxation powers. It is extremely difficult to say where this development will stop.
-    The *solutions* will be typically Belgian and any reference to foreign examples is not very relevant in this sphere.
-    Relations between the two entities, within a 'Bipolar (Con)federation' will be inspired less by abstract ideas such as the

general interest, national unity, solidarity, etc. than by a reasonable balance between mutual material interests.[23]

The Development of Political Tendencies

The outstanding factor is perhaps the 'decline of the traditional political parties and the emergence of small ecological or nationalist parties' (a trend observed in other European countries).

The three large traditional political groups (Christian, Socialist and Liberal) only represent 70% of the electorate today, against 78% in 1985. The analysis of the poll over a long period (30 years) at a national level, shows since 1987 an inversion in the relative weight of the parties. The Christian group (24.5% of the national electorate) is being overtaken to a small extent by the Socialists, with the Liberals maintaining over recent years around 20% of the vote. This development is due to the tendency to decline on the part of the Flemish Christian Socialists, who went from 50% in 1961 to 27% of the Flemish electorate in 1991. This was accompanied by a certain increase in political fragmentation in Flanders. This is not the case in Walloon, where four parties share the parliamentary representation, but where the Socialist Party, with 39% of the Walloon electorate, continues to outdistance the other parties.

The last elections saw the traditional parties penalized by the electorate. The extreme right established itself everywhere, but particularly in Flanders, and the ecological movement made an advance in Walloon. This seems to indicate that social problems (security, immigration, the environment, solidarity) have become a priority for the population.

If the analysis is taken a little further, it is noted that there are no longer national parties,[24] or even *traditional* parties, but rather *political groups*, which whilst often adopting common points of view on ethical matters, are profoundly divided on certain problems, particularly community problems.

What Developments can be Anticipated for the Future?

In the long term, regrouping resulting in new political parties is not to be excluded even though up to now the swings observed occurred less amongst parties which took part more or less regularly in power than in

---

23 In this respect, see further on the considerations relating to the financial fluxes between regions.
24 Belgium is the only federal country which presents this distinctive characteristic.

the new small parties, the success of which has, up to now, been largely short-lived. The principal factor for examination is without doubt the medium-term future of the CVP[25] in Flanders. If the latter continues to recede, it could cease to be the undefeatable partner around which the alternative coalition governments traditionally organize themselves. The changeover of power itself could thus be compromised.

The Development of the Role of the State and the Future of the Public Sector

The Role of the State

The role of the State in economic life has increased in Belgium as in many other industrialized countries, particularly since the crisis. At the beginning of the 1970s, the share of public spending in GNP was in the order of 40%: it increased to 58% at the beginning of the 1980s, after which it went back to 50%.

With the persistence of the crisis and the consecutive rise of unemployment in industry, the State was forced to become more and more involved in the activity of enterprises, to the point, for example, of becoming the proprietor of the largest iron and steel works in the country. At the same time, systems of social protection (prior pensions) were established to facilitate voluntary exit from the workforce and numerous jobs were created in the civil service (either directly or in the form of subsidizing 'parallel channels' of work). At the beginning of the 1980s, in order to re-establish the competitiveness of the Belgian economy, the State in addition intervened directly in wage negotiations, until then an exclusive sphere of the two sides of industry. It has retained this possibility of intervening through the law relating to 'the protection of competitiveness', passed in 1989.

It should also be noted that during this whole period, regionalization continued to be established, and today a third of the Central State's budget is regionalized, half of this budget being devoted to the overall level of debt. In the end, the latter will still weigh heavily on the budget of the National State, which will have to remain confined to the major traditional functions, which are the functions of law and order, education, infrastructure, welfare payments, without however forgetting an increased role in the protection of the environment, the fight against social exclusion, etc. With regard to economic policy, its margin of manoeuvre,

---

[25]   Christian Popular Party.

which is already very reduced in monetary and budgetary policy, will be even more reduced within the framework of EMU.   Alone under its jurisdiction will be incomes policy and so-called *structural* policies.

The Future of the Public Sector

This is certainly closely linked with the conception and development of the role of the State, which has just been discussed.

Moreover, it is advisable to distinguish clearly between the Government itself and State companies.

As far as the Government is concerned, the record and the prospects are hardly encouraging:

- At the same time there are too many and too few officials in the departments.
- It is lacking in organization; lacking in transparency, insufficient productivity.
- De-motivation, resulting in particular from the proliferation of ministerial advisors and the political nature of the nominations.
- Failure of previous endeavours to improve efficiency.

Whilst the recent Government declaration is well-intentioned, in particular with regard to a better governmental integration in the decision-making process, better productivity as a result of greater mobility, enhanced training and increased computerization, it is improbable that these reforms will have a significant effect in the short term.

In so far as 'the State companies' are concerned, it is necessary to distinguish between the problem of the State companies in the economic and commercial sector and the public credit establishments.

'With regard to the first', which are present in particular in the sector of transport and communications and whose profitability can vary widely (e.g. RTT and SNCB), the tendency towards privatization which began at the beginning of the 1980s as a result of an increased concern for efficiency, was made concrete in Belgium by the effective privatization of certain segments of the public enterprises (e.g. RTT terminals) and in particular by the decision to grant greater autonomy to the State companies (RTT, SNCB), linked with their shareholders through management contracts.

'In the sphere of public credit establishments', significant restructuring (concentration of the establishments around two poles crowned by majority public holding companies) is in progress and measures are anticipated with a view to establishing competition conditions equivalent to the private sector, with a view to the single market of 1993, whilst retaining significant State control.

This restructuring does not resolve however the problem of the insufficient profitability of certain establishments and its overall effectiveness remains the subject of controversy.

'In both cases, the reforms instituted have not put an end to the debate on privatization', although this does not have the same acuteness as in other countries and although the unions and the Socialist Party oppose it fiercely. A recent study has rekindled the controversy, attempting to put figures on the contribution that the sale of certain assets would make to the realization of the objectives of reduction of the budgetary deficit imposed by the Maastricht treaty.

North-South Financial Transfers and their Political Implications

The problem has been clearly posed since 1980 in Flemish academic circles, around the time when the first law of institutional reform was approved.[26]

It has come up again since 1988 and 1989, at the time when the reform of the State took a decisive turn in granting the Regions and Communities wide-ranging powers of jurisdiction and considerable financial means.[27]

Principally focused on social security,[28] it has more recently extended to

---

[26] See in particular:

P. Van Rompuy, A. Verheirstraten, *Regionale herverdeling en financieringsstromen, Leuvense Economische Standpunten*, No. 14, KUL, 1979.

P. Van Rompuy, A. Verheirstraten, F. Uyttebroek, *De regionalisering van de overheidsontvangsten en uitgaven en de interregionale financiële stromen - 1975-1978*, KUL, CES, 1980, and by way of response from the French-speaking community:

D. Weiserbs, A. Kervyn, *Essay on regional division in relation to the State*, IRES Bulletin No. 58, 1980. *Essay on regional division in relation to private individuals*, IRES Bulletin No. 59, 1980.

[27] See in particular P. Van Rompuy, V. Bilsen, *Tien jaar financiele stromen tussen de gewesten in Belgie*, Leuvense Economische Standpunten, No. 45, 1988.

[28] See in particular:

S. Leblanc, *The Federalization of Social Security*, CRISP Weekly Post No. 1282-83, 1990.

P. Defeyt, *From the regionalization of Social Security to the community application of health care*, IRES Bulletin No. 154, 1991.

H. Deleeck, L. De Lathouwer, K. Van Den Bosch, *Verschillen in sociale zekerheid tussen Wallonië en Vlaanderen*, Economisch en Sociaal Tijdschrift, 1989/1.

the sphere of the national debt.[29]

Excluding the debate on the figures, their interpretation and the various scenarios of total or partial regionalization of social security or the national debt which may be devised for the future, there are 'four major considerations':

- Whilst discussion can continue interminably with regard to their importance, there are undeniable 'transfers of solidarity' from Flanders to Wallonië, particularly with regard to spending relating to social security and the national debt.

- Through all the ambiguities which surround the debate, what is evident is the 'differential in growth between the North and the South', which has favoured Flanders for some fifteen years. This is shown particularly in the very much higher unemployment rates in the South, which imply transfers. Moreover there is a more rapid ageing of the population in Wallonië and its industrial past (e.g. occupational disease) means that invoking solidarity is in favour of the Walloon Region, also with regard to pensions and health care.

A revival in commercial activity on the Walloon side would restore a certain equilibrium, but Walloon, as a result of its marked de-industrialization and its aged population, remains too dependent upon a large non-commercial sector, whilst Flanders can count on a strong industrial potential.

- The problem remains *unsolvable* and will be at the centre of the 'Community to Community dialogue' which has just opened between the political parties. It will be an important test for the future of Belgian-style *bipolar and centrifugal* federalism (see above), of which one of the last binding factors is precisely the fate of social security and solidarity.

- Paradoxically, whilst the budgetary development of the last years has consolidated the acuteness of the debate, the budgetary discipline imposed by the Maastricht Treaty for 1996-97 could also, by the probable reduction in welfare payments which it entails in the medium term and the reduction in the national debt in the long term, involve a reduction in North-South transfers in Belgium.

---

29   P. De Grauwe, *Denkoefeningen over de regionalisering van de Belgische overheidschuld*, Leuvense Economische Standpunten, 1991/6.

7. Denmark: Shaping Factors*

INTRODUCTION

This report emphasizes the main factors that are more or less specific for Denmark in the post-1992 Community, and examines how they are likely to affect business strategies. The following aspects are underlined:

- Macroeconomic performance and capital structure.
- Industrial relations.
- Natural resources.
- Infrastructure.
- Demographic changes.
- Values.
- Regional context.
- The Environment.
- Industrial policy.
- The political system and the European context.

MACROECONOMIC PERFORMANCE AND CAPITAL STRUCTURE

In recent years the short-term macroeconomic prospects for Denmark have improved somewhat. There is a surplus on the balance of payments. Inflation is low. Wage claims are moderate. Profitability has improved. Unemployment is high, but only just a little over EC average levels and it could be reduced considerably during the 1990s. There is no structural budget deficit. Compared to the situation in the mid-80s when many observers considered Denmark an economic basket case this turnaround is remarkable.

Cynics argue that this was all due to a long cyclical downturn 1987-91 in domestic demand, the favourable climate of the international economy

---

*   Dr P. Nedergaard and Dr S. Thomsen.

1983-1990 and an abnormal demand-pull effect of German unification. According to this view, the balance of payments equilibrium was paid for by high unemployment, and nothing fundamental has changed. On the other hand optimists may argue that Danish tax reform and subdued inflationary expectations have caused a lasting change of attitudes towards increased private savings and wage moderation.

There is little disagreement that the present favourable circumstances will make a medium-term economic recovery possible in the 1992-96 period. But in the absence of further structural change, the upswing is expected to increase inflation accompanied by falling export market shares, reduced savings and a renewed deficit on the balance of payments. Consequently, a new downturn and rising unemployment could be expected after 1996.

Several structural reforms to overcome these problems are being discussed.

Public expenditure (as a share of GDP) may have to be reduced through increased public productivity: market-like incentives, privatization, wage reductions, etc. Expenditure cuts, increased private social security contributions and environmental taxes will finance tax cuts which could help increase savings.

Structural unemployment may be attacked by measures such as privatized unemployment insurance, decentralized wage negotiations, increased wage differentials and more post-graduate training. It has even been provocatively suggested, for instance, that Danish companies should be obliged to hire one unemployed person for every ten employees. This would almost certainly increase unit labour costs. Another unconventional suggestion of greater political impact has been to let the unemployed work part time for their unemployment allowances, which would still be paid by the government. This would mean a free source of labour, but could have the unwanted effect of decreasing ordinary employment.

The balance of payments deficit has traditionally been the overriding concern of Danish macroeconomic policy. In 1991 there was a surplus which may be sustainable, and although the stance of fiscal policy may be expected to remain tight to sustain this position, further belt tightening may not be necessary. In addition it is possible that some of the stop-go-instability which has characterized domestic demand, may be avoided. Furthermore, the relevance of the balance of payments objective will clearly decrease in the face of European economic and financial integration (even considering the *no* at the referendum on 2 June 1992).

For the same reasons low Danish savings ratios will probably become less of a macroeconomic (balance of payments) problem. A reduction of tax deductibility of interest on household debt seems to have had a strong influence on the propensity to save. However the ageing of the population implies a strong need for pension saving which may not be served by the current low savings ratios.

Economic Structure

The strategies of Danish companies will doubtlessly be affected by three important structural features of the Danish economy.

(i)   The large public sector (i.e. the Welfare State).
(ii)   The continued importance of the food-producing sector.
(iii)   The predominance of small firms in the Danish economy.

This section deals with each of the three subjects in turn.

The Public Sector

The Danish public sector is large in EC comparison. Conversely, private industry and services account for a smaller share of employment than the EC average.

This raises a number of strategic perspectives. Is a large public sector sustainable in the face of European integration? Will it put an intolerably heavy tax load on Danish companies? With a constant labour force, will there be labour shortages up to 2010? Will privatization raise new opportunities for private service companies?

At present there appears to be a broad political consensus in Danish politics that the public sector should not grow larger. A possible scenario is that the public sector will diminish relative to the rest of the economy, as government employees retire, and employment in the private sector will grow. But the Danish labour force is not projected to grow significantly up to 2010, so increased private sector growth must necessarily come from reduced unemployment. It remains to be seen to what extent the business sector can absorb the unemployed. How much of the Danish unemployment is 'natural'? How much can unemployment fall without inflationary pressure? A likely scenario is some upward pressure on real wages. How many of the unemployed can (re)acquire the skills necessary for productive employment? This will be a major task for the personnel and training policies of Danish companies (as well as for public policy).

Privatization is an alternative solution to the problem of the large public sector, which entails significant business opportunities, especially in the private service sector, e.g. insurance companies.

Complementary to the 'no further expansion' consensus there seems to be a political consensus that hostile privatization or lay offs will not be attempted. This is understandable since the Welfare State is ingrained in Danish culture and since public employees and income recipients account for a sizeable share of the electorate. Rather privatization could be *friendly* stemming from a gradual growth of private revenue in public institutions and a growing wish on the part of individual institutions to be freed from the bureaucracy (e.g. wage policies) of the public sector.

The Food Cluster

Traditionally, agriculture has played an important role in the Danish economy and especially for Danish exports. In the manufacturing industry, food processing and supporting industries are still relatively important. The strategic challenge seems to be whether it will be possible to revitalize this sector by (bio)technology and new product development.

The relative specialization in food products and related industries is often considered part of an export specialization problem: a large share of national exports being low-growth/low-income elasticity goods. Danish companies have above-normal world market shares of pork meat, dairy products, etc. and supporting industries (farm machinery, food additives, etc.).

However, the importance of the agro-industrial *development block* is decreasing, since food accounts for a decreasing share of production and exports. The strategic problem is that many Danish companies may be caught in low-growth/profitability sectors such as food, construction products and transport equipment (e.g. shipyards). Will it be possible to revitalize the food sector by new (bio)technology and new more differentiated products with a higher value-added? Some modest public policy measures have been taken to support such a revitalization, among them a 500 million kroner food research programme. Within the food industry, mergers between some of the largest food companies have been motivated by achieving the critical mass presumably needed for R&D to develop new products. For example, Danisco, a merger between three food cluster conglomerates in 1989, aims to double its turnover in the 1990s. A particularly strong horizontal concentration has been taking place among the cooperative bacon factories, motivated primarily by scale economies at the plant level and in marketing.

Furthermore, there is reason not to exaggerate the food cluster problem. As a share of gross national income the food industry accounted for approximately 4% in 1990, whereas the iron and metal industry accounted for 6% and the total manufacturing sector for 18%.

Small-Scale Industry

Small businesses predominate in Danish industry and there are few Danish *industrial locomotives* (large manufacturing companies). This is sometimes considered a strategic problem since European integration will intensify competition and small companies may not reap the economies of scale and scope.

Export intensity (exports/turnover) rises with firm size (at least up to a certain level), and so does R&D intensity (R&D expenditure/turnover). Consequently there is some concern that the small Danish firms may not enjoy the benefits of returns to scale in R&D, marketing, distribution, etc. and that this problem will be aggravated by the internal market and increasing competition. This perceived need for more Danish *industrial locomotives* played some role in an outburst of mergers and acquisitions between 1989 and 1990.

From a strategic perspective one would expect further concentration in Danish business up to 2010, primarily through national and international mergers and acquisitions. Some large Danish companies have announced ambitious growth targets (e.g. to double their size up to the year 2000 as mentioned above in the case of Danisco). An important assumption behind the presumed gains of the internal market is that such a concentration process will in fact take place, creating net benefits by economies of scale.

Capital Market Influences

The capital structure of non-financial Danish companies lies somewhere in between the high debt/equity ratios of German and French companies and the low ratios in Anglo-Saxon countries. 'Long-term debt' is supplied primarily by building societies and banks, which suffered huge losses in the downturn of the late 1980s. This may lead to more restrictive loan policies during the 1990s. 'Equity' is supplied by many institutional arrangements which differ somewhat from international standards.

Stock markets, too, lie somewhere in between the well-developed Anglo-Saxon markets and the modest continental tradition. The market value of companies listed at the Copenhagen stock exchange was approximately 240 billion DKK or 30% of GDP (810 billion DKK) in 1990, far lower than in the UK, but much higher than in Italy or Austria. Of this, 79 billion kroner (30%) were held by financial investors (of this two-thirds, 20% by institutional investors).

Some analysts argue that the Danish capital market is segmented from international markets, and that this means higher costs of capital for Danish companies. If correct, this implies an obvious business interest in European financial integration, for instance mergers between different European stock exchanges.

Among the financial investors, institutional investors (pension funds) hold more than 20% of the total market value. As in most other countries, institutional investors have increased their ownership share over time, up from 12% in 1980. This tendency may be expected to continue as many new pension schemes are currently being implemented. However, due partly to government regulation, the majority control of institutional and other financial investors has so far been negligible.

The majority of even relatively large Danish companies are owned by families/entrepreneurs and private foundations. Private foundations are sometimes a tax shelter for family ownership, but in many cases they are independent with the sole objective of continuing the company's activities.

The primary mechanism for keeping control is to issue stocks with limited voting rights (B-shares of typically one-tenth vote as contrasted with 'one share-one vote' A-shares). This means that the 13th company law directive limiting B-shares to 50% of equity is a sensitive issue in Denmark. In the long run it could mean radical changes of the ownership structure or alternatively a shortage of equity capital, if owners refrain from issuing new stock for fear of losing control.

Institutional investors, of which many are linked with labour unions, have heavily criticized the B-share system, which effectively keeps them out of control. Employers argue that a mixing of labour and financial objectives leads to conflicts of interest. Union pension funds may be subject to political pressure and could for instance find it difficult to close down plants in which their members are employed.

In any case, changes in ownership structure (institutional investors, internationalization, harmonization) are likely to cause important changes in corporate strategy-making. Greater emphasis may be put on long-term strategic plans, not because institutional or international investors are necessarily more farsighted, but because strategic plans have an important function as an information base for financial investors. The traditional company wealth maximization may increasingly be replaced by stockholder wealth maximization. Share prices will matter more to management with the possible risk of more myopic decision-making.

INDUSTRIAL RELATIONS

Industrial relations in this context are about relations between employers and employees. On both sides, the degree of affiliation has traditionally been very high in Denmark. It is, however, expected to fall somewhat in the next 20 years. On the one hand, nothing like the quasi-elimination of trade unions in, for example, France is foreseen in Denmark, a major reason being the Danish tradition that labour market regulations are a task for the labour market parties themselves rather than the Government.

So, even when wage setting is being decentralized, when job functions become more individualized, and when trade unions lose their functions as class organizations, there will still be room for trade union influence. It is even expected that trade unions in Denmark will get new roles in relation to future pension schemes, education, training, and funding of the unemployment benefit schemes.

Strong Trade Unions

Traditionally, Denmark has had strong trade unions. All in all, the percentage affiliated to a trade union is nearly 80% for the labour force as a whole compared to an international average of about 50% in 16 OECD countries. The highly organized labour market implies that a large number of decisions on wages and working conditions are made at a centralized level rather than at the firm level by individual negotiators. At the same time, strong labour market organizations have made it possible for Government and Parliament to avoid much of the detailed labour market legislation that is seen in other countries of the

Community. Regulations in relation to holidays, minimum wages, pregnancy, etc. are almost the sole responsibility of the Danish labour market organizations.

In the 1970s, the percentage affiliated to the trade unions in Denmark grew very rapidly until a figure of about 85% was reached in 1984. The explanation was the growing unemployment after the economic crisis in 1973/74 which in a Danish context implies higher trade union affiliation because of the combined membership and linkage of trade unions and the unemployment benefit schemes. However, since 1984 the degree of affiliation to the trade unions has fallen about six percentage points.

New Roles for Labour Market Organizations

The relatively fewer members of the trade unions reflect a general trend among OECD countries. Employees become less and less class oriented, more individualized in their occupations, and interested in more education rather than higher wages. In order to meet these new post-industrial trends, most Danish trade unions have tried to create new niches. As a result of their bargaining power, many trade unions are able to offer insurances, holiday trips, and even ordinary supermarket goods at a discount. Many trade unions have offered an increasing number of cultural events to their members.

To describe the new roles for trade unions, a concept of being a '24-hour trade union' has been coined by HK (office and retail employees). The development of trade unions has, too, been described as a development from the class organization of yesterday, to the interest organization of today, aiming at the service organization of tomorrow. On the other hand, in a recent survey members of trade unions indicate that they want trade unions only to take care of the working environment, education, personal consultation in situations of crisis stemming from the work place, and (mostly unskilled workers) wage negotiations. So, it seems that there is a growing dilemma for the trade union leadership in seeing their traditional roles vanish and the trade union members wanting them to stick to these roles. All in all, however, environment, personal consultation, and education in a broad sense seem to be the playing field for the trade unions of tomorrow.

As for the employers' organization, a rapid concentration process is taking place in the beginning of the 1990s. Today, almost all employers in the Danish industry are members of the organization called Dansk Industri. Even though it has been tried, the same degree of restructuring has not been possible within the wage earners' organizations due to a certain degree of organizational conservatism. However, a new federation of trade unions called CO-Industri has been formed that will, perhaps, sooner or later be amalgamated into a true trade union for all persons employed in Danish industry.

Both trade unions and employers' organizations are expected to take a greater responsibility in financing the unemployment benefit schemes. Today, about two-thirds of the unemployment benefit schemes are publicity funded, and the insured wage earners provide collectively the remaining one-third. A decreasing engagement on the part of the public purse is expected, and likewise a closer relation between unemployment risk and contribution to the unemployment benefit schemes is to be expected. A greater contribution (and influence on administration of the schemes) on the part of the employers has been suggested, too, e.g. by some employers' organizations themselves.

A greater engagement is also foreseen from the labour market organizations in financing future pension schemes. From 1991, almost all employees are covered by common labour market pension schemes as they are extended to the blue-collar labour force. This supplement to the public pension schemes is moderate in the beginning but a continuous build up is taking place in the 1990s. Thereby, the trade unions as a general rule are indirectly responsible for investing the private pension funds, and become players on the capital market.

The decreasing engagement on the part of the public (and tax-financed) contribution to the unemployment benefit and pension schemes is expected to lead to a reduction in the relatively high personal taxes in Denmark. In the beginning of the 1990s there seems to be broad consensus that this shift should take place. However, there is some disagreement on the speed and certain technicalities.

Education/Training

Trade unions will play an increasing role in the education and training of skilled and semi-skilled workers. Already today, heads of the local branch of e.g. the Metal Workers' Federation are often chairmen of the board at the local Technical Schools training skilled workers, basic engineers, etc. At the same time, the trade unions' head offices engage themselves in formulating general policies for education and training and in lobbying the Parliament and Government in order to spend more on their particular educational interest. At the shop-floor level, the shop steward is seen to play a central role in formulating new objectives in the field of education when looking at the technological development of the firm, in transforming these objectives into educational planning within the firm, and in supervising the education which takes place.

Conclusions: Implications for Business Strategy

In short, the changing industrial relations of the future include a slightly lower degree of affiliation among the employees, and trade unions become less influential in traditional areas, but, on the other hand, new roles will be played by the labour market organizations.

Business will have to handle more wage issues at the firm level, i.e. to argue for wage differences, to compromise in wage disputes, etc. These issues are going to be solved less and less at a central level.

At the same time, in the future, Danish business has to take a greater social and financial responsibility for the workforce than now. In that respect, firms will have to find a *partnership role* with the employees and the local trade union branch in order to increase motivation and upgrade the education of the workforce. Danish trade unions are eager to play this new role and the firms that let them play it will automatically get an advantage.

NATURAL RESOURCES

Historically, Denmark has been a country of very few natural resources - except for a relatively fertile soil. Therefore, until about 20 years ago, agriculture was the only resource-based business. Today, however, considering the world-wide agricultural surplus and scarce energy resources, Denmark's most important natural resource by far is her potentially big oil and natural gas reserves in the North Sea. It is estimated that Denmark's present energy resources will make a considerable contribution to Danish energy consumption in the next 20 to 30 years.

For business, Danish oil and natural gas production has had three effects. Firstly, as a safeguard of future oil supply, especially when considering the energy infrastructure constructed in the 1980s and 1990s. Secondly, as an input in the manufacturing industry in order to make oil-based products. Thirdly, as a welfare source for the country, and therefore as an indicator of a lighter tax burden in the future.

Oil

Today, Danish production of crude oil is close to the total consumption of oil products. In the year 1990, oil production in the Danish part of the North Sea totalled 256 peta-joule. The corresponding self-sufficiency degree was 72%.

Oil reserves in 1990 were estimated to be in the neighbourhood of 183 million cubic metres. These energy reserves are defined as reserves that are exploitable with the present technology and already well-defined production projects. Besides, it is realistic to increase the reserves by using better technology.

In general, it is difficult to exploit the Danish oil fields because of specific geological conditions. Today, only about 14% of the total amount of oil in Danish fields is exploitable. By using *all* existing technologies, it is possible to exploit nearly 50% of the existing amounts of oil. However, considering the technological *and* economic possibilities, a realistic guess is that it will soon be possible to exploit 20% of the total amount of oil in the Danish offshore oil fields.

Natural Gas

In 1990, total Danish natural gas production was 116 peta-joule. That corresponds to a Danish self-sufficiency degree of more than 100%. All in all, it is estimated that Danish reserves of natural gas are 176 billion cubic metres. Of this, it is possible to exploit 35%. Due to the already high percentage of exploitation, it is estimated by the Ministry of Energy that only a few possibilities exist to raise this percentage.

Welfare Benefits

Besides a high degree of energy security in the next 20 years, Danish production of oil and natural gas improves the Danish balance of payments and the Danish public finances. In an economic and monetary union, Danish balance of payments figures become less relevant but, still, the contribution to the national public finances exists. In these years, carbon dioxide taxes, corporate taxes, and royalties on oil and natural gas production will contribute 13 billion kroner to the Danish public finances from 1991 to 1996. At the same time, investments in natural gas infrastructure are being constantly written off.

To business, an unknown factor in the future energy policy is whether the Community will adopt CO_2/energy tax in response to the greenhouse effect. Already a moderate, but purely national, carbon dioxide duty has been adopted by the Danish Parliament. A Community duty would further harm the competitiveness of the Danish industry since it is relatively more dependent on oil and natural gas as an energy resource than neighbouring countries like Germany, Sweden, and the United Kingdom. The reason is the lack of nuclear power stations in Denmark. A common Community tax, however, is much preferred by business to a purely national one.

Conclusions: Implications for Business Strategy

The present Danish oil and gas reserves in the North Sea will make a considerable contribution to the Danish energy consumption in the next 20 to 30 years. In most of the years until the year 2010, Denmark will face self-sufficiency in these two energy resources. For business, the implications are, firstly, that the future supply of oil and natural gas is safeguarded, secondly, that production of Danish oil-based products might become cost advantageous, and, thirdly, that the public tax revenue from carbon dioxide taxes, royalties, and corporate taxes from oil producers will slightly lighten the present tax burden, *ceteris paribus*.

INFRASTRUCTURE

In the next 20 years, huge investments will be carried out in the transport infrastructure in Denmark. The regions on each side of the Great Belt, the Sound (Øresund), and Femern Belt will be linked by bridges and tunnels. As a side effect, a number of follow-up investments in motor-ways and railroads are planned. Besides, the overall Danish road network will be built up. Therefore, the markets for goods, services, and labour between Eastern and Western Denmark, between Eastern Denmark and Southern Sweden, between Denmark and Northern Germany, and across Jutland will be much more integrated.

The Overall Traffic Infrastructure

In the 1960s and until the mid-1970s, a number of investments in the Danish traffic infrastructure were carried out. Of these investments, new roads and ferries made up a large proportion. In the rest of the 1970s, however, and especially in the beginning of the 1980s, public investments in infrastructure became still more scarce. Balance of payments problems, making it necessary to cut public expenditure, were a main reason for restrictive public investment policy.

The 1990s marks a change compared to the 1980s with regard to the increasing investments in the overall infrastructure. A reason is that investment in infrastructure is seen as an engine to create new employment, now that the Danish balance of payments poses no problems. The most expensive investment is supposed to be the permanent link for trains and vehicles across the Great Belt.

From the perspective of firms, traffic infrastructure is relevant for business rationalization and a better management of transport, distribution, and storage. The importance of the transportation sector can be seen from the fact that in Denmark about 100 billion kroner (about 12 billion ECUs) are spent on transportation every year. Out of the 12 billion ECUs, 70 billion kroner are spent on road transportation corresponding to 10% of GDP.

Danish Road System in the Year of 2010

In the year 2010, the *great H* is to be implemented as the skeleton of the overall Danish road system. In the same period, a system of so-called motor traffic roads are to be established, too, where there is insufficient trifacial or political pressure to establish real motorways.

All in all, according to the Ministry of Transport, the expected total length of the motorways will be about 1200 kilometres by the year 2010. At the same time, 600 kilometres of new roads are expected to be constructed. Hereafter, the Danish road system will have integrated the country into a whole.

Increasingly, the road system will be financed by user payments. For different types of roads, different types of payments will be used. For example, it will cost more to drive in the cities than on the motorways. On the other hand, taxes on fuel and registration will be harmonized to the European average.

Fixed Link: the Great Belt

In Denmark, there is a tradition of making social cost-benefit analyses before making big traffic investments. For traffic investments like bridges, construction costs will have to be judged against saving costs from running the ferries and saved time for the travellers. In calculating the value of saved time, the logistic-conditioned benefits for business are only partly considered. Non-calculated benefits are, for example, improved distribution and storage functions, a more flexible customer base, and labour market, and a more rational exploitation of the transport facilities.

Therefore, social benefits from traffic investments are tendentiously underestimated. That happens to be the case, not least when *bottlenecks* like ferries are substituted by bridges. At present, the Great Belt is a fundamental barrier to traffic and economic transactions between Funen/Jutland on the one side and Sealand/Lolland-Falster on the other side. As a consequence, traffic across the Great Belt is almost exclusively long-distance traffic. Inter-regional and short-distance traffic is almost non-existent. In the other direction, however, there is intensive traffic between Funen and the so-called *triangle area* (between Fredericia, Kolding, and Vejle) in the form of commuting and goods transport. On the other hand, the traffic between Funen and Western Sealand, is very limited.

Today, only 11,000 cars cross the Great Belt between Western and Eastern Denmark. The number of cars crossing the Danish-German border are four times as big, and the number of cars crossing the Little Belt bridge are three times as big. Hence, considerable economic benefits are expected to come from a permanent link across the Great Belt.

A/S Storebæltsforbindelsen, the company responsible for the construction of the Great Belt bridge, has made a cost-benefit analysis of the project under construction. (Logistics benefits have been partly integrated into the calculations, even though in a very superficial way.) This cost-benefit analysis shows a socio-economic yield of 11 to 12% t p.a. from an investment of 18 billion kroner in 1988 prices. Compared with a real interest rate of approximately 5% p.a. it seems that there is a considerable surplus from the investment in the Great Belt bridge. The immediate impression is even strengthened by the fact that the bridge is supposed to stand for at least 100 years.

Fixed Link: the Sound

A/S Storebæltsforbindelsen has made another analysis, too, showing the socio-economic benefits from a permanent road and train link across the Sound. Using the same method as when calculating the cost and benefit of the Great Belt link, it shows that an Øresund bridge gives a real socio-economic yield of 6% p.a. alone. On the other hand, when a Sound bridge is combined with a permanent link across Femern Belt, the remunerativeness of the Sound bridge rises to 8.25% p.a.

In the calculations above, there is not supposed to be any general increase in traffic intensity after the opening of the Sound bridge in 2000. If, however, the traffic intensity is supposed to increase 1% p.a. after the year 2000, e.g. as a response to increased economic integration of the Scandinavian and Baltic States with the rest of Europe, the economic return of the Sound bridge alone increases from 6% p.a. to 6.25% p.a.

However, the above-mentioned calculations of the benefits of fixed links across the Sound should be regarded as too pessimistic. In fact, both among scholars and decision-makers, there is a growing consensus that big cities have important roles to play as dynamic regional centres in a more borderless Europe. In the case of Copenhagen, the Sound link (especially when Sweden joins the European Community) will make it possible for this city to become the metropolis of Denmark and Southern Sweden, i.e. a region of 8-9 million people.

Today, all surveys indicate that economic, personal, and cultural links across the Sound are very limited. Today, Copenhagen has 1.6 million inhabitants (number 32 among the cities of Europe), and a *Gross-Big-City-Product* in 1988 of $33.6 billion (number 16 among the European cities, or in a group of cities like Randstadt, Amsterdam, Den Haag, Rotterdam, Utrecht, etc.). With a fixed link, however, Greater Copenhagen (the big city on both sides of the Sound) expands to 2.3 million inhabitants (number 20 among the European cities). In terms of economy, the rise of future Copenhagen is even more impressive: from number 16 to number 8 when calculating the *Gross-Big-City-Product*. Furthermore, Greater Copenhagen becomes number 5 on the list of the most creative cities in Western Europe (calculated in resources spent on industrial and scientific R&D plus communication facilities) after London (including Oxford and Cambridge), Paris, Randstadt and Rhein-Ruhr (Dortmund, Essen, Duisburg, Düsseldorf, Köln, Bonn, etc.).

Fixed Link: the Femern Belt

If one includes all potential but realistic benefits from a permanent Femern link, from a moderately increased traffic intensity after 2000, and from logistic gains like those of the Great Belt, the permanent link across the Femern Belt will give a total socio-economic benefit of nearly 11% p.a.

Contrary to the Great Belt link and the Sound link, no calculations have yet been made to estimate the socio-economic benefits from a permanent link across the Femern Belt, only some preliminary investigations about the technical possibilities of establishing such a link. On the other hand, it is difficult to imagine that the effect on society and business will be less than the effects from the Great Belt bridge and the Sound bridge.

In connection to the Femern Belt link, it is planned to make the railroad net from Copenhagen to Rødby part of the trans-European high-speed network with a maximum speed of 300 kilometres per hour.

Conclusions: Implications for Business Strategy

The infrastructural development within Denmark and between Denmark and its neighbour countries makes it still easier for firms in Denmark to reach markets in the neighbour countries on the one hand, and to reach Danish markets from the outside on the other hand. So, the net result of the new infrastructural investments depends - to a large extent - on the future competitiveness of firms situated in Denmark. If Danish firms are (or become) relatively more competitive than firms in the neighbouring countries, Denmark will face a large net gain in employment, production, etc. If, however, the opposite situation is the case, Denmark might face a net loss and become what has been labelled a 'transit country'. For the region of Northern Europe as a whole, however, there is no doubt that the extensive development of the region's infrastructure is advantageous.

The huge investments in infrastructure binds Scandinavia and Continental Europe to each other. In other words, *missing links* will no more be an obstacle to investments in Denmark and the rest of Scandinavia.

DEMOGRAPHIC CHANGES

Among the decisive factors of future Danish business strategies, demographic changes are significant for a number of reasons. The size of the population, and the age distribution, are at the same time equivalent proxies of the number of domestic consumers and the age composition of the labour force. Another question is whether or not an *ageing* population is putting an extra tax burden on the productive population and thereby making the labour force and the firms located in Denmark less competitive.

The Size of the Population

The size of the Danish population is not supposed to change much in the next 20 years. In the year 1990, there were 5,175,417 inhabitants in Denmark. In the year 2007, there is expected to be about 40,000 persons less.

In a broad perspective, there are only minor changes in the relations between the group from 0 to 19 years, from 20 to 74 years and the group of more than 75 years. Thus, it is suggested that there is only a limited change in the so-called support burden.

When disaggregating the figures some more characteristic demographic changes show up. The first of three clear tendencies is that the group from 15 to 30 years is reduced drastically in the period from 1990 to 2007. The reduction will be 24.1% which corresponds to 281,000 persons. This development will first and foremost affect the education sector and lead to a still smaller infusion of younger people into the labour market. Secondly, the number in the group from 55 to 65 years will increase dramatically. In 2007, there will be 39.9% more persons in this age group. The corresponding number of extra people is 200,000. This development will have a major impact on the need for retraining. At the same time, one can foresee a big increase in the demand for special products for this age group. Thirdly, one can expect a sharp increase in the number of the very old. Although in real numbers the increase is only of minor significance, the number of people of more than 85 years is expected to increase by nearly 30,000 persons from now until 2007. That is an increase of about 37.2%. This development will especially affect the public sector. But, on the other hand, there will be a growing demand for products directly focusing on this age group, too.

All in all, no *old-age boom* is expected. Even though the number of the very old will increase, this growth is more than outweighed by the growth of the people from 55 to 65 years who are still regarded as being in their 'productive age'.

Demographic Changes and the *Age Dependency* Ratio

An important part of the demographic changes concerns the question of how the demographic changes will affect future public expenditures. The answer is that in the period from now and until 2010 they will only have a limited impact, increasing public expenditures by only about 0.1% per year.

Therefore, the demographic changes in Denmark do not by themselves create problems for financing pension schemes in the future.

Demographic Changes and the Labour Market

From 1958 to 1990, the labour force grew about 36%, and in the period from 1979 to 1990 alone the growth was 12%. Under no circumstances can such a growth be expected for the future. On the contrary, as mentioned above, the labour force is expected to shrink a little over the next 20 years.

In theory, such a decrease should not create any trouble. (In any case, there seems to be political consensus that the demographic changes can by no means be used to justify extensive immigration.) First of all one could point to the number of unemployed. Then there is the possibility of motivating more than 600,000 part-time working people (especially women) to shift to full-time work. One could also raise the pension age that is in reality close to 60 years for a growing number of people.

Probably, one or more of these methods will be used when firms experience trouble in finding the right persons for the right jobs. On the other hand, a massive increase in training and education for adults is needed, too, in the years to come. The reason is that there is no single labour market. Perhaps labour market segmentation is even more salient in Denmark than in most of the other European countries. Therefore, a fear is that there will be a rising number of bottlenecks within the labour market if resources are not allocated to training and education for adults as the possibilities of filling (potentially) vacant positions with young people become more difficult.

Conclusions: Implications for Business Strategy

A still smaller infusion of young people in the labour market and an ageing population could lead to possible labour shortages, rigidities, and bottlenecks, especially in *new* and growing occupation areas. However, unemployed, part-time working women, and/or a rising pension age can fill the gap if the necessary education and training are provided.

The dramatic increase in the group from 55 to 65 imply increasing funds spent on retraining of this group.

A sharp increase in the number of the very old (more than 85 years) implies extra public spending (and taxes) for this group, partly to supply a growing demand for products directly focusing on this age. However, the demographic changes in Denmark do not by themselves create problems in financing the overall pension schemes in the future.

VALUES

It is difficult to talk about changes in attitude and values in any precise way. And forecasting seems a virtually impossible exercise. But value changes are important to business strategy, and therefore it is attempted here to outline some possible perspectives. For present purposes we stress two important dimensions in social value systems. The degree of materialism and the degree of traditionalism. Basic material needs such as food and shelter are contrasted with immaterial needs such as leisure, culture and entertainment, status or self-actualization. Traditional values such as family ties and social norms are contrasted with modern individualism.

The general direction of value changes in Denmark seems to be towards less material and more individualistic values. The primary driving forces are economic growth, rising standards of living and an increasing level of education. Secondary change agents are changes in the Welfare State, European integration, immigration, etc. In a Maslow framework the Danes have become less motivated by a basic need for food, comfort and security.

In Denmark, as in other industrialized nations, the family as a social institution has been on the decline since the beginning of the century. Female work participation ratios have grown, fertility has dropped, more people live alone, and tight family networks have been uprooted by urbanization and a more mobile, dynamic society. One indicator is average household size.

Table 7.1   Average household size (persons) 1900-1990

1901	1900	1930	1940	1950	1960	1970	1980	1990
4.3	3.7	3.2	3.1	2.9	2.7	2.4	2.2	

However, the decline in family size is further advanced in Denmark than in most other countries. The female work participation ratio is exceptionally high, the average household size is exceptionally low.

Institutions taking care of traditional family tasks such as nurseries, kindergartens and homes for the elderly have exceptionally high coverage ratios.

If the Welfare State is no longer considered a viable alternative to the family, this raises a number of important questions for corporate strategy. First, some new business possibilities are opened. Secondly, to what extent should companies play a family role - supplying for instance kindergartens, leisure facilities and entertainment, pension and retirement schemes, and old boys' clubs. And more profoundly, should the company work to be a second home for employees to identify with, implementing for instance lifelong Japanese employment schemes, and building a strong corporate culture? This may increase loyalty but could also increase family-type conflicts.

In the long run, the family-company interaction would seem to indicate a more important social role and responsibility for the company as an institution. How important this role is appears less certain.

The decline in family size seems to be one sign of a fundamental transition from 'traditional' to 'modern' values exemplified by the high female work participation ratio, the rising level of education, the number of non-married couples, etc.

There are also some signs of a transitional trend towards a less materialistic culture.

-    Consumption of 'culture' has been increasing. People read more books, go more often to the theatre and to concerts, art exhibitions etc. The popularist futurist J. Naisbitt predicts a 'golden age of the arts' in the 1990s, and there seem to be some tendencies in this direction. However, the consumption of 'fine arts' is still modest compared with mass culture such as going to the cinema and watching television.
-    Leisure network organizations such as clubs and societies are very important in Denmark and other Scandinavian countries compared to international activity levels. Their importance has increased further during the last 25 years.
-    Personal health matters more. There has been a dramatic rise in the number of people doing regular physical exercise.

It should be noted that these tendencies do not cover the whole population. In international comparison, Denmark is a homogenous country, partly because of its small size. But there are subcultures.

REGIONAL CONTEXT

Basically, the regional context of Danish business will change in two ways in the next 20 years. Firstly, the character of Nordic collaboration will change because of the *Europeanization* of the Nordic countries. Secondly, the Baltic area - to which most Nordic countries belong - is undergoing major changes after the end of the Cold War.

The Present Nordic Collaboration

Nordic collaboration is both formal and informal. Perhaps, the most unique feature of Nordic collaboration is the intensive and informal communication networks across the borders of the Nordic countries. All of these networks are based on the common linguistic and cultural roots of the Nordic countries.

The institutionalized part of Nordic collaboration consists of the Nordic Council that was established in 1952. The Nordic Council is made up of parliamentarians from all Nordic countries who meet to discuss subjects of common interest. The Governments are, however, not committed to implement the recommendations made by the parliamentarians.

Inspired by the Council of Ministers in the European Community, a Nordic Council of Ministers was set up in 1971. This new institutional creation has by no means meant much progress in Nordic collaboration, which has not had a 'golden age' since the 1950s. It was in this period that, among other things, the common labour market (dating back to 1954), the Passport Union (from 1958) and the Nordic Social Convention (dating back to 1955), were adopted. Probably the most important part of Nordic collaboration is the common labour market. Today, about half a million Nordic citizens work in another Nordic country.

Changes in the 1990s

In the 1990s, the Nordic countries will have to face drastic changes in their relations *vis-à-vis* the European Community. Most probably, other Nordic countries will become members of the European Community as early as 1995, 1996, or 1997. Sweden has applied for membership, and Finland did the same thing in the spring of 1992. Norway will also apply.

On the other hand, it is less certain that Norway and Iceland will become members like Sweden and Finland before the end of the century.

Therefore, if Sweden and Finland join the European Community in the mid-1990s, Nordic collaboration will be put in a difficult situation. More than 75% of the Nordic population will then be Community citizens while 25% will be left outside.

However, it is possible that some of the traditional Nordic subjects of collaboration will by then already be absorbed by the new institutions that follow the adoption of the agreement on the European Economic Area. Certainly, it is expected that these institutions will have to handle all 'heavy' issues that also relate to Nordic collaboration.

Until 1995/1997, the EEA agreement will probably make up the framework for the relations of the Nordic countries towards the European Community. Perhaps Nordic collaboration will become even stronger in this interim period when the Nordic countries have to find a role for themselves in Europe. There is still, however, the possibility that the European Community will not be enlarged until the mid-1990s. The EEA arrangement will then become a more or less permanent relationship between the Nordic countries and the European Community. If that happens, the Nordic collaboration is almost doomed to weaken when all of the EFTA countries (including Austria and Switzerland) have to speak with one voice.

Economic Interests of the Nordic Countries

Even though Nordic countries have many cultural links, and even though they do try to find a common political platform in Europe, their economic interest as countries is far from the same. It is not least the different business structure that means that they have to exploit different economic interests in any type of collaboration:

Denmark has an interest in the other Nordic countries joining the European Community because of the large number of barriers in the other Nordic countries to Danish agricultural exports (due to protectionism and political preferences for self-sufficiency, barriers that will subsequently have to be lifted). On the other hand, in case the other Nordic countries join the EC, Denmark can no longer play the role of a Nordic *investment bridge* to Europe.

Sweden has the most European business-industrial structure among the Nordic countries. This country, therefore, has a lot of interests in common with the most industrialized Member countries of the European Community.

Finland has a large export based on primary products even though manufactured goods make up an increasing part of Finnish exports. Earlier about 20% of Finnish exports went to the former Soviet Union. Today it is only 3-4%. As a result, Finland has become correspondingly more dependent on the EC/EEA market.

Norway has an emphasis on exports of energy and primary goods. These products are sensitive to business cycles but less dependent of the internal market of the European Community. It is estimated that less than 20% of the Norwegian goods production is sensitive to the internal market regulations and that only 50% of industrial production is sensitive to the EC as a whole.

Iceland is characterized by a very great dependency on fisheries. The economic interest of Iceland can be reduced to a question of tariff-free export of fish products.

As can be seen, the Nordic countries have differing economic interests in their relations to the European Community. They all want free access for their exports. But they want free access for different kinds of exports. Therefore, in practice, one cannot expect to see a close Nordic cooperation in order to influence the economic regulations of the EC.

Political Interests of the Nordic Countries

In spite of the differing economic interests, the Nordic countries have common political interests in strengthening the Nordic region in Europe. In that respect, the Nordic region mirrors the regionalization trend in Europe that is also seen in Central Europe (*Mitteleuropa*), in the Benelux countries, and among the European Mediterranean countries. Already, a precedent has been established for such geographic subgroups in the EC in Article 233 in the Treaty of Rome. When the EC is expanded, this article becomes even more relevant.

If all Nordic countries join the European Community, it means that they will probably get 16 votes in the EC Council of Ministers and 25% of all presidencies of the Council will be occupied by Nordic countries. These figures should be compared with the fact that the total populations in the Nordic countries are only 22-23 million. On the other hand, as mentioned above, it is by no means certain that the Nordic countries will make up one bloc in the questions on economic regulations. Already, however, discussions are under way on how the Nordic Council can be used to find a common Nordic position in the EC on a number of political welfare state issues when most of the Nordic countries are EC members.

The Baltic Region - Before and Now

Historically, countries around the Baltic Sea have been a more important region in economic terms for most Nordic countries than the Nordic region. After the end of the Cold War, it is not unrealistic to assume that the Baltic region will once again overshadow the Nordic region as the most economically relevant region. Possibly, the old Hansa economic collaboration is recreated in new clothing in the 1990s - this time with Northern Germany as a fellow player.

In the negotiations, the Nordic countries have accepted an extraordinary responsibility for those parts of the former Soviet Union and Eastern Europe that are situated along the shores of the Baltic Sea. A close institutionalized collaboration can be foreseen between the Nordic Council consisting of five Member States and the newly established Baltic Council consisting of ten Member States, although the Baltic Council is still very weak and a purely consultative forum. At the same time, *ad hoc* collaboration is already flourishing between e.g. Denmark and the individual Baltic countries at all levels of the society.

It is not, however, realistic that Denmark will get any kind of economic leadership role in the Baltic area. Already, both Sweden and Germany have closer economic ties to most countries in the area. On the other hand, Copenhagen is the traditional gateway to the Baltic Sea. Before the First World War, Copenhagen was the junction for trade with countries in the Baltic area. Copenhagen can probably regain some of its former position, even though bulk traffic has made the need for harbour facilities less important.

The Baltic area can be defined as the following regions: Denmark, Sweden, Estonia, Latvia, Lithuania, the St. Petersburg and Kaliningrad region in Russia, Suwalki, Olstyn, Elblag, Slubsk, Koszalin and Sczcecin in Poland, Mecklenburg-Vorpommern in the former East Germany and Schleswig-Holstein in the former West Germany. All of these regions have direct access to the Baltic Sea. The area covered is 1.2 million square kilometres, and the total population is about 41 million.

So defined, the Baltic area has 45 cities with more than 100,000 inhabitants which mirrors the fact that most of the population lives in cities. On the other hand, there are only four cities with more than one million inhabitants in the region. In a physical-geographic sense, the living conditions of the people in the Baltic region are almost the same.

Infrastructure in the Baltic Area

Even though low wages is a necessary condition for Danish industrial investments in, for example, Poland, it is not a sufficient condition. A well-functioning infrastructure in a broad sense is a precondition if economic transactions are to increase.

Earlier on, the *new* market economies had a low capacity in telecommunication. So, communication was an effective restriction for the exchange of information and thereby for trade. Problems exist in this area but progress is continuously being made.

Still, the physical transportation means limiting the intensity of goods exchange. The railroad networking is overloaded in Estonia and in Russia while it is only lightly loaded in Finland, Sweden, and Denmark. On the other hand, the roads of the Baltic states are only lightly loaded while the roads of the former East Germany especially are heavily overloaded. Changes for the better are expected in the short run in East Germany while changes in the other *new* market economies may take place but only in a medium-range perspective.

Evidently, the possibility of using the waterways of the Baltic Sea calls for special attention. This possibility is even expected to increase in importance when some of the military facilities, like the port of Kaliningrad, are left for civil use, and if consequences are drawn from the fact that sea transport is the environmentally least harmful way of goods transportation.

Trade in the Baltic Area

The Danish trade with the *old* market economies around the Baltic Sea is relatively intensive. On the other hand, the *new* market economies have been trading almost exclusively among themselves. Trade between the former political *East* and *West* in the Baltic area has been very limited - except for Finland.

The *old* market economies exchange machines, raw materials, and semi-manufactured goods. The intra-sectorial trade is well developed. Conversely, when *East* traded with *West* earlier on, raw materials were almost exclusively going West while technology products went East when allowed to do so by the COCOM regulations.

Now, when the political barriers between the countries around the Baltic Sea have disappeared, potentially there are more possibilities for exploiting the comparative advantages that each individual country may have. The former planned economies in the Baltic region have a great need to *pick up* their economic activity. For a number of consumer goods like television sets, cars, refrigerators, and telephones, there is less than half the number per 1,000 inhabitants in these countries than in, for example, Denmark.

On the other hand, the low and even decreasing level of incomes means that the consumer markets of the *East* are shrinking in the short term. When the economic transformation period ends, i.e. after the mid-1990s, trade between the *East* and *West* of the Baltic area is expected to flourish. In Poland, already, Danish exports have risen to a level of 4-5 billion kroner.

Another example can illustrate the trade potential. In 1933 Danish exports to Estonia, Latvia, and Lithuania amounted to 660,000 kroner, 1,025 million kroner, and 1,055 million kroner respectively. Danish exports to Finland were about the same size as to the three Baltic States. Today, Danish exports to the three States are negligible whilst Denmark exported 5.6 billion kroner worth of goods and services to Finland (2.7% of total Danish export) in 1989.

Conclusions: Implications for Business Strategy

The changing regional context of Denmark means that business situated in Denmark will move from the periphery to the centre of Northern Europe. In other words, business in Denmark will have easy access to the markets in the Nordic countries and the new markets in the Baltic area. In this connection, historical, linguistic, and cultural ties are assumed to reduce market transaction costs.

Danish agro-business has an interest in the other Nordic countries joining the European Community because the large number of barriers in the other Nordic countries to Danish agricultural exports (due to protectionism and political preferences for self-sufficiency) will then be lifted. To a certain extent, new markets in the Nordic countries might 'save' Danish agriculture after a GATT reform. On the other hand, in case the other Nordic countries join the EC, Denmark can no longer play the role as a Nordic *investment bridge* to Europe.

The changes in the social fabric of the Baltic area imply that Danish firms get a nearby pool of cheap labour. Of course, there are commercial and other policy restrictions on how to exploit the labour in the *new* market economics. In practical terms, it is especially the Danish textile and metal industry that will relocate parts of the labour intensive production to e.g. Poland. In a medium time perspective, trade based on cheap labour in the *new* market economics is likely to become the basis of most trade in the Baltic area.

THE ENVIRONMENT

The Danish public pays increasing attention to environmental issues. In a 1988 opinion poll on Danish core values, one-third chose *nature* as their core value second in popularity only to *family and friends*. Close to 10% of the population are members of green grass roots movements. The Green Party is not represented in Folketinget, but this may largely be explained by the large extent to which old parties have adopted *green views*. Green values produce a political pressure to 'do something' about the environment. But they do not necessarily channel this effort in the right direction. Furthermore environmental protection is often an international problem which needs to be attacked at a supranational level.

An increasing number of companies take a proactive rather than reactive stance towards environmental protection. New management methods are needed to face the challenges. That means, for example, *cradle-to-grave analysis* of production processes in which the energy and material flows at each stage are assessed as to the environmental consequences. In addition, companies need to strengthen their *environmental image* for marketing reasons and to attract qualified personnel as well as investors. Many institutional investors have begun to consider explicitly the environmental damage done by companies before they invest in them (*green capitalism*).

Environmental protection is also becoming a business in itself (e.g. equipment for environmental protection), and Danish companies are generally thought to be competitive in this line of business. However Danish companies may have lost a good portion of their earlier lead, because the industry is fragmented (small companies). A modest programme of 130 million kroner from the Ministry of Industry ('industrial application of environmental protection technology') aims at creating networks and public-private sector cooperation, but it will hardly be sufficient.

INDUSTRIAL POLICY

Industrial policy has never been important in Denmark. Government subsidies for industry are modest, and in recent years (1989-91) they have been further reduced. The total budget of the Ministry of Industry has been cut from 2 billion DKK in 1990 to 1.5 billion in 1992, and further cuts seem likely.

However, the present government as well as the opposition have recently advocated *active* industrial policies - i.e. indirect and horizontal measures such as large investments in infrastructure, R&D, education, etc. Hence old industrial policies (subsidies) are being replaced by a *new industrial policy* implying a broader view of government business relations very much in line with new theory (Porter 1990) and the EC Commission's proposals for a European industrial policy for the 1990s.

The general direction of the *new industrial policy* is to reduce selective government subsidies whereas horizontal measures not directed at particular industries are preferred. In effect this implies reductions in the budget of the Ministry of Industry whereas resources and initiatives are delegated to other ministries (Education, Traffic, Finance).

The net effect may be lower government expenditure and some see the *new industrial policy* as a step towards *laissez-faire*. Thus, new policy measures have been modest in economic terms.

THE POLITICAL SYSTEM AND THE EUROPEAN CONTEXT

The political system in Denmark is characterized by the same trends that are seen in most Western European countries: the political parties lose members and more voters shift their votes from election to election. On the other hand, the Danish political system has some specific features: near-permanence of minority governments, consensus orientation with often very small differences between the political left and right, relative stability between a socialist bloc (about 45% of the votes) and a non-socialist bloc (about 55% of the votes), an anti-elitism political culture perhaps more sensitive to shifts in political sentiments and to opinion makers outside the political establishment, and a strong sense of non-interventionism in relation to business. One of the major shifts in the second half of the 1980s is seen in the political parties' attitude towards integration in the EC. In short, Danish political parties have become more like political parties in other EC Member States.

Fragile Minority Governments

Except for short periods, Denmark has been ruled by minority governments in the last 30 years. That happens to be a record in Western Europe. On the one hand, and especially in certain periods, that has led to destabilization of the national economy. In the 1970s and in the beginning of the 1980s, governments were unable to cope with increasing balance of payments deficits and public budget deficits. As a result, after these years Denmark ended up having the highest foreign debt ratio per capita among the OECD countries. In the same period, a build up of the public debt was seen, although Denmark was never in the forefront.

On the other hand, the permanence of minority governments has strengthened the consensus orientation of Danish politics. A lot of the present Danish legislation is a result of what is called 'broad political agreements'. These 'broad political agreements' have an almost mythical status in Danish politics and they are often seen as an end in themselves no matter what the substance of the agreements.

The preference for broad political agreements in Danish politics implies that no haphazard legislation is adopted, but legislation aiming at structural reforms is also difficult to implement because it will almost always hurt specific groups of the society that are represented in the political consensus. Therefore, structural reforms and reformative legislation in Danish politics need to have a consensus status before they are adopted. Then, however, implementation seems to create smaller problems than in most other countries.

Another positive effect of the consensus orientation of Danish politics is the ability to make a substantial change in the direction of the country if and when the consensus changes. The shift in economic policy from the end of the 1970s to the beginning of the 1990s is an example of such a change. At the end of the 1970s Denmark was one of the OECD countries with the biggest trade balance deficit, whereas in the beginning of the 1990s Denmark is one of the OECD countries with the highest balance of trade surplus. So, in recent years, the minority governments have had no trouble in getting acceptance for a *hard-line* economic policy.

Bloc Permanence

Even though Danish voters show increasing liability, the political blocs in Danish society remain relatively constant. Therefore, whether the government has a Social Democratic or a Liberal Conservative colour is more or less up to the centre parties to decide. If they support a Liberal Conservative prime minister as the head of government, as they have done since 1982, the government becomes Liberal Conservative. On the other hand, if the centre parties choose a Social Democrat as their preferred candidate for prime minister, as they did from 1975 to 1982, the government becomes Social Democratic.

At the same time, the more or less constant blocs of socialist and non-socialist votes further strengthened the consensus character of Danish politics. One explanation of the bloc permanence might be that the attitudes of a majority of the Danish population cross traditional party ideologies. In short, it seems that most Danish voters favour a right-wing economic policy, a Social Democratic redistributive policy, and a *green* environment policy that do not hurt Danish competitiveness. Also when asked about their view on the functioning of the political system and the way the democracy works, the Danish people are the most contented people in all of the Member States in the European Community.

Political Culture

The fact that Denmark is a country of few big multinational firms, of many small- and middle-sized firms, and a strong and influential sector of middle-sized farmers not so many years ago, is the background of both egalitarianism and economic liberalism in Danish society today.

Another and connected reason for this anti-elitist (or often even populist) and anti-interventionist political culture is deeply rooted in the particular national romantic tradition of N.F.S. Grundtvig. If a single person has to be named who has had the greatest influence on the political culture it is undoubtedly him. As a theologian, writer, and public spokesman in the nineteenth century he founded the tradition of Danish folk high schools without examinations, of agricultural cooperatives, of a Danish anti-intellectualism, and of free enterprise as the foundation of the economic life in society.

In that respect, it has to be remembered that in the last century Denmark lost a third of its territory to the German Empire. Compared to the size of the country, that was the biggest loss of all the German neighbours. Economic and cultural development (however, not by more resources spent on defence) were seen by Grundtvig as the two major and interconnected ways of overcoming the loss.

The ideas of Grundtvig have been influential until today. Many Danes still regard themselves as Gundtvigians, especially within the theological arena, but normally at least one or two ministers (no matter the colour of the government) are declared Grundtvigians. A sign of the influence of Grundtvig and the mythical status he put in the word 'people' (*folk*) can be seen in the many ways that the word people is used in Denmark: the national church is called The Peoples' Church, the public libraries are called The Peoples' Libraries, the primary school is called The Peoples' School, the Parliament is called The Peoples' Parliament (*Folketinget*), etc.

All these traditions are strong even today. Ten thousand Danes or more take courses at the folk high schools each year, almost all big (and multinational) Danish dairies and slaughterhouses are farmer-owned co-operatives, and anti-intellectualism is still seen in the fact that the quality of skilled workers' education is of high quality, whereas basic research is perhaps of less profound quality. Besides, the root of the strong free business climate (almost absolute freedom to dismiss employees, to fix prices, to start a business, etc.) is partly Grundtvigian. Also there is no doubt that the still relatively strong anti-EC sentiments in the population and among theologians, writers, teachers, etc., have their roots in the national romantic tradition and economic liberalism of Grundtvig.

Attitudes Towards the EC

One of the major shifts in the second half of the 1980s is the shift in the political parties in their attitudes toward European integration. Not least the change in the Social Democratic Party (38% of the votes in the election in 1990) has been profound. In 1986, when a Danish referendum was held about the Single European Act, the Social Democratic Party officially recommended a *no* vote. In 1992, however, the Social Democratic Party recommended a *yes* vote to the Treaty on the European Union in the referendum held in June. A number of factors explain this shift.

Firstly (and probably most important), the unification and *normalization* of Germany have led a number of Social Democratic leaders to believe that a Germany deeply integrated in the European Community is in the political interest of Denmark. Secondly, after the end of the Cold War, there is no longer any barrier to a European Community becoming the *anchor* in a broader European political architecture and what the Danish Social Democrats have labelled 'An Open Europe'. Thirdly, after the *negative* (eliminating barriers to trade, etc.) integration of the internal market, the European Community now needs a *positive* (i.e. new policies and institutions) integration in order to adjust or correct the market mechanism of the internal market according to the Social Democratic Party. Fourthly, in the meantime, some of the most influential trade unions have put strong pressure on the Social Democratic Party to become more pro-European (in spite of what is seen in other Northern European countries some strong Danish trade unions, like the Metal Workers' Federation, are more to the right in economic policy matters than the Social Democratic Party with which the trade unions have strong organizational links).

To the left of the Social Democratic Party, the Socialist People's Party (8% of the votes in the election in 1990) is still officially against the EC and the European Union. However, in the youth organization of the Socialist People's Party a large number of the members and leaders are now in favour of a closer European integration because of the potential benefits for the environment and the need for a stronger control with multinational companies. The main reason why the Socialist People's Party (like other Nordic left-wing parties, but contrary to most left-wing parties in the other EC Member States) is against the EC is that the integration is seen as a threat to the traditional Nordic Welfare State with its costly tax-financed redistributive policies.

To the right of the Social Democratic Party, the small centre parties, Christian People's Party (2% of the votes in the election in 1990), Centre Democrats (5% of the votes), and Radical Liberal Party (4% of the votes) differ in their attitudes towards the EC and European integration on the whole.

The Christian People's Party traditionally was pro-EC and pro-Single European Act, but the party has been split on the European Union issue. The Radical Liberal Party, on the other hand, recommended a *no* in the 1986 referendum, but is now in favour of a European Union for reasons similar to those of the Social Democratic Party. The founder of the Centre Democrats originally split from the Social Democratic Party in the beginning of the 1970s, partly because then there was too little enthusiasm on behalf of European integration in the Social Democratic

Party. Since then the Centre Democrats have been known for their strong pro-EC attitudes.

Both parties in the present Government, the Liberal Party (16% of the votes in the election in 1990) and the Conservative People's Party (18% of the votes) have always been strongly pro-EC. While the Liberal Party has maintained its position as the most pro-European political party (together with the Centre Democrats) in Denmark, within the Conservative Party some scepticism of the speed of European integration has arisen. In a way, the Conservative Party has dug up some of its traditional patriotic roots again.

On the right wing, the populist Progress Party (7% of the votes) is pro-EC, but officially against the European Union and recommended a *no* in the Danish referendum in June.

As can be seen, parties representing an overwhelming majority of the voters are in favour of the European Union. Among the voters in general, however, the situation is much more blurred. On the other hand, more than two-thirds of the voters claim to be pro-EC.

Gradually, the Danish population has become pro-European; especially among the younger generations, pro-European attitudes are strong. That does not mean that the scepticism about European integration will disappear altogether, especially if European integration takes a centralist direction. Therefore, much depends on the future interpretation by the Commission and European Court of the subsidiarity principle now in the Treaty of the European Union after pressure from e.g. the Danish Government during the Maastricht summit.

Another Danish worry is the defence provision in the Treaty on the European Union. All opinion polls show that a majority of the voters are against Danish membership of the WEU, even though some of the non-socialist parties are in favour of membership. Contrary to the situation in, for example, Norway and Sweden, pacifist attitudes are relatively strong in Denmark. The Socialist People's Party and the Radical Liberal Party are pacifist parties, but pacifism is also relatively strong in the Social Democratic Party.

Therefore, the strongest and most broadly accepted arguments in favour of full Danish participation in the European integration process have always emphasized economic benefits whereas in Norway (not least in the Norwegian Social Democratic Party) defence political arguments in favour of participation in the European integration process are often more accepted than the economic ones. In Norway, the WEU is seen as an opportunity to safeguard the defence of the country.

Also an issue like EMU is not a generally popular one among the Danish people, not for substantial reasons, but for symbolic reasons because it is necessary to give up the present notes and coins in kroner.

Conclusions: Implications for Business Strategy

The specific features of the Danish political system have implications for business in different ways. Firstly, there is no doubt that the political system in Denmark is a very harmonious one in international comparison. So, from a business perspective strategic and long-term decisions can be made without fear of any serious or radical political disturbance.

Secondly, the egalitarian political culture in Denmark puts some limitations on business, e.g. how can one motivate the labour force, how can one operate the business (flat hierarchies or networking are preferred), etc. Of course, these features may cause some problems for non-Danish firms operating in Denmark, unless they adapt. On the other hand, some of these cultural features are often mentioned as post-industrial values of the future.

Thirdly, because of the strong tradition for economic liberalism, it may be difficult for foreign firms to get the 'special treatment' from the administration and politicians that they might be used to. Probably a large number of foreign direct investments in Denmark have been lost on that account.

8. France: Shaping Factors*

INTRODUCTION

Anyone attempting to chart the future course of French society must at least first identify the forces which induce it to accept (actively or passively) or refuse the changes in question, as well as the areas in which it will be required to make these choices. In other words judgements have to be made about the forms of modernization and the adjustments necessary to obtain a relatively favourable position. It has become customary in many countries, including France, to cite the *outside world* as the single most important reason for moving down new paths, and to regard any change as entirely exogenous.

In actual fact, the policy of opening up to the outside world, pursued by France since the Monnet Plan has been a source of constant pressure in favour of change - change in methods of production as well as in patterns of consumption; and the incentive has continued to grow as markets and competition have become increasingly globalized and commercial borders increasingly permeable. In addition to this process of globalization there began to emerge, from the late 1950s onwards, a dynamic movement aimed at the gradual construction in Europe of an economic area without internal borders where, from 1993 onwards, goods and services, capital and people could move around freely.

Quite clearly, although they have occurred in very different ways, globalization and Europeanization are two vital engines in the development of French society, which will most likely continue to influence it and generate change even if the French people themselves are not always fully aware of the fact. Such change, however, will not occur in just any direction. It will depend to a large extent on the manner in which society decides or refuses to adapt.

The point is that socio-cultural changes give the distinct impression of being largely endogenous, in the sense that it is difficult to see for

---

*   R. Fraisse, B. Cazes, F. Descouyete and J.L. Levet.

example how from 1964 onwards, foreign influences could have caused the prolonged decline in fertility rates in every Western country, thus putting an end to the *baby-boom*. The fact that endogenous changes abound, however, does not make them any easier to detect in advance, because they are the - normally unexpected - product of an interaction between stable cultural traits[1] which represent what can best be termed *Frenchness*, the maximizing behaviour ascribed to *Homo oeconomicus*, and individualist-libertarian values, which are normally associated in France with May 1968 even though they date back much further than that.

Faced with this multiform pressure for and against change, France, like the other European countries concerned, has responded by seeking to partially modify its *modus operandi* in order to adapt to new needs - in short, by trying to modernize - while at the same time preserving anything that appeared too precious (or too jealously guarded) to be sacrificed on the altar of modernity. The main point to stress is that this modernization has gradually acquired a broader meaning.

The word was initially used in the 1945-65 period in a distinctly 'economic sense', to denote the constant updating of the economic system, in both material and human terms. During these two decades economic modernization was widely perceived as being of universal benefit, even though it invariably penalized certain sectors, technologies and skills, now rendered obsolete.

While support for economic modernization is perfectly understandable, since it is directly linked to the desire to regain the capacity to produce (and to act, more widely), after being crippled by defeat and German occupation, 'socio-cultural modernization', which surfaced both as an aspiration and a way of life from 1968 onwards, is more difficult to explain. Perhaps, as L. Roussel suggests,[2] we should see it as the delayed result of a long, slow process of demythification of social norms, which gradually robbed them of their transcendence by reducing them to the level of arbitrary conventions. This was to the great detriment of institutions such as marriage and the family, which had ensured the social integration of those who obeyed their rules. Another difference in relation to the previous type of modernization lies in the fact that the reference to foreign models, although not completely absent (witness the fascination with the Californian lifestyle in the 1950s) was secondary compared to the desire to get rid of as many collectively imposed

---

1   In the sense that in 1960, General de Gaulle concluded, after hearing a report on the changes occurring in the Japanese economy and society, 'at the end of the day, Japan will always be Japan!'

2   L. Roussel, *La famille incertaine*, Paris, Odile Jacob, 1991.

interdictions, sanctions and obligations as possible. This included an economic rationality whose behavioural implications (in terms of work, consumption, saving and attitudes to the environment) were for a time equated with the dictates of a repressive society. Modernization in those days, meant updating the rules which govern interhuman relations within marriage, families, at work, at university, etc. so as to make them more transparent and more egalitarian.

More insidiously, because here there was no warning shot of the May 68 variety, the past few years have seen a growing tide of feeling that what France needs now is 'political modernization', i.e. a review of the fundamental characteristics of the French political system, its 'referents and principal means of regulation' (Y. Mény).[3]

This third type of modernization, which has scarcely begun, is the most difficult to pinpoint because it seems to have been prompted by widely differing motives. Foremost of these is the economic motive, similar to that which underlies the first of the three types of modernization: the French tradition of a State which is 'a single player, prioritising and coordinating all activities relating to the common interest' (M. Crozier) often seems outmoded in a fiercely competitive world where one of the prime functions of the authorities is to assist civil society in its ongoing battle for innovation and competitiveness.

Then there is the socio-cultural motive: this same Unitarian, centralized State is increasingly perceived as incompatible with an individualist-consumerist concept of how public utilities should be run, i.e. just as in the case of commercial consumption, the 'client' should have his say and even a bit more. Then there is a rather special motive, linked, we believe, to the conviction that the sphere of political legitimacy does not necessarily coincide with the territory of the Nation State but may - and should - pertain to a wider area, such as the European Community framework, or even the entire planet, where one finds a higher form of legitimacy (that of human rights, or even the rights of the ecosphere, for instance). A. Touraine's historical interpretation[4] makes the point that while France has progressed from a period marked by socio-economic issues to the current period geared towards socio-cultural issues and identity-related concerns similar to the globalization of the economy, its political model has not adapted to accommodate this shift in the collective debate; so much so that France must now reinvent a national political

---

3   This report has used contributions from external experts, academics and research centres. The names mentioned in parenthesis in the text correspond to these contributions some of which are included in Volume II of the full report.

4   Interviewed by the compilers of this report.

model which reconstructs a positive link between economics (the international) and the socio-cultural-identity-related issues (the internal).

SECTION 1: THE FORCES OF CHANGE: PROSPECTS FOR THE FUTURE

As an initial analysis, it seems sensible to base our prospective study on those *shaping factors* which occur earliest on in the cause-and-effect sequences, in other words the forces of change themselves. We identify the following:

-    The 'trend towards the globalization' of trade and competition may develop in any of a number of ways. Although the consequences for Europe as a whole will obviously differ markedly from one scenario to another, the impact of each scenario will hardly vary at all from country to country. As a result, we can simply observe that, for better or worse, France will have to either continue adapting to the challenge posed by economic globalization, or endeavour to overcome the adverse effects of any refragmentation of the world market.

-    The 'dynamics of European integration' call for somewhat similar comments: a range of possibilities can be identified using long-range scenarios, but it still equates to the need for France to respond to any 'future shock', i.e. the continuation of the post-Maastricht deepening process (ibid.), accompanied however, relative to the previous force, by a more marked effort to adapt than in other countries.

-    Thirdly, we have 'endogenous changes', the workings of which have proved a source of fascination for social scientists, pollsters and business consultants alike, although it has to be said that their ability to anticipate the results has not made much progress since G. Berger first coined the term 'prospective study' in 1959. For the purposes of this study however, we will use the three stages suggested earlier: the inmost depths of the French personality, classic economic values, and the new values ('post-materialist' in R. Inglehart's terminology).

At the lowest level lies the 'French identity', a sort of genetic code, oft-mentioned yet seldom analysed, which has grown up over the centuries around the French language, humanist cultural heritage, republican values and the belief in the universal significance of Frenchness. According to the dominant view, the attachment to national identity is perceived as a sign of cultural archaism, which becomes increasingly significant the further down the social ladder you go. In the case of the French, things are more complex, because while it is true that the anti-immigration attitudes currently fuelling support for the National Front produce much nationalistic-xenophobic rhetoric, some observers believe that at grass roots level, the level of support for the National Front is not so much an indicator of the intensity of French nationalist feeling as an outlet for poorly educated, low-skilled groups haunted by the dual threat of unemployment, crime and social exclusion - and convinced that it stems from an overly lax immigration policy for which they alone are having to pay the price. There are other signs too, that nationalist concerns are not confined in France to the lowest levels of society: witness the so-called 'veil'[5] affair, which led many members of the professional classes to rediscover how much the separation between religion and the secular is still an integral part of the French political model, or the mixture of irritation and confusion periodically caused by the constant infiltration of the English language, in commercial and scientific fields.

More generally, we will posit the theory that everything that bears the stamp of 'tradition' - local political means of regulation, economic activities with strong, territorial roots such as farming - will be destined to appear as 'either obsolete or counter-productive, or on the contrary, will be perceived as hallowed traditions, to be safeguarded at any price' (Y. Mény). Two opposing forces will come into play: on the one hand, as J.-P. Rioux points out, 'people adrift in a state of social weightlessness' because less dependent than before on their membership of a particular class for their self-definition, will probably find themselves confronted with the issue of national identity. On the other hand, there will be constant tension between the defence and illustration of such and such a 'symbolic feature of the French character', particularly in the cultural sphere - the quality of spoken and written French, the place accorded to the classic humanities in an ever-changing school curricula, and the anti-elitist attitudes which underlie the quest for socio-cultural modernization, or the heavy emphasis on scientific and technical culture inherent in economic development.

Whatever obstacles lie ahead however, 'this search for an identity' cannot proceed without taking a long, hard look at what J.P. Rioux terms

---

5   Controversy which arose in 1990 over the wearing of the Islamic veil by some Muslim girls at state schools.

'the old factors of antagonism and division which for more than a century have kept alive an internal Franco-French war' (ibid.), whose periodic flare-ups give the French a feeling of being (still) very much a breed apart.

The intermediate stage - 'the attachment to material interests' - has often been interpreted as a sign of obsolescence, in much the same way as identity-related concerns: as general living standards rise, it was thought, qualitative concerns and in particular the desire to have more free time would prevail over the desire to acquire more material possessions. The answers gathered over the past ten years in the *Aspirations* surveys compiled by CREDOC,[6] however, would seem to suggest otherwise since between 1981 and 1991 the proportion of respondents who said they would prefer more purchasing power rather than more free time increased from 58% (compared with 41% choosing the other option) to 66% (compared with 33% making the opposite choice). You might well ask yourself however whether this balance between work, money and leisure (no doubt influenced by the actual change in purchasing power over the period) adequately expresses the profound trends in most French people's attitudes to material possessions. Another series of opinion polls, this time from SOFRES,[7] gives the distinct impression that through seemingly inconsistent choices made from a list of economic concepts with a strong ideological slant, the French clearly reaffirm:

> What they have been calling for in opinion polls for the past thirty years: despite the division of political life into two opposing camps, they want to see an economy, a society which promotes competition and participation, freedom and social justice.

Isn't this remarkable syncretism of aspirations in some way connected to the shift in French society towards a complex process of stratification, where the old tripartite structure of society - peasantry-proletariat-bourgeoisie - (cf. below) looks set to disappear ?

The most recent stage, 'socio-cultural values' favouring libertarianism, putting down roots, authenticity - or autonomy - throws up two paradoxes which might have weighty implications for a futures-oriented analysis.

The first paradox concerns the gap between the actual and the apparent significance of these values, in terms of their ability to take account of the

---

6   They were analysed in the paper commissioned by the CGP, submitted to the Forecasting Unit - cf. p. 95.

7   R. Cayrol, in SOFRES, *L'état de l'opinion*, Paris, Le Seuil, 1992.

changes in demographic patterns resulting from the advent of the 'permissive society'[8] which began in the mid-sixties, and evidence of which can be seen in the changes in birth rates, the number of marriages and the proportion of births outside marriage. Interestingly, the modernism/traditionalism indicator devised by CREDOC[9] shows that in the course of the 1980s, the modernists initially gained five points (from 11 to 16%) only to end up back where they started by 1990. The traditionalists meanwhile lost five points in total (from 15 to 10%), without benefiting from the setback suffered by the modernists. By the end of the decade, both groups were still very much in a minority, like the 'materialist' and 'post-materialist' categories borrowed from R. Inglehart and used in the regular surveys conducted by Euro-Barometer.

The second paradox lies in the fact that towards the mid-eighties, the 'age' variable ceases to correlate, at least in France, with the answers to a question about whether the respondent would prefer gradual changes in society, radical changes or things to remain as they were. Up until 1982-83 the preference for or against 'radicalism' varied according to the age groups, with support for radical changes going hand in hand with youth. Today it can be seen that for all age groups combined, the division occurs between people with few or no qualifications and those educated to A-level standard and beyond. The same inversion moreover can be seen, albeit less noticeably, in the favourable or critical opinions expressed with regard to the running of the judicial system or technical progress.

Curiously enough, this paradoxical correlation in the 'level of education' variable recurs, in a completely different context, in the SOFRES[10] surveys which highlight the increasing role played by the level of education in shaping public opinion on certain major issues such as immigration, economy, social mores and international matters. One less obvious result of the new role played by education is that the Left is attracting growing support among the educated classes, whereas the Right can now count on more support from people with few or no qualifications.

All this is bound to have far-reaching implications for the future course of French politics.

---

8   See the CGP report, *Entrer dans le XXIème siècle,* Chapter 2, Paris, La Découverte/ Documentation Française, 1990.

9   The term *modernist* is applied to respondents who consider that the family is not the only place where one can feel happy and relaxed, that marriage can be dissolved just through the agreement of both parties, that women should always work, or at least if they so wish. A traditionalist is someone who takes the opposite view: the family is the only place, etc., marriage is an indissoluble union, women should never work (or at least not if they have young children) (Op. cit.).

10   J. Jaffré, *Le gouvernement des instruits,* in L'Etat de l'Opinion 1992, op. cit.

SECTION 2: THREE TYPES OF MODERNIZATION IN PROSPECT

Three types of modernization must be considered: economic, socio-cultural and political.

The chronological gap which separates the advent of these three types of modernization should not mislead us into thinking that the oldest, 'economic modernization', has become the least topical, even though it has shifted its ground. As far back as forty years ago, when preparations for the 2nd Plan were under way, the Commissaire-General for the Plan, E. Hirsch, explained to F. de Wendel,[11] who was wondering how after all the investments already made, there could be any question of modernizing iron and steel firms still further, that 'modernity is not a definitive state', but rather on ongoing process.

Despite the anxiety which invariably accompanied each new stage in the process of opening up to the outside world, the French economy has certainly risen to the challenge of globalization: as the fourth-largest world exporter, with OECD countries accounting for more than 80% of its export sales, France is well ahead of Japan in terms of exports per capita ($3,215 compared with $1,950 for Japan). In thirty years, the wealth generated in France has increased threefold, while consumption per capita increased nearly as much between 1975 and 1990 as between 1960 and 1975.

It would be unwise however, particularly from a long-term perspective, to dismiss certain trouble spots or structural difficulties, which are a continuing source of concern.

Firstly, France has a 'growing foreign trade deficit' in certain key areas such as 'electrical and electronic engineering and domestic appliances', a problem admittedly shared by other European countries.

France also seems to be suffering from a 'lack of competitiveness' in a number of sectors with a high proportion of SMEs, such as the processing of materials, mechanical engineering and everyday consumer goods. According to the BIPE,[12] there is a high risk that this could undermine the country's industrial fabric and seriously hamper major groups who rely on SMEs for supplies or services.

More generally, the speed of technological change and the degree of competition tend to reduce the number of jobs and increase the rate at

---

11   Chief executive officer of a large iron and steel firm.
12   Bureau d'Information et de Prévisions Economiques, a leading consulting firm.

which human resources are rendered obsolescent. In the case of France, this has led to an increased preference for capital rather than labour, a tendency to take on young, low-skilled workers for longer periods of time, with no guarantee of permanent employment, and an increase in the number of early retirements for employees of a certain age, regarded as incapable of adapting to technological change. As the pool of workers diminishes for purely demographic reasons, firms will have to compete more fiercely to attract the various skills deemed vital in both intra- and extra-EC competition (scientists, engineers, technicians, researchers and salesmen).

Meanwhile we will see growing disparities within the workforce between those who have sheltered employment (through statutory job security and barriers to entry), and those who are regarded as less employable, and are hence confined to the fringes of stable employment, insecure jobs and unemployment (C. Seibel).

These concerns, as we have seen, are not confined to economic modernization. Past experience suggests in fact that the boundaries between the three types of modernization are not as clear-cut as previously thought. Firstly because the *aggiornamento* of institutions or procedures have objectives which are more than just economic (in France in particular, schools have throughout modern history been a means of integrating culturally disparate communities and a means of detecting future public and even private elites), and secondly because the reforms thus implemented have widely differing repercussions, which are not always easy to gauge.

Has 'socio-cultural modernization' reached its natural term? The extent of the changes which have taken place in the status of women (cf. below) and in the family sphere would suggest that it has, subject to a close look at those points where further change is needed (sharing duties between husbands and wives?). On the other hand, there is a strong feeling that in certain areas of key importance to economic activity such as human relations within the firm, inter-company relations and training, the current situation is far from optimum, 'although it is unclear how we should set about improving it'.

Whether it be a question of 'social relations within firms or links between firms', company managers appear to be divided between two coexistent models: on the one hand, there is the so-called 'integrating' model, based on job security, pay scales established by means of agreements, strong staff commitment to the corporate values, and partnership-type relations with banks, suppliers and sub-contractors;

alongside this, we have the liberal model, or rather the 'commercial' model, which favours a flexible workforce and little personal involvement on the part of the staff, with relations with other firms being conducted on an essentially contractual basis. The obvious parallel between the so-called integrating model and Japanese and German firms undoubtedly adds to its appeal, but the fact that it is rooted in a specific culture only distantly related to French culture makes it very difficult to transpose, except in the form of some hybrid version which combines the best of both. The debate on the modernization of the France's socio-productive model has only just begun.

The French 'education system' is similarly torn between, if not models, at least fairly incompatible aims, which are aptly summed up in two words: consistency and excellence. According to F. Gaussen[13] the French education system has come closer to achieving the 'reforming Utopia' than any other European country because thanks to its high degree of centralization, it has managed to combine two systems within a single school, mass education and the selection of elites which in the rest of Europe have basically remained separate. In the view of many French people, this has led to a 'hybrid pedagogical compromise, with an average standard which is too demanding for the weakest yet too low for the best', because it provides for neither a gradual initiation into social integration nor close monitoring of the most able pupils. Vocational training fares no better, in so far as the technical colleges which provide it within the framework of the National Education (France is one of the few countries in the world where this is so) are hamstrung, despite their efforts, by insufficient links with industry (ibid.), a situation which is no doubt partly to blame for the extremely high level of unemployment among young people in France.

'Political modernization' appears under a very different guise from the two previous types. The reference for economic modernization is towards the 'state of the art', although this is beyond the actual level being sought to be made up. The latter is determined on the basis of widely accepted cost-benefit criteria. What's more, these same criteria influence microeconomic behaviour at grass roots level, in such a way as to eliminate any obsolete practices. Although in the case of socio-cultural modernization the weight of the past and tradition are certainly more keenly felt, it is nevertheless true that micro-social behaviour criteria which were governed by more 'modern' values have year after year

---

13   *La formation: le 'modèle français' dans la concurrence internationale*, in R. Lenoir et J. Lesourne (eds.), Où va l'Etat?; Paris, Le Monde Editions, 1992.

ignored established social norms, and the sheer numbers involved have prompted legislators to seriously consider whether the law should not be updated. Conversely, it can be seen that in areas of social activity such as labour relations, where any questioning of the rules was only temporary and sporadic, modernization - whatever that may mean in this particular instance (see page 212) - has made much less headway.

Political modernization is in some respects similar to the previous type. In many cases the institutions and regulatory mechanisms at stake have considerable symbolic value: consider the emotional impact, in France at least, of the three short words 'government of judges', which were used to pour scorn on the Constitutional Council or the EC institutions! Consider too, the decentralization which began in 1982 in favour of local and regional authorities and the anguish which it has caused over the principle of the unity of public authority! Thus it is that accusations of obsolescence or counter-productivity can be rejected in the name of some fine-sounding principle, to ridicule which would allegedly be to strike at the very core of the French identity.

There is a strong likelihood however that the *grass roots* changes which have rendered many of the norms and conventions in conjugal and family life obsolete will also occur, *mutatis mutandi,* in the public domain, thus rendering certain long-standing rules defunct. One such example is the French model of public policy, whereby the State intervenes on a sector-by-sector basis and professional groups of experts, operating within the Administration (civil servants) or outside the government (e.g. the farming profession)[14] look after the interests of the people concerned. One clear symptom of this crisis is the fact that the 'non-sectorized' areas - cities, poverty, unemployment, the environment, rural areas - where the traditional, sectorized State has great trouble finding credible, consistent solutions, are giving rise to the emergence of public policy making at the local level to *bypass* the faltering state-corporatist system and take its place (even to the extent of repeating its mistakes).

This *bypass* strategy does not have all the answers however, as will no doubt become increasingly apparent as time goes on. The judicial system, it would seem, is already a case in point. It has been pointed out for example[15] that in France, the lawful State remains incomplete, despite recent improvements, in so far as the Constitution does not recognize judicial power but merely judicial authority, based on a Jacobin concept of sovereignty which makes it very difficult to develop arbitration through

---

14   See article by P. Muller, Revue Française des Sciences Politiques, 1992-2.
15   B. Barret-Kriegel, *La République insuffisante*, Libération, 25.3.92.

law.   Viewed from this angle, 'the current insurrection by the magistrature' is not a short-term phenomenon but rather 'the result of the inevitable tension between the democratic need for law and the political refusal to substitute judicial arbitration for administrative authority'.

The future of French society, such as we have tried to understand it through the various forces of change and modernization at work in the country, can now be more closely defined, by considering the following in turn:

- The French and their territory.
- Their main institutions.
- The future of certain social groups.

SECTION 3 : THE FRENCH AND THEIR TERRITORY

'France's long-term socio-demographic development' is much the same as in other EC countries (with the exception of Ireland), i.e. a low fertility-rate (which has stabilized at around 1.8 children per woman), longer life expectancy and shorter working lives.   As a result, the age structure becomes inverted, with an increase in the number of elderly people and a steady decline in the number of young people: assuming that the fertility-rate remains at 1.8 and that mortality decreases at a faster rate than past trends suggest, the over-60s and under-20s will, for the first time in history, account for the same percentage, 23.5%, whereas in 1990 the respective shares of the two age groups were 19% and 27.5%.   It seems likely that France, whose family policy devised at the time of the Second World War is better suited than elsewhere to current needs (increase in the cost of having a child, high number of working mothers), and Sweden, which has been pursuing an original family policy for the past ten years, will be the only two Western countries where the new generations born in the 1950s, will produce 'sufficient offspring to ensure population replacement'.

The 'grey revolution' will have numerous long-term repercussions.   Its impact on pension schemes and healthcare systems has already been extensively studied,[16] even if practical measures aimed at redirecting collective efforts (caring for elderly relatives, preventing social exclusion, revising methods of financing pensions) are slow in coming.

---

16   Cf. in particular the White Paper on pensions, Paris, La Documentation Française, 1991.

Changes in the overall population likewise affect the 'potential working population'. The latter is tending to grow increasingly slowly, and from the nineties onwards should start to fall off, going from +150,000 per year to +90,000 by the beginning of the next century. The reversal in the trend could be delayed by fifteen years or so by a rise in the number of working women, to match the number of working men by the year 2000 (for average ages 25-55 years), but this would clearly require major 'changes in childcare arrangements'. Similarly, if the future health of our pension schemes is to be preserved, the 'retirement age for men will probably have to be raised', as is already happening in Northern Europe, the United States and Japan. In France however, this would mean a significant departure from the pattern of the past fifteen years, whereby more and more fifty- and sixty-year-olds have been taking early retirement. This ageing working population, with its low replacement rate, will in turn pose the problem of 'adapting to technological progress': will it mean a huge number of underqualified people? Will it be possible to retrain a workforce which has good *on-the-job* skills but whose standard of formal education is undoubtedly weaker than in other countries such as Germany? (C. Seibel).

Having long believed that it enjoyed only the best aspects of 'rurality and modern urban life', thanks notably to its omnipresent agriculture and low-profile industrial fabric, France is now undergoing a gradual, yet irresistible change whereby it could well lose out on both fronts, through a simultaneous dearth and welter of people; and this applies as much to the French islands and overseas territories as it does to France itself.

Firstly, the natural areas with which France is so liberally endowed (they make up 95% of the national territory and account for a quarter of the EC's natural areas) are being slowly but steadily eaten away by urbanization and infrastructures, while the spread of farmland going-out of production is causing the land to degenerate by turning it into wasteland.

At the same time, the way in which the population is distributed over the territory is becoming increasingly unbalanced. Very roughly, we can assume that in 1900, 50% of French people occupied half of the territory. On the eve of the Second World War, the ratio was 60:40. By 1970, i.e. thirty years later, it was 70:30. It took just twenty years to reach a ratio of 80:20, and 'it is perfectly possible that by the end of the century, 90% of French people will be living on one tenth of the national territory'. This powerful trend seems to be linked to the globalization of markets and the rise of the tertiary sector, but it is also influenced by the highly discriminating effects of high-speed public transport facilities (motorways, air connections, high-speed trains) which create a loosely-knit network in which the *hub* towns and cities derive an enormous advantage in terms of speed and frequency of access. This 'dismemberment of the territories'[17] generates very high investment and running costs: it is estimated that Parisians lose 7.5 million working hours every day due to traffic jams, i.e. the equivalent of one working day for the population of Lyons. It may also be partly to blame for the 'growing decline' of numerous 'suburbs', where poverty tends to become hereditary and goes hand in hand with social marginalization.

This hyper-concentration leads in turn to under-population in the most remote rural areas, where the shrinking number of inhabitants makes it increasingly expensive to maintain a minimum level of public services (an extreme example being provided by the department of Aveyron, where in order to pick up schoolchildren, 900 coaches have to make a daily trip of 40 kilometres, which is equivalent to the circumference of the globe).

The strategies needed in order to redress this imbalance will not come from any traditional French solutions, in other words, a combination of sectoral public policies. Instead they will emerge from this new *troika* - State, local authorities, European Community - which is gradually taking shape and which will require a firm commitment to adapt from each partner. The State will have to learn other rules and in so doing, get used to the new 'European public area'[18] defined by subsidiarity and the social market economy. Local authorities, which must overcome the serious handicap of a century old past where local elected representatives' ability to implement public policies was systematically curbed, will for their part have to concede that continued decentralization cannot indiscriminately benefit the 36,500 French towns, but primarily the regions and cities. This would be followed up, with a view to maintaining the overall cohesion, by an evaluation of local public policies and reinforcement of jurisdictional controls by local authorities.[19] As for the EC authorities, they must realize that they will be passing up the chance to recreate a more balanced urban fabric if they too yield to the obsession with vast metropolises and/or give free rein to the trend towards greater concentration, engendered by high-speed transport: better to adapt *all* towns to new criteria in terms of competition and solidarity than to end up with a Europe dominated by a few prestigious cities (C. Lacour).

17　J.L. Guigou, *La dislocation des territoires*, Le Monde, 3-4 May 1992.
18　P. Muller, op. cit.
19　Y. Mény, in *Où va l'Etat?*, op. cit., pp. 132 etc.

SECTION 4 : INSTITUTIONS GREATLY INFLUENCED BY ECONOMIC GLOBALIZATION AND CHANGING MENTALITIES

Institutions are a difficult proposition. Some give the impression of being immune to change, whereas behind this outer veneer of stability radical transformations are under way. Others by contrast affirm their commitment to modernization yet nevertheless continue to trundle along in their present groove as long as circumstances allow. Not forgetting those institutions whose credibility seems to have been badly undermined and whose actual situation is as serious as it looks. France offers fertile scope for observation in this respect, with a wide variety of situations.

First and foremost, one notes a marked decline in certain 'symbolic institutions' (H. Mendras) such as the Catholic Church, the Army, the trade unions and the Communist Party which, in days gone by, inspired equally fierce loyalties and aversions. Within this fairly disparate group, 'trade unions' are particularly relevant to us because of their pivotal role between economy and society, and because their long-term decline would mean that French society will be entering the next century with a system of consultation which is ill-equipped to act as an instrument of dialogue between management and workers. It is worth noting however that alongside the growing doubts cast on the credibility and representativeness of the unions, the percentage of employees who believe that they do not have enough influence rose steadily throughout the past decade, 'a sure sign that a trade union revival is possible, providing the ways and means are used to good effect'.[20]

The institution of 'marriage', in France as indeed in the whole of Northern Europe (with the South lagging slightly behind), is losing ground to contracts negotiated between private individuals and which can thus be rescinded at any time by either partner. With sexual relations made easier thanks to the pill, which eliminates the risk of unwanted pregnancies, marriage is becoming less and less a formal prelude to sex, living together and having children.

This type of contractual relationship moreover does not just govern conjugal life but tends to permeate 'the general system of the family',[21] and in particular, parent/child relations: in the absence of any cast-iron criteria, parents will tend to forbid their children from doing only those things which actually 'threaten the health of the child or his education.

---

[20] R. Soubie, in SOFRES, L'Opinion publique, Le Seuil, 1992
[21] L. Roussel, op. cit.

What's more, their children will take little or no heed' (ibid.). Within a few decades we have thus seen an entire institution - marriage - decline both quantitatively and in terms of its prescriptive role, thereby transforming the institution of the family, and giving a whole new meaning to the word. While in terms of its central core, the family unit appears to be dwindling and coming apart (fewer instances of different generations living under one roof, fewer children, couples separating), it tends to be expanding vertically, due to the fact that grandparents are living longer. Three-generation families have become the norm and four-generation families are increasingly common; within this family network, there are still strong bonds, which play an important role in times of crisis (J.- C. Chesnais).

Strictly speaking, the group of totally or partially non-market-related activities covered by the 'Welfare State' comprises four main functions - the elderly, healthcare, unemployment, the family. In a society where the proportion of elderly people is steadily rising and where national insurance contributions are seen to be of a less 'fiscal' nature than tax, the performance of these first two functions has helped preserve the Welfare State from the fate suffered by the symbolic institutions. Despite the widespread support regularly expressed in the opinion polls however, every now and again the Welfare State attracts sharp criticism, for a variety of reasons:

-    Its recurrent financial problems due to increased spending on pensions and sickness benefits.
-    Its poor performance in terms of redistribution (to the point that the RMI scheme had to be set up alongside it).
-    And finally, its alleged role in aggravating unemployment, owing to the fact that it is funded by national insurance contributions which increase the cost of labour.

The State as 'creator of the social link' (P. Rosanvallon) will also no doubt come in for its fair share of criticism, because the goals which it will be called upon to pursue are in themselves fairly incompatible. In education matters, a function which France has traditionally regarded as the sole preserve of the central State, families expect the latter to maintain a high standard of excellence, to ensure that as many pupils as possible gain the *baccalauréat*, leading to higher education, and to integrate those elements of society which are most resistant to socialization, with a teaching profession where pay is linked to qualifications much more than classroom performance.

The last group of institutions is in a sense the most important as it encompasses both large- and medium-sized 'firms' and the 'Nation State'. Unlike the first group, it has lost nothing of its sacred aura (quite the reverse in fact where firms are concerned!). Nor has it been threatened by the *privatization* of husband-wife relations noted in connection with the formation of households, or the rather cynical *consumerism* which often plagues the Welfare State. Both businesses and the State however, are 'under pressure to become denationalized' as it were, a process which ultimately tends to remove them from any allegiance or reference to a particular national framework. The two exogenous forces mentioned earlier - globalization and Europeanization - contribute to this process in varying forms and degrees, with widely differing reactions.

'French firms', assisted moreover by major improvements in efficiency in terms of transport facilities and communications, have in fact proved that they were perfectly capable of transcending national borders and choosing where to operate from according to which site offered the best value for money in terms of materials and, above all, human resources in each geographical area. What's more, the efforts made by many firms (and not just in Japan!) to adapt their internal organization in order to remain competitive, and in particular to *detaylorize* their manufacturing processes, are evidently in keeping with the vocational expectations of the youngest and most educated members of the working population.

On the other hand, owing to its historical territorial roots, and its enduring symbolic value for the French people, the 'Nation State' still has enormous problems coping with the challenge of *denationalization*. Coming up with a credible response which is neither desperate withdrawal into the national sanctuary nor docile renunciation of any legitimate identity is one of the most important tasks for *futures* studies.

SECTION 5: THE SOCIAL GROUPS: A 'CENTRAL CONSTELLATION' WITH NUMEROUS SPLITS

Echoing the decline of the symbolic institutions, there are signs of a gradual erosion in the sociological divisions which have long split society into three homogenous and antagonistic classes - the middle class, the working class and the peasantry. In its place, a much less disparate structure is beginning to emerge, where a fairly high number of socio-professional groups gravitate around 'a central constellation' of managers, engineers and intermediate professions.[22]   This silent shift is accompanied, logically enough, by more uniform, market driven, consumer habits, with the majority of French people concurring in their tendency to increase (or reduce) the relative share of the same consumer items, show the same fascination with fitness and health and devote 40% of their free time to watching TV.   When interviewed by pollsters, moreover, an increasing number seem to think that the distinction between Right and Left is no longer any guide to the stances adopted by the different parties and politicians (33% in 1981, 55% in 1991).   The majority, too, express their support for a good honest mixture of competition and participation, freedom and social justice, the raising of moral standards in public affairs and a greater sense of responsibility towards the environment (SOFRES 1992).

The fact that the classic tripartite social structure is giving way to a looser set-up, however, does not mean that the social fabric of French society is becoming increasingly uniform.   What we are in fact seeing, is the emergence of socio-demographic groups which, linked as they are to differentiation by age and gender, have always existed yet have certain original features which encourage us to see them if not as new social classes, then at least as a sign of things to come.

The most difficult group to pinpoint is 'young people', because any reference to a supposedly 'young' age group is bound to be rather arbitrary.   The interest devoted to this category is not due to the fact that it displays a degree of cohesion and self-awareness similar to that formerly ascribed to the working class.   Rather it is a question of highlighting a qualitative change which occurs in the transition between leaving full-time education and entering adult life, as marked by two 'rites of passage', the start of one's career and marriage.

Twenty odd years ago, this transition, which was relatively brief moreover, was usually over by the age of 24.   A combination of factors - the raising of the school-leaving age, greater problems finding a stable job after leaving full-time education or military service, people getting married for the first time later and later (if at all) has meant that the intermediate period between adolescence and the entry into adult life has been postponed and extended, a period 'between 16 and 28 when young people live in unstable circumstances, with the help of social welfare and their parents'.[23]

---

22   cf. H. Mendras, *La seconde révolution française 1965-1984*, Paris, Gallimard, 1988.
23   L. Dirn, *La société française en tendances*, Paris, Presses Universitaires de France, 1991.

It is not so much a specific age group therefore - the 16-28-year-old - which gives this group its distinctive character as the 'relatively unstructured nature of the social environment in which young people move'. By the same token, it is perfectly possible that this period might extend beyond the age of 28 for those who fail to find jobs, or begin earlier than the age of 16 for those who experience serious family and/or education problems. Young people (*lato sensu*) can thus be regarded as a high-risk group because they are at the intersection of several trends whose combined effect could be highly disruptive: looser and more precarious family structures which make it harder to integrate children into society, a labour market which has little to offer first-time job seekers in the way of secure employment, plus of course the probable spread of crime, practised on an increasingly global scale, and perfectly capable of providing not only drugs to combat the despair experienced by some young people but also a lucrative career for which no formal qualifications are required.

Unlike young people, whose relative share of the total population is steadily declining, 'the elderly' - conventionally defined as those over the age of 65 - are growing in both absolute and relative terms. This trend, which can be seen in all the industrialized countries, is one of those rare stable factors on which a twenty-year study can safely rely. What is less certain is how best to tackle the two main issues raised by this general trend towards an ageing population:

(a)   A society where people over the age of 65 account for more than 20% of the population has no historical precedent on which to draw when it comes to planning its future. Is there a risk that it will become less and less receptive to technological innovation and cultural diversity, as Alfred Sauvy feared? Or should we share H. Mendras' belief that these 'new-age pensioners' will be so different from their predecessors from the point of view of material resources and standard of education that they will succeed in forming a 'leisure class', inventing new lifestyles?

(b)   How will we reconcile these two conflicting forces, whereby workers deemed to be too old will be edged out of the job market at an ever earlier age in order to make way for younger workers who represent better value for money for their employers, but whose pension rights will be increasingly jeopardized by the financial difficulties besetting the Welfare State? Admittedly, in the long run, slower growth followed by decline in the working population will lessen the effects of the first trend.

Viewed overall, *women* have not only gained a significant and thus far growing advantage over men in terms of longer life expectancy. From a future development point of view, the crucial factor is that their economic role and their place in society have undergone a sea change over the past thirty years, in both the private and professional spheres.

With regard to the conjugal and family sphere, we need merely point out that the status of women has changed with dramatic improvements in their standard of education (in many cases higher than that of their partner), the revolution in contraceptives (which gives women control over family planning) and financial independence (despite the remaining differences in pay). After years of being treated as minors, women have gradually acquired new rights. They 'have also greatly reinforced the formally paternal role with regard to children'.[24] In so far as behind all the instability of present and future demographic trends the mother figure represents the permanent element for the child, a 'matrilinear matrimonial model'[25] is beginning to emerge. Once again, this model has no precedent and as such is bound to affect the way children are integrated into society. Brought up differently, in many cases with no brothers or sisters despite the high-number of remarriages, these children will be different from their elders. What we are seeing therefore, is the emergence of a new social matrix, which produces a new type of person. Whether or not he or she will be any better equipped to cope with the complex private and vocational environment which lies ahead remains to be seen (J.- C. Chesnais).

From a professional point of view, women's determination to achieve independence by pursuing a career appears equally irreversible. Current projections for the working population cite women as a major source of growth in the labour pool, although there is major uncertainty over the long-term importance of part-time jobs. This growing proportion of women in the workforce may well come as something of a shock to human resources managers, whose approach has always been based on situations where the workforce was predominantly male. Perhaps in the long run it will trigger a new dynamism, as an antidote to the effects of an ageing population.

---

24 E. Sullerot, in Futuribles, 1991, op. cit.
25 L. Roussel, op. cit.

It would be going too far to speak of 'immigrants' as a fourth emergent social group. France, after all, has been taking in immigrants for more than a century now in order to offset its dwindling birth-rate, although it was loath to admit the fact. The novelty lies not in any change in the proportion of immigrants in the total population, the current figure being similar to the pre-1914 percentage or that recorded in the 1930s. It has more to do with changes in the demographic origin of the immigrants, non-European countries and in particular North Africa, Black Africa and more latterly, Turkey, having accounted for a growing share in the period 1960-75.

There is no doubt that the socio-cultural characteristics of these newcomers have created and will continue to create greater adjustment problems than previous waves of immigrants from European countries. The fact that immigration has become the focus of heated political debate and that one party in particular has made anti-immigration policies its main platform should not mislead us into thinking that this is the country's number 1 problem, which could be solved by restoring 'France to the French' and sending the foreigners back where they came from.

If the immigration issue is of anything other than temporary significance, it is because it highlights two closely linked aspects of French society, which merit our attention:

- Alongside the immigrants, the growing number of people who also have a real problem with 'integration',[26] or more accurately, 'exclusion'.
- The diminishing capacity of certain institutions to create a social bond between French people, either because they are not really attuned to the spirit of the times, or because - as with the institution of marriage - they are tailored to the expectations and aspirations of those sections of society for whom the problem of integration hardly ever arises.

From a purely societal point of view therefore, immigrants are but one manifestation of a central problem which affects all so-called post-modern societies, namely the co-existence in their midst of two seemingly conflicting trends: on the one hand, the gradual uniformization of life-styles (beyond the charming idiosyncrasies which individualism tends to

---

[26] Meaning 'the process whereby individuals participate in collective life through work, learning the norms of consumption, adapting their family and social behaviour patterns, establishing relations with others' (D. Schnapper, *L'Europe des immigrés*, Paris, Editions F. Bourin, 1991, p. 18).

generate) according to a common model born in the United States, and on the other, the division of society into three strata, namely a relatively homogenous central constellation which practises a sort of ideological syncretism, a professionally mobile *superclass*, steeped in a cosmopolitan culture and finally, a poorly integrated *underclass*, with a disproportionate number of young people, immigrants and unskilled people, and who unlike the previous two groups are susceptible to extreme points of view.

This dialectic between domestic socio-cultural dynamics and exogenous driving forces is also operating in the wider Community context. National specificities, undoubtedly as lively as in France, will interact at the European level. But what kind of Europe will result?

French Economic Players and the Future of European Integration

Although European integration in the immediate future as far as companies are concerned is a matter of rules, regulations and the single market, on the other hand, twenty years from now, what matters to them will obviously be the degree of consistency attained by industrial Europe, which for them is the backbone of the European design.

Indeed, the questions and strategic views of large French companies operating in a competitive field (irrespective of whether their shareholding public is public, private or mixed) with regard to European integration by 2010 can today be differentiated into three main categories:

* Firms which have succeeded in acquiring a 'solid national base' and are in a position to become Europeanized (groups in the manufacturing sector, for example).
* Firms 'in the process of Europeanization' already possessing a multinational organization and identity (Sommer-Allibert in plastics processing, GEC-Alsthom in the railway industry, BSN in agri-foodstuffs, CMB Packaging).
* Firms which have already achieved the *status* of European champion, 'and which are currently in the process of globalization' (e.g. Saint-Gobain, Usinor, Schneider).

It can nevertheless be seen that French firms, including small- and medium-sized enterprises (SME) and small- and medium-sized industries (SMI), have something in common in their vision of European integration and in their expectations in this regard. This results from asking oneself four different questions: What long-term objectives do they set themselves within the European framework? What are the structural changes they would have to face up to? What resources would they wish to have at their disposal in order to respond to these needs? What role could public sector/private sector dialogue play?

Firms' Objectives

The vast majority of French firms, with the exception of some SMEs and SMIs which have been considerably destabilized by the economic recession, a priori are confident as to what the creation of an economic Europe can bring them. The majority consider that the various measures contained in the Single Act will have a favourable and lasting impact on their business. Mutual recognition of standards and the harmonization of national policies with regard to third countries are identified as the most important stakes.[27]

This optimism over Europe is not borne out by the facts however, because more than 50% of industrial firms still realize most of their turnover in France. Even among France's top 300 industrial groups (except for the top 20), 20% still realize more than 50% of their turnover on the home market. With international expansion still a long way off, firms are very much alive to the issue of European integration. Their strategy revolves around three main objectives.

Objective Number One: To Rediscover at European Level the Advantages of Proximity Offered by a National Market

This does not mean working within an expanded domestic market protected from world competition as was formerly the case in France. On the contrary, firms consider - and the facts moreover indicate that they are right - that France is now one of the most open markets of the EC countries and, on a wider scale, of all the industrialized countries: 31% of France's domestic market is covered by imported industrial products, as against, for example, 29.2% in Great Britain, 24.8% in Germany and 22% in Italy.

Consequently, a great many French firms whose domestic market will be subject to very strong competitive pressures and which have had a tendency to promote the advantages of proximity which a national market offers (relations with subcontractors, fluidity of exchanges of experience,

---

[27] The *France 300* study carried out by Bain and Co. at the request of the Department of Industry confirms these points.

a coherent fiscal system) would like to rediscover these advantages at European level. Three expectations are clearly perceptible here.

Gradual Installation of the Single Legal and Fiscal Market

Following installation of the single market in 1993, this should make the conduct of business throughout the whole of the European territory fiscally neutral as well as enabling fiscal integration to be organized to facilitate industrial development.

Exchanges of Know-How and Skills

Of all the factors explaining the extension of the sphere of activity of firms at world level, 'technology' is judged to be the most important in the long term. Because of the increase in costs of research and size of risks, a great many developments will only be affordable in the future if they are planned for a large number of markets. The dispersion of sources of technology will compel firms to disseminate their research centres where the best skills are situated. Furthermore, the rate of development of the technologies will no longer enable markets to be attacked one after the other: products become obsolete too quickly and patent right protection rules are too fragile for this approach to remain effective.

Access to know-how, exchange of skills, and mobility of people will thus be determining factors in firms' competitiveness. Development of sound industrial connections between main contractors and subcontractors, between big groups and small- and medium-sized businesses, and between industrialists and distributors will ensure for the economy the necessary strength and flexibility to enable both better mastery of the European market, stronger resistance to external shocks and greater attractiveness for the world capital of groups looking for new locations. The single European market must provide such advantages and be built on the basis of the multiple ties developed between the spheres of 'education, research, production, distribution and banking'.

A Favourable Financial Environment

French companies are all the more aware of this subject since they consider that in France they are generally placed at a disadvantage in comparison with their foreign competitors. The excessive level of short-

and long-term interest rates is the main handicap cited by these companies. They also suffer badly from the strictures of the French banking system (in terms of flexibility and costs), even though the banks are their indispensable partners and are still their main moneylenders. They therefore expect of European integration that the effects of greater competition will contribute to improving the services offered by the banks. Finally, they consider that free movement of capital will be one of the beneficial effects of European integration.

Objective Number Two: To Defend the Interests of French Companies in Europe

In April 1992, fourteen big French companies - including Rhône-Poulenc, EDF, Usinor-Sacilor and Lyonnaise des Eaux - announced the creation of the French Association of Companies for the Environment and decided to devote 15 billion francs to cleaning up discharges of toxic products. Indeed, a new industrial lobby has just been born. In effect, industrialists are realizing that their 'systems of influence' in the French administration are no longer adequate, nor suitable for environmental matters. It is in Brussels that the standards governing emissions of gas by automobiles are fixed; it was at the Planet Earth summit in Rio in June 1992 that the idea of a tax on emissions of carbon gas, responsible for global warming, was fought for.

More generally, the French Association of Private Companies, which includes the biggest French companies, a few years ago created a body responsible for defending their interests in Brussels on fiscal and legal matters, etc. French groups have recently started to provide themselves with permanent agencies in Brussels. These initiatives, however, fall far short of those of their European competitors, and even the Japanese: companies such as Fiat or Mercedes Benz have 50 to 100 people in their permanent delegations. Of the 4,000 lobbyists present in Brussels, the French represent less than a hundred. French companies are, nevertheless, gradually becoming aware that Brussels has become a decision-making centre in its own right. They will have to participate far more in development of the European administrative environment and they must have influential power equal to that of their competitors.

French companies are also keen that, parallel to their individual and collective initiatives, the French Government should have effective relays in order to have their essential interests respected: in particular, they consider that France's presence is too weak in certain areas of the Commission which they regard as strategic.

Objective Number Three : To Harmonize the Conditions of Competition Between Europe, Asia and North America by Balanced Concessions

> The car industry represents 10% of European employment and I cannot see why we should sacrifice a million people in France on the altar of a free exchange system which only exists in speeches made by the naive and hypocrites. It is a question of reciprocity: today we sell ten Japanese cars in Europe as against one European car in Japan, whereas on markets where true competition exists, we do at least as well as them declared J.Y. Helmer, a Director since 1989 of the Automobile Branch of PSA.[28]

Behind the pugnacity of these intentions and beyond the opinions of various French employers, one finds an acute perception of the new relations of power within the world economy (and of new forms of protectionism by certain industrialized countries), which call for new strategies. There can be no question of creating an isolationist Europe, refusing foreign capital and technologies, but neither can there be any question of operating a unilateral type of 'disarmament'.

French entrepreneurs therefore expect Europe to equip itself with real technological and industrial power in order to negotiate as an equal with its trading partners. This new awareness has, for example, been reflected in the EC/Japanese agreements concerning the automobile industry, or again in the firm positions which European negotiators defend within the framework of GATT, especially on the subject of aeronautics, agri-foodstuffs or industrial property rights. There is every reason to believe that this state of mind is destined to last and that it will lead to pressure being put on the European authorities with a view to a balance of relations in the Triad, whilst seeking, for this objective as for the two previous ones, a constant and intelligent partnership with those responsible for European policies.

---

[28] *Revue Science et Technologie*, No. 20, November 1989.

Structural Changes Required

In order to become successfully internationalized, the majority of French companies will have to make several determining structural changes, mainly concerning the opening up of capital, development of partnership, the integrating role of technology and ever more sophisticated management of their organizations.

It is necessary, however, to make a distinction between the SMIs and the big groups.

With regard to the SMIs, the majority will be faced with the need to strengthen their capital or transfer their assets, in view of the average age attained by company directors who are very often the principal shareholders. The SMEs/SMIs offer quality products, but their structurally deficient financial situation does not allow them to carry out on their own the necessary updating of their production. The development of 'technological and commercial cooperation' with European associates, favouring mutually improved knowledge and great flexibility of cooperation, can provide these SMIs with interesting opportunities and make them better able to cope with more intense competition.

In the case of big groups, Europe forms the starting point of a world strategy; with this aim in mind, all the strategic industries of the Community are currently in the process of restructuring. The French firms still have to grow, since, with only a few shining exceptions (Michelin, L'Oréal, CGE), they are undersized. The take-over of Américan Can by Pechiney in 1989 received approval, as did the take-over of the European subsidiaries of the American group RJR Nabisco by BSN (the most important offensive abroad in French history, with 17 billion francs); this is a sign that the international dimension is receiving increasing consideration from public authorities and the community. It is likely that it will become a priority, since 'alliances with European groups' is a major strategic axis of the same importance as research and development or exporting.

In the Europe of the single market and single currency, two factors will help boost this trend. The first is connected with the scale of the process, with the disappearance of technical differentiations such as geographical compartmentalization and also with the concentration of technological skills. The second factor is connected with the decompartmentalization of financial markets, which will stimulate investments. It should be remembered that the European financial markets as a whole are as important as those of the United States or Japan, admittedly with stock market capitalization of lower values, but with a much higher number of listed companies.

When they have more or less completed their restructuring, French firms should then be starting to globalize from solid bases (Usinor, Bull, Thomson, Rhône-Poulenc, Matra) or consolidate the process. They will be in a position to negotiate the development of European partnerships on an equal footing, giving them a better foundation for growth. For their respective shareholders, they will call on European operators, competitive or otherwise, giving preference to the industrial approach.

Finally, organization, information systems, creation and utilization of skills are the privileged tools of globalization which the big French companies are going to have to incorporate in their strategy. Their traditional structures were based on the principle of unity of authority and responsibility: the global organization of the future is, on the contrary, based on the development of transnational skills, on a capacity to 'manage transfrontier', enabling them to remain attentive to local situations whilst optimizing human, financial and technological resources on a world-wide scale: the entire French socio-productive model[29] will thus have to undergo a radical transformation.

This 'revolution of powers' in companies is not, however, without its risks. The dual hierarchical dependence of each responsible member of staff within the framework of a matrical organization, rigid behaviour patterns, and the defence of established positions are just so many factors of possible ways in which the formal structure and the actual running of a company may be out of step, which will have to be constantly corrected in the communicating and integrated company of tomorrow.

The Means

To build up an economic, technological and industrial Europe, to develop themselves there and utilize this large internal market with a view to globalization, the vast majority of French companies tend to consider that the way to achieve this lies largely in the preparation of a European industrial strategy, with the required resources and, if necessary, declaration of a system of Community preference.

---

29 *L'usine du futur* (The factory of the future). Report by the Commissariat-General for the Plan, 1990 (French Documentation).

A European Technological and Industrial Strategy

The first step will be to 'reconcile policy on competition and industrial strategy', frequently presented as belonging to two incompatible spheres, both conceptually and practically speaking. A good many French operators consider that this opposition has been very largely overcome by present economic developments and must give way to a pragmatic complementarity: on the one hand, in effect, the failure of policies based on measures of state control compels a redefinition of state intervention - the legitimacy of which is not denied - with a view to intervening in respect of market imperfections and various external factors (R&D, investments, networks, qualifications); on the other hand, the logic of competition needs to be resited in a new, world-wide environment where competition and cooperation are closely connected; it is in this sense that any moves towards greater concentration must be controlled.

As to the preparation of a technological policy on a European scale, this is perceived by French companies as designed to favour the installation of flexible programmes, combining many partners on precise objectives and taking into consideration the various phases of innovation, including product marketing, or to encourage stronger technology networks and networks of European alliances.

The Question of Community Preference

Giving preference to own-country companies, in tenders, for example, occurs in the United States, and also in Japan. A price difference of 10% is applied by the EFTA countries, whilst in the US this price difference varies depending on the State, from 6% to 25%, in order to favour local firms: symmetry of rules within the Triad will be increasingly demanded by entrepreneurs.

Europe and the World

French companies will play the European field but are at the same time keen to broaden their horizons. To ensure their international development, they are hoping to develop an increased presence in certain areas of the world whilst at the same time consolidating home bases.

On the first point, they will attempt to play the *trump cards* which French networks abroad, public and private, give them. On the second point, they will endeavour to benefit from the advantages of proximity afforded by a strong position in the country of origin, as demonstrated by the examples of German or Japanese firms.

Many of them are aware that these two trump cards are extremely useful, yet at the same time insufficient. Hence the interest they are paying to the European part of their strategy, which is likely to bring them, between rear base and place of operations, the strength they need.

The Public Sector/Private Sector Debate: European Public Corporations

The French notion of the 'mixed economy' represents a historical compromise between the market and the economic projects of the Nation State. However, neither in France nor even in Europe does a solution of total continuity exist between private sector and public sector. Of course, the two extremes can be seen, consisting of the purely private firm on the one hand, and the administrative departments of the State and local authorities on the other, as well as corporations and organizations incorporated under public law: the *établissement public* in France, the *Anstalt* in Germany, the *Ente* in Italy, the Public Corporation in the United Kingdom. Between these two extremes, however, a continuous range of private companies exists which are highly or exclusively dependent on public orders, joint bodies responsible for collective functions, mixed capital companies, nationalized companies and, over and above the public corporations, departments of the State or local authorities engaged in industrial and commercial activities, and finally, the 'third sector', represented by mutual companies and the social economy.

Right from the start, the European Community has always been afraid of Member States using measures with public and private corporations of a sort which can interfere with competition (Article 90 of the Treaty of Rome). The Single Act and the Treaty of Maastricht however, are silent on the subject of 'public corporations'.

This situation appears doubly paradoxical. First of all, against the background of this stony silence, a renewal of Community activity can be seen on matters which chiefly concern public corporations: State participation in capital, transparency of financial relations with the States, markets. Secondly, Economic and Monetary Union, by improving and deepening the process of economic integration of the Member States, involves innovations which will have a profound effect on the evolution of national public sectors, leading to more efficient management and causing them to restructure their objectives by seeking European partners.

Obviously French public corporations will expect European Union to provide a definition of a 'prospective concept of the European public sector', whether this relates to infrastructural activities, that part of research not ordered from *downstream*, non-commercial sectors of natural monopoly or solidarity which, in order to be managed at national level will nevertheless call for a strategy on a European scale.

Sooner than wait for the standardized definition of a 'European public corporation', the state sector will probably prefer a more pragmatic approach, based on the establishment of a sort of 'code of good conduct' for public corporations, which is capable of providing a common framework of action, making it easier for national behaviour patterns to converge and avoiding suspicions or conflicts harmful to overall European economic efficiency. This would possibly enable gradual definition of the reality and purpose of a European public sector with a global strategy in 2010.

9. Germany: Shaping Factors*

INTRODUCTION

If one broadly distinguishes between economic, political and socio-cultural shaping factors, 'then we are inclined to predict a predominance of economic matters' for the coming 10 to 15 years in Germany. We do so even at the risk that our judgement might be attributed to a professional deformation that perceives money to make the world go round. We identify four big issues which are all economic in nature - though, of course, highly political in consequences - and which are likely to remain in or move into the limelight of society's attention; these are:

-   The economic transformation of Central and Eastern Europe and its implications for trade policy and migration.
-   The economic legacy of German unification.
-   The further stages of EC integration, especially the steps towards monetary union, a social dimension of the common market and a new industrial policy.
-   Environmental concerns for a sustainable development of the world economy.

As far as politics outside the economic realm is concerned, the main factors will be the natural consequence of the dramatic political changes in Europe in recent years, namely:

-   In foreign policy: the search for a workable definition of the international role and responsibility a united Germany is to take up in the future.
-   In domestic policy: the gradual convergence of all major political forces towards a middle-of-the-road pragmatism.

---

*   Dr K.H. Paqué and Dr R. Soltwedel.

Similarly, the main socio-cultural challenges will be that German society - firmly rooted in Western values, but geographically located at the East/West-crossroads of cultures - has to become more cosmopolitan to fill its new role.

Naturally, the issues related to German unification are specifically German factors, which have no direct counterpart in other EC countries, although they may be far from irrelevant for the outside world. In this respect, the Germany of the coming decade - and possibly beyond - is really a special case, much more so than West Germany used to be until the Wall came down. Things look different as to the economic liberalization of Eastern Europe, which directly concerns all EC countries, albeit to very different degrees with Germany receiving the most forceful impulses from the East. In turn, the future EC integration including monetary union will affect all EC countries. And environmental problems also have important transfrontier and even global dimensions.

In Germany, neither politicians nor academics and not even thinktanks are used to make explicit rankings of what the future will bring in the next two decades. As far as one can judge from the diffuse picture which public opinion offers, our hierarchy of broad issues may be regarded as a rough-and-ready approximation of general expert opinion. We shall successively consider in each case the external and the internal challenges for Germany.

SECTION 1: EXTERNAL CHALLENGES

Economic Aspects

As to external challenges, it is the transformation of Central and Eastern Europe which will have the most far-reaching repercussions on Germany. Partly related to what will happen in Eastern Europe is the migration challenge to which Germany is particularly exposed because of living standards, geographical proximity and to some extent, cultural affinity. And given the high degree of openness of the German economy, it is of extreme importance whether it will be possible to stem the rising tide of protectionism in the trade regime. Finally, Germany is quite perceptive to the pervasive environmental problems. In all these instances, it is more than economics that is at stake; these global factors will definitely harness or even shape the trends in the political and socio-cultural arena.

The Transformation of Central and Eastern Europe

From this hazardous process, Germany is likely to be affected more than other EC countries, both with respect to the transition problems and the long-run growth prospects of the Central and Eastern European countries. Germany will not only be an important trading partner and a major source of foreign direct investment for the East, but also the prime choice for emigrants, who try to escape the hardships of the economic and maybe also the political turmoil in their countries. It will also be the country most directly exposed to security risks, be it the malfunctioning of nuclear power stations or the outburst of political conflicts. Hence, Germany will further grow into a natural advocate of concerns of Eastern countries within the EC and beyond, an advocate whose population may be slightly more prepared than others to trade off short-run sacrifices against long-run benefits of opening to the East.

As to benefits, Germany's traditional strength in high-quality investment goods will again pay off handsomely once the investment boom in the transformation countries is in full swing. On the other hand, in the period of transition, the sacrifices will be substantial and long drawn-out. They will comprise not only money hand-outs, the costs of which can be broadly dispersed, but - even more importantly - real adjustments in the German economy with a marked incidence on specific sectors. Intensified East-West trade in the sequel of a freer market access for Eastern products will hit most the classical protected sectors of the German economy, namely agriculture and coal mining as well as steel and textiles, so that major German lobbying groups may clash with widely shared political imperatives, much more so than they did in the past.

Migration Pressures

In all of Europe, the increasing migration pressures have called forth xenophobic reactions. These ubiquitous right-wing obsessions are being fuelled by the fact that a large part of immigration is taking place in the form of asylum applications and the high costs of processing these applications and providing care to asylum seekers. There is a clear indication that the EC Member countries in general and Germany with its extremely liberal asylum law (and practice) in particular will have to convert from *de facto* to *de jure* immigration countries and to obey the need for an immigration policy. For that, it is necessary:

(i) To disentangle humanitarian refugee policy from immigration policy, which is basically part of general economic policy.

(ii) To clearly define criteria for taking in additional immigrants - by no means an easy legislative task.

However, it will be increasingly realized that the immigration threat will, to some extent, turn into relief once the demographically-determined ageing of the West European societies materializes in growth-impeding labour market shortages and a substantially heavier age burden (with Germany taking the lead). However, immigration policy will not suffice to reduce permanently emigration pressures in the source countries. To this end, international trade policy regime is far more important.

The Multilateral Trading System

The international economic environment of European firms is characterized by a steady erosion of GATT principles, both with respect to trade policy instruments and to regional trading arrangements. Which way the pendulum will swing in the future depends to a large extent on the outcome of the Uruguay Round, and in particular on whether the US and the EC can forge a compromise on agriculture support policies. Even assuming a successful conclusion of the Uruguay Round, the international trading system will suffer from weaknesses in GATT rules and regulations, thereby loosening the principle of multilateralism.

The German Government has long since been committed to an open international trading environment and MFN treatment. There are no indications that this basic trade policy stance has changed or will change in the near future, despite the rather passive role that Germany has played in the Uruguay Round until recently. However, the German Government will increasingly realize that trade policies in the 1990s are deeply intertwined with other issues such as security policies, burden-sharing in restructuring Eastern European economies, and financing international compensation funds for protecting the environment, and is thus pushing towards a cooperative game.

However, the Government's view does not necessarily reflect a consensus in society: obviously, the well-organized agricultural lobby opposes any trade agreement which would require further adjustment in the agricultural sector.

And industrial lobby groups - traditionally supportive to liberal trade policies - are having second thoughts on the pay-offs of this attitude under mounting pressure of especially Japanese competition in important branches of manufacturing such as the motor car industry and electronics.

Industrial Policy

Industrial policy is likely to become one of the most controversial topics of the future discussion of economic policy in Germany. At present, the front line against industrial policy seems to be weakening, as a growing part of the political establishment feels increasingly attracted by the ideas of strategic industrial policy. Even despite the rather cheerless prospects for a success of industrial policy, it can be expected that the ongoing shift in attitude in German industry will eventually translate into a corresponding shift in government policy sooner or later - sooner if the Social Democrats take over in 1994, later if the Christian Democrats and Liberals stay in power. The result could be a certain reconciliation in the design of future EC politics between the traditional German position and the more *étatiste* Franco-Roman standpoint on the role of state intervention. The outcome could be a division of labour in industrial policy between the German Government - concentrating on programmes for mitigating structural unemployment - and the Commission of the EC focusing on the support of advanced technologies and strategic industries. In any event, there are serious doubts whether the EC Commission and national governments can successfully restrict strategic support to Community firms in the environment of globalization of markets and ever intensifying international division of labour in production and knowledge creation.

Political Aspects

The most obvious consequence of the end of the Cold War is the need to reorient and restructure foreign and defence policy. Within this context, the unified Germany will have to redefine its responsibilities and to find its international role. The main lines of expert reasoning about the final outcome may read as follows: Germany will gradually take over the standard role of any other medium-sized European power like Britain and France though with the important and permanent difference that its defence will remain strictly non-nuclear. As this role will also cover a military contribution not only to international peacekeeping forces, but also to military task forces of the UN or - in a not too distant future - the EC, the German army will undergo a thorough reorganization. Roughly speaking, it will be transformed from a large, draft-based and purely defensive army into a much smaller professional army with highly specialized units for out-of-area deployment.

At present, these issues are still the object of a heated political controversy between (and partly within) the main political parties, and this is likely to remain so for quite a few years. As to Germany's international responsibility, the political right and the centre take a positive attitude, while the Greens and the Social Democrats - especially their pacifist-leaning left wing - are still very cautious. As to the restructuring of the army, the lines of dissent are more complicated: roughly speaking, the left and the right still favour the draft as the basis for a defensive 'people's army' while the Liberals and an increasing number of 'single voices' of all colours speak in favour of complete professionalization. It is a good guess that the camp of the proponents of a purely professional army will become larger, the more clear-cut the range of future responsibilities will be defined in the course of the 1990s. Whatever political forces will form the government after the next federal elections, it is hard to imagine any other long-term outcome than the one sketched above. Note that the rethinking of Germany's international responsibilities has been speeded up considerably by the rather unfortunate role which the country played during the Gulf War. In particular, the political left with its traditionally strong pacifist leanings was shaken in its all too naive vision of a peaceful world after the end of the Cold War. While, at present, the Social Democrats are still not ready to go beyond contributing German manpower to UN peacekeeping forces - before the Gulf War, they did not even agree to that - they will probably move towards a compromise in the coming years. Quite a few foreign observers have voiced the fear that a unified Germany is likely to become an ever more parochial country - internally absorbed with the many *petty* problems of a population of almost 80 million and externally throwing its weight around without due regard for broader responsibilities. This prospect is often contrasted with the positive development which the country took - *nilly-willy* - after having shrunk to its Western part after the Second World War. In our view - and in the view of the majority of analysts and observers - this gloomy picture of future parochialism is at least heavily exaggerated, if not simply mistaken. To be sure, Germany will take more explicit account of its specific national interests in foreign policy, particularly in its European stance which will be likely to have - in British and French eyes - a bias towards 'Eastern concerns'. However, both developments seem quite natural parts of a process in which

Germany redefines its role after the end of an artificially imposed post-war order. Given the sheer extent of the transformation problems in Eastern Europe, German politics will be confronted head-on with severe international responsibilities which it cannot escape. Although, in the short run, there has been some reluctance to accept the new role - notably before and during the Gulf War - the political class and the population at large by now seem to have realized that there is no way to duck the new challenges. If the international community - especially the United States, Britain, and France - continues to demand a more active role of Germany in international politics, there is hardly any doubt that there will gradually grow a broad consensus on this matter.

SECTION 2: INTERNAL CHALLENGES

German Unification

Outside observers might be inclined to regard German economic unification as no more than a short-term distraction of German politics which will phase out as soon as the transformation of the post-socialist East German economy has been completed. To be sure, huge public investments - mostly financed by the West - will certainly remove the most urgent bottlenecks in the physical and the administrative infrastructure so that the present extreme capital shortage of the East German economy will be largely overcome after five to ten years from now. In other respects, however, there are good reasons to expect German unification to have sustained consequences for Germany's economic and, hence, political future. Broadly summarized, the most likely medium- and long-term changes may read as follows.

The Rising Fiscal Burden

In the first wave of political euphoria after the Wall had come down, the economic costs of unification were vastly underestimated by the political class and large parts of the public. By now, it should be altogether clear that the great public tasks - building up a modern physical and administrative infrastructure, mitigating disastrous environmental damages, privatizing and restructuring a decrepit industrial capital stock, and supporting a rapidly rising number of unemployed people within the framework of the generous Western welfare state provisions - have turned out to be much more expensive than expected, not the least because the collapse of production in the East has surpassed all prior predictions. The drastic increase of public expenditures, which is partly hidden in newly created (and euphemistically named) funds outside the official budgets, was at first regarded to be strictly temporary. However, all economic indicators now show that this will most probably not be the case so that the steps taken so far - the sharp rise of gasoline taxes, the prospective rise of the standard value added tax rate from 14 to 15% by 1993 and the imposition of a (temporary) income tax surcharge - levied for just 12 months - and the rise of payroll taxation will not be remotely sufficient to balance the books in the medium and long run.

As a consequence, the question of consolidating public finances will become something of a permanent theme of German politics again, as it used to be for a while in the late 1970s and early 1980s, with the likely outcome being some rather *ad hoc* combination of expenditure cuts in the Western part of the country (especially of subsidies), a postponement of further tax reductions notably on business profits, and maybe some further tax increases, and, most importantly, a permanently higher fiscal deficit. To be sure, the deficit will not be monetized by the central bank which is likely to stick to the not unpopular German-style policy of tight money and low inflation; in view of the prospective convergence targets of macroeconomic stability in the EC to be met by the mid-1990s, the German Bundesbank will have an easy political justification in public to defend an uncompromising stance. Hence, real interest rates - at record levels already - may well continue to stay high in the coming years which will allow Germany to 'export' part of the adjustment burden to other countries, just as the Reaganomics in the early 1980s did for the United States. If - a big if - the real rate of return on investment in Germany - notably in East Germany - is sufficiently high, such a policy may well be justified as it would then tend not to undermine the still excellent credit rating of the German Government and the locational attractiveness of the country for foreign investment. However, as a large part of the transfers to the East go into private consumption, things may look different: given the extreme inertia of social spending, which is politically very hard to cut back once *institutionalized* as, e.g., in the form of unemployment benefits, the odds appear to be well in favour of a worsening in the attractiveness of the country for foreign investment, at least in the medium-term, but maybe also in the longer run.

Economic Dualization

By the mid-1990s, there will emerge a dual economy in the East consisting of a rather modern, highly capital-intensive segment and a subsidized old one with long-term unemployment remaining much higher in East Germany than in the West. The basic reason is that collective bargaining in unified Germany has opted for a very rapid equalization of wages between West and East in major industries by 1994, despite the vast and obvious labour productivity differential. These terms reflect the endeavour to avoid mass migration and wage competition. The burden of creating incentives for private investment in the East was thus put on public subsidization. The Federal Government in fact swiftly provided a large and generous menu of investment aid items which amount to an effective rate of subsidization of between 30 and 50%, seconded by comprehensive labour market measures to mitigate social disruptions in the adjustment of hopelessly overmanned enterprises. In the medium and long run, this emergency help will be fiscally unsustainable and will give way to more moderate aid packages. In addition, even if the Treuhand-Anstalt (the holding company of East German formerly state-owned enterprises) finishes up its prime task of privatization on schedule, i.e. in 2-3 years, there will no doubt remain a significant residuum of unsaleable industrial capacity which will be heavily concentrated in certain Eastern industrial regions. Pressures will mount that this capacity should continue to operate at high rates of subsidization.

Basically, this will be a replay of the structural crises witnessed in Western regions like the Ruhr district and the Saar Valley in the mid-1970s and early 1980s. The difference will be the sheer extent of the crisis and its long-term consequences: while, after restructuring, the sunset regions in the West were left with still tolerable unemployment rates of 10-15%, the rock bottom of non-cyclical unemployment in the East may easily amount to more than 20% of the labour force. Hence, while the transformation of the Eastern economy may be basically successful in initiating a sustained revival of industrial activity, it is unlikely to be powerful enough to lead to a full-scale reintegration of the Eastern workforce at Western wage levels.

The dualization of the Eastern economy will be further accentuated by what may be called the vintage effect of investment: as the industrial capital stock in the East is renewed at an unusually fast speed, the average vintage of technology and thus the average level of labour productivity (output per man-hour) will turn out higher in the East than in the respective industrial activity in the West, at least for a possibly rather long period of transition.

Only after the gradual rejuvenation of Western industrial capacity through reinvestment and the gradual ageing of the Eastern capital stock has re-established a balanced age structure - say, in two decades - will the East/West vintage and productivity gap be closed. In the meantime the East will have to live with a segment of industry, which is hyper-modern even by Western standards, side by side with the run-down capacity remnants of socialism. To some extent, such a vintage-dualization is certainly the unavoidable consequence of any transformation from socialism to capitalism and thus *per se* nothing to worry about. However, to the extent that the sheer presence of a hyper-modern sector in the East helps to drive up wage demands in the East, there will be a negative side-effect on the labour market. Unfortunately, this is likely to be the case since unions tend to orientate their wage demands not at the state of a (regional) labour market; in addition, the employers' side at the bargaining table is likely to be dominated by an odd coalition of *new* firms operating with a highly modern capital stock and of highly subsidized *old* firms so that wages are unlikely to take due account of high and persistent unemployment. Hence the prospects for a self-correction of labour market dualization in Eastern Germany may be bleak, even in the longer run.

Experience in Germany shows that - once fixed - collective agreements are hardly adjusted *ex post* to the detriment of the employed workforce, even with sky-rocketing unemployment. In particular, pronounced and sustained regional disparities in the jobless figures do not trigger any corresponding inter-regional wage differentiation. Hence, it is highly unlikely that collective bargaining will be flexible enough to take account of the remaining long-term gap in unemployment between East and West. Instead, pressure on government to continue subsidization will mount. However, whereas in earlier structural crises, these pressures could be fiscally accommodated without too much turmoil, the extent of unemployment in the East will make much more drastic fiscal measures necessary, with the Federal Government most likely to foot a large part of the bill. In the same vein, the structure of German-style fiscal federalism will have to be completely overhauled to the advantage of Eastern regions. All this will add a sizeable permanent burden to the public budget. In this sense, Germany will not be quite the same again: as a unified country, it will have to endure larger internal economic disparities and somewhat tougher redistributive quarrels over tax money than its Western part ever had to in the past.

Digression: the 'Treuhand': Record and Prospects

The Treuhand was founded in March 1990 by the late GDR Government as a holding company of basically all East-German state-owned enterprises. In practice, it started its work after German unification (3 October 1990) when it was assigned three major tasks, namely the restructuring, the privatization, and the demonopolization of existing firms. The legal task assignment does not provide any guidance to the hierarchy of these aims; in particular, there is no explicit priority given to privatization. Therefore, in practice, much depends on the strategy of the Treuhand's management and its supervisory board as well as on the governments on the federal and the state level, notably the Federal Minister of Finance, who sets the frame in which the Treuhand is extended credits and credit guarantees; in addition, the Federal Government has a major influence on the choice of the Treuhand's supervisory board. Hence, although legally no political institution, the Treuhand is bound to be subject to the political will of the government and to all standard political pressures from outside lobby groups.

Given this uneasy political framework, the Treuhand's record up to the present looks remarkably successful. As of late February 1992, the privatization of firms in the service sector had long been completed. In industry, 38% of all firms had been privatized, 2% had been taken over by local governments (*communitization*); only 2% had been closed down. Note that, to some extent, these numbers are misleading since many firms were split into different parts in the course of privatization so that the number of remaining non-privatized firms continued to grow. In terms of jobs, 25% of all employees of the Treuhand firms in industry now work in firms which have been privatized, another 7% in other private firms, while about 40% are still with the Treuhand; the remaining 28% have become unemployed, retired, self-employed, or are participating in training programmes.

While the record is quite impressive as to privatization speed - it amounts to 400-500 privatized firms per month - the problem is that this speed is likely to slow down considerably in the near future. This is so for economic and political reasons. Economically, the commercially most attractive firms could be privatized first so that the remaining stock will have an ever rising share of plants which suffer either from conflicting property claims or from particularly run-down capital equipment. Politically, the resistance of employers, unions, and state and local governments will grow with the likelihood of massive lay-offs which will be concentrated in certain branches and regions. A good case in point is shipbuilding in the northernmost Eastern State of Mecklenburg where the scheduled privatization led to a genuine political crisis in early 1992. In short: the more the Treuhand approaches the hard core of the matter, the slower and the more politically controversial will any further privatization become. A likely scenario seems to be that the Treuhand will rather easily proceed in privatizing the bulk of the smaller firms. In turn, it will become particularly difficult to privatize those larger firms which are concentrated in backward regions such as Mecklenburg, parts of Thuringia, and the area to the West of the border to Poland, in branches with very severe transformation problems such as chemicals or mechanical engineering, and in branches which face bleak long-term prospects anyway such as shipbuilding, mining, iron and steel as well as textiles and clothing. These will turn into a long-term burden which will form the gloomy part of the dualized economy sketched above.

New Regional Growth Patterns

German unification together with the economic transformation of Eastern Europe is quite likely to have initiated a profound change of the regional growth prospects in the future, both in the Western and in the Eastern parts of the country.

In the West, the last four decades have been a time of a rather stable pattern of regional growth, with the industrial centres of the Rhine/Ruhr and the more Southern Main/Neckar valleys quite persistently figuring as the pacemakers of development. Only two major trend changes could be observed:

(i)   The gradual loss of growth dynamics during and after the two oil price shocks in the regions where major sunset industries were concentrated, namely the Ruhr and the Saar valleys with coalmining and the steel industry, the Northern coastal shore with shipbuilding, and, to a lesser extent, Westfalia with textiles and clothing.

(ii) The rise of Southern Bavaria, especially Munich, and of the Frankfurt metropolitan area, as major centres of manufacturing and services which profited most from the decline of West Berlin, the

Western part of the former capital, that lost part of its manufacturing base due to its geographic and economic insulation.

Of course, there were some perennial 'problem regions' whose economic performance quite consistently lagged behind the average in terms of per capita income and/or of unemployment, most of them areas with some inherent locational disadvantages; apart from Berlin, these were the coastal shore and hinterland of the North and the Baltic Sea, and - most importantly - a 50-100 km strip of land along the Iron Curtain, reaching from the city of Lübeck at the northern most point of the inner-German border down to the Bavarian Forest neighbouring Czechoslovakia. Even with ample public support for these regions - above all the so-called horizontal fiscal equilibration (*Finanzausgleich*) between rich and less well-off states - the economic gap between them and the rest of the country could never be substantially narrowed.

German unification and to a lesser extent the prospective transformation of Eastern Europe have brought some definite changes to this pattern. With the re-establishment of trade and transport links to the East, all artificial handicaps of locations along the former Iron Curtain have disappeared or will disappear in due course. In fact, some of the previously handicapped locations now enjoy distinct advantages from the standpoint of a potential investor. This is certainly true for the capital Berlin, which, apart from becoming the seat of the German Government, now finds itself geographically well placed to resume its pre-war role of a metropolis right at the crossroads between Europe's East and West. It is also true for the industrial areas near the former inner-German border, e.g. in Eastern Lower Saxony, Northern Hesse, and Northern Bavaria, which are turned from the Eastern periphery of West Germany into Central regions of a united Germany, with a complementary industrial hinterland in the Eastern states of Brandenburg, Saxony-Anhalt, Thuringia, and Saxony.

The most likely losers in this reshuffling of growth potentials will be precisely those regions which profited most from the division of Germany in the first place, notably Southern Bavaria, the Rhine valley and the Frankfurt metropolitan area: in particular, many firms may return their headquarters from Munich, where they had moved after the Second World War, to their traditional home Berlin, and many government-close service branches are likely to follow the trek of bureaucrats and lobbyists from the Cologne-Bonn urban area to the new (and old) capital, Berlin.

Within Eastern Germany, the industrial heartlands of the pre-war period which are to be found in the states of Saxony, Saxony-Anhalt, Thuringia and Southern Brandenburg will enjoy similar locational improvements to their counterparts in Lower Saxony, Hesse, and Northern Bavaria. Notwithstanding the chronic structural problems of labour market dualization, which have been described above, they will certainly be the most attractive locations for industrial investment in the Eastern part of the country. However, due to their relatively high wages compared to neighbouring regions to the East - notably Bohemia with its formidable industrial tradition - they will not be the favourite place to establish 'extended work benches' for Western firms to save on labour costs. The economic prospects will look more gloomy for the Northern regions of East Germany: while the State of Brandenburg will still profit from the growth dynamics of the city of Berlin, the northernmost State of Mecklenburg is likely to remain the country's poorhouse as it used to be in the pre-war period. Hard hit by the deep crises of its main economic sectors - shipbuilding and agriculture - and lacking the strong locational advantages of the regions south of Berlin, Mecklenburg will have to rely very much on exploiting its tourist potential - the coast of the Baltic Sea, a large number of lakes and a thinly populated green countryside - and on developing transport facilities linking Scandinavia to East Germany and Southern Europe. However, this potential is hardly sufficient to prevent unemployment to emerge on a scale which is unknown in other parts of Germany.

Since German unification, many fears have been voiced that the prospective resurgence of Berlin as a European metropolis and as the German capital will lead to a new unwelcome trend towards centralization, i.e. to the days of the Kaiserreich and the Weimar Republic when Prussian dominance had very unwelcome consequences; this picture is then often contrasted with the high degree of decentralization which characterized West Germany and the Bonn republic, with a strong dose of federalism injected into the political system, and a relatively large number of about equally sized urban centres scattered all over the country competing for economic excellence. On closer inspection, this argument does not carry much weight. Politically, the strongly federal constitution of the Bonn republic has been fully preserved in the course of unification, and there is not a single large state such as Prussia in the Kaiserreich or in the inter-war period which could dominate political decision-making. While the system of fiscal equilibration between the states (*Finanzausleich*) needs a thorough overhauling, the basic structure of

German-style federalism is certainly not endangered.[1] Economically, the fear seems to be just as misplaced: although certainly an industrial centre before the Second World War, Berlin never dominated the German economy in the sense Paris dominates the French one; rather it was a kind of north-eastern counterweight to the industrial power concentrated in other regions like the Ruhr valley in the West, Saxony further South, and Silesia in the South-East. It is likely to resume some of this prior function which should be welcome in view of the desperate lack of growth poles in the East. In this sense, the often-made comparison to Paris and the Ile de France is beside the point; rather Berlin may take over an economic role similar to the one of Rome in Italy, i.e. of a metropolis, which is located at the doorsteps of an economically backward region, and if anything, gives that region a growth impulse. However, just as Rome undermined neither the industrial vitality of the rich Northern provinces of Piedmont and Lombardia, nor the dominance of Milano in trade and finance, so the resurgence of Berlin is very unlikely to develop such strong centripedal forces so as to degrade the rich West and South to shadows of their past power in industry and services.

To sum up, the new growth pattern to be expected after unification in the long run should not be viewed as distorting anything like a harmonious regional pattern of economic activity. Rather it removes some most artificial economic consequences of the division of Germany and of Europe.

Political Pragmatism

Due to German unification, the next 10 to 15 years will be a time of rather unideological, pragmatic policy-making. The reasons are basically economic ones: as described above, the 1990s and beyond will remain a period of an economic East/West gap within Germany, i.e. of a clearly defined geographical imbalance. Typically in such times, the political cracks and rifts do not tend to coincide with party boundaries so that manifold implicit grand coalitions may become ever more frequent facts of political life, at least for those many *multidimensional* issues which concern federal, state, and possibly also local governments at the same time.

---

[1]   In this respect, recent concerns voiced in the Anglo-Saxon press seem to be exaggerated. See, e.g., *The Economist* of 25 April 1992, 'Germany's struggle to keep federalism on the road'.

The trend towards pragmatism will be further supported by the small, but significant impact which the new German *Länder* are likely to have on the 'balance of ideologies' in united Germany. While there is no doubt that the main orientation of major parties is basically determined in the Western part of the country, the more subtle inner-party shifts and their long-term effects should not be underestimated: whereas the Christian Democratic Party (CDU/CSU) and the Liberals (The Free Democratic Party, FDP) have merged with Eastern partners of a somewhat more left-wing tradition (less pro-business and more in favour of the Welfare State and an active industrial policy), the SPD and the Greens have relatively conservative Eastern partners with a strong background in the Protestant church and in so-called civil movements, but rather little attachment to traditional left-wing ideas. If these inner-party rifts will be overcome by some sort of compromise in the long run, then the ideological baselines of the parties will tend to move closer together and thus facilitate pragmatic multi-party cooperation. However, within the parties, the potential for conflict is likely to rise, especially within the CDU and the FDP which have become parties with political strongholds in the East. The recent debate on the reform of the legal treatment of abortion, which saw the Eastern CDU favouring a rather liberal practice and the Western CDU by and large defending the status quo, may be a first foreboding of the future conflict potential.

Of course, a more general reason for the trend towards political pragmatism is that outright socialism, so far the main ideological ingredient of politics, has been largely discredited. As a consequence, socialist-leaning political forces like the Greens and the left wing of the Social Democratic Party (SPD) will more and more move away from their German-style anti-capitalist stance which used to be a combination of anti-American pacifism, ecological radicalism, fabian welfarism, and what may be called lifestyle libertarianism. While they will, of course, retain the traditional tinge of their political identity, they will become ready to allow for much more pragmatic solutions in all sorts of coalitions. To be sure, this tendency will be a straight continuation of trends which began in the 1980s and which seem to prevail in other advanced industrial countries as well.

While a fair dose of pragmatism may be welcome in view of the traditional strong and often stubborn party adherence in German politics, the likely price to be paid for it should not be overlooked: with implicit grand coalitions looming behind many issues, the political resistance against the bribing of special interest groups may be reduced and the call for budgetary discipline may thus further weaken. Note that the trend towards a cooperation of the large parties will be further harnessed by the appearance of new parties and formations at the fringe of the political spectrum, notably on the right wing of the political spectrum. The recent polls in Baden-Württemberg and Schleswig-Holstein are a conspicuous case in point.

Demography and the Welfare State

Virtually the whole industrial world will experience a quite dramatic ageing of its population in the coming decades.   This will have far-reaching consequences for the financing and the structure of the Welfare State since it is likely to entail a sharp rise of the number of retired people relative to the active labour force.   As demographic forecasts and scenarios tend to be somewhat easier to make and somewhat more reliable than in other fields of the social and economic sciences, we shall first give a brief quantitative sketch of what the demographic future looks like for the EC countries in general and for Germany in particular. We then draw some more tentative conclusions on what all this means for the future of the Welfare State.

Facts and Forecasts

The ageing process is already well under way in all EC countries; it will accelerate considerably until 2010, and it will culminate at about the years 2030-40 when the baby-boom generation of the years 1960-75 will finally reach the retirement age. The reasons for this trend may be interpreted both as sociological and economic: sociological in the sense that they go back to a sweeping change of value systems towards a more radical indivi-dualism which is less ready to sacrifice personal ambitions and career prospects for child care and family life; economic in the sense that this value change typically evolves in industrialized countries with higher income levels and some sort of social safety net which helps to substitute formal institutions of health and old-age insurance for the more traditional intergenerational support within the family.

The marked decline in fertility rates[2] in all EC countries, which began in the North (Germany, Denmark) and then spread to the South (Italy, Spain, Greece) has levelled off in recent years.   In some of the Northern

---

2   Net reproduction rate: a value of 1 corresponds exactly to a stable population size in the long-run steady state.

countries, there are even signs of a moderate recovery which is believed to be not only a short-run phenomenon. Nevertheless, a future rise of fertility rates in the EC back to or even above the replacement ratio seems to be extremely unlikely. Nor will immigration be powerful enough to turn around this trend: a full compensation of the domestic 'birth deficit' for the Community as a whole by immigrants (more precisely: by immigrant women in the reproductive age) would require an annual net influx of migrants of the order of at least 5 million people.[3] This would probably overstretch the absorptive capacity of the EC countries as it would imply a total of 50 million immigrants in a decade, i.e. about 15% of the present total Community population.

Following estimates of EUROSTAT which are based on national forecasts under slightly differing assumptions (see the table below, which excludes East Germany) the 'age burden'[4] of the Community, which stood at 21% at the beginning of 1990, will have increased to 27% by 2010 and to 31% by 2020. The 'child burden'[5] may decline from 27% (1990) down to 24% in 2010 and 23% in 2020. In addition, mortality rates are expected to fall further throughout the Community so that the age group '80 years and over' will experience by far the highest growth rates. All this has to be seen against the background of a general *dejuvenation* of the active population whose average age will increase considerably.

As to the situation in Germany, one has to make an explicit distinction between the Western and the Eastern part of the country. The population in the Western part of the country is clearly leading the ageing process in the Community (see Table 9.1), and this should remain so at least until 2015/20.

The fertility rate of the West showed by far the sharpest decline of the EC countries from 1.18 in 1965 to a low of 0.60 in 1985; thereafter it rose gradually to an estimated 0.69 in 1991. In a quite realistic - though maybe somewhat optimistic - scenario, we expect this slow rise to continue so that in 2010 the fertility rate in the West may approach 0.75; it is based on the assumption that the future will bring considerably more flexible working arrangements which enable young couples to combine their professional careers with the raising of children in a way that requires fewer personal sacrifices (especially for women) than in the past.

---

3   Assuming an age and sex structure for migrants as prevailed for ethnic Germans from CIS-republics in recent years.

4   Defined as the number of people of the age group 65 years or more divided by the number of people of the age group 15-64 years.

5   Defined as the number of people of the age group 0-14 years divided by the number of people of the age group 15-64 years.

Table 9.1 Demographic Trends in the EC and in Western Germany, 1990-2020 (mill.)

Age Groups (years)	1.1.1990		2000		2010		2020	
	EUR 12	Dwest	EUR 12	Dwest	EUR 12	Dwest	EUR 12	Dwest
0 - 14	59.6	9.44	58.2	10.36	53.2	8.35	48.4	7.60
15 - 64	220.2	43.63	221.6	42.93	220.2	41.20	211.1	38.20
- (15 - 29)	76.8	14.41	64.1	10.12	59.5	10.77	56.7	9.67
- (50 - 64)	55.1	11.76	58.3	12.54	64.9	12.75	72.0	14.70
$\geq$ 65	47.2	9.61	54.2	11.01	58.9	12.75	65.0	13.02
- ($\geq$ 80)	11.0	2.39	11.9	2.44	15.4	3.07	17.0	3.70
Total population	327.0	62.68	334.0	64.30	332.5	62.30	324.5	58.82
Child Burden (0 - 14)} as %	27.1	21.6	26.3	24.1	24.3	20.3	23.0	19.9
Age Burden ($\geq$ 65) of	21.4	22.0	24.5	25.6	26.7	30.9	30.8	34.1
- very old ($\geq$ 80) } (15-64)	5.0	5.5	5.4	5.7	7.0	7.5	8.1	9.7
Total Burden (child + age)	48.5	43.6	50.8	49.7	51.0	51.2	53.8	54.0
Dejuvenation and ageing of the potentially active population								
- (15 - 29) as % of	34.9	33.0	28.9	23.6	27.0	26.1	26.9	25.3
- (50 - 64) (15 - 64)	25.0	27.0	26.3	29.2	29.5	30.9	34.1	38.5

For Germany (West) a constant birth rate, a further increase in life expectancy and a cumulative net immigration of 2.84 mill. (including immigration from Eastern Germany) from 1990-2014 (thereafter: 0) has been assumed.

Sources: EUROSTAT, Demographic Statistics 1991, Luxembourg 1991. - Own calculations.

Sharper future increases of fertility rates could be imaginable only if there were a real breakthrough in changing the present tax and transfer system in favour of families with children. However, this seems to become ever less likely to happen the longer the process of ageing persists as the ever increasing share of the elderly in the total electorate will tend to resist any such changes.

In the Eastern part of the country, the age structure of the population is somewhat more favourable to the financing of old-age pensions than in the West because there have been considerably higher fertility rates in the former GDR, (0.80 in 1988) due to a strictly pro-natal policy of the Communist Government in the last two decades. At the same time, an almost comprehensive system for baby and child care provided the basis for reaching and retaining a very high female labour participation. After the fall of the Iron Curtain, in particular after unification, the fertility rate in the East dropped dramatically to less than 0.45 in 1991 with the number of marriages halving from 1990 to 1991 alone. A fall of nearly 50% in the birth-rate in less than five years is an altogether unique event in German demographic history; it even exceeds by far the respective decline observed in the German Reich during the Great Depression in

1929/32. Apparently, the uncertain future prospects especially in the labour market and in housing, which are the consequences of the abrupt change from a command system to a market economy, induced the majority of young couples to postpone child-birth until the economic outlook turns more favourable.

Provided that labour market prospects in the East will improve considerably from the end of 1992 onwards, we expect the fertility rate in the East to recover soon from the trough which may last until 1993/94. In numerical terms, we assume the Eastern fertility rate to move up from 0.5, the rough average for the period 1990-94, to nearly 0.9 in 1995-99. Thereafter, i.e. when the births postponed in 1990-94 are partly recouped, the fertility rate in the East might fall again and stabilize at around 0.7 from 2000 onwards. This is considerably below the level under the socialist regime because the pro-natal policy of these times will find no adequate substitute under market conditions.

Taking a weighted average of the fertility rates for the East and the West yields an aggregate fertility rate for unified Germany, though admittedly a rather tentative one: it is expected to fall from 0.69 (1989) to 0.64 (1991/92), then to rise to 0.77 in the years 1995/99, before it will stabilize at a level of about 0.74 beyond the year 2000 (more than one-fifth above the Western minimum arrived at in 1985). This scenario has basically two implications:

(i)   Since the fertility rate for total Germany remains all the time far below the replacement rate, German population - barring immigration - will shrink with rising rates of decline after the year 2000. The ageing process as well as the dejuvenation of the labour force will accelerate considerably. According to an independent estimate of the Deutsches Institut für Wirtschaftsforschung (DIW) - see Table 9.1 - the age burden of unified Germany could increase by as much as 60% from 1989 to 2020.

(ii)   The dramatic switch in the birth-rate of the East will be echoed about 15-20 years later in the East German labour market: around 2010 there should be an extreme trough, around 2015 a very pronounced maximum of new entrants. More stability of the inflow into the domestic labour supply of the East will not be regained before 2020.

Any more comprehensive demographic forecast for unified Germany must be interpreted with great caution since it involves the merging of separate scenarios for the two parts of the country with a quite different record to be expected. One such forecast has been prepared by the Institut für Arbeitsmarkt und Berufsforschung (IAB) of the Federal Labour Office. Some selected results of it are shown in Table 9.2.

Under the assumption of a constant fertility rate and a cumulative net immigration of 4.55 million until 2010 - consisting of 1.85 million ethnic Germans predominantly from CIS countries, 1.62 million asylum seekers and 1.08 million other foreigners - but no further net immigration thereafter, the population in total Germany would increase moderately from 79.5 million (1990) to 81.8 million in 2000. Beyond that year total population would decline, until 2010 only marginally (80.5 million) as immigration would partly compensate for the domestic population shrinkage; thereafter, due to the assumed absence of further net immigration, the decline would accelerate (2020: 76.4 million).

The estimated labour force more or less tracks the path of population: a near-stagnation at about 41 million until 2010, thereafter a shrinkage to 38.2 million in 2020. To illustrate the vigour of the domestic demographic contraction process, one might alternatively think of a no-immigration scenario (all other assumptions about birth- and death-rates remaining unchanged): in that case, the total population in Germany would decline from 79.5 million (1990) to 78.0 million in 2000, 74.6 million in 2010 and 70.1 million in 2020.

In view of these prospects, the crucial question of the coming decades for unified Germany in the field of demography will be to what extent the country will accommodate the consequences of the ageing and the shrinking of the domestic population by replacement immigration. In the past, official Germany has firmly denied being an immigration country. We expect this to change under the combined pressures of the dwindling domestic population and the strong demand for immigration from outside (ethnic Germans and asylum seekers from the CIS, migrant labour from Eastern Europe, etc.).

Implications for the Welfare State

It is quite safe to predict that the ageing of the German population will lead to severe financial problems for the social security system. Above all, the compulsory old-age insurance, which is based on the pay-as-you-go principle, is heading for troubled times: so far, benefits have been more or less indexed to wage growth, with a routine parliamentary decision legally enforcing the annual increases. As described above, the ratio between the number of retired people and the labour force will almost certainly rise and so will the percentage share of the gross wage which will have to be devoted to payroll taxes unless there is a thorough structural reform of the system.

In view of these rather bleak long-term prospects of the pay-as-you-go system, some reform measures have been decided upon in 1989. Beginning in 1992, the benefits are indexed to wages net of payroll and wage income tax. This means that old-age benefits after a complete 'working life' (defined as 45 years) with average wage income are fixed at a level of 68% of the average take-home pay of the employees. Besides, the retirement age will be raised gradually in the future. Beginning in 2001, the standard retirement age - at present between 60 and 65 - is to be raised to 65 in 2017. In addition, there will be more leeway for the individual choice of the retirement age on an actuarially fair basis.

According to the projections of the government for a 15-years period,[6] the revenues will suffice to cover the expenditures for the retirees, survivors, disabled, etc., if the payroll tax rate (17.7% in 1992 with half being paid by the employer and half by the employee) is raised to 20.7% in 2005 and if the Federal Government's subsidy (amounting to about 20% of total expenditures of the old-age insurance system in 1992) is raised in line with the increase of gross wages and the rise of the payroll tax rate, i.e. in line with the contributions of employees and employers. To be sure, these projections are based on rather conservative forecasts of immigration; assuming a higher number of immigrants, the respective tax rate for the year 2005 would be somewhat lower, but still higher than at present.

On the other hand, the projections do not include any negative effects of an increasing payroll tax and thus of a rising wedge between the consumer wage (take-home pay) and the producer wage (gross remuneration) on labour supply and labour demand which may aggravate the problem.

The compulsory health insurance (covering more than 90% of the population) will face problems similar to those of the old-age pension system. The problems might be even somewhat more severe because the share of the very old (people aged 80 or more), which is of course a top-risk group, will go up markedly.[7] Hence, the payroll tax rate for compulsory health insurance (12.5% in 1992 with half being paid by the

---

6 Bericht der Bundesregierung über die gesetzlichen Rentenversicherungen (Rentenanpassungsbericht 1991), Deutscher Bundestag, 12. Wahlperiode, Drucksache 12/1841.

7 Sachverständigenrat für die Konzertierte Aktion im Gesundheitswesen, Jahresgutachten 1991, Das Gesundheitswesen im vereinten Deutschland, Baden-Baden 1991.

employer and by the employee, respectively) will rise considerably in line with the ageing process if no thoroughgoing policy reform takes place.

Table 9.2 Demographic trends in Unified Germany and in Eastern Germany, 1990-2020 (million.)

Unified Germany	1990		2000		2010		2020	
Total Population(a)	79.47	100.0	81.80	100.0	80.54	100.0	76.43	100.0
- potentially active (15 - 75 yrs)	61.03	76.8	62.90	76.9	62.98	78.2	58.85	77.0
-inactive (0-14 and >75 yrs)	18.44	23.2	18.90	23.1	17.56	21.8	17.58	23.0
Estimated Labour supply(a,b)	41.06		40.88		41.40		38.19	
- as % of (15 - 75 yrs)		67.3		65.0		65.7		64.9
Age Burden(c) (≥ 60 yrs as % of 20-59 yrs)	35.2 (d)		42.2		47.8		55.6	
Eastern Germany								
Total Population(e)	16.25	100.0	15.51	100.0	15.30	100.0	14.50	100.0
- (0-14 yrs)	3.17	19.5	2.51	16.2	2.10	13.7	1.91	13.2
- (15-64 yrs)	10.92	67.2	10.76	69.4	10.48	68.5	9.73	67.1
- (≥ 65 yrs)	2.16	13.3	2.24	14.4	2.72	17.8	2.86	19.7
Estimated Labour supply (e,f)	9.40		8.22		8.25		7.51	
- as % of (15 - 64 yrs)		86.1		76.4		78.7		77.2
Dejuvenation and ageing of the estimated labour supply (e,f)								
- (15 - 29) as % of total supply		31.0		24.8		25.3		20.2
- (≥ 50) as % of total supply		24.3		20.9		25.3		30.4

(a) Forecast of the Institut für Arbeitsmarkt- und Berufsforschung (IAB) of the Federal Labour Office under the assumption of constant fertility rates, further declining death rates and a cumulative net immigration of 4.6 mill. from 1991-2010.

(b) IAB-Forecast under the same assumptions as referred to in (a) and in addition by postulating a moderate increase in labour participation ratios in Western Germany (Eastern Germany: see under (f) below).

(c) Estimated by the Deutsche Institut für Wirtschaftsforschung (DIW, Berlin) for 2000-2020 on the basis of calculations of the Federal Statistical Office for 1989.

(d) 1989.

(e) IAB-Forecast under the condition that fertility and mortality rates in Eastern Germany will adjust to the ones in Western Germany, and that from 1991-1995 there is a net emigration from the East (mainly to the West) of 205 000 (1996-2010: net immigration into the East (mainly from foreign countries) of 477 000).

(f) The until 1989 extremely high labour participation rates in the East are assumed to adjust to the much lower rates of the West especially in the case of married women.

Sources: Institut für Arbeitsmarkt- und Berufsforschung of the Federal Labour Office.
Deutsches Institut für Wirtschaftsforschung, Berlin. Federal Statistical Office. Own calculations.

The most recent Health Reform Act of 1988, which was a most painstaking uphill struggle in the political arena, did not entail any lasting effect for the most important kinds of health expenditures; in addition, the very important hospital sector was excluded from the reform initiatives. Without reform measures the health payroll tax rate is expected to rise to at least 15% within a 10- or 15-years period.

All in all, the social security system is shaping up to a first-rate challenge that bears the risk of running out of control. The question of how to cope with the financial difficulties associated with population ageing will remain on the agenda of the economic policy debate for decades to come, despite the recent first reform steps taken. The relevant options are not difficult to detect:

(i)   Policy might react by simply raising further the rate of payroll taxes for the old-age and the health insurance system. This option has the obvious drawback that it may lead to more wage pressure if workers and unions do not accept an equivalent cut of their take-home pay, but rather insist on recouping the real income loss by a rise of the gross wage. The concomitant increase in labour costs might then lead to a rise of equilibrium unemployment, thus to higher payroll taxation for unemployment insurance and to a lower employment and income base to tax in the future. Under unfavourable macroeconomic circumstances, a genuine payroll tax-wage-spiral may set in which may undermine the basis of the welfare system. This is why some further cautious increases may be politically envisaged, but a great leap forward to a new dimension of payroll tax rates looks rather unlikely.

(ii)   Obvious alternative policy options are a further rise of the retirement age and/or cuts in benefits. Within the limits of what an inert popular consensus on social security deems as reasonable, these options will be used. However, the limits of change are rather narrow, not least because any more drastic measure would be highly unpopular in view of the growing share of the elderly in the voting population. Therefore, it is likely that only minor reductions of the benefit levels will be discussed and finally enacted in the coming 10-15 years.

(iii)   Most probably, a different option will be on top of the policy agenda, namely a change of the immigration laws. In the face of the demographic challenges of a shrinking domestic labour force, it will be realized increasingly by the public at large that a more liberal immigration policy may help alleviate pressure from the social security system and may keep at bay the need for overhauling the otherwise popular pay-as-you-go model of social security. To ever more people and voters, the option of extending the intergenerational contract to a new cohort of young people from abroad will look increasingly attractive, not least in the light of emerging labour scarcities. Thus the question of reforming the social security system will more and more blend with the broader issue of making Germany an immigration country, with a carefully designed policy of screening potential entrants to maximize their positive external benefits in the form of taxes and social security contributions.

Apart from its detrimental effects on the financing of the social security system, the unfavourable demographic trend will certainly lead to a rise of expenditures for existing tax-financed social services. Apart from the medical needs of the very elderly, there will be a growing demand for more long-term care facilities, both public and private ones. Given a continued trend away from intra-family care for the elderly which is reinforced by the demographically-caused shrinking or intra-family ties, an ever growing number of people will need help from outside institutions. This trend is reinforced by the growing participation rates of the female labour force, which reduce the individual leisure time to be used for care of the parent generation. It is widely expected that the government will supply some kind of tax-financed public help to alleviate this problem. It is also likely that, in a few years' or even months' time, some sort of compulsory insurance for the care of the elderly will be added to the social security system. According to most recent announcements by the Government any additional expenditures are to be financed by equivalent cuts of existing benefits; given the present outcry from the public in view of the proposal of reducing the rather generous sick leave benefits (since 1970 100% of wages, beginning with the first day of illness), however, the Government may in fact refrain from making its announcements come true.

Labour Markets and Collective Bargaining

In speculating about the future features of the German labour market, one should distinguish sharply between two types of tendencies, namely those emanating from *exogenous* trends common to more or less all advanced industrial societies and those arising from the peculiar German situation of a unified country covering two very different economies.

Three general trends are likely to continue in an unabated manner. First, due to the combined effect of productivity growth, shifts of private demand at rising income levels and a changing division of labour, employment in the tertiary sector - notably in private services - will grow faster than in industry. By international standards, Germany will continue to have a relatively large industrial sector due to its traditional pattern of intersectoral specialization, but the employment share of services will grow more or less as it did in the past two decades, even if there are no severe supply shocks hitting industry as the two oil price hikes in 1973/74 and 1979/80.

Second, female labour force participation will keep growing due to sociological trends in favour of a more balanced division of labour between the two sexes. In this respect, Germany still lags somewhat behind most other advanced countries with comparable income levels and one might expect this gap to narrow since other countries, notably in Scandinavia, have already reached an almost equal employment participation of men and women.

Third, there will be a continued trend towards more flexible working time including part-time work caused by a combination of three factors, namely:

(i)   Structural change from industry to modern services which have a less rigid time-bound complementarity of capital and labour in production.

(ii)   The increasing labour force participation of women who have a 'natural' preference for combining household duties and employment.

(iii)   A sociological trend towards more individualized working relations which appears to be characteristic of advanced societies at high levels of income and a strong preference of people for leisure and mixed forms of work and leisure.

These trends are likely to be overlapped by quite different forces originating in the economic unification of Germany. At present, the East is going through a drastic transformation process which involves an abrupt cut of industrial employment, with the large female industrial workforce, which had extremely high socialist-type participation rates, being particularly hard hit. Optimistically speaking, a forceful re-industrialization may set in by the mid-1990s - somewhat contrary to the long-run trend - but it is unlikely to be the female labour force which will profit most from it. Rather one might expect the participation rate of women to drop permanently to the standard of the West. In any case, economic policy-makers are likely to be obsessed with the aim of rebuilding the industrial base in the East, with the growth of the service sector remaining a side issue.

Probably for a whole decade, this will make the policy debate resemble the one in the early 1950s when overcoming capital shortage unemployment due to the influx of refugees and war-time destruction was the focus of policy interest.

Whether all this leads to a further tightening of labour markets in the West and to a sustained improvement, i.e. something like a return to full employment in the East will depend on at least four sets of factors, namely:

(i)   The growth of the labour supply.
(ii)   The economic success of the large-scale subsidization of the East.
(iii)   Labour market deregulation.
(iv)   Trade union behaviour.

Labour Supply

Demographic changes will almost certainly pull towards a shrinking labour supply, a trend which will only be mitigated, but not neutralized by rising female participation rates. In this respect, united Germany in the 1980s and beyond (both West *and* East) will have features of West Germany in the 1960s. However, there will be growing immigration pressures from Eastern European countries which might take a similar *safety valve* function in industrial boom periods as the *guest workers* from Southern Europe in the 1960s. Whether they can serve as anything like close substitutes for domestic labour - especially the skilled part of it - is doubtful so that, at least in the West, a secular tightening of labour markets might be felt from the mid-1990s (incidentally leading to large-scale internal East-West migration).

Public Transfers to the East

By the mid-1990s, the vast public investments in the East carried out with taxpayers' money from the West will certainly have removed the worst infrastructure bottlenecks, both as to the physical and the administrative infrastructure. Whether the massive subsidization of private investment in the East will be successful enough to close the 'capital gap' of post-socialism is much more doubtful. It will crucially depend on how labour costs develop which, in turn, will depend on collective bargaining.

Labour Market Deregulation

All through the 1980s, the deregulation of labour markets had been a persistent theme of the policy debate on how to reduce unemployment, with the only tangible political result being a law in 1985 which generally allows fixed-term contracts up to two years and which is now set to expire by 1995. With labour markets tightening again in the West by the late 1980s, the discussion finally died down, and it is unlikely to be revived again in the 1990s, despite the mass unemployment in the East[8] and despite a general trend towards an individualization of labour contracts. The main reason is that the debate had been embedded in the larger discussion on deregulation which was a big topic in the poor growth climate of the early 1980s but which is simply eclipsed by the vast transformation problems of post-socialist Eastern Europe and its integration in the world economy by the 1990s. Yet, while it is unlikely that there will be a new legal offensive in the field of labour market deregulation, there may well be some *de facto* deregulation in segments of the labour market due to a rising share of immigrants who are ready to work at conditions below the contractually fixed minima.

Trade Union Behaviour

It is, of course, extremely difficult to predict how unions will react to the set of exogenous challenges emanating on the labour market and beyond. At best, some major informed guesses are possible.

Given the above mentioned trends of structural change towards service employment and flexibility of employment conditions, unions will in general find themselves on the defensive. In the long run, they will face a strategic choice: either they stick to their traditional norms of horizontal equity and tight union control of working conditions so as to preserve their identity - thereby risking becoming increasingly unpopular with their

---

8   Those instances, rare anyway, where labour market regulations are not stringently applied to East Germany, are only temporary deviations in the transformation process and do not flag a reconsideration of the basic provisions.

own clientele - or they adjust to the new conditions and allow for more flexible, individualized agreements - thereby taking the risk of sacrificing their own identity which, at least in the eyes of the public, heavily depends on ideas of collective standardization. In practice, the unions are likely to strike a compromise line as they did in the past, with the public rhetoric and the broad outline of their stance remaining 'conservative', but with some flexibility sprinkled into collective agreements as to working time and conditions, which helps accommodate the new trends.

As in the last decade, this will be a very uneasy position somewhere between the Scylla of degenerating into a mere service organization of employees, and the Charybdis of losing the contract to the new generation of more relaxed young employees. All this adds up to a position of vulnerability of the union movement with no prospect for a reversal of the gradually falling union participation rates noted in the 1980s and the 1990s.

Whether this will lead on average to more or to less militancy in wage bargaining is open to speculation: more militancy may be due to the fact that unions tend to show more muscle in one field (remuneration) if other fields begin to slip out of their grip (working time etc.). This view is consistent with the off-hand observation that German unions were rather moderate in wage claims at times when they had important other aims on their agenda like co-determination in the early 1950s and the shortening of the working week all through the 1980s. By the late 1980s, the switches had been set towards the 35-hour week to be realized in the next few years; no comparably spectacular aim is in sight for the coming decade so that unions may focus again on their traditional main battlefield, that of wages. Other aims such as overhauling the structure of wages between ill-defined professional groups are presently discussed in union circles, but obviously, they will remain technical side issues.

On the other hand, it is hard to imagine unions flexing their muscles at a time which will basically have an anti-union tinge: after all, the only dramatic 'wage revolution' in West German post-war history happened in the period 1969-74, a period of growing union popularity, sharply rising union density rates and a union-friendly government which fostered a social democratic reform enthusiasm. Even if the Federal Government became again social democratic/liberal in 1994 or 1998, the very strong union influence of earlier times is unlikely to be repeated. A more realistic scenario seems to be that unions periodically step up wage demands in boom times such as in 1990/91 and in the present wage rounds, but do refrain from an ideologically-fuelled massive redistribution from 'capital to labour'.

The only major macroeconomic trend which seems to work in favour of unions' aims and aspirations will be the demographic changes to be expected from the mid-1990s on, with successive waves of retirement leading to a drastic *exogenous* reduction of the domestic labour supply. On closer inspection, however, even this trend will have double-edged consequences for the unions' strategy, since it is likely to require more internal wage differentiation. In the lower segments of the labour market, the ensuing shortages will be rather easily accommodated by attracting foreign workers or immigrants from Eastern Europe, Turkey, and maybe also increasingly - via France and Italy - from Northern Africa. In the upper qualitative segments of the market, this will not be possible to the same extent so that structural disparities in scarcity between different types of labour, which already exist, will be further accentuated. Naturally, upwardly mobile skilled workers - mostly German ones - will profit most from these trends, and they will call for a more pronounced wage stratification between skilled and unskilled labour. As an important union clientele, they will put pressure on the union leadership to allow them to cash in their scarcity rent.

In turn, this will push unions into another variant of their basic strategic dilemma: either they will give way to the internal demand for wage stratification and thus further erode their traditional reputation as representatives of the broad masses of (unskilled) blue-collar workers, or they will stick to an egalitarian philosophy and thus risk appearing as a defender of the rights of fringe groups, notably of immigrants and foreign labour. In many respects, these conflicts may resemble the dilemma of unions in the 1960s when the extreme shortage of skilled labour led to massive wage drift, i.e. to a much faster growth of actual earnings than of contractual minimum wages. It finally ended in a wage revolution with the union leadership bending to the call of the rank-and-file for more militancy. As argued above, however, such a gloomy outcome seems to be much less likely in the future simply because the unions' power base is gradually eroding for other reasons anyway.

The really big challenge to unions in the 1990s is a structural one, namely the transformation crisis in East Germany. To the great surprise of many observers - especially foreign ones - pilot wage agreements in East Germany settled for an equalization of contractual wages in major industries between West and East by about 1995. There are basically two reasons for these altogether unreasonable terms: first, the employers' side was represented by heavily subsidized, not yet privatized firms which faced a very soft budget constraint and thus could effectively externalize the future costs of the agreements. Second, German unions tend to take it as an utmost priority to avoid anything like a long-term regional differentiation of wages which could violate the maxim 'equal pay for equal work'. In fact, the inter-regional wage structure turned out rigid in earlier periods of crisis as well, even if the incidence of structural crisis was heavily concentrated in specific regions like the Ruhr valley or the Saar. In this sense, unions took the transformation in the East as another regional problem not to be accommodated by regional wage restraint.

Clearly, it will be of crucial importance for the prospects of the East German labour market whether this misguided wage policy will be reversed or not. If not, all the burden of creating incentives for private investment in the East will continue to lay on public subsidies which, due to unprecedented fiscal constraints, can hardly do the job alone. The danger will then rise that East Germany will be stuck with a dramatically higher equilibrium unemployment rate than the West. The big question of German labour markets in the 1990s will be whether such a disastrous 'dualization' of labour markets into a full employment Western and a long-term unemployment Eastern part can be avoided.

Probably the only way is to renegotiate wage contracts for the East; whether unions will be ready to reopen negotiations - which would be unique in the history of German collective bargaining - depends on the sheer extent of the crisis and, most importantly, on the prospective fiscal consolidation of the federal budget which may cut heavily into the transfers to the East. At any rate, an uncompromising stance of the unions might become very unpopular in view of a deepening crisis and mounting public pressures, both in the West and in the East. In the West, the average man in the street and the average union member may begin to realize that his/her tax bill is in fact a direct function of Eastern wage levels. In the East, the worker may increasingly acknowledge the fact that his/her market prospects depend heavily on a persistent wage differential between West and East.

From a more long-term perspective, German unification may amount to a very serious challenge to the unions' prominent role in society. After all, the East German population shares the anti-collectivist attitude which now predominates all over the former communist countries in Central and Eastern Europe: with the union movement having been instrumentalized and thus thoroughly discredited by communist regimes ('Solidarnosc' in Poland being the exception to the rule), people are very reluctant to join again any collective organization which pretends to further their individual interests. In fact, virtually all unions presently complain about the great difficulty of recruiting new members in the East, a difficulty which is not only due to high unemployment, but also to a general scepticism *vis-à-vis* any form of collectivist tutelage. Even if labour markets in the East will tighten up in due course, this scepticism is likely to remain a characteristic feature of the East German labour force. In this respect, East Germany of the 1990s will resemble West Germany of the 1950s, when the so-called 'sceptical generation', who had vivid memories of the Nazi-style collectivism, kept aloof from large-scale interest groups, with the unions facing very low popularity ratings and declining density rates. Note that this anti-unionism has a direct political parallel in the rather poor showing of the Social Democratic Party: as in West Germany in the misery of the late 1940s and the early 1950s, voters in East Germany today tend to flock behind the conservative/liberal wing of the political spectrum, which appears to promise more economic competence to further their personal and mostly material interests.

10. Greece: Shaping Factors*

INTRODUCTION

It is evident that a number of issues like trade or environmental pollution, will have a bearing on the Greek economy, but these problems cannot be solved by Greece alone. This chapter analyses only problems that require national initiatives. We successively analyse the economic, social and political factors.

SECTION 1: ECONOMIC FACTORS

Nominal Convergence and Real Growth

For a prolonged period that ended with the second oil shock the Greek economy was growing at a faster rate than the rest of OECD economies. The gap between Greek and the average EC standard of living was being closed at a reasonable pace. But since the second oil shock the climate changed in the early 1980s. The Greek economy faced stagflation and high fiscal imbalances, as well as occasional balance of payments crises. The reasons were a fast expanding and inefficient state sector, unsustainable income demands and the increasing regulation of market forces.

A high PSBR absorbed financial resources, thus reducing investment in productive capital and entailing high real interest rates. Equally the falling rate of return on capital (which was actually negative in the mid-1980s) further reduced investment and held back technological progress. From here on, the Greek economy started *diverging* from its Community partners.

This change cannot be explained either by past performance, or by the international situation, as it occurred during the 'longest peace time expansion' of the world economy. This allows us hope that it was

---

*   Prof. G. Economou, N. Tsaveas and P. Politis.

266

peculiar to that period and can be easily reversed.

A three-year stabilization programme was enacted in 1990 and a more radical 'convergence' plan is being prepared for the future. The aim of both these plans is to rein in the state sector's expansion. It is to be hoped that the reduction of public deficits, the promotion of competition and deregulation will restore the market mechanism as a way of disseminating information and allocating resources. The plan will also strengthen incentives for productivity increases and reduce the slack in the economy. Reduced demand from the state sector and increased supply, coupled with a reduction in market inelasticities, will help fight inflationary pressures.

A rather strict economic policy over the next few years will produce excess supply conditions in the markets for goods and labour. This will also be necessary in order to infuse a sense of realism to producers and trade unions who were not previously exposed to market discipline. The policy of currency appreciation will also continue. The final aim of this process is to bring drachma into the ERM in time for the Third Stage of EMU. The hope is that this policy, if sustained, will force individuals in Greece to realize that the rules of the game have drastically changed. Borrowing the EMS's credibility the Greek Government hopes to change expectations and influence private sector behaviour.

There has already been substantial progress in liberalizing the labour market. The indexation of wages has been abandoned and greater flexibility in the determination of employment is now allowed. A much greater source of optimism comes from the new realism shown by trade unions. Trade unions in the private sector (but not in the public sector) have accepted a two-year wage plan that involves substantial wage restraint. A rather centralized wage bargaining framework has forced trade unions to face up to economic problems, and they have responded quite successfully, compared to a rather militant past. Eighteen years after the fall of the dictatorship the trade union movement is now coming of age. Private sector trade unions are now giving greater thought to maintaining a stable employment level instead of pressing excessive wage demands. Minimum wages will probably remain low, in order to help absorb youth unemployment. These developments lead us to hope that the increase in unemployment will not be as large as could be expected from the unavoidable harshness of the adjustment programme. Unfortunately this new realism does not extend to the public sector unions, and there is no sign yet that they are coming to terms with the changed conditions.

The Macroeconomic Environment

While all other EC countries managed to stabilise and restructure their economies, Greece had to adopt a stabilization programme in 1990. This happened after another stabilization programme during 1986-87 was dropped, which had it been continued would have created the conditions for some success. The success of the current stabilization efforts will be judged by the degree to which we attain the targets which have been set on reducing the inflation rate and the public deficit as well as creating the right conditions for faster growth.

This time the Greek Government seems to be obliged to follow this effort to the end, the main reason being that restructuring and stabilization are preconditions to the country joining the economic and monetary union.

The growth rate of the Greek economy, for the period up to 1996, is expected to be low since priority is given to the stabilization and the restructuring of the economy. According to the convergence plan, there will be an increase in GDP only in the range of 2.5% and 3.5%. But from 1997, or 1999 at the latest, an acceleration of the growth rate for the Greek economy is expected. This will come from the capability of the domestic industry to compete effectively, both in the domestic market as well as abroad. Greek industry needs not only to expand its markets, but also to attract resources especially from the rich Western European countries. An important factor to succeed in this area is improving the infrastructure (public transport, telecommunications, energy, banking etc.) and especially the educational system, the public services and the labour market. Special attention should be given to the lifting of certain perverse incentives which would help in attracting foreign investment.

Studies at IOBE have shown that the slowing down of the economic growth in the Greek economy after 1973, and the complete absence of any growth in the 1980s, which increased the income per capita differences between Greece and the other European countries, are due to a number of interlinked structural factors. The increase in public spending, incomes policies which were not based on productivity and the exchange rate policies are the factors identified which led to the reduction of the return on capital used in the industrial sector.

The relative success of the stabilization plan of 1986-87 which involved austerity measures and incomes policies, and the right handling of the exchange rate seems to justify the IOBE's suggestions.

These observations also seem to apply to the current stabilization programme, and explain the lack of effectiveness of it. It seems that the programme does not cope with certain structural problems, especially those that concern the competitiveness of the Greek economy. A recent econometric study at IOBE, shows that the observed slowing down of convergence, and the recent divergence can be explained by four crucial factors: the exchange rates, the rate of return on capital, the PSBR, and the real interest rates.

Simulations also showed that a different mix of policies, which would have taken care of these four factors, would allow a differential rate of growth and increase it by at least 2%. But it seems there are no political or structural conditions which will facilitate a faster convergence. This can also be seen by the fact that the convergence plan allows a growth rate of only 2.5-3.5% for the above period (1993-96).

The Greek economy seems likely to go through the following phases: it is likely that the de-industrialization and the zero growth observed in the 1980s will be replaced by a slow growth path, something which is also predicted by the convergence plan in the 1993-96 period. This will offer the right conditions for a faster growth for the period beyond 1997. It is likely that the difference in Greek growth rates with the EC average will not exceed the 2% level or even approach the 1.5% of Portugal.

This is, of course, given the inadequacy of the political conditions and the structural transformations necessary for an accelerated convergence, and the prediction that the EC will succeed in improving the structural changes according to the Maastricht agreement.

It is more likely that a differential growth rate between the rest of the EC and Greece of just 1% will materialize, which would be consistent with slow convergence. This will raise the per capita income from 50% of the average EC to 56% by the year 2010.

An alternative faster route to the convergence of the Greek economy to the European will necessitate drastic changes in the political and social system, in education, the public service, the labour market and the infrastructure generally of the country. These changes are unlikely to happen without a political consensus as well as support from the Community.

As far as the labour market is concerned, it does not look to be an obstacle for economic growth. It is predicted that a satisfactory increase in the size of the labour, a higher participation rate of women, as well as training programmes will increase the elasticity of supply and reduce the natural rate of unemployment. For the period beyond 2000 a drastic fall in unemployment and an increased role for women in the labour market are likely.

This prospect of a lower unemployment rate will not be realized if:

(a)   The convergence programme turns out not to be a success.

(b)   Immigration from Eastern European countries is not checked.

On the other hand a low population growth could turn out to be a constraint for the economic growth, unless the right demographic and economic policies are taken both domestically and at the European level. As far as the economy is concerned the following could be of importance: the share of agriculture both in terms of production and employment will fall. This will happen at an accelerated rate, especially in view of the reforms of the Common Agricultural Policy and the GATT Round.

However, the reduction of employment in agriculture could slow down, if new Community programmes give the incentive for new opportunities for full or part-time employment in this sector.

During the last ten years there was an almost zero growth in the Greek manufacturing. This was mainly due to the sudden opening of the market to international competition by means of lower tariffs and protection, as well as the bad macroeconomic conditions which prevailed. This tendency is likely to be reversed and the share of manufacturing in GDP will increase, from about 18% in 1990 to maybe 20% in 2010. This share, however, will continue to be the lowest in all Europe. Employment in manufacturing is likely to remain at the same level or perhaps to fall slightly, as a result of improved productivity. Deregulation and the cleaning up of debt-ridden companies will also work in the same direction.

There are likely to be many changes in the structure of Greek industry, due to the creation of the common market and increased competition. Not only the relative importance of sectors will change, but also the conditions prevailing within any one of them. Mergers, take-overs and cooperation agreements are likely to be substantial.

Some traditional sectors with relatively low technology seem to be undergoing restructuring and they are likely to continue to be the backbone of the Greek manufacturing sector. Others like the shoe industry have a tendency towards negative growth whilst textiles can still cope with competition from cheap imports from LDCs. The Community's proposals for the textile industry are also likely to reduce these external effects. The growth of high-technology sectors will largely depend on the technological policies of the Community, as well as the ability of the country to attract innovation-rich investment. Studies at IOBE show that business seems to be optimistic about these prospects. The proper macroeconomic environment, some structural changes, and improved infrastructure seem to be the main factors needed to allow the industry to improve its competitiveness. Under the regime of fixed exchange rates, the role of incomes policy to advance competitiveness will remain important.

The prospects of the Greek industry are also closely related to the prevailing conditions in the labour market and, therefore, the degree of responsibility in pay negotiations.

Although industry will remain the most strategic sector, which will facilitate growth, services will take on an ever increasing importance. European integration is also likely to increase the relative importance of tourism in Greece. Shipping, which is one of the most dynamic sectors, production of information technology, the banking sector, and education will advance and become the base for sustained growth. Education seems to be a basic way to improve services at large, and the adoption of common policies in Europe will advance the restructuring of these sectors.

Greek Comparative Advantage

Greece's expansion, in the past, was based on certain dynamic sectors like shipping which is typical of a sector with a high capital requirement, but also one with low sunk costs. Competition, therefore, was always typical in this sector, and the quality of the service, human capital, and Greek entrepreneurship were the driving forces. Resources were transferred, through taxation or investment, to other sectors which were predominantly the food industry, chemicals and construction.

Today's characteristics of Greece are different. There is no single sector which will finance the expansion of Greece, nor a typical technology. As in the case of shipping, the human capital remains the most important factor. Despite the variation in quality of the Greek education, there is a large number of graduates, covering all specializations. A lack of resources makes the use of specific technological possibilities obligatory, but is by no means characteristic of the Greek economy. It seems that, in conditions where the profitability of the industry falls, companies, in order to survive, use the factors that they can acquire relatively cheaper. If capital is expensive, they choose labour-intensive technologies. Human capital is, therefore, a determining factor for future expansion, which together with entrepreneurship help to use different technologies at different times.

Today it is obvious that, despite the fact that Greek manufacturing has recently realized zero growth, there is a dynamic part which not only struggles to survive in extremely adverse conditions, but also expands both domestically and abroad.

It is also characteristic that this dynamic part of the Greek industry is not confined to certain industry sectors, but is spread across the spectrum. Information Technology with low capital requirements, but with extremely skilled labour demands is expanding fairly quickly, as are parts of the food industry with high capital requirement, a large number of differentiated products, and human capital of variable quality. The same is true for the production of cement, where new technology was adopted and an advantage gained.

The marketing of the products is improving, and there are more efforts to discover niche markets. Lately, the tendency to expand to the East European markets has been observed, by providing goods and services of relatively good quality but cheaper than Western European companies can offer. This is also helped by friendly relations with most East European companies in the past.

The Greek Merchant Navy

Greece has a long and successful history as a country with a strong mercantile navy. It has the largest merchant fleet in the Community. Moves towards the common market and freedom of movement will affect Greek shipping.

Cabotage restrictions cover three branches of domestic shipping services in Greece:

(a)   Regular passenger and ferry services to the islands.
(b)   Mainland-to-mainland cargo ship services.
(c)   Cruising and yachting. The latter is closer to the tourist industry than shipping *per se*.

It is likely that following the adoption of the Maastricht Treaty the issue of cabotage restrictions within the European Union also will be resolved. The Portuguese Presidency in the first half of 1992 put forward proposals that envisaged two lines of action:

(a)   Liberalization of restrictions associated with specific derogations.
(b)   The imposition of public service obligations by operators such as those that exist at present for remote or underpopulated islands.

Mainland-to-mainland cargo ship services are likely to be liberalized by 1 January 1993. This is not expected to have any significant impact on the Greek economy, given the limited volume of cargoes involved, especially bearing in mind the continuation of restrictions for ships smaller than 650 gt., until the year 2004.

Island cabotage is likely to be liberalized by 1999. For regular passenger and ferry services to the Greek islands, cabotage restrictions are expected to be retained until the year 2004. The lifting of these restrictions is expected to have a negative effect on the defence capabilities of the Greek Aegean Archipelago, since the Greek authorities will not be able to have full control of sea transport services to the islands in case of an emergency.

Cabotage restrictions in cruising concern only *cyclical cruises*, i.e. passengers embarking and disembarking at Greek ports. This is only a subsection of the Greek cruise market. Its liberalization will produce increased competition for Greek operations in that market. The main handicap that will have to be removed is their obligation to have a full Greek complement, including their on-board 'hotel type' of services since their foreign competitors can employ low-cost crews from developing countries. Nevertheless, increased competition in that latter market will be to the benefit of the tourist sector in Greece.

On the other hand, activities of the Greek cruising sector are likely to expand to other markets (e.g. the Caribbean), and therefore create a favourable environment for the business.

Public Administration

The structure and workings of the Greek civil service have been pivotal in influencing the economic and social transformation of the country. On the one hand, a strong, centralized civil service has in the past helped forge a unitary and homogeneous state with very little regional differences with a high degree of geographic and social mobility and imbalances. But more recently we are becoming increasingly aware of its shortcomings:

(i)   Its bureaucratic mentality, inefficiency and centralized decision-making.
(ii)   Its overstaffing in tandem with strong and militant unionization.
(iii)   Politicization, which makes the civil service often the servant of the party that happens to be in government.

Local authorities suffer from the same illnesses and, in addition, they face the lack of independence (from central government), restricted financial resources, and very little leeway in deciding about their own affairs.

The above shortcomings are leading to increasing squandering of the revenues under public control (60% of GNP), but they also have adverse spill-over effects, in reducing private sector productivity to the extent that the latter is regulated or influenced by the state sector. The solution to the state sector's problems can be achieved through an overhaul of our political system, with a move towards more consensual policy-making, and the immunization of the civil service from party interferences.

Two further developments are working in that direction:

(a)   The increasing computerization (to a large extent financed by Community transfers) is making the flow of information easier and decision-making more transparent to outsiders. This makes it easier to bring civil servants and their political masters to account.
(b)   The need to adhere to the Maastricht rules on budget deficits. It is clear enough for everyone to see that we cannot reduce PSBR to 3% of GNP without :

-       Reining in on the ever expanding civil service, and reducing its numbers.
-       Increasing the productivity of the public sector.

Furthermore, the Maastricht Treaty had a more profound effect. It forced on all the parties the message that Greece was falling behind, and that the spiralling costs of the state sector were mainly to blame. There now seems to be sufficient consensus that the era of pork-barrel politics, influence peddling and patronage has to come to an end. There is broad agreement that we need a streamlined, more efficient and smaller civil service, although there remain differences as to the extent and speed of the adjustment.

The Social Security System

Greek social insurance institutions are integrated, in that they provide both health and pension insurance. To the extent that longevity is correlated with good health this arrangement implicitly effects a hedging of competing risks. The main problem of Greece's social security system is the multiplicity of institutions. Apart from the three main organizations (for civil servants, private-sector employees and farmers) there exist a multiplicity of small or inefficient institutions, either for special categories of the population or supplementary ones that provide top-up benefits or cover special risks. As a result, labour mobility is reduced and scale economies are not fully taken advantage of.

Since the mid-1980s, an elementary National Health Service has been in operation. It has provided health cover to a small part of the population previously uninsured, but it has also led to sky-rocketing costs. There is a feeling that the management of health services has deteriorated. There is also a feeling that there have been too many appointments of non-medical personnel in the National Health Service, managerial incompetence, political interference, coupled with vocal and militant trade unions. As a result, the inflated costs have not resulted in a better health service, and in some cases some overall deterioration has occurred.

The pension insurance funds suffer from explosive debts. This is due (among other reasons) to the ageing of the population, the reduction in the pensionable age, evasion of social security contribution, and to the extension of cover to categories of the population which had not contributed towards their pension. The main problem is that pensions were allowed to rise much above their actuarially fair level, as an ill-conceived way to promote income redistribution.

There has been a substantial change in the pensions system in 1990. This has temporarily halted the cost increases, but more fundamental measures will have to be adopted soon.

The modernization and rehabilitation of the social insurance system is extremely difficult, as it is interrelated with Greece's political system and is bound to hurt politically strong groups. The general consensus between the two main parties is bringing hope that a reasonable solution will be found, especially under the pressure to converge to EC standards. There will be a reduction in the ratio of pensions to social security contributions towards actuarially fair levels, stricter requirements for getting a pension, insureds' participation in paying for health costs, the amalgamation of the smallest institutions, and greater operational autonomy for the remaining ones. The difficulties stem:

(i)   From the long gestation period until those measures bear fruit, during which time social security deficits will be financed by the central government.

(ii)   The need to enforce substantial reductions in what people considered fully guaranteed benefit levels.

A source of relative optimism is the private sector. Despite being discouraged in the past, pension insurance companies are booming. The younger population is realizing the problems of the state sector and is increasing fast its demand for private insurance. We are now seeing private pension insurance companies expanding into health provision and other related areas like banking and financial services. There have also been successful efforts to export health management services to East European countries. The private insurance companies are and may well continue to be one of the most dynamic sectors in Greece.

The Family and the Economy

The Greek family is quite tightly knit. There is reason to believe that the internal organization of the Greek family will be loosened over the next years.

The family can be viewed as a mechanism for intergenerational trade and insurance. Parents accumulate assets that will be enjoyed by their offspring and in turn they expect that their children will look after them. In an overlapping generation model it would be elementary to show that this intergenerational trade allows the economy to increase its savings rate and move closer to the optimum.

If the family loses its internal strength, savings can be expected to decline. Many of the incentives of accumulating assets to pass on as bequests, dowries etc. will be weakened. We can expect that savings will be depressed correspondingly. We can expect that some other institutions will be called upon to fill this vacuum, such as (pay-as-you-go) pension funds.

There are also a number of secondary issues, that may affect the efficiency of fiscal policy or the government's receipts from inheritance tax, but these are probably of second order.

The loosening of the family ties will have some important effects on poverty and income distribution and will affect public attitudes. We may expect that a number of old-age people will be less supported by their family, especially if fewer children per retired person means that they will have to carry a much more onerous burden. How will the society respond to an increase in old-age poverty?

Equally, university students are currently expected to be supported by their family for much longer than in other countries. A 25-year old student is supported by his family. If this support vanishes, the society (state) will be required to provide scholarships high enough to pay for all their expenses as in most Western economies. There will also probably be pressure for shorter university courses.

Finally, the unemployed are usually supported by their family, and possible given some secondary jobs in family business. This has allowed Greece to keep unemployment benefits at the lowest level in Europe without experiencing substantial social unrest, despite substantial unemployment increases in the late 1980s. If this support is reduced, the unemployed will fall into poverty, and the demand for unemployment benefits is also likely to be increased. The market wage will become more responsive to unemployment.

If the family starts losing its strength, and younger generations move out of their parents' houses, there will inevitably be an increased demand for housing, especially small rented apartments to cater for those young home-leavers.

Becker has maintained that the family is the best channel for transmitting human capital from one generation to the other. The close-knit Greek family performs this task as required; even more than that, it transmits social values: children are usually expected to follow in their parents' footsteps and accept their values.

The extremely high demand for university education is the result of this; educated parents wish to send their children to university, even if this university is in Bulgaria, Romania etc. A less strong family would reduce this demand for education, especially abroad. It would also permit some greater mobility between places; children would not be expected to stay near their parents' place. On the other hand, it may increase youth delinquency and inner city violence, especially if it coincides with increasing youth unemployment.

Telecommunications and Transport

The development of infrastructure was delayed in the past by the expansion of the state sector. The large public sector deficits absorbed a significant proportion of national savings and left little for investment in infrastructure which is necessary in order to renovate the crumbling network. The convergence programme now in operation will inevitably pose further problems as the need to consolidate the fiscal situation will further restrict the availability of funds.

The evolution of the telecommunications sector will be determined by technological factors and the need to converge to the Community standards. The main emphasis will be in the dissolution of the state monopoly, as well as the promotion of new services.

The state-owned Telecommunications Organization of Greece has significantly improved its financial position over the last couple of years, but this has not resulted in any appreciable amelioration of its services. The liberalization of the telecommunications market will impose significant strains on the state sector, due to the loss of its monopoly power. The hope is that this will be more than compensated by the influx of private capital and entrepreneurship. There has already been developed a significant industry supplying telecommunications equipment, which may gain from the opening of new East European markets. There is also a need to introduce mobile communications, digital equipment and optic fibres.

That part of Greek foreign trade that depends on road transport through Yugoslavia has been disrupted by the civil war. There have been attempts to divert the flow of trucks through Bulgaria and Hungary but with the effect of inflating costs. Even if the situation in Yugoslavia stabilizes eventually, Greek trucks and trains will have to go through at least five border controls, instead of only one, in order to reach another EC country (Italy).

The best solution would be to develop the direct axis Greece-Italy and Greece-France by sea. This will necessitate changing the structure of the road system of Greece and large investments will be needed in port facilities financed by public as well as private funds. Greek industry has largely been located on the Eastern coast, along the Athens-Thessaloniki axis. The new orientation of Greek exports towards the Community and the transport problems in former Yugoslavia will necessitate a major relocation effort towards the West.

A major project is the building of the Egnatia motorway, linking Thrace and Macedonia to North-Western Greece as well as the integration of the Thessaly road network to Western Greece. There is bound to be a relocation of economic activity from the East towards the (as yet less developed) Western part of Greece. Part of this new infrastructure will be financed by Community funds, which will have to play an important part in this long-term policy of formulating new trade roads between Greece and the rest of the Community. In the medium-term Greece will have to think about a rail link from Igoumenitsa to Volos and a bridge connecting the Peloponese to Western Greece.

Finally, we have to mention that an environmental tax that will increase the cost of fuel and, as a result, of transport, will increase the costs of transporting goods between Greece and the rest of the Community.

SECTION 2: SOCIAL FACTORS

The main theme prevailing in Greek society in the next decade will be the effort to modernize, i.e. to converge to the form of economic, social and political organization that can be roughly described as West European.

Modernization is a deep-rooted desire in the country. Great thinkers of the past and politicians have tried to change society, bringing it closer to the Western model of social organization. Statesmen like Trikoupis in the late nineteenth century and Venizelos, during the inter-war period, initiated reforms towards that aim.

Today the voices calling for modernization are numerous and can be found everywhere: in all political parties, in the trade union movement, in the employers' organizations. They all conclude that participation in the European Union dictates, besides economic convergence, a radical change in social attitudes and values, which in turn will influence and be influenced by economic progress. There is a widely shared and well-defined sense that Greek society should leave behind practices of the past and adjust to the new conditions.

Central to the idea of modernization is the notion that the role the State has played in Greek society in the post-war period should change. Differences of opinion still exist, but they reflect varying estimates about the extent of the necessary changes rather than disagreement on principle. Modernization in the broader sense is seen as a process of transition from the public to the private, from protection to competition, from the group to the individual. As such, it constitutes a powerful ideology that is very likely to become dominant in the Greek society of the 1990s and thereby radically affect social norms of thinking and behaviour in the future.

Factors Inducing New Social Attitudes and Practices

Apart from ideology, there are also important real factors that can play a decisive role in changing social attitudes and practices.

The first is the fact that the State, mainly for economic reasons, can no longer function as it did in the past. The economic system that produced a certain typology of social responses has reached its limits and it is not sustainable any more. The retreat of statism in the real world dictated by the needs of the economy will certainly change people's ideas about what the State can and what it cannot do. It is indicative to note that public opinion polls conducted in the period of the last two years show: a suspicious public *vis-à-vis* the State and its initiatives; an increase of calls for law and order; demands for efficient public management; a considerable retreat of the support for government intervention practices, in favour of private initiative and the firm.

The second important factor is the existence of a small but dynamic private sector that has already transformed itself, has forged strong ties with the rest of Europe and has adopted the West European ethos. A relatively significant part of Greek society has learned to live and work in an international environment, embracing new values. This part can form the nucleus of an important social force exerting strong influence on the society as a whole in the future.

The *third* factor is the opening up of Greek society to the rest of the world and, more importantly, the country's participation in the EC. The specific cultural characteristics, a language that is the oldest in Europe, but spoken only in Greece, a long history of religious adversity to the West as well as to the East and the way Greeks experienced the country's relation with other nations throughout their modern history, contributed to the formation of a society that presented strong *defensive* elements. A defensive culture is reluctant to accept changes and influences. It becomes entrenched in its own system of values and develops mechanisms to keep the *other* out. If however, channels of communication are opened up, defensive structures are eroded. This is the phase Greece is going through, a process that is expected to accelerate rapidly in the years to come. The most important channel of communication is the country's participation in the EC, through which important changes are introduced, not only in the form of institutions or economic practices. The EC also serves as a powerful paradigm. It is argued convincingly that the decision to enter the EC was for Greece the most important political decision in its post-war history with far-reaching consequences in all aspects of economic, political and social life. Communication with the EC, in the broadest sense of the world, involving large numbers of people and institutions, is estimated to have a growing positive influence on the process of modernization in the future.

A Difficult Transition

The factors listed above will be pivotal in shaping new social behaviour, practices and norms. However it will not be a smooth transition, as it is expected to meet with strong resistance particularly at the social level. The argument however for less state control, that has come to be synonymous with modernization, does not have in Greece the class or political connotations that it has in other countries. It transcends political ideologies and social groups and proponents of one or other solution can be found everywhere. Consequently, the conflict around modernization is not expected to become *political*. It will remain mainly social in character reflecting demands of social groups to be shielded from change.

To identify the loci of resistance and the potential for social tension it is useful to refer briefly to the structure of Greek society and the way it can affect the process of modernization. This structure presents some important differences compared to most of the other European nations. It has the following crucial characteristics:

First, there is still a large agricultural population, amounting to some 25% of total active population, i.e. three times higher than the community average.

Second, wage earners represent only one-third of the active population. Most of them are employed in the public sector.

Third, there is a large number of self-employed people, roughly equal to that of wage earners. Their percentage in the active population is again the highest in the European Community.

Fourth, there is widespread multiple employment, usually part-time employment, often in the large shadow economy.

Fifth, there is wide resource to family employment and income strategies, with families and not individuals functioning as income maximizing units.

This framework of social relations has the following important consequences:

-   A large number of people rely directly or indirectly on the State expecting it to intervene in their favour. The belief that personal or group welfare can come from the activity of a benevolent state prevented till now the formation of a civil society that can function autonomously. Thus the level of social organization is very low and its functions are delegated to party politics.

-   The absence of clear-cut stratifications, the weakness of the civil society and the high degree of social mobility transform the notion of class antagonisms. Social groups direct their demands mainly towards the State asking for favourable treatment or protection against other groups. Social conflicts reflect more often antagonisms for the distribution of state protection, privileges and exemptions, than strife between classes.

-   There is a diffusion of economic and social power among many groups that undermines the State's ability to implement its general policies, bypassing corporatist demands.

This social structure and the attitudes it fosters present serious obstacles to modernization. Resistance will be stronger and more persistent among those who are directly dependent on the State in one form or the other. But the ideology of statism in general will gradually retreat, under the influence of the factors listed above, weakening the strength of this resistance.

Moreover some of the social characteristics, infused with a new attitude, can be proved to be beneficial in the future.

The preference e.g. of Greeks in favour of becoming self-employed or working in small enterprises (possibly partnerships between friends or relatives) which was a negative factor in the process of heavy industrialization, may well prove a blessing in disguise for the future as the newer technologies require smaller units of operation and closer cooperation between similarly-minded people.

The parallel or shadow economy, will continue to play an important role as a social buffer, providing the means of survival for those becoming unemployed in the primary market.

Finally one should note that the diffusion of social and economic power, together with the existence of strong family ties has sheltered Greek society from significant social problems. Relative to other Western countries up to now there has been almost no racism and very little problems of youth delinquency, hooliganism, etc. It is quite probable that we shall see some such phenomena in the future, but as long as the current recession is not prolonged they are probably going to remain of minor importance compared to other countries' experience. On the other hand, there is bound to be some lessening of family ties, but for the foreseeable future they are going to be strong enough so as to remain the chief way of providing social insurance. Income distribution may change in favour of those who would undertake business initiatives in all sectors, but a strong trend towards the emergence of a dual society cannot be envisaged.

Concluding, one can safely assume that Greece is moving towards being a much more market-driven economy, a fact that is expected to have important consequences on the prevailing social values. There are serious indications that this process is irreversible and that it will be a constant factor in the future. The transition however is not expected to be smooth. Severe conflicts may arise at the social front around the role of the State and society's relation to it. On the other hand the existence of modernizing tendencies across all social groups points to the possibility of a new social partnership including all the elements that adopt the same *European* perspective. A very significant development towards that direction is the rapprochement of employers and workers in the private sector that has taken place in the last two years, resulting in the virtual elimination of strikes in the private sector in a period of strict incomes policies and widespread labour unrest in the public sector.

SECTION 3: POLITICAL FACTORS

The International Environment Security Issues

Greece is situated in the most advanced point of contact of the Community with third European states. It is the nearest meeting point with Asia and the only Member State neighbouring as many as four countries, each of them presenting strong particularities in their political, economic and social structure. Moreover, Greece has no land frontier with any other Community country.

Therefore the country's relations with those neighbouring states will be a decisive factor not only for Greece itself but for the Community as a whole. There are three important areas of concern: first, Greece's position in the sub-system of international relations in the Balkans, second, relations with Turkey and third developments in the Mediterranean.

Greece and the Balkans

The countries of the Balkan Peninsula constitute a sub-system of international relations in Europe, strongly influenced by the developments in the continent, but with its own distinct features and peculiarities.

This sub-system is today both in crisis and unstable. The reasons of instability stem both from domestic and international factors: as the Warsaw Pact has disintegrated and NATO is going through a process of fundamental changes, old bilateral issues, based on ethnic contradictions and historical cleavages are gaining importance in the Balkan Peninsula.

These processes have the potential of affecting the whole structure of international relations in the region and exert a strong influence on the bilateral relations of the Balkan States. In the next decade the new situation is likely to produce territorial claims, religious and ethnic conflicts and renewed security risks for Europe as a whole.

The factors which determine the present crisis and are likely to persist in the future are:

- The disintegration of Yugoslavia.
- The creation of new state entities from former Yugoslavia. It is however certain that these new states will be confronted with the following problems:

- Insufficient local resources.
- An insignificant internal market.
- Population not numerous and decreasing due to migratory trends.
- Their borders becoming the object of international disputes.

Of particular interest to Greece are the conflicts that may arise in the so-called 'Republic of Macedonia'. The establishment of such a state does not guarantee the elimination of instability. On the contrary some basic facts, already evident, contain the seeds of future conflicts:

- Albanian and Bulgarian claims to some parts of the region have already been expressed. Serbian political leadership, regardless of ideological persuasion, insists that the inhabitants of Skopje are Southern Serbs.
- On the other hand, the leadership of Skopje also maintains long-standing territorial claims against Bulgaria and Greece. The

insistence on the use of the name 'Macedonia', together with the constitutional amendment which identifies the Democracy of Skopje as the 'historical motherland of all Macedonians' lead to the conclusion that the new State aspires to wide areas of Bulgaria and Greece.

- Finally, the structure of the political and ethnic forces in the new State points to an acceleration of partitioning tendencies rather than the establishment of a national identity. The territorial narrowness of the new republic as an enclaved state, the lack of military capacity and economic capabilities are expected to contribute even further to that trend, forcing Skopje to operate as a pendulum between neighbouring countries.

Thus, on this new State converge all the domestic and international factors which can turn it into a destabilizing element of conflict between all the countries of the region.

The Security Problem of Bulgaria

The collapse of the Warsaw Pact left Bulgaria in a strategic vacuum. For a long time the basic premises of Bulgarian foreign policy were the *Turkish threat* and the historical animosity with Serbia.

The main point of conflict with Turkey has always been the Muslim minority in South Bulgaria. A recent trend of rapprochement between Turkey and Bulgaria is again based on this minority, through the Turkish minority party, the Movement of Freedoms and Rights.

It will be particularly important for Greece in the future if Turkish-Bulgarian *détente* is realized at the expense of Greek-Bulgarian cooperation, that for a long time has been close and constantly improving.

Finally, a factor which will be of great importance is the development of the economic relations between Bulgaria and Turkey. The establishment of the Black Sea Cooperation Zone and the liberalization of capital and workers' transfers, as proposed by Turkey, will create a new situation and will give a predominant position to Turkish capital in the Bulgarian economy.

Albanian Nationalism

Nationalism has been one of the main characteristics of the Albanian communist regime. It followed a policy of repression towards the Greek minority in South Albania, imposing additional restrictions (religious, linguistic etc.) on it. Although some progress has been achieved after the collapse of that regime, the traditional repressive state mechanism in the region where the Greek minority lives is still functioning and the Government of Tirana has given no indication that it intends to dismantle it. Albania, suspicious of the intentions of the Greek Government, has declared that it also has its own minority in Greece.

In Skopje the parties representing the Albanians of the republic promote, under the influence of Tirana, the idea of political and cultural autonomy. Albanian nationalism is expected to be in the future a crucial destabilizing factor in the Skopje region.

Greece and Turkey

Turkey is a major military force in the region. The strategic and military significance of the country has been upgraded since the Gulf War as well as after the disintegration of the Soviet Union. The United States and other Western countries are supporting Turkey's efforts for a more significant presence in the wider region: Turkey is the only member of CSCE that has been authorized to exempt, under the Agreement on Conventional Forces in Europe (CFE) and because of its proximity to the Middle East, almost one-third of its territory from any CSCE control on military material, personnel and manoeuvres.

In the future Turkey is expected to play an increasingly important role in Balkan developments, aided by the existence of Muslim minorities in Greece, Bulgaria, Bosnia-Hercegovina, Kosovo and Albania. The concentration of those minorities in neighbouring areas, their high birth-rates and their susceptibility to Turkish nationalist propaganda can provide Turkish foreign policy with options that cannot be foreseen. It seems however quite possible that Turkey can assume the role of the leader of the Muslim forces in the Balkans, exerting pressure on the European Community from the South.

Greek-Turkish relations are presently overshadowed by two issues: the Cyprus problem and Turkish claims for the Aegean Sea. These problems have been considered very grave by all Greek governments, because they are directly related to questions of sovereignty and security. On several occasions these problems have led to severe crises between the two countries. The crisis of 1987 prompted a reassessment of the relations between the two countries and since then there have been some efforts to reduce tension. Until now, however, diplomatic procedures and political contacts have brought about only marginal and temporary improvements. The tension in the relations with Turkey is expected to be a more or less permanent feature in the future, affecting Greek foreign policy.

Greece and the Mediterranean

With the radical transformation of East-West relations there is a widely shared, but still ill-defined, sense of the growing importance of the Mediterranean and its regions. Europe as a whole, and the US are beginning to look at the Mediterranean with new interest and concern, thinking about it as an area of strategic consequence in its own right and not as a critical adjunct to aims elsewhere. The movement of the centre of gravity away from Central Europe and the existing and potential problems in North Africa, the Balkans and the Middle East suggest a future in which the Mediterranean region is becoming more important for the security of Europe as a whole.

Apart from issues such as immigration and economic and political developments one should also consider the possibilities of the rise of fundamentalist movements in North Africa, the expansion of arsenals (nuclear or conventional) along the Southern and Eastern shores of the Mediterranean and the resulting potential for political friction and possibly military conflicts that constitute what has already been called a 'threat from the South'.

The Southern European countries, among them Greece, will be an integral, indispensable, part of the new European policy towards the Mediterranean basin. By virtue of geography and traditional political and economic relationships with North Africa and the Levant they are well placed to play an active role in this process.

The evolution of Greece's strategic role as part of a comprehensive European policy towards the South is likely to be a major shaping factor in the future affecting strongly the political, economic and security outlooks, making them increasingly *European*.

Conclusions - Policy Responses

The security issues analysed in the preceding paragraphs lead to the following conclusions:

First, the strategic imbalance that exists today in the Balkans and the greater Mediterranean region is expected to persist for some years.

Greece, being in the middle of an unstable environment will have to respond by maintaining its defence capability.   Defence spending that presently amounts to some 6.5% of GNP will probably remain high in the next decade.   It is therefore unlikely that Greece will enjoy a direct peace dividend resulting from the end of the Cold War.

Second, the response of Greece to the new situation in the region will depend very much on the form that the EC takes: a move toward a broader EC and/or the development of bilateral relations of the EC countries with the new democracies would probably dilute the value of EC as an important strategic factor in the region and perhaps tend to reinforce the importance of Greece's bilateral relations with US.   On the other hand, the continuation of the trend towards deepening integration among the existing members would encourage the growth of a European approach to security matters.   In that case Greek foreign policy will gradually become Europeanized.[1]

Third, the emerging security environment in Europe will be characterized by problems of regional stability that cannot be addressed effectively in the absence of a multilateral approach.   What is needed to promote security in the Mediterranean region is a range of institutions that can address political and economic, as well as military requirements. The EC is the most important of these institutions.   In such areas as the Balkans, where there is potential for instability, the influence and the prestige of the EC may give it a unique role.   In such a case Greece, as the only EC member in the region, should have a keen interest in restoring stability, and building a workable basis for multilateral economic and political relations with all countries.

Fourth, 'economic diplomacy' can contribute greatly to stability in the Balkans and the Mediterranean. A constellation of association agreements around the Community and assistance through multilateral programmes, opening the door to bilateral cooperation, would certainly help to avoid situations of conflict.   Greece is well placed to assume an active role in strengthening economic ties between the Community and the new States. A most promising area of cooperation is that of joint-ventures between

---

1   It is important to note that Greek foreign policy shows increasing convergence with that of the other Community members.   Since its accession to full membership (1981) - in about the same time as the institutionalization of the European Political Cooperation - Greece has participated in various degrees - as all other Member States - in the elaboration of a coordinated foreign policy.   There had been some hesitation in the beginning, but since 1988 the list of voting patterns in the United Nations and other international fora, established every semester by the presidency, is witness to the degree of convergence and consensus on a wide range of important foreign policy issues.

Greek and local firms to improve and expand production for the domestic and foreign markets. This can be greatly helped by Community policies in the framework of its 'renewed Mediterranean policy'.

Immigration

In 1988 there were some 8 million non-EC foreign nationals living in the EC, representing 2.5% of the total population.

The problem for Greece is already acute. There are today some 250,000 foreigners living in the country, most of them illegally.

The usual path of immigration to Greece is by the sea: Turks, Iranians, Filipinos, Pakistani, Egyptians, Iraqi and other Arabs arrive in Greece by sea with the intention of continuing their travel to other more prosperous European countries and to the United States. The number of arrivals varies according to the economic and the political situation in the respective countries.

A parallel movement of persons has taken place mainly from Yugoslavia, Romania and Bulgaria during the last decade, but the great Albanian *exodus* - the term being used by the Albanian authorities - to Greece began in 1991 and is still continuing to a lesser extent even today. About 150,000 Albanians, overwhelmingly economic rather than political refugees, are undocumented.

Among the Albanians entering the country legally or illegally are a number of members of the Greek minority of Albania.

It should also be noted that a number of Greeks, about 500,000, live in the former Soviet Union (Russia, Georgia, Ukraine, Uzbekistan) and that their arrival in Greece is directly linked to the situation in these republics.

It is expected that the migratory pressures into the EC in general and Greece in particular will continue to increase in the future. Due to rising unemployment in Eastern Europe, it is estimated that as many as 8 million people may want to leave Eastern Europe in the near future. Equally, unemployment and a steep rise in birth-rates in North Africa may increase migratory pressures from the South.

At the same time the demographic figures in Europe as well as in Greece show that a decline in the workforce will be increasingly felt. This shortage of manpower will constitute a pull factor for immigration. Immigration will definitely be an important shaping factor in the future affecting not only the labour market but social attitudes as well. The presence of non-Greek residents is increasingly felt and is giving rise to conflicts.   Although Greece has a long history of racial and ethnic tolerance we might witness in the future a hardening of attitudes *vis-à-vis* immigrants.

These of course will in turn depend on the political response to immigration. Will there be a consistent policy of integration of immigrants or an effort to keep them out of the country?

This is a question that can no longer be answered by any country alone. Traditionally migration policies have been a matter of national policies. But the elimination of border controls to allow for the free movement of persons within the internal market will render national immigration policies ineffective. The need for a common approach by the Twelve and the need to cooperate has been widely recognized. Immigration is a perfect example of a policy which can only be dealt with at EC level. There is a genuine need for an EC immigration policy. Moreover, if there is no common immigration policy, there is a risk that Member States will not agree to the complete abolition of border controls. This policy must set the rules for legal immigration and take all the necessary steps for the integration of immigrants. On the other hand it is absolutely necessary to establish adequate and effective controls at the external borders of the Community to combat illegal immigration.

The latter is especially important for Greece for reasons of geography alone: the land frontier with Albania extends to 285 km; with the former Yugoslavia, 236.8 km; with Bulgaria, 480.5 km and with Turkey, 139 km. The Greek coastline totals 15,000 km, and much of this includes a common maritime frontier with Turkey. This situation makes the control of mass illegal entries a very difficult task, that should be undertaken in close cooperation with Community authorities.

11. Ireland: Shaping Factors*

INTRODUCTION

In this chapter, we shall firstly analyse the various dimensions of the socio-economic shaping factors, the cultural and historical factors, and thirdly, the political dimension. Then, we shall consider the balance between national and Community factors, as well as the domains of consensus and divergences about these factors, in the Irish case.

SECTION 1: SOCIO-ECONOMIC FACTORS

Structure of the Irish Economy

The evolution of economic activity in Ireland between now and 2010 will be shaped to a very large extent by the current structure of the Irish economy. The sectoral structure of the economy can be summarized as follows.

Agriculture

A sector employing approximately 15% of those in employment. The sector is highly concentrated in products supported by the CAP and is highly export oriented. The internal structure of the sector, and its relevance for the evolution of the Irish economy, including manufacturing, will be considered in more detail at a later stage.

Industry

Approximately 29% of those at work in Ireland are employed in industry - about two-thirds of which is manufacturing. The manufacturing sector in Ireland exhibits a significant element of dualism - between foreign-owned

---

*   Dr R. 0'Donnell.

segments in, mostly, high-growth industries producing for international markets and indigenous firms in slower-growth segments which, for a variety of reasons, face difficulties in achieving a firm foothold in international markets. This somewhat dualistic structure of the Irish manufacturing sector is a fundamental structural characteristic of the Irish economy which will shape developments in the post-1992 period (see below).

Services

The service sectors account for over 55% of Irish employment. The service sector produces just over 50% of Irish GDP.

This sectoral structure, and a number of other characteristics of the Irish economy and society discussed below, are summarized below in the box of basic statistics.

Table 11.1   Ireland basic statistics (with comparable EC 12 figures)

	IRELAND	EC 12
Population, 1991, m.	3.5	328.7
Population density, per sq. km.	51	145
Relative GDP per head of population, 1991, PPS	69	100
Relative GDP per worker, 1991	89	100
Unemployment rate 1991, %	16.8	8.6
% Employment by Sector, 1989		
Agriculture	15	7
Industry	28	32
Services	57	61
% Gross Value Added by Sector, 1988		
Agriculture	10	3
Industry	37	35
Services	57	61
Exports of goods as % GDP, 1991	56	22
do. Intra-EC	43	14
do. Extra-EC	13	8
% Population 14-24 in Education, 1989	50	43

Demographic Developments

Three demographic trends will be of particular significance between now and 2010.

-    Inflows into the labour market arising from natural increase which exceed current and past rates of job creation. This pattern will continue until the early years of the next century.

- A gradual ageing of the population relative to the age structure found in recent years. However, this ageing will remain less advanced than in other EC countries.
- Emigration will remain a significant factor in Ireland's development.

Social Class Structure and Unemployment

A very important factor shaping Ireland's evolution is the social structure which has emerged in the period since 1960. While high rates of emigration have been endemic in Ireland since the early nineteenth century the social structure within which emigration occurs has altered significantly (Breen, et al.,[1] Sexton, et al.[2]).

After 1960 the occupational structure shifted dramatically - with a decline in the number of agricultural and unskilled opportunities and a sharp increase in the opportunities available to the middle class and skilled manual groups (Breen, et al.).[3] While these developments shifted the emphasis from family inheritance to education as a key determinant of occupational position, they had some negative consequences which are of the utmost importance for development of the Irish economy and society. Chief among these is the emergence of a significant set of residual classes 'stranded in the course of industrial development, especially farmers on marginal holdings and labourers without skills' (Breen, et al., p. 59).[4] It is these groups which account for much of the unemployed and especially, the long-term unemployed. It has been shown that:

> Today's class structure contains a substantial number of positions that are viable only in so far as they are underwritten by State social welfare programmes and from which, especially given present economic circumstances, there appears to be no exit (ibid).

Long-term intergenerational consequences are likely to result from the interaction between the structure and high level of unemployment. The fact that nearly half the unemployed are long-term unemployed, and that

---

[1] R. Breen, D. Hannan, D. Rottman and C.T. Whelan, *Understanding Contemporary Ireland,* Dublin: Gill and Macmillan, 1990.
[2] J. Sexton, B. Walsh, D. Hannan, D. McMahon, *The Economic and Social Implications of Emigration,* Dublin: National Economic and Social Council.
[3] R. Breen, D. Hannan, D. Rottman and C.T. Whelan, op. cit.
[4] R. Breen, D. Hannan, D. Rottman and C.T. Whelan, op. cit.

unemployment is predominantly concentrated among the less educated and skilled, gives rise to the danger of fostering a deprived underclass which will transmit these handicaps to the next generation.

Moreover, in these conditions, the persons involved become so detached from labour market processes that they exert no influence on collective bargaining, so that the fact of their remaining unemployed imposes no moderation on the level or structure of wage claims.

While casual observation, and even analysis, suggest that long-term unemployment has limited economic, political and social consequences for the system, as a system, it is not possible to ignore explosive potential of so serious a social problem on this scale. History, in both Ireland and in other Western countries, suggests that serious social problems may be tolerated for long periods, but that the explosion when it happens is sudden, traumatic and unpredictable.

Overall there can be little doubt that the high level of total unemployment, and of long-term unemployment, and the attendant poverty, constitute a major shaping factor for Ireland. The way in which this will bear on economic and social development will emerge in the course of the analysis.

Public Finance

Ireland enters the 1990s with a high level of outstanding national debt and a taxation system which is widely agreed to be sub-optimal. While this situation can, in large measure, be attributed to poor macroeconomic and public finance management in the late 1970s and early 1980s it has been argued by the tripartite National Economic and Social Council (NESC) that the fiscal crisis has some longer-run determinants. The NESC have pointed out that the other side of the coin of structural problems in the economy is low income per capita and high dependency rates, which tend to require higher baseline levels of social expenditure also.

This line of argument leads to the recognition that 'there is a public finance dimension to the developmental problems of the economy' (NESC, p. 200)[5].

The ratio of employment to population in Ireland at 31%, is among the lowest in the EC. The cost of supporting this high level of dependency is one of the fundamental reasons why public expenditure and taxes are relatively high in Ireland for a country at its level of development. The low employment ratio also largely accounts, at least in an arithmetical

---

5   NESC, *A Strategy for the Nineties*. Dublin: National Economic and Social Council, 1990.

sense, for the divergence in living standards between Ireland and the EC. In 1991 GDP per employed person in Ireland was little more than 10% below the EC average, but because of the small proportion of the population in employment, GDP per capita in Ireland was only 69% of the EC average (see Table 11.1). Although the employment/population ratio is influenced by demographic factors also, the major underlying explanation is the poor labour market conditions, as manifest particularly in the high unemployment rate, which is now the highest in the EC.

Unemployment and Public Policy

Sustained high unemployment will continue to shape profoundly the economic and social environment in which policy is formulated and business is conducted. It places severe constraints on the scope for reducing taxes or government expenditure. The continued pressure on government and state agencies to be seen to be doing something to create employment makes it very difficult to give adequate attention to key policies in areas where the fruits in terms of employment can be expected to mature only slowly (e.g. development of indigenous manufacturing industry). There can be pressure for short-term palliatives, some of which could make the labour market conditions even worse in the long-term. This factor is intensified by the volatility of the Irish labour market, and its sensitivity to conditions abroad, especially in the UK, due to the long-standing ease of outward and return migration. Thus any given policy mix can be put under severe short-term strain by a worsening labour market in the UK, resulting in a sudden change in migration behaviour.

Migration

Ireland's migration history is virtually unique in Europe (let alone among the EC-12) and this will undoubtedly remain a most important shaping factor (L. Mjoset).[6]

However, analysis of the social and economic consequences of emigration has only recently begun (Sexton, et al.).[7]

While some understanding of the social consequences of emigration has been achieved, the economic effects have not been adequately explored.

---

[6] L. Mjoset, *The Irish Economy in a Comparative Institutional Perspective*, NESC, mimeo, 1991.

[7] J. Sexton, B. Walsh, D. Hannan and D. McMahon, op. cit.

Recent developments in international trade theory and regional theory provide analytical approaches which could be used.

International Growth

The development of the Hermes model has, in recent years, brought to light some of the complexities in the relationship between international growth and Irish economic performance. These arise because of the significance and sensitivity of migration and foreign direct investment. (Bradley and Barry,[8] Bradley and Fitzgerald, 1991[9]).

International Patterns of Production and Location

All Community countries will be enormously shaped by the evolving international patterns of production and location.

Yet it is most important not to confuse internationalization, or even globalization, with the emergence of uniformity or spatially even economic development. One of the most interesting aspects of recent geographical and regional studies is the analysis of the interaction been the global nature of enterprises and markets and the local/unique nature of each of the places where production and consumption take place. It follows that these international patterns will have specific consequences in various Community regions, including Ireland.

Public Finance and Tax Reform

While a number of Member States have public finance problems similar to Ireland's, there is a definite sense in which these are specific to each country. This arises, first and foremost, because taxation, expenditure and debt remain, for the time being, under the control of national politics.

Both expenditure and taxation reflect social, economic and political structures and traditions. In Ireland's case the issue of tax reform raises questions about the effectiveness of both the political and administrative systems (see below).

---

8   J. Bradley and F. Barry, 'On the Causes of Ireland's Unemployment', *Economic and Social Review*, I. Begg and D. Mayes, 1992.

9   J. Bradley and J. Fitzgerald, *The Role of the Structural Funds: Analysis of Consequences for Ireland in the Context of 1992*, Dublin: Economic and Social Research Institute, 1992.

Developments in Agriculture

Agriculture and food processing form an important part of the Irish economy. Consequently, there can be no doubt that Ireland's evolution in the post-1992 period will be shaped to a considerable degree by developments in agriculture. While it is common to analyse this by reference to reform of the CAP and possible changes in international food markets, this would be a partial approach. Nowhere is the 'interactive vision' which informs our approach more relevant than in the area of agriculture. Irish social scientists have, in recent years, begun to explore the relationship between the dominant, exporting, agricultural sector and the indigenous economic and social structures and policies (see Breen, et al.,[10] Kennedy, et al.,[11] NESC[12]). While these relationships are by no means adequately understood sufficient progress has been made to allow the current CAP reform to be analysed in the correct context.

Some of the relevant considerations are the following. First, while Ireland's national income is dependent to a considerable degree on the value of agricultural exports, the problem of rural development which Ireland faces is only partially an agricultural one. Second, the current phase of CAP reform constitutes a continuation of a reform process which has been in operation since 1977. Third, Ireland's long-run competitiveness in international food production requires the removal of structural impediments. This depends more on domestic policy than Community policy. Fourth, the continuing problems of low and volatile incomes among a sizeable segment of Irish farmers are due to structural characteristics which could only have been addressed by national policy (though a strong case can be made for some Community financial support). Fifth, while the CAP has provided considerable net transfers to Ireland, it hindered rather than helped the development of a strong food processing industry. Indeed, those features of the CAP which inhibit the development of a food industry producing high value-added products will not be fundamentally altered in the current reform. Sixth, the Irish food industry continues to face the challenge of diversification and development of high value-added products; this is akin to the problems which all indigenous industries face, rather than one to which the current CAP reform proposals have particular relevance.

---

[10] R. Breen, D. Hannan, D. Rottman and C.T. Whelan, op. cit.
[11] K. Kennedy, T. Giblin, D. McHugh, *The Economic Development of Ireland in the Twentieth Century,* London: Routledge, 1988.
[12] NESC, op. cit.

These observations have important implications for how the likely implications of CAP reform should be measured. They suggest that analysis should focus not only on changes in agricultural output and incomes but also on the economy-wide effects, including the implications for the food processing industries. Furthermore, just as the effects of past CAP instruments can be measured only by reference to some alternative regime (see A. Matthews)[13] so the likely effects of the current CAP reforms must ultimately be identified by comparison to some realistic alternative policy scenario.

A static analysis of the impact of CAP reform can be derived by assuming that everything stays constant except the policy instruments to be changed in the Mac Sharry proposals.

The main immediate effect would be to reduce farm output - which is not surprising since a key objective of the proposals is to reduce agricultural production by means of a combination of price reductions and direct supply controls. The effect on real farm incomes will depend on the balance between output and price reductions, on the one hand, and direct compensation and reductions in input prices, on the other. Estimates vary from a small real income decrease to a fairly substantial fall. It is of considerable significance that the effects of the reform will not be uniform throughout Irish agriculture.

The negative effects will be greater in the beef sector than the dairy sector. Estimates of the static effects suggest that 44% of farms would gain while 56% would lose. However, most farms would be only marginally affected by the proposals. The direct compensation payments will tend to go to the smaller, more extensive, farms and the main losers will be larger, more intensive and efficient farmers (Leavy and Heavy).[14]

A more dynamic analysis of the implications of CAP reform would take account of responses within the farm sector and the food processing industry. Since there have been very significant changes in the CAP in the past fifteen years, this experience provides a guide to the likely pattern of response in the coming years. Farmers' responses, including reduced fertilizer usage, will tend to reduce the impact of the reforms on both output and incomes. If the reform succeeds in reducing the supply/demand imbalance in the EC, then market prices will strengthen. Other possible responses include pursuit of off-farm employment, migration and, where these are not possible, reliance on social transfer

---

[13]   A. Matthews, 'Common Agricultural Policy Reform and National Compensation Strategies', *Journal of the Statistical and Social Inquiry Society of Ireland*, 1988.

[14]   A. Leavy and J.F. Heavy, 'Interim Analyis of the Proposed Common Agricultural Policy Reforms', *Journal of the Statistical and Social Inquiry Society of Ireland*, 1992.

payments. Analysis suggests that given that similar income losses have been experienced in the past, the present reform may be 'expected to underpin the continued, gradual, attrition of the farm labour force'.

Changes in agricultural policy are also likely to induce responses in the food processing industry. This industry accounts for almost 30% of employment in Irish-owned manufacturing, and over 20% of total manufacturing employment. For a variety of reasons the industry is primarily involved in the production of commodity products and relies on high-volume and sales into intervention. The reduction in agricultural output will reinforce current pressures for cost cutting - suggesting the likelihood of further rationalization and job losses. While an alternative, and highly desirable, response to supply constraints would be to move into higher value-added products, there are a number of factors which may prevent this. Irish food processing firms have a number of structural problems and face barriers to entry which are common throughout indigenous industry.

However, it is now understood that the CAP reinforced these difficulties by providing non-commercial outlets (i.e. intervention) and by accentuating the already strong seasonality of raw materials supply in both the beef and dairy sectors. What is most significant is that the CAP reform will not fundamentally alter these characteristics of the system and may, indeed, reinforce seasonality.

The reform of the CAP will also have economy-wide macroeconomic effects. These have been estimated using the ESRI's HERMES model of the Irish economy. That analysis suggested that the loss in farm income (after compensation) would be roughly equal to the gain in consumer income. Given the fairly modest face in agricultural output, the major macroeconomic effect may result from the effect of the reform on prices. The reduction in agricultural and food prices will reduce the overall price level in all Member States. Indeed, the final real macroeconomic effects may depend on the relative size of these price reductions and the consequent gains and losses of competitiveness. If the price fall was uniform throughout the Community, and if all prices were fairly flexible, then the long-run impact of the Mac Sharry proposals on the Irish economy may be to reduce long-run real GNP by perhaps 0.3% to 0.5% below what would otherwise prevail. If, on the other hand, European interest rates did not fall in line with prices, then Ireland's loss of GNP would be somewhat greater.

These estimates of the likely effect of the reforms are based on the package as formulated in July 1991. If the compensation payments inherent in the Mac Sharry proposals were to be abolished, then the costs to the Irish economy would be increased. Recent economic analysis suggests that the larger immediate fall in farm incomes may be less serious than the long-run implications. In particular, the proposed mix of supply controls and price reductions would prevent Ireland from exploiting its competitive advantage in dairy and cereals. This is so, largely because the supply control element of the reform package arises precisely in those sectors - dairy and cereals - in which Ireland could exploit comparative advantage.

Environmental Developments

While environmental developments and policy responses will have some influence on the development of all EC member countries this factor may not be of particular importance to Ireland. This reflects Ireland's geographic position, low population density, lack of heavy industry, low average income (by EC standards) and relatively clean environment. This raises questions about the use of the new cohesion fund - which has been designated for transport and environmental programmes.

In assessing the relevance of the environmental factor it seems advisable to break the idea of *the environment* into its separate parts. The various types of air pollution, water pollution, pollution of food, congestion and decay of the natural and built environment, operate at different spatial scales and impact on various interest groups in different ways. While there is, among some Community citizens, an ideology which lumps these together to form a *green consciousness*, it seems unlikely that this can adequately reflect the complexity of the issue or resolve the conflicts of interest which arise.

Probably the most important environmental issues for Ireland are those of water pollution, urban and rural planning and meat production. The problems in these areas go to the heart of the Irish political system. Only in recent years has the argument been made that low standards in these areas are actually harming Ireland's economic interest by damaging water resources used for tourism, limiting the kind of economic regeneration achieved in many cities in other countries and undermining the image of Irish food exports. While this is accurate it, in turn, reflects a dependent mentality that is part of the problem. While it is important now to do whatever is necessary to protect Ireland's advantage in these areas, the literature on international competitive advantage suggests that, in general, the process works the other way round. That is, countries tend to develop an international competitive advantage in activities which they perform to a high standard for themselves. This is yet another example of the interaction been indigenous and global forces in the shaping of any country's role in the international division of labour.

SECTION 2: CULTURAL AND HISTORICAL FACTORS

The cultural and historical factors which may shape Ireland's developments in the years to 2010 are, in many ways, the two sides of the one coin. The chief historical factor is the economic and social structures, created in the disastrous nineteenth century, and the political reaction to this of the Irish people - the push for, and achievement of, owner occupancy and political independence. In the course of these economic and political developments there emerged a particular cultural pattern which probably still has relevance. Some of the characteristics of this culture are listed below:

Language

The Irish people lost their own language in the course of the nineteenth century and are now overwhelmingly English speaking.

Linguistic and Musical

Irish culture is highly linguistic and musical, with far less emphasis on the visual arts and crafts than some other European cultures.

Land

The culture contains a very strong attachment to land ownership and occupancy. Indeed it has been argued, more generally, that twentieth-century Ireland has a 'possessor ethic' rather than a 'performer ethic'.

Religion

The Catholic religion was virtually a defining national characteristic during much of the period since the mid-nineteenth century.

Family

The family remains the centre of social organization to a degree, and in ways, which differ from other Northern European countries. Yet there is evidence of rapid convergence towards Northern European patterns of family formation and size and sexual mores.

Migration

Mass emigration has been a most significant factor in Irish society for two centuries. However, it remains difficult to interpret its social and economic significance and consequences. At one level it definitely makes the Irish one of the most internationalized peoples in the world. It would be quite mistaken to see Ireland's problem as lack of access to the international economy. Nevertheless, despite continued emigration, the period from political independence to the 1960s does seem to have been one in which the society in Ireland became more closed, and the period since then, including Community membership, to have been one of increased openness to international cultural influences.

Education

For various historical reasons Irish people put a very high value on education. However, academic training and qualifications are valued much more highly than technical subjects.

Sport

Ireland retains two indigenous, highly popular field games - one of them of ancient Gaelic origin. Indeed, sport in general is an important part of Irish culture: over 500,000 people (or 1 in 7 of the total population) were on the streets of Dublin to greet Ireland's football team after their quarter-final defeat by Italy in the World Cup. A week later in Germany 50,000 greeted the victorious German side.

Political Culture

The formation of the Irish nation in the early nineteenth century was virtually simultaneous with, or perhaps shaped by, the development of highly effective mass politics (see below).

While each of these cultural characteristics has an economic dimension this does not mean that they are, or will be, causal factors in Ireland's economic evolution. In recent years an important debate has developed concerning the relative significance of cultural, structural and political factors in explaining the economic failure of independent Ireland (K. Kennedy).[15] The 'interactive vision' which informs this paper suggests that, even if we tend to prefer a structural explanation, the cultural and political dimensions probably retail some validity.

SECTION 3: THE POLITICAL DIMENSION

The world geopolitical dimension is of minor significance to Ireland - largely by virtue of its size and location. By contrast, the domestic political dimension and the political development of the Community are of the utmost importance. Two aspects of domestic politics seem important if Ireland is to achieve its major economic and social goals: the development of a national political process capable of formulating and implementing strategic programmes and some rationalization of the relationship between local and national politics and administration. A third political factor is the conflict in Northern Ireland.

Political Culture and Strategic Policy-Making

A political culture which was highly sophisticated and successful in the struggle for owner occupancy and national independence has been much less effective in the expression and resolution of domestic conflicts and the formulation of strategic goals and policies. At its best this political system failed, from independence onward, to maintain Ireland's relative economic position and failed to solve the problems of unemployment and mass emigration; at its worst it resorted to extreme pragmatism and resolved problems by reckless foreign borrowing - so driving the country to a severe fiscal crisis which has only been partially resolved.

Whatever the explanation for this political failure the most important attempt to move beyond it has been the willingness of the social partners and some political parties to develop a system of social and political concertation which allows the resolution of conflicts in the context of coherent strategic approaches. While the tripartite National Economic and

---

[15] K. Kennedy, 'The Context of Economic Development' in J. Goldthorpe and C.T. Whelan (eds) *The Development of Industrial Society in Ireland,* Oxford: Basil Blackwell (forthcoming), 1992.

Social Council has expressed the social partners' interest in this, and promoted its development, it has also become aware of how demanding a project it is (see NESC, Chapter 15).[16]   An important debate has developed on whether a system of consensus or social concertation, along the lines found in several highly successful small European countries, can succeed in Ireland (N. Hardiman,[17] L. Mjoset,[18] W. Roche[19]).   While some doubt has been created as to whether Ireland's political, trade union and employers' organizations can sustain such a system there is a strong case for the view that its development is potentially important.

Local Democracy and Administration

The second political issue which will shape Ireland's evolution is the question of sub-national politics and administration.   Ireland has a highly centralized political and administrative system; the abolition of domestic rates in 1977 removed the vital link between local administration and democracy (T. Barrington).[20]   In recent years the case has been made for the development of a more independent system of local government and democracy.   The Commission has also advocated substantial local involvement in the formulation, implementation and monitoring of Regional Development Programmes.   So far the Irish Government has responded to arguments for local government with extreme caution and has met the Commission's requirements in a perfunctory and formal sense only.

Northern Ireland

Developments in Northern Ireland will inevitably shape Ireland's evolution in the years to 2010.   The conflict of the past twenty years has had a number of effects.   It has influenced Irish Politics - but hardly in a

---

16   NESC, *A Strategy for the Nineties*, Dublin: National Economic and Social Council, 1990.

17   N. Hardiman, *Pay, Politics and Economic Performance in Ireland 1970-87*, Oxford: Clarendon Press, 1988. 'The State and Economic Interests' in J. Goldthorpe and C.T. Whelan (eds) *The Development of Industrial Society in Ireland*, Oxford: Oxford University Press (forthcoming), 1992.

18   L. Mjoset, 'The Irish Economy in a Comparative Institutional Perspective', NESC, mimeo, 1991.

19   W. Roche, 'The Liberal Theory of Industrialism and the Development of Industrial Relations in Ireland' in J. Goldthorpe and C.T. Whelan (eds) *The Development of Industrial Society in Ireland*, Oxford: Oxford University Press (forthcoming), 1992.

20   T. Barrington, *Local Government Reorganization and Reform*, Report of the Advisory Expert Committee chaired by T. Barrington, Dublin: Stationery Office.

way which enhances the ability of the political system to identify problems, mediate conflicting interests and execute strategic policies. The issue was frequently used in low-level political competition, so distracting attention from more mundane economic and social matters; when it was occasionally treated seriously it was politically damaging also, because it drew high-level political attention away from other critical issues. It has undoubtedly influenced economic development to some degree, by absorbing public resources, by severely damaging Ireland's tourist industry and, possibly, by influencing the rate of inward investment. It has clearly shaped Irish-UK diplomatic relations in ways which do fully reflect the nature and density of social and economic relations between the two countries. Irish-British relations are different in the State and in civil society.

If any of these influences were continue, then the problem in Northern Ireland would be a significant shaping factor. However, this somewhat technical description passes over the main reason why people in the Republic will be concerned. That concern arises because a significant number of people are highly aware of the problems in Northern Ireland and feel involved in a political, cultural and ethnic way. In looking at public and private sector responses to major shaping factors, consideration is given to the potential for North-South economic cooperation.

Disarmament

There are some factors which will have particularly little relevance for Ireland. The most obvious of these is disarmament.

SECTION 4: A SPECIFIC BALANCE BETWEEN NATIONAL AND COMMUNITY FACTORS

In recent years there has been some advance in our understanding of the implications of EC membership for Ireland (NESC,[21] P. Keatinge,[22] R. O'Donnell[23]). One of the findings of that body of work is that the effects of membership, and the associated loss, or sharing, of sovereignty,

---

[21]   NESC, op. cit.
[22]   P. Keatinge, *Ireland and EC Membership Evaluated,* London: Pinter, 1991. P. Keatinge, B. Laffan and R. O'Donnell, 'Weighing up the gains and losses' in P. Keatinge (ed.) *Ireland and EC Membership Evaluated,* London: Pinter, 1991.
[23]   R. O'Donnell (ed.), *Economic and Monetary Union,* Dublin: Institute of European Affairs, 1991.

must be evaluated by reference to an appropriate concept of sovereignty. The meaning of sovereignty differs from one Member State to another, and over time. It follows that the extent and meaning of loss of sovereignty can be quite different in each Member State. This implies that in analysing factors shaping development in the post-1992 period the balance between Community, or international, factors and indigenous factors will be seen to be different in each Member State. This may be particularly so when considering factors which require political initiatives. Indeed, one implication of this is that correct application of the principle of subsidiarity may not imply the same allocation of policy functions to each Member State.

In Ireland's case the analysis of the balance between international and domestic factors reveals an interesting pattern. When considering socio-economic factors the analysis strongly suggests that international factors and Community policies have particular relevance. Although we have cited many areas of domestic policy which are essential to success it is also the case that there are definite limits to Ireland's economic policy autonomy, some of which arise from Community membership. However, when considering historical/cultural and political matters, we find relatively few global factors that will shape Ireland's development or, at least, it is not easy to identify what factors will do so. In part, this reflects Ireland's location and small size. In a more general sense, it reflects the fact that, except for superpowers, the significance of some factor for a given country is dependent on that country's significance for the factor in question. This reflects the predominance of interdependence in the world. In Ireland's case this interdependence tends towards the dependent end of the spectrum and this accentuates the significance of global economic factors and diminishes the significance of global cultural and political factors.

SECTION 5: CONSENSUS AND CONTROVERSY IN IRELAND

There is agreement that the following socio-economic factors will significantly shape Ireland's development.

- Structure of the economy.
- Demographic trends.
- Unemployment.
- Public finance.
- International economic growth.

- Agricultural reform.
- Environmental development.
- EC enlargement.

There would not be complete agreement on how these factors will bear on future development. Some analysis of these causal relationships constitutes the ultimate objective of the study, but we are aware that it encompasses some of the major debates on Irish society.

There is controversy on the relevance of the following factors:

- International production and location patterns.
- All the cultural and historical factors discussed above.
- The need for a system of consensus/concertation.
- The need for more developed local government and democracy.

Intuition suggests that these controversies will be resolved, or at least progressed, by conceptual rather than empirical innovation. For example, in the debate on the relative significance of cultural, structural, political and administrative factors, each of the protagonists has presented his interpretation with detailed historical material. A new conceptual approach, or application of an approach which has not yet been brought to bear on the Irish issue, could open the way to a fusion of some of the horizons. Mjoset's work for the NESC is in this vein and it is also likely that recent regional theory, seldom cited in Ireland, offers some hope of enlightenment.

12. Italy: Shaping Factors*

INTRODUCTION

Today Italian society often seems to lack solidity, to have virtually no firm basis from which to meet the challenge of international reality. There is a tendency to underestimate the growth of the last forty years and to consider instead that the changes have been too fast and too intense not to involve a corresponding burden of contradictions which are now exploding and making us weak.

It seems likely that the shift in what we have become is due less to cultural change than to today's levelling and the cultural inability to think in terms of long-term trends. However, anyone genuinely familiar with Italian reality knows that the changes of recent decades have not been random or transient but have followed substantial, structural logic, and that it is this logic which has made Italian development a model of rapid mass development.

The first long-term logic is the 'proliferation of agents and attitudes which has led to a diffused society with horizontal dynamics'.

-   The proliferation of small- and medium-sized businesses and self-employed and independent work.
-   The corresponding proliferation of non-institutional forms of work.
-   The formation of a number of labour markets.
-   The rapid growth of the service sector.
-   The sustained expansion of residential areas and the continuous appropriation of land.
-   The growth of small and medium economic localisms and the renewed importance of suburban areas, also at political and administrative levels.
-   The increase in territorial mobility and the flow of transfers.
-   Social segmentation and the development of new professional and

---

* N. Delai and A. Mairate.

social groups (and their representation).
- The increase in consumer goods with resultant segmentation and personalization.
- The growth in needs, expectations and desires (economic, social and cultural).
- The development of the theme of individual rights (citizenship, attitudes, etc.).
- The strong trend towards internationalization (first emigration, then exports, then tourism).

It is a diffuse society which perhaps has been and still is confused, which has experienced development as an invasive phenomenon, but which has had a mobilizing effect on it for years. It still has a high charge of proliferating vigour if we bear in mind that many of the phenomena mentioned above have made further advances in recent years (particularly consumer segmentation and personalization, the increased interest in rights, the expansion of housing, etc.).

Of course a society experiencing diffuse development ends by operating according to 'the logic of the pre-eminence of individual agents', the elementary cells of the system. In this respect the following should be remembered:

- The consistent centrality of individual decisions and attitudes (with regard to work, consumption and rights).
- The importance of the family, particularly as an economic agent (from the point of view of income, consumption, savings and investment).
- The growing importance of business which has even led to talk of the *commercialization* of the system.
- The progressive assertion of more restricted and compact professional associations.
- The growing pressure of localisms not only in economic terms, but also as a focus of social and political identity.

The phrase 'the triumph of the individual' is based on this logic of the growing importance of society's elementary agents, but such logic embodies something more: there is a basic mobilization, a growing awareness of responsibility in the various social segments, a sense of personal involvement in every major social and economic process; there is also a varying degree of awareness that a society which embraces so many subjects, so many attitudes and so many areas of decision is a strongly democratic society in more than conventional terms, an open society which allows a mobility and progress unimaginable in more vertical, more highly structured societies.

Inevitably these characteristics provide a third major logic of the long-term trend: 'continuous adjustment'. A society proliferating on the vitality of millions of subjects cannot be brought back to unitary schemes, designs or regulations. It has to rely on continuous *feed-back*, even though this is sometimes conflicting and often expensive. This can be seen from the continuing influence of the following phenomena:

- Emulation and pursuit (in terms of consumption and wages).
- More or less inventive adaptation to more or less recurrent crises.
- Combination strategies (in the entrepreneurial and the family cover of social needs).
- Self-organization of various agents (particularly from the point of view of services, from transport to postal services).
- Recourse to an informal flexibility based on the individual's capacity to adapt or the social cohesion of the various local realities.

These different incarnations of the logic of feed-back and continuous adjustment, justify the claim that, whether aware of it or not, society has found a market dialectic, at least at the level of social behaviour. It is this market dialectic which has produced an advanced Western country, a country which, although embodying much public intervention, deep down is far more under private control than we imagine: by private interests, private attitudes, private regulation of every economic and social impulse.

Perhaps this is almost too much the case, in respect of the fourth major logic governing the development of the last forty years: the 'socio-economic finalization and instrumentalization of public action'. Precisely in those decades of consistent call for policy to lead the way, public action has failed to achieve independence and has broadened simply to aid, assist, safeguard and motivate private action. This can be seen from the following:

- How the need for individual and family security caused an increase in the growth of the Welfare State and social spending, haphazardly and without a unified plan.
- How the widespread growth in housing and manufacturing has

created a need for services and a demand for public intervention in various sectors (telecommunications, transport, infrastructures, energy, etc.).

- How business has always looked to public action in situations of crisis, reorganization and renewal (from redundancy funds and early retirement funds to research costs, etc.).
- How many social conflicts have been controlled (resolved or prevented) by calling on public intervention.
- How it has been necessary to have recourse to the proliferation of supply in terms of public intervention and to related public expenditure to deal with old and new territorial imbalances and social inequality and deprivation.

Thus we see that today's major problem for the Italian model of development is the uncontrolled growth of public spending. It is a model in which the three vital components (the proliferation of agents and processes, the strength of individual agents and continuous adjustment) have to find their way across the gulf between the constant cover of public action which meets their interests and needs and another which presses direct responsibility upon them; but these components resist by trying to extend the cover as far as they can. It seems highly likely, instead, that there should be increasing recourse to the pure market, to the growing responsibility of the private dimension of socio-economic dynamics, even though the laws of the long-term trend show that a strong public presence will always be a feature of Italian society.

It would, however, be unjust and quite wrong to concentrate only on the problems of the stratification of so many interventions and so much public expenditure. In the present-day reality in Italy, complex imbalances also play a special part in the obstruction of our long-term development process, in part linked with the careless management of some of the long-term logic mentioned above.

The first of the major imbalances of the system is, in fact, the surplus and the sometimes contradictory overload of agents, processes and attitudes, stratified as a whole according to the logic of their proliferation. We have, in fact:

- A clear surplus in the service sector and inflationary costs (at least in relation to the quality of its output).
- Congestion of the subjectual dimension of the business system.
- Over-concentration of ownership of real estate and personal

property.

- Congestion (in space and time) of the consumer-based model of society.
- Growth (and increasingly difficult management) of the waste and residues from consumer products.
- Lack of a structural pattern of rights and expectations in the cover of welfare needs.
- A steady trend towards selfish and regressive attitudes *vis-à-vis* the environment.
- A growth in projects of all kinds (infrastructure, service centres, reform and counter-reform) which is not leading to concrete operational action.

An uncontrolled surplus, producing more inflation than strategy, creates a second great imbalance in our present economic and social system: the relative inability to create added-value (whether in terms of quality or innovation). It almost seems that imagination and creativity, where Italians excelled for many years, have given way to mediocrity which is certainly hampering Italian competitivity on the international stage:

- The service sector is expanding, but even its so-called *advanced* sectors are unable to give high quality input, and indeed are unable to create much added-value.
- Manufacturing businesses, perhaps because they are too numerous, and of excessively limited dimensions, cannot make significant product innovations (except in highly specialist areas).
- Local economic markets seem to have lost their identity and specificity, their appearance and their dynamism.
- The large range of consumer products is still of variable quality, in terms of both the supply of products and services and the organization and effectiveness of their distribution.
- The increase in supply and expenditure in the social sector is not accompanied (in education, health, the social services and welfare) by the necessary innovation and quality of the supply itself, so that there is a genuine 'poverty gap in the social sector'.
- The quality of land resources (due to considerable misuse by the inhabitants as well as the total lack of a maintenance culture) is very low, almost to the point of inevitable deterioration of value rather than added-value.

The platitude that failure to advance means not standing still, but losing ground, is also true in this field; a surplus gives rise to a ballooning effect, not quality, and the enlarged balloon created may collapse.

The whys and wherefores of the third great imbalance present in the system are now understood: the tendency of the various decision-making centres to lose their sense of responsibility, being now marked more by the primordial mechanism of appropriation than by the pressure to innovate, to provide quality, to compete at a high level. On this point one only needs to look at the more striking aspects of this imbalance:

- The appropriation of territory and environment which is taking place daily without any responsible agents to guarantee their proper use.
- The dramatic appropriation by organized crime of entire regions or major urban hinterlands with an obvious loss of accountability of the local administrative and economic structures.
- The inability to decide on resources, on the infrastructure and on the services necessary for development or at least for the consolidation of productive local economic markets.
- The lack of accountability which characterizes social intervention, both in its increasing avoidance of serious, *hard* requirements and in its failure to create an undertaking of economic responsibility, to the limits of its control, in the agents of social expenditure (within local organizations, users, sector operators, etc.), as well as in its failure to structure requests and offers of intervention adequately.
- Finally, the trend towards unaccountability which is beginning to permeate even the usual attitudes of agents which were more vital in the past, such as families ever more ready to consume than to invest or save and ever less attentive to future needs (using resources for today and, as a result, taking them away from future generations).

Understandably, if the prevalent mechanism is one of lack of accountability and acquisitiveness, then the main victim will be public intervention. In fact, one of the most visible (partly because it drains the others) and most dramatically perceived is now the increasing ineffectiveness of public action, accompanied by a corresponding, almost uncontrollable, increase in its cost.

However, often we only dwell on the financial aspect of this crisis: the costs. It would, in fact, be more fair to focus on the fact that the crisis has a quality motive: the *open door* aspect of public action and the relative spiralling number of interest groups (who are becoming more aggressive in their lobbying). Public action, in other words, does not follow a strategy of its own, but is an open door for the ideas, needs and strategies of economic and social agents; and providing an open-door policy on one hand increases the queue of claimants and, on the other, indirectly increases the number of formal representations and lobbying activities, without, however, increasing the quality of their accountability. On this point, it should be remembered that:

- Today there are no sectoral policies (in industry, infrastructure or scientific research) which are not becoming gradually depleted by open-door rules and financing projects invented in an entrepreneurial environment.
- At the same time, the conditions for autonomous responsibility of regions and local authorities do not exist; these, in practice, should make pressing requests to the Government/open door for specific interventions (by special laws or financing).
- Intervention in the social sector, even when it appears tendentiously rigorous (even with tickets) is now structurally an intervention action in relation to needs, by means of an extremely expensive stratification of the supply.
- All public intervention is tied up by a bureaucratic machine which is not only excessive and expensive in relation to the services actually provided, but also a prisoner of category actions between the various internal bodies, which, basically, see public intervention as a means of obtaining hand-outs which are in some way almost reserved for the privileged.

In this situation, which seems to give formal cover to part of the *acquisitive* tendency existing in our country, it is understandable that there should be pressure to push into the queue at the counter and to elbow one's way through in order to get more. As a result, the representations of ever more individual interests, both of the union and lobby type, have grown with very fast segmentation, with the overall effect of increasingly uncontrolled public expenditure, increasingly ineffective political action, and representative systems which are increasingly fragmented and in crisis.

SECTION 1: THE STRUCTURAL FACTORS OF THE SYSTEM

At a time when the Italian socio-economic system has to face difficulties which are both structural and related to economic competition, it is legitimate to query the validity, in a development perspective of what have been seen, for a long time, as the strong points of the system:

- In the first place, the strong pressure for the formation of real territorial systems with diffused entrepreneurship have been found to be reliable producers of wealth.
- In the second place, the proven ability to operate in extremely flexible conditions, assisted by the availability of a dimensional advantage which current opinion considered to be a disadvantage, but which, instead, turned out to be a success factor at a time when it permitted the setting up and dismantling of the production processes in relation to the stresses of highly subjective, erratic market demand.
- In the third place, the superimposition, in relation to more formalized models of civil service and big business, of a series of labour markets with a diminishing degree of institutionality, which have generated a highly elastic potential supply.

During an important stage of development, the vitality of the system coincided with an explosion of economic subjectualism, which, at times, could not be efficiently contained within the production process, and was often short-lived, but which has always provided an undoubted impetus, linking together economic opportunities.

The cycle of proliferation of agents has cut across the socio-economic space of Italy, producing a rich fabric of resources and structures:

- In the business system, which is still dominated by a large number of small and very small units, both in industry and in the service sector.
- In the service sectors which have witnessed an extraordinary process of growth for almost twenty years.
- In professional opportunities, with accelerated mobility of working conditions (between sectors, levels and geographical areas), as a result of the expansion of the opportunities themselves and the progressive linking up of the labour market.

It would be churlish to deny that these trends still have a dynamic impetus, but today their disadvantages can also be seen, corresponding to a certain verifiable slowing down of their life cycle:

-    In the attenuation of the processes of generation of new entrepreneurship in the manufacturing sectors.
-    In the processes of restructuring local districts, which in some cases have caused outlays of considerable contributions from entrepreneurial agents.
-    In the process of technological development and the gradual pre-eminence of the quality factors which have to a great extent cancelled the advantages, in terms of flexibility, of small companies and have exposed the quality defects of a production process which is often aimed at saturating the market rather than governing it.
-    In the labour market, where demographic factors, with a tendency to be subjective, are bringing back conditions of rigidity not found on the institutional side (either from regulatory or contractual origins) or through feeble attempts to slow down the opposition, reducing *de facto* the potential store of flexibility which is not compensated by a sufficient flow of new professionalism.
-    In the weakening of the rapid rise of the service sector which, in the second half of the 1980s, saw a considerable decline in the rates of growth of employment, and now seems to be developing along lines of restructuring and qualification, giving precedence to the sector of sophisticated services for businesses and families, rather than to further expansion.

The beginning of this phase of settlement of the proliferation of agents does not mean in itself an incipient depletion of the lifelines of Italy's economic fabric. In fact, many of the processes of progressive restructuring which we are seeing contribute to introducing the system selectors necessary for more rational and qualified lines of development, which might otherwise lead to a dead end.

SECTION 2: THE PRESENT BOTTLENECK

Notwithstanding the obvious progression of this process of compaction, the inertia of the impetus towards diffusion of agents and opportunities on one hand and the sharpening of competition on the other have contributed to forming a series of bottlenecks in relation to which the system now seems no longer to be in phase.

Today we are seeing a growth in unit costs which is not matched by a proportional growth in productivity, with the result that the terms of trade are deteriorating. The difficulty in transferring the growth in costs to product prices means an imbalance between costs and production prices which has a negative effect on the profit margins and reduces investment capital.

The large number of small companies in Italy relative to its main European competitors is a powerful brake on raising its competitivity profile because of the structural difficulties in obtaining financial resources for investment. The consolidation of small businesses, both from the point of view of organizational strategy and in the scale of the turnover developed, is thus a vital route for completion of the processes of modernization already positively set in motion by smaller firms in the 1980s.

However, even here, a further inconsistency arises; there is still a wide gap between the perception of the problems of growth, which small businessmen today tend to share widely, and the concrete activation of the instruments which affect these bottlenecks.

Alongside the effects of inconsistency of the proliferation of businesses, various, substantial contradictions characterize the interface between manufacturing and services, following an excessive impetus in the growth of services, only feebly accompanied by adequate attention to quality aspects.

On this point, it is emphasized that:

- In a system with a high degree of integration of industry and services, the costs of the latter become highly important in the calculation of overall costs.
- The cost of credit, distribution and some primary services to businesses shows a varying disadvantage in comparison with Italy's main European partners.
- The excessive 'open-door mentality', which, in recent years, has characterized the approach of the public system to supporting businesses, a supply surplus, scarcely able to penetrate business culture, resulting in large areas of dissatisfaction in the businesses which benefit, accentuated by considerable bureaucratic and administrative disorganization.

Finally, there are inconsistencies in the development of the traditional local economic market. It is all too obvious that continuous external pressures have, little by little, weakened the internal nucleus of territorial cohesion in the manufacturing districts, enlarging, at extra local level, the network of references - production, services, market - which support the balance of the businesses in the area.

All this heightens the need for resources (service, professional, etc.) for local companies which come up against a qualitatively rigid supply. A series of critical junctures for the development of the districts, combined with the low efficiency of the infrastructural networks and the low availability of human and financial resources, adds up to a new competitive disease.

SECTION 3: FACTORS OPERATING AT TERRITORIAL LEVEL

The Importance of the Territorial Dimension

If one looks at the country's socio-economic development in recent decades, the part played by the territorial variable appears to be central. It is in fact in territorial terms that the twofold process of growth has taken place:

- The diffusion in the hundred and more productive localisms of the modern logic of setting up business (crafts, industry, services).
- The maturing of business resources able to combine company organization and the local network of socio-economic relations.

In recent years, the linking up and territorial differentiation of the socio-economic fabric have undergone a process of reorganization and consolidation. This process has gradually led to the overcoming of restricted local confines, identifying more extended territorial areas as a new scope for modernization.

Various determining factors have led to a movement which, while not completely setting aside the force of local radication, has defined real, enlarged territorial systems. The need to operate in an increasingly translocal dimension has, in fact, been justified:

- By company strategies, aimed at combining various geographical openings of the market, technology and services.
- By infrastructural policies, as the efficiency of the individual

company or urban area must be supported by adequate communications networks.
-   By environmental management, pollution (its prevention and removal), being a problem which is intrinsically of extra local value.
-   By institutional engineering, as the extended dimension of territorial references has had to be matched by an enlargement of the group of subjects involved (communes, mountain communities, metropolitan areas, provinces and regions).

And it is due to this process of sub-system organization that it is possible to find, in the socio-economic geography of our country, areas of territorial concentration:

-   The North East, embodying three regions which are similar from historic, economic and socio-cultural points of view, and at the centre of the major trans-European axes (the vertical axis of the Brenner Pass and the transverse Barcelona-Trieste-Budapest axis).
-   Lombardy-Veneto, as areas of excellence and growth due to the merger of industrial and service enterprises (first and foremost credit and commercial organizations).
-   The North West, as an industrial sub-system with strong internal integration, but increasingly exposed to the magnetic attraction of external poles (Lyons and the South of France, first and foremost).
-   The Adriatic line, as a geographic extension of a model of development centred on small businesses (industry and craft) and on traditional manufacturing specialization.
-   The Rome-Caserta axis, as a territorial continuum of productive presences (agricultural and industrial) and housing (in urban centres and built-up areas).

SECTION 4: THE FACTORS OPERATING IN THE SOCIAL SECTOR

The Large-Scale Growth of the Social Sector

Incoherent growth and stratification as a whole are the most obvious characteristics of the development of the Italian social system in the last 25 years.

The stratification is evident in a series of long-term trends, in particular:

- The continued growth of wealth.
- Extemporaneous growth of social hardship and deprivation (at least up to 1976) and the renewal of the processes of economic inequality in recent years.
- Continuously rising public expenditure (from 20% of the GDP in 1976 to 27% in 1991), above all a considerable lack of coordination and bad timing in relation to needs.
- The increase in the awareness of individual and collective rights and the more or less spontaneous and formalized forms of associationism and voluntary service.

The incongruities of development and incoherent growth point to the need for a deeper analysis of the many junctures which give substance to the imbalance. The questions spring to mind of where the snags are hidden, and where the unsolved questions are to be found which determine the lack of coherence between demand trends and social supply.

The Ageing of the Population

From various forecasts carried out, it can be assumed with certainty that in the coming decades the process of ageing will be consolidated; the only uncertain factor is the rhythm of ageing and, as a result, the ratios of the various age groups in the future.

The ageing of the population, which affects the whole Western world, has taken place in Italy, too, in an unforeseeably short time, and, moreover, with very different trends in the Centre/North and South. In under thirty years the over-sixties have increased from under 7 million to over 11½ million and they will be in excess of 14 million in 2020 (of these, some three million will be octogenarians).

In 1960 there were 37 elderly people for every 100 under-15s; in 1987 the ratio had shot up to 73% and in 2020 for every two young people we will have three elderly. International comparisons place us among the countries with the highest rates of old-age people, preceded only by Sweden, the UK and the German Federal Republic.

This 'grey phenomenon' will thus tend to become, unless a coordinated programme of intervention is worked out in time (town planning, pensions, welfare services, labour policy, leisure, etc.), one of the major shaping factors governing the development and the quality of life in Italy.

The more immediate consequences of this situation depend on one hand on the inadequate flow of contributions which, in a social welfare system, is essential for payment of current pension services; and on the other the fear, even if limited to how many will actually remain in Italy, of having to pay, in future, a higher number of benefits to people who have never been insured, or only partially insured (invalidity, welfare pensions, etc.).

Further elements to be considered, which have a direct impact on welfare problems, relate to the changed life expectancy of the various age groups and the diversification of the composition of the nuclear family. The former have grown gradually and, in connection with the reduction in disease and the improvement of sanitary conditions, they will grow further in the coming decades; then we will not only have more old people, but we will have them for a greater number of years.

Between now and 2005, the average life expectancy of a sixty-year-old will increase by two years and that of a seventy-year-old by one year, and this relatively limited increase affects the need for a rise in the pension age; this may be necessary due to the progressively increasing ratio of the elderly to people of working age; it may be appropriate due to the improved state of health of today's (and tomorrow's) sixty-year-old in comparison with those of the past; but it will certainly lessen the burden with regard to life expectancy, i.e. to the period during which, on average, the pension will be received.

The Generation 'Overload'

There is a considerable uncertainty of relationship between the generations. Unexpectedly, at a time when we thought that the questions and problems of previous cycles of the human story had been left behind, we once again find ourselves up against one of the *primordial* elements of existence, namely intergenerational relations.

Today we have a society *stretched* between two poles: the *lone* generation classes (with no parents or children, 6.2% in 1991); and the generation classes who have another three generations in front and behind (individuals with parents, children and grandchildren, 14.3%). The figures for the simultaneous presence of two generations (33.8%) and three generations (45.7%) come in between.

The generational imbalance is found to some extent within each of the typologies indicated but is particularly present where the simultaneous presence of generations means a real overload for the intermediate generations.

The Poverty Threshold and the Redistribution Stalemate

Another inconsistency can be found in the permanence of a solid threshold of material and non-material poverty and in the stalemate of economic distribution. According to the most reliable estimates, in Italy 3,800,000 families, 18.9% of all Italian families, exist below the poverty line. Of these 1,105,000 live in conditions of real misery.

It is not only the scale of the problem, but the differentiation and quality breakdown of poverty in Italy which are striking. These can be grouped together into five main areas:

-     The traditional economic poverty of lack of income, housing, food.
-     *Hard* poverty; lack of physical self-sufficiency, handicap, drug addiction, Aids.
-     Relational and affective poverty, loneliness etc.
-     The poverty of cultural and psychological marginalization, such as tramps, exploited foreigners and immigrants, the mentally ill etc.
-     Institutional or second-level poverty, in other words poverty caused by a serious lack of services.

Immigration Between Exclusion and Solidarity

Especially in recent years, immigration in Italy has been a mobile, continually growing phenomenon, and has taken on the proportions of a real emergency.

We are certainly confronted with a highly complex phenomenon, of which the demographic component is only the first indicator. In particular, we are faced with an increase in the demand for services, as the immigrants bring with them needs characterized by urgency and multi-dimensionality.

The characteristics of foreign immigration can be summarized as follows:

-     The immigration flows broken down into various types of presence, mobility and future prospects differ from each other.
-     Immigration which is temporary, and which is directed mainly towards returning to the country of origin or emigrating to other countries.
-     Immigration which is mainly regular from the point of view of residency for which the irregular employment rate is in any case

lower than forecast.

With regard to the political and cultural impact, investigations have revealed the following:

- There is strong pressure exerted on Italy by the developing countries, especially in North Africa, in demographic, economic and social terms.
- The ethnic, linguistic and religious complexity characterizing groups of immigrants, which raises entirely new cultural and social problems.
- The level of education and civil awareness - in some cases particularly high - which impose a high level of pressure for action.

With regard to the reactions of Italian society, the widespread phenomena of sensationalism, dismissal and apathy seem to prevail, with policies providing a low level of response to the emergency. But, in the meantime, there is also the growth of a culture of solidarity and hospitality, due above all to the work of associations and voluntary organizations.

The emergence of this new category of 'unprotected persons' and the complexity of the motivations, expectations and needs expressed by the immigrants, are presented as a new challenge, both for students of social problems, politicians and administrators and for all those who, professionally, privately or voluntarily, operate in the services.

The subject of rights of citizenship needs to be revised, not focusing so much on the *abstract* rights of man, but on the rights of the individual citizen, understood in turn as rights of diversity (of ideas, of culture, of lifestyles) and of equality.

The strategy to be adopted in the face of this new challenge is that of a tone of modern normality, otherwise there is a risk of dealing with immigration only as an emergency, one of the many which have been afflicting Italian society for some time. In reality, it is necessary:

- To review our welfare system in a modern manner, in the new multicultural modernity.
- To review the relationships between Italy and the other Mediterranean countries (e.g. co-operation for development).
- To enter, as protagonists, the cultural debate which will develop at European level on the many problems of *European society*, which

include the multicultural question.

The Voluntary Services: a New 'Social Lung' of Solidarity

The 1980s were years of great expansion of subjectivity and individualism, to the point of suggesting the theory that solidarity was inevitably in decline or that only the *me* culture was growing.

The expansion of *subjectivity* was, however, not accompanied, as if by entropy, by a reduction in solidarity, but subjectivity and solidarity grew together, as:

- On one hand the growth in subjectivity represents the tendency to simplify social reality, placing the circle of one's own needs and interests at the centre, as a privileged place through which to interpret it.
- On the other the growth of *solidarity* represents the tendency to simplify the relational system making relationships between subjects more direct and immediate.

In the field of social policy, the success factors which determined the affirmation of this reality were:

- Faced with the proliferation of needs and the growth in social complexity, which have caused a crisis in the traditional models of welfare, the voluntary services have offered immediate, flexible responses.
- In relation to the inability of social policies to respond adequately to the new forms of deprivation and alienation, the voluntary services have been thrust into the front line, placing emphasis on innovation and experimentation in intervention.
- Faced with the crises of public finance, which have also affected the social welfare system, the voluntary services can count on free human resources and a strong independence in terms of financial resources (the most usual form of financing is self-financing).
- Finally, the voluntary services have been able to count on a considerable store of generosity and solidarity idealism originating from the young.

One of the most innovatory elements which has characterized the development of the organized voluntary services of recent years is the trend towards a new approach to the public sector.

If we look, therefore, at the specific nature of its role, as it evolves, this form of association no longer simply represents a simple laboratory for social solidarity experiments but, in a social reality which is ever more exposed to the impoverishment of the relational dimension, the voluntary sector may represent a privileged channel for putting elements of sharing and reciprocity back into circulation in the social system.

SECTION 5: FACTORS OPERATING ON THE POLITICAL/ INSTITUTIONAL LEVEL

From Proliferation to Concentration

A long march towards decentralization of competences, under the banner of proliferation, has characterized the last thirty years' development in Italy.

The result has often been one of widespread fragmentation:

- Fragmentation of territory, with a multiplication of many micro-institutions.
- Fragmentation of participation, which has become ever more individualistic and conflictual (in the 1970s) and ineffective (in the 1980s).
- Fragmentation of the channels of representation of interests, with a huge multiplication of independent trade union agents and of spontaneous forms of representation of all kinds.

Certainly a sort of progressive *horizontalization* of Italian society has taken place, following the growth of subjectivity on one side and the loss of the unifying characteristic of the traditional *verticalities* (parties, ideologies, opposing blocs) on the other.

Parallel to the trend towards proliferation/fragmentation, in the case of local and regional organizations, responsibility for identifying resources (which are almost exclusively attributed to them by the Centre) has been attenuated.

More horizontality and less responsibility have become a *mix* which has created problems which are ever more obvious and which today make clear the growing need to find new and more appropriate forms of *concentration*, i.e.:

- Concentration of responsibility around local government, which should be given the task of distribution, monitoring and accountability of the resources to be spent in order to create a healthier self-regulating process with regard to expenditure.
- Territorial concentration in relation to the existing fragmentation which may lead to the formation of associative groupings between different regional realities (on the example of what is happening in the North East, which groups together Veneto, Friuli, Trentino and Alto Adige).
- Concentration of the elective and decision-making processes, a direction in which work needs to be done, in order to leave the purely proportional system in the first case and to arrive at a form of direct election of the mayor and, perhaps in the future of the head of state himself.

The main medium- to long-term consequences with regard to the EC might be at the level of reinforcement of the role of the regions and of the associations between regions. For the purpose of European integration, new experimentation with innovatory policies (in this connection, some steps are being taken within the Italian North East, which is considering joint activities with the bordering regions of other countries, regardless of whether they are members of the present Community) is to be encouraged.

The Opportunities and Dangers of the East and the Mediterranean

Italy has gone through key moments of tension in relation to migrants:

- The *regularization* of the Martelli law (1990), consisting mainly of counting and integrating those already present (mainly from outside the Community, from many different Southern countries of origin, today amounting to approx. 2 million individuals).
- The arrival of 20,000 Albanian refugees (1991) which brought back into the limelight the subject, the size and potential of the problem.
- The present situation of the arrival of Yugoslavian refugees, the flow of whom will probably increase in the future.

After the first *heated* reactions, the matter seems to have entered into the collective consciousness as an everyday affair, albeit a controversial one.
There is, however, a feeling that, in fact, we Italians are much better

regulated than other EC countries and that, as a result, there is a strong need for a coordinated presence.

In particular, there seems to be an increased need for a Community initiative (like the 'European Immigration Fund') which does not leave in isolation our country which, in turn, is exposed to unexpected and over-large flows of migrants.

At the same time attention to the opening up towards the East has increased, which has led to two recent legislative measures, the last of which was very recent (Law No. 212 of 26 February 1992), promulgated by the Ministry of Foreign Affairs, which opens up interesting prospects for cooperation between regions of North-East Italy and Central European countries.

The attention to the Mediterranean, on which a suitable initiative should be reformulated, is more limited.

In the long term a joint initiative by the EC and the countries of Southern Europe should be consolidated and improved.

The Permanent North/South Contrast and the Prospects for Growth of the System

There is still a North/South divide which affects the overall economic development of Italy.

Over the last twenty years, however, both the awareness of the question and the inadequacy of the traditional approach have grown.

In the first place the real development of the South has increased to form:

- On one hand an initial nucleus of areas/regions which have moved significantly closer to the Centre/North, and which today need further support, in order to be able to transfer, almost through *contiguity*, the developments which they have achieved to the less developed parts of the South (according to a principle of 'regional integration' of growth).
- And on the other, a sort of *South of the South*, which has serious, direct need of intervention, both on the economic and social fronts.

In the second place, there is an increasing awareness that more money may mean greater prosperity, but not necessarily greater development.

This has led to the need to review the logic of support to the South, so that it takes account of this awareness. However, it also seems useful to find in the EC a line of reasoning on the revision of the many 'Southern Governments' which can use the growth which has taken place in these years to deal with the problems which still remain unsolved.

13. Luxembourg: Shaping Factors*

INTRODUCTION

Lacking in natural resources, except for iron ore, suffering from the disadvantage of a numerically small workforce, and possessing only limited physical and financial capital, such are the main handicaps facing the Grand-Duché. One may ask how such a constrained economy should have been able to generate such a rapid, strong and lasting growth which has achieved one of the highest standards of living per inhabitant in Europe, as well as the bonus of a very low level of unemployment.

Since its creation, Luxembourg has been able to lay down the foundations of economic and industrial development and progressively establish an original social and economic model, one of the keys to which is an organization of links in society which are based on dialogue and the pursuit of social compromise. A major part of the effort of businesses and of the Government has been focused on the capacity to attract and retain scarce resources which were lacking in the country: financial and physical capital, and qualified and unqualified manpower. National sovereignty is the key tool which enabled the social accord to be structured and decisions to be taken on the allocation of resources. In effect it was this sovereignty which was the source of the freedom to manoeuvre on a legal, fiscal, social or political level.

The economic and social model rests on the positive dynamics of a rapid and strong internal growth driven by a growth in export of goods and services. This growth lies at the origin of the increase in budgetary revenue. Revenue has on the one hand enabled the financing of public consumer expenditure and investment (the development of host infrastructures, of transport and telecommunications, training, education, research, etc.) and, on the other hand, the accumulation of major reserves (except during five years: 1963, 1964, 1967, 1968 and 1983). The increase in revenue was, however, bound to slow down due to the

---

* S. Allegrezza.

generous tax concessions allowed in the tax reforms in 1991, to both companies and private individuals. If there is no let up in the rate of increase of public spending, Luxembourg should experience some budgetary deficits in the years to come.

In order to appreciate the scale of the deficit, which may reach 3% of GNP in 1991, the level of public debt should be considered in relation to GNP. This ratio has been less than 5% since 1988. The margin for manoeuvre, in the light of the criteria established by the Treaty of European Union which opened up access to economic and monetary union, remains of importance in the medium term. An increase in compulsory levies (taxes and contributions) could undermine the positive dynamics of Luxembourg's growth if the flow of direct foreign investment should dry up as a result of this increase.

The price competitiveness of companies in the Grand-Duché, measured in terms of unit wage cost, is about the Community average. This is a consideration amongst those factors favouring the creation of new companies. The consensus management of social relationships (in other words the joint resolution of problems between those involved at society level), which does not moreover exclude localized sectoral conflicts, has contributed to the fact that the accumulation-distribution mechanism is never obstructed while competitiveness needs are still met.

In the course of the last twenty years, the increase in GNP and that of employment has been very strong, and has generally remained significantly above the average for the EC. The standard of living has constantly improved and the country as a whole has achieved a high level of well-being. Further evidence of this is the virtually permanent low level of unemployment (which remains under 2%), despite a period of recession during the 1970s where the level reached 5%. Between 1970 and 1990 the elasticity of economic growth in Luxembourg corresponds to 1.27 the average GNP volume growth of the EC. In other words, when the average growth of the Member States of the EC improves by 1%, that of Luxembourg increases on average by 1.27%. The fluctuations in the world and Community economy's have powerful repercussions on the fluctuations of the small open economy of the Grand-Duché.

The policy of economic diversification represents the *leitmotif* and avowed objective of Luxembourg economic policy. It consists of creating new business activity in Luxembourg. This policy seems to have borne fruit since the diverse portfolio of sectors has reduced the amplitude of the fluctuations: the flexibility of the growth of the economy in Luxembourg, in relation to that of the EC, has become less during the 1980s, even with an elasticity greater than 1.

The price of success is growing larger and larger because it has been driven by political pressure groups with a direct or indirect influence on public opinion and the political chessboard which cannot be neglected: we should cite, amongst others, the problems of urban congestion, the high prices of building land and land for accommodation.

While the country is often presented as a tax paradise *par excellence,* and accused of being a predator on the resources of neighbouring countries, in particular the border regions, and suspected of being a *free-rider,* it is, on the other hand, a certain fact that accumulated wealth and a standard of living whose fragility cannot be emphasized enough, do multiply the number of the jealous and the envious.

A strategic commercial rationale can be seen in all this, in the sense of Krugman's new theory of international business, which tends to add impetus to those new companies, in new sectors, even if the financial tax and natural advantages diminish progressively. By virtue of the irreversibility of certain undertakings and the difficulty of getting out of certain markets and by virtue of exit costs, new companies, once established, should be encouraged to plan their development on the basis of their decision to site themselves in Luxembourg.

Furthermore, the large companies are generally - with the exception of the iron and steel group ARBED and the CFL (Compagnie Ferroviaire Luxembourgeoise) - subsidiaries of multinational groups: it is normal that such companies would be pursuing a global strategy, at EC level or beyond. Company managers and executives of the parent company or of the group will be making their decisions on the basis of variables for the whole group of countries for which they operate, variables over which Luxembourg has only scant influence. Luxembourg can only follow a policy of availability which will tend to conserve the competitiveness of its location in terms of economic viability - the unit cost of production - and in terms of financial viability after taxes on capital invested and on revenue distributed.

Luxembourg may become a victim of its own success if it cannot manage the secondary effects thereof and focus the extensive growth of sectors in which it will benefit from the greatest relative advantages. It does not have the option, on the other hand, of taking specialization too far; this objective would run counter to the aim of the policy of diversification. This balance between the highest possible return and the minimization of risk, interpreted as a minimization of the fluctuation in economic activity, taking into account social preferences, has been translated into a norm according to which 30% of value-added comes from the manufacturing sector. This confirms that contrary to a widely-held belief, Luxembourg does not consist uniquely of a financial centre.

In order that it should remain on a path of strong growth and high living standards, the peculiar nature of the economic dynamics and the structure of its production suggest that companies in Luxembourg must continuously adjust to the changes in their institutional environment.

The new developments of European integration, with the completion of the single market and the realization of economic, monetary and political union, will influence a series of factors which cannot fail to have repercussions at macroeconomic level and more specifically at mesoeconomic level, on certain sectors but also at the microeconomic level for a certain number of companies.

HISTORICAL FACTORS

Several factors have enabled the launch of Luxembourg: amongst others the policy of mine concessions, the discovery of iron ore in the south of the country and the entrepreneurial spirit of Luxembourg industrialists, who were able to take advantage of these deposits through the use of the *Thomas Gilchrist* process.

The danger of monolithism in the production apparatus of the Grand-Duché, focused solely on the iron and steel industry, caused the Government to undertake the diversification of the industrial fabric of the country, in order to relax the strong correlation between international fluctuations in the steel market and economic fluctuations in the country. Other industries have been established, especially in the chemical sector, in rubber, glass, and to a lesser degree in the electronics sector.

As in several countries, the 1970s were characterized by structural economic prices which hit the iron and steel industry hardest. Fortunately, a well-planned policy has enabled service sector industries to develop, especially banking and insurance. The latter have now taken over and become a new and powerful growth area for the economy.

Efforts in the direction of diversification in the service sector were in turn made, at the first signs of a slowing down: at that time the objective was to attract new service activities based on activities in the financial market and, on the other hand the development of other branches of the communications sector, for example the audio-visual sector. Two companies are dominant:

- The Société Européenne des satellites (SES), currently running two satellites, is a particularly eloquent example which stems from the strategy outlined above.
- The Compagnie Luxembourgeoise de Télécommunications (CLT), which is known as an exporter of radio and television broadcasts (RTL).

Integration into larger economic environments - Zollverein, The Union Economique Belgo-Luxembourgeoise, and finally the Common Market - has been an urgent necessity throughout the history of the Grand-Duché. This small country, with a very small domestic market, is obliged to export almost all (exports/GNP = 90%) of its production.

Luxembourg benefits from its location at the heart of the traditional economic centre of Northern Europe, which is delimited by the Paris-London-Amsterdam triangle and the Ruhr basin. However, another focus of development is under way, engulfing the prosperous regions of Southern Germany, Northern Italy and rapid growth areas like the South of France and the areas around Barcelona and Valencia. The urban economies and services offered to companies, and the quality and productivity of the labour force should continue to attract companies interested in proximity with clients and suppliers at the industrial heart of Northern Europe. But this focus of development also runs the risk of ever greater competition from the development of Southern Europe.

THE SINGLE MARKET AND THE EMU

The completion of the internal market will, without doubt, refine the workings of the market and extend it. Large industrial companies in Luxembourg are already major exporters and are highly integrated into the Community market; because of this, the completion of the internal market should pose no particular problem to them, and on the contrary, the completion of the internal market should stimulate still further exports.

Despite everything, the completion of the market, in as much as it must go through the phase of harmonization of taxation and contributions, is fraught with possible difficulties for Luxembourg. Let us take two examples:

- The recent modification of VAT rates. Anticipating the convergence towards a closer range of VAT rates within the

Community, and decided at the Luxembourg summit of December 1991, Luxembourg changed its VAT rate upwards and downwards: the maximum changed from 12% to 15% from 1 January 1992.

- The modification requested by the Commission, under the general regime of State assistance for companies, of a valuable instrument in Luxembourg's policy of commercial diversification, which, all things being equal, will make in-roads against the advantages of the Luxembourg location as an attractive magnet for direct foreign investment.

In all, the work of harmonization, which seems to have been a necessary prelude to the completion of the various markets, conceals a series of threats to the newer economic sectors in Luxembourg whose progress may thereby be hampered.

In spite of everything, monetary and economic union seems not necessarily to entail too many changes in the Luxembourg economy: it defines a series of macroeconomic constraints, the greater part of which already exists in the macroeconomic management of the country. In fact the margin for manoeuvre in terms of macroeconomic policy has always been very restricted: the economy of the Grand-Duché has always been determined by international factors and influences.

From a strictly macroeconomic point of view it is a fact that the Luxembourg economy is - at the moment - a very good pupil in the class of Europeans, satisfying the criteria of convergence required for the establishment of a single currency.

The stability of parities is viewed favourably. Luxembourg, which has long been in a state of monetary and economic union with Belgium, has scarcely had the option of devaluation. The sudden devaluation of the Belgium franc in 1982 was not requested by Luxembourg but was imposed by its partner who in turn was subject to the general economic stagnation of the time. This devaluation added spontaneously to the inflation that was running in Luxembourg and made necessary the partial indexation of salaries from the price index. In fact the automatic indexation clause which links salaries and the price index has the effect of more rapidly diffusing the impact of imported prices or increases in salaries than in other countries, where these fluctuations have repercussions on production costs and the price index itself. In spite of everything inflation has remained very low in recent years.

Political Union, in the transfer of sovereignty which it entails, has two contrasting effects: on the one hand, it gives Luxembourg the possibility of having an influence, albeit a small one, on the events at Community level as a whole, and on the other hand, it ultimately risks the loss of the autonomy which had enabled the Grand-Duché to forge its social consensus and high standard of living as well as a tax policy designed to attract and develop diverse activities in Luxembourg itself.

But, the debate on the ratification of the Maastricht Treaty which has recently blown up concerning whether or not and how the constitution should be amended, seems only to have concentrated on certain of the more innovative aspects of European citizenship.

DEMOGRAPHY AND THE JOB MARKET

Luxembourg is the smallest Member State of the EC if measured by the yardstick of its population (380,000 inhabitants) or by its area (2700 km^2) The natural surplus of births against deaths remains low from the point of view of population increase. Despite the presence of non-nationals (28% of the population), traditionally with a higher birth-rate, the natural movement of the population was negative between 1972 and 1978. The growth in population is principally due to the migratory balance. The change in patterns of births has changed the distribution of population by age. Even so, the number of active individuals is currently very favourable (63% of the inhabitants are between 20 and 64) thanks to the creation of employment right up to the borders.

Significant technological progress and strong growth during the last twenty years has required a significant increase in the workforce. The growth of the national population has been largely inadequate for this. The natural surplus (births to deaths) is low. In that time the increase in the active population has only been possible through sustained flow of immigrant workers and cross-border workers. The proportion of foreign population is currently 28% of the total population and the proportion of cross-border workers is 18% of the total workforce. The limited size of the resident workforce entails the regular recruitment of cross-border workers.

There is a long history of immigration. The different waves of immigration date back to the beginning of industrialization and have settled migrant workers of different origins: France, Germany, Italy and more recently Portugal.

The demographic situation has had the result of a limited availability of a qualified workforce and the need to pay a premium to compensate for the non-appropriateness of work and for the supplementary cost entailed (e.g. transport cost). This has increased salaries, while at the same time the reservoir of cross-border workforce has dried up. This will increasingly be the case when the neighbouring regions or Portugal experience a stronger economic development such that they retain their own workforce within their borders.

Luxembourg's great problem is certainly its future demographic structure, in respect of reproduction and the increase in the workforce required by economic growth. 28% of the resident population are non-natives, and together with cross-border workers, they occupy 44% of jobs. A simulation study carried out by STATEC, the statistics institute, shows that given certain hypotheses, the non-Luxembourg part of the population could grow between 1990 and 2020 to platform out at 28.8% and in an extreme hypothetical situation the quota of foreigners could reach 43.8% of the total population.[1]

The use of a foreign workforce, in itself, does not bring with it significant problems, but even so certain features which will directly or indirectly affect management of companies should be highlighted: (a) the level of social security contributions by virtue of the fairly generous old-age insurance which is currently financed by a strong level of active population, (b) the management of human resources within companies between nationals and non-nationals and (c) the initial and continued training problems, even though cross-border workers are generally highly trained.

CAPITAL, LAND, TECHNOLOGY AND FOREIGN DIRECT INVESTMENT

The diversification of the economic structure of Luxembourg has been achieved by virtue of foreign direct investments: American, Japanese and European. A diverse panoply of aid - in terms of tax, finance and

---

[1]   This refers to several simulated annual figures carried out under different birth-rate, mortality, migration balance, national status options/naturalization hypotheses (*Journal of STATEC*, no. 4, 1991).

zoning[2] - not to mention the advantages offered by the productivity of the workforce and the central location of Luxembourg, have enabled it to attract capital and foreign know-how.

In the context of its policy on competition, the EC has invited the Luxembourg Government to revise its general regime of assistance to investment, having reproached it for creating a distortion in competition to the detriment of less developed regions, which runs counter to the objective of cohesion pursued by the EC.[3] It is, however, doubtful that Luxembourg State aid will create any distortions given the low level of investments on a European scale and their negligible weight in intra-Community exchanges.

The continuance of the policy of diversification presupposes that the EC does not become a fortress and will in fact allow the Member States the freedom of formulating their own industrial policy. The regime of investment aid will therefore be modified towards greater selectivity. Henceforth industrial policy will take into account:

- The criteria for assistance to research and innovation.
- The size of companies, giving priority to small- and medium-size enterprises.
- The rational use of energy and protection of the environment.

The creation of capital results from investment financed by profits retained within Luxembourg. Tax on company revenues, on savings and on the income of individual persons also plays an important role. Assistance to investment is a means of indicating to international investors who may be seeking a production site in Northern Europe that Luxembourg is an option.

---

2   The tools used to encourage investment are: close advantages, State guarantees, capital subsidies, tax relief, land and building acquisitions and developments, equipment credits, long-term loans, participative loans, innovation loans, export credit, and financial involvement. The range of tax and financial measures originated in the draft law of 2 June 1962 which aimed at improving the general structure and equilibrium of the national economy and stimulating expansion, extended to service industries in 1973, and regionalized in the revision of the law of 14 May 1986, which is about to be modified following initiatives of the EC Commission (SNCI, 1991).

3   Aid allocated by Luxembourg to the manufacturing industry was only at a level of 0.7% of GNP (PC: 0.9% of GNP) in the period 1986 to 1988. Aid given to the railways on the other hand reached the highest level of any grant measured in ECU/traveller-kilometre. This situation is due to the small size of the network and to enormous fixed costs. The overall quantity of aid given by the State gives the impression that Luxembourg has been the most prodigious in subsidies (4% of GNP, double the average in the EC).

The ability to receive foreign investment requires the development of industrial zones of transport infrastructures and communication networks, as well as an increase in residential property. The management of space poses problems of balance between alternative allocations of an area limited to 2,500 km^2. Currently 1.9% alone of the land is occupied by industrial zones. The lack of space is a positive hindrance to the growth of companies which will become worse in the medium and long term. The inventory of sites needed for the years 1990 to 2020 and the sites currently available at national, regional and communal level highlight the fact that supply and demand of sites need balancing.

If the standard of living is to be maintained in the long term while avoiding an escalation of prices for property and land, Luxembourg will need to show an increasingly effective control of its use of space and of its attendant externalized assets, which are a source of social costs, due to urban congestion. The frequently cited example in this context is that of the Saarland which has an area comparable to that of Luxembourg but double the population. This example would suggest that Luxembourg is still counting on a significant reserve capacity for accommodating new growth. The lack of space, all other things being equal, runs the risk of down-grading the framework for the quality of life and thereby diminishing the attractiveness of Luxembourg as a location.

Transport infrastructures by road or rail, the telecommunications networks and their associated services, the electricity supply and the collection circuits for industrial waste contribute to the structure of this space. It is the quality of these infrastructures which will determine the competitive advantage of the location of Luxembourg for production.

Cross-border cooperation in the context of the Grande-Région, in particular the *European focus of development* is an alternative to the shared rational use of land for industrial purposes.

Research is also increasingly a productivity and competitiveness factor. Lack of a university and a centre for applied and theoretical research in Luxembourg may prove to be a handicap for development and research in companies and for technology transfer, despite recent initiatives by the Government.

In-company research is not the only source of innovation, which may arise from *learning by doing or learning by using* or through the purchase of licences as new foreign companies establish themselves, bringing with them new technologies and technology transfer between subsidiaries of the parent company. Despite the structural limits of Luxembourg, there remains a certain margin for error for companies but it does favour indigenous development within Luxembourg, especially if the subsidiaries of major companies decide to establish their research centre in Luxembourg itself. All initiatives favouring transfer, appropriation and the use of scientific information and technical know-how are favourable factors.

Finally, as a small open economy, exchanges with the outside world are vital. In fact, while production has to be massively imported from border regions - Lorraine, the Rhine, Saar, the Belgian Province of Luxembourg - exports are aimed at even larger areas, Germany, Belgium and France in the main.

Luxembourg's main partners are therefore its neighbouring countries. Opportunities for investment, exchange and collaboration with Eastern European countries have only been partially explored but should assume increasing importance as information on the opportunities becomes better, or conversely less important if information ceases to be available and if the legal framework is able to offer the judicial and financial security required for trade.

Cross-border trade in certain products which are subject to high VAT in the cross-border countries and/or are subject to high excise levies, like alcoholic beverages and tobacco, may suffer significantly from the levelling out of tariffs at European level.

The Regions of Europe present an additional spatial challenge for Luxembourg, itself a sovereign *State-Region*. Still more so for its companies given that Luxembourg's greater commercial autonomy is translated into a higher degree of flexibility and an increased margin for manoeuvre which all make the country a focus for direct foreign investment.

PRICES, COSTS AND TAXES

The tax and social position of cross-border workers in the country of the employer constitute an important aspect of the financing of public expenditure linked to the infrastructures and financing of social security (health insurance, old-age insurance). In fact the introduction of the principle of taxation in the country of residence would be balanced by a fall in tax revenue and revenue from social security for Luxembourg. The probable consequence of this for companies in Luxembourg will be an increase in tax on companies or on employers' contributions.

Luxembourg is one of the few countries having *automatic indexation* of salaries to increase in prices. Despite this adaptation of salaries to the cost of living, inflation has remained very low and is below the average for the Community and even below the average for inflation in countries with which Luxembourg is principally involved in commercial exchange. One may be forgiven for thinking that although a delicate subject, from a political and social point of view, the impact of inflation like that experienced by the Luxembourg economy during the 1970s and during the devaluation of the Belgian franc in 1982, has more rapid repercussions and is even accelerated with an automatic salary indexation system. If the indexation system is able to accelerate the diffusion of an inflationary shock-wave, it may to some degree lead companies to retain lower profit margins and also trade unions to exercise a certain degree of moderation in salary claims in tandem with increases in productivity, given that neither party to collective bargaining has any interest in stirring up the indexation system.

The achievement of economic and monetary union which in principle at least favours greater stability in prices, should also lessen the danger of damaging inflationary spirals which threaten social harmony and the price competitiveness of Luxembourg companies.

Finally, in comparison with other countries of the OECD, obligatory levies are very high in Luxembourg, in particular tax on income (of residents), whereas contributions to social security are relatively less.

However, there are significant differences between incomes and pensions in the public and in the private sector. These differences seem to be very markedly in favour of the public sector at least for lower-paid and medium-income professions. This inequality is one of the reasons why union organizations in the private sector and certain political groups are seeking an increase in pensions. This factor in itself tends to increase the obligatory levies for the purpose of financing public transfers to social security insurance and pensions.

POLITICAL FACTORS

There is considerable value in describing the historical background of the State of Luxembourg. The comté of Luxembourg, founded in 963 by Count Sigefroi, was to develop through the centuries to become a duché and subsequently a Grand-Duché.

Luxembourg had an important role to play in the middle ages through the various dynasties related to the House of Luxembourg (Henry VII,

Charles IV and Wenceslas of Bohemia).

Luxembourg was occupied several times by the Burgundians, the Spanish, the French and the Austrians, and has been under foreign rule for 350 years of its history. At the Congress of Vienna in 1815, Luxembourg became a Grand-Duché, but was separated from the region of Bitburg and the Rhineland. When Brussels revolted against the North of the Netherlands, Luxembourg rallied to the Belgian cause in 1830. The Treaty of London in 1839 divided Luxembourg into two parts, one became the Belgian province of Luxembourg and the other became an independent State.

This brief overview emphasizes the fact that Luxembourg, which was born out of an accident of history, has accepted the challenge and undertaken the construction of a State. The population's attachment to the concept of this State, and the major difficulties it has had to suffer throughout two world wars have culminated in a strong national feeling.

A very important cultural factor merits emphasis here: before the division of 1839, Luxembourg had two linguistic areas, the one, a francophone area, was ceded to Belgium and the other, a germanophone area, remains in the new independent State. French has been maintained as the administrative and cultural language. For some time now there has been a noticeable resurgence of cultural, literary and theatre activity in the Luxembourg patois, and this has been increasingly accessible to foreigners, as many people study this language. This patois has served to underline the national feeling and conveys an individuality and perhaps also a motivating force, through the sharing of common values. But language too can also constitute a cultural barrier to non-Luxembourgers.

Luxembourg's greatest wealth is its sovereignty. This enabled it on the one hand to have a voice in the gathering of the nations, and on the other hand to have a certain room for manoeuvre in the direction of its economic policy, in the organization of the State and the structure of its administration. For example, sovereignty enables Luxembourg to decide between equity and effectiveness, in the structure of its public finances. This freedom, in the context of democratic institutions, has enabled a social consensus in economic policy and social affairs to be established and expressed - and this has been called the *Luxembourg model* - and has also influenced the organization of the State, which also encompasses fiscal and budgetary policy.

Political Union as far as citizenship is concerned will give the *right to vote to EC citizens* in local and European elections. The relatively high number of immigrants, *more than 28%* of the population, has been the cause of some alarm for some of the population.   Despite the various dispensations allowed for in the Treaty of Maastricht, there are fears in some quarters that non-native electors and elected individuals will achieve a dominant position in certain communes, and, in general, on national policy-making authorities.

The ratification of the Treaty of Union signed at Maastricht should not give rise to many concerns.   There is a degree of consensus over the importance of integration of the Luxembourg economy and society into the structures of the Community of Europe.   Some parties like the pressure group *5/6* have suggested that the ratification of the Treaty should be subject to a national referendum.   The Democratic Party (Liberal), the largest opposition party, also seems inclined to this point of view.   But the Communist Party and the two green parties have declared themselves against a referendum.   The referendum procedure, which has rarely been used throughout history, runs the risk of being *tainted by political ulterior motives which are entirely foreign to the true issues of European Union*, as the President of the Government Mr Jacques Santer emphasized in his debate on the State of the Nation (L.W. 23.4.92).   It is true that themes of a demagogic or populist nature, notably as far as the right to vote of resident citizens of Member States of the EC is concerned, could quickly assume disproportional importance to the cost of economic, social and cultural interests.

The great challenge for Luxembourg is to ensure the cohesion of Luxembourg society by creating a European and *multicultural* socio-political structure which integrates foreign residents, who are in any case mostly citizens of the Member States of the EC.

At the legislative elections of 1989, the three most important parties (Christian-Social, Socialist and Liberal) saw a decline in their votes. They were competing against various ecological candidates and the *5/6* initiative, which fought the increase in pensions for the private sector, following the example of the pensions of administrative staff who receive almost 5/6 of their last salary.

This degree of autonomy in the Grand-Duché, which has been reduced by the new stages of European integration, which on the other hand has certainly been moderated by the theoretical principle of subsidiarity, risks being undermined.

CONCLUSIONS: THE MALTHUSIAN TEMPTATION OF A NATION OF INDEPENDENT MEANS?

This paper has helped to bring to the fore some of the main features of the social and economic model of Luxembourg as well as the driving force behind its dynamics together with the attendant explosive risks, but also risks of implosion in the event that Luxembourg loses its economic and social advantages which guarantee its autonomy based on sovereignty.

It cannot be denied that public opinion would gladly be seduced by options seeking a slowing down in economic growth, as well as in urbanization and population density, under the guise of respect for the natural environment or preservation of a certain *national identity*, which is in itself a notion which is quite difficult to define for the Grand-Duché of Luxembourg. Given that these aspirations have not found a political voice, except perhaps, to some degree, in the green tendencies and nationalist tendencies, the traditional parties carrying the social and economic *Luxembourg model* remain, broadly speaking, committed to the current model of development.

The International Monetary Fund, in its last report devoted to Luxembourg's situation,[4] seems to lend support to those seeking a reorientation of economic policy and industrial policy in particular. In its report the IMF highlights the resources allocated for attracting economic activity to Luxembourg and the fact that these will be increasingly characterized by a fall in marginal effectiveness of investment and asks the question whether these resources, in particular the budgetary resources, would not be better invested in a portfolio of international assets which might offer a better return. This would lead straightaway to the beginning of the nation of *independent means*.

The unbridled growth of GNP, driven by external demand arising from the arrival of new companies, and by the policy of economic diversification, must be eventually substituted by more sustainable growth (R. Goebbels)[5] rather than the slowing down that certain philosopher-ecologists would like to impose. The challenge, which is a very difficult one, is the control of the detail of this growth, and of its orientation and consequences.

---

4   IMF, *Luxembourg-Staff Report for the 1991 Article IV Consultation*, October 1991.

5   R. Goebbels, *Investir dans l'avenir*, Made in Luxembourg, no. 40, October 1991, Letzebuerger Land.

Subsidiarity is a principle to which Luxembourg is very committed. In fact, if it is the case that a series of problems cannot be resolved other than through the plurality of the States, certain problems which reflect collective preferences, like for example the relationship between direct taxation and indirect taxation (the latter being considered as regressive), should be expressed and concretized. Harmonization, if it is to be accepted and encouraged, may well be achieved on the basis of a competition of regulations which in turn causes institutions to become competitive and organize themselves in a competitive way. But the differentiation of these institutions means that the regulations will never be identical from one country to another.

Reciprocity is another important principle for Luxembourg, in particular in its social and economic relationships with the surrounding region, the aforementioned Grande Région Saar-Lor-Lux. Having been accused of stockpiling the human resources of its neighbouring countries, Luxembourg will also have to examine the possibility of a series of actions, in the framework of Community programmes which provide for the redistribution of value-added other than in the creation of employment throughout the neighbouring regions. This interdependence has already emerged through the EC's regional policy and through involvement in the European focus of development.

The construction of a political Europe is something to be favoured, as the Nobel prize winner for economics, Maurice Allais, recently proposed at a conference in Luxembourg. Certainly from this point of view also, Luxembourg will have to undergo some loss of sovereignty, but for a small neutral non-aggressive State, without a colonial past or military deterrent, this loss will be extremely relative.

14. Netherlands: Shaping Factors*

INTRODUCTION

In the next decades business in the Netherlands and other European countries will face important problems, opportunities and challenges. This report attempts to identify the key general factors which will drive the European business environment during the next 20 years. Specifically, it will concentrate on those developments that are of importance to the Netherlands. The *leitmotif* is that the future business environment will be determined not only by market forces, but also to a significant degree by the success or failure of EC countries to adapt to new circumstances.

The coming years will be of critical importance for the future of the European Community as a leading player in world markets. The creation of a single market will improve Europe's economic position *vis-à-vis* the American and Japanese economies. Nevertheless, European companies will have to perform as well as American or Japanese competitors if they are to survive. The single market is a necessary condition but not a guarantee for improved economic performance.

Competition *within* the EC will also increase, not only between companies but between (national and regional) communities as a whole. The single market will leave companies fewer opportunities to hide behind national barriers and institutional arrangements. Certain institutional differences among nations, regions and communities will, however, remain. With further integration, authorities will have to focus on combinations of natural and infrastructure-related environmental and institutional conditions to attract economic activities to their territories, in order to enhance national prosperity. The efforts of national actors to optimize and create business environments that are attractive to both domestic and foreign investors, will lead to increased *policy competition*. Economic conditions will not be the only instrument in the process of competitive policy-making. Social and political stability, a well-

---

*   J.C.F. Bletz, W. Dercksen and K. van Paridon.

345

functioning labour market, stable industrial relations, innovative capacities, progress on environmental issues and diplomatic ability will also be of importance here.

Thus, European integration can in itself be considered a main shaping factor for the future business environment. The position of Europe in the world, the emergence of market economies in Central and Eastern Europe, the future architecture of Europe, the consequences of European Monetary Union (EMU), European Political Union (EPU) and the single market are important aspects in the international arena, affecting the position of the individual Member States. There is no reason to believe that the Netherlands will be affected by these developments in a deviating way. It is not necessary therefore to discuss international developments separately in this chapter. The consequences of German unification might be an exception to this, because of the strong trade ties between the two countries.

On the basis of expert knowledge, inside and outside the Scientific Council,[1] seven key areas have been selected for more detailed discussion:

-     Geography, natural resources and physical infrastructure.
-     The public sector.
-     Socio-economic relations.
-     Socio-cultural relations.
-     Technology.
-     Environment.
-     The private sector.

The following sections will sketch the main developments in each area, the way in which Dutch firms, government and society anticipate expected changes in policies and behaviour, and the areas in which the Dutch feel that the European Community has an important role to play.

As all futures research does, this report labours under present reality, in that it tends to project today's concerns on tomorrow's world. Present assumptions may in the longer term seem less relevant, while at the same time, unforeseen circumstances may influence the outcomes. The authors

---

1   In recent years the Council has produced in-depth studies on labour market policies, environment, technological developments, urban problems, agricultural policies and law enforcement. For this report, these sources and others from outside the Council have been used. The outcomes of this study were compared with a report on long-term economic development in the Netherlands: Central Planning Bureau, *The Netherlands in Triplo*, The Hague, 1992.

do, however, feel reasonably confident about the choices they have had to make, since most of the developments traced are solidly rooted in the (sometimes distant) past. Whereas many things will change, they do not necessarily alter. It might be tempting to consider the advent of the single market as not only a new beginning, but also another *end of history*. It does not, however, seem prudent to exclude historic continuity from the many factors that will shape Europe after 1992.

GEOGRAPHY, NATURAL RESOURCES AND PHYSICAL INFRASTRUCTURE

At the moment, new products, new production methods, new materials and new markets are all emerging in rapid succession. Other important elements, however, remain relatively unaffected. This section will address three such factors: geographical location, availability of natural resources, and physical infrastructure. These all have an effect on business strategies. Their importance is equalled by their *policy resistance*.

Key Features

The geographic position of the Netherlands is considered an asset. Certain trends, such as a shift of the main transport arteries in Europe towards the South, might, however, decrease its importance. Because the Netherlands is a small, open and trade-oriented economy, the size and quality of physical infrastructure are obviously crucial to the overall competitiveness of the Dutch economy. In order to attract economic activity and hold on to the major share in a rapidly changing transport market, attention must therefore be focused on infrastructure and logistics. The traditionally strong position held by Dutch firms in the European transport market can only be maintained through timely and sufficient investments in both road and rail infrastructure, as well as in the two mainports Schiphol Airport and Rotterdam Harbour. At the same time, increasing environmental problems resulting from transport will have to be adequately addressed.

The Netherlands is not known for its wide range of natural resources. It is, however, a major producer of natural gas. The Netherlands has become a very important supplier of energy to several countries in Western Europe. The country is responsible for about 10% of the primary energy production of the Community.

Recent Trends

Internationalization affects the comparative advantages which the Netherlands derives from its geographic position. The fast growth of the Southern German *Länder*, the rise of Lombardy in Italy and of the regions around Toulouse and Lyons in France, combined with the decline of traditional industries in the Ruhr area and the United Kingdom, could lead to a gradual shift southward of Europe's economic centre.

Furthermore, the rise of new technologies and use of new materials have generally diminished the importance of the traditional geographic factors on which the Netherlands has always relied so much. It has not, however, weakened the corresponding traditional skills possessed by Dutch transport entrepreneurs. Companies are now much less dependent on the proximity of raw materials or markets, and have a far wider choice of locations. The emphasis on knowledge-intensive production, supported by sophisticated logistics (*just-in-time* production), has resulted in changes in the modal split of international trade and transport. Cheap, bulk-oriented (sea) transport declines, while more expensive, but much faster and more reliable air transport shows a very strong increase. Competition in this growth market is fierce and there are no geographic factors which might favour Schiphol Airport the same way they favoured Rotterdam.

Higher incomes, increased scales of production, new forms of intra-firm organization and changes in the modal split have all led to a higher demand for transport, both private and public. In the Netherlands, road transport has become the most important means of transport, both for passengers as well as for freight. In 1990 about 75% of traffic measured in passenger-kilometres occurred with cars; the percentage for domestic cargo was about the same. The increase over the past decades has been tremendous, especially because of the increase in the number of cars, but also due to higher mileage rates. Road infrastructure has changed much less dramatically, however. As a result, traffic intensity has risen considerably, by more than 45% since 1980.

Natural gas has become the major source of energy for domestic heating. It is also by far the most important energy source for electricity production; its share in the manufacturing sector is currently more than 30%. The presence of such a cheap and abundant energy source has contributed to a rather high energy use in this country, compared with other EC countries.

Policies

Natural gas has not been properly used to increase the structural competitiveness of the Dutch economy; investment decisions by firms were based on undervalued energy prices, and government policies favoured consumption rather than investment. Much attention has been paid to changing the energy content of production during recent years, resulting in some partial success. The same can be said of efforts to better utilize combined heat and power generation. The reallocation of funds within the government budget, aimed at investment instead of consumption, is proving very difficult indeed. Both changes must continue in the near future.

The Dutch Government has recently decided to earmark revenues from exploration of natural gas for an infrastructure investment fund. The Government is also investigating the options of improving and accelerating planning procedures aimed at speeding up the construction of new roads or railways.

Current government policy regarding the infrastructure is directed towards improving existing roads and building a few new tunnels to relieve the biggest bottlenecks, instead of expanding it much further. More emphasis is given towards changes in the modal split, aimed at using all available types of infrastructure as energy-efficient as possible. Major improvements in public transport systems will have to be realized in order to cope with the rush-hour traffic. Related measures currently being considered include: reducing available parking in towns, creating better facilities for switching from private to public transport, introducing a road-pricing system in the region comprising The Hague, Amsterdam, Rotterdam and Utrecht (Randstad) in order to generate more efficient use of the existing infrastructure, limiting office construction in areas which cannot easily be reached by public transport, and further increasing the price of petrol (as part of an energy tax programme). For this to succeed, it is imperative that public transport become at least as competitive as private transport by automobile, with regard to speed, comfort and price.

Both the domestic road and railway structure are essential links in global transport chains, with Rotterdam and Schiphol acting as important mainports. Both have shown very impressive growth rates in the last decades and are planning to make huge investments to be able to maintain their prominent position in fast growing but also quickly changing markets. The Government wants to facilitate further expansion; new areas are made available and physical infrastructure is improved or created. An example is the plan to extend the TGV network to Schiphol.

The business sector responds by means of new investments in both mainports. At the Rotterdam docks, new terminals are being constructed for containers and specialized products such as fruit. Many new firms are also making investments in the Schiphol area, with an eye to using the location for efficient distribution of their products within Europe.

Prospects

The EC must play a part in European infrastructure, transport and environmental policies. A desirable Community reaction for the Netherlands would be to stress the necessity of certain essential links in the continental infrastructure. This would include completion of the Rhine-Danube Canal and construction of a standardized, European high-speed train system. It is expected that the single market will open several domestic road-freight markets for Dutch firms. The Netherlands would then be able to improve its already strong competitiveness on the European transport market, while at the same time the Community could profit from handling cargo at the lowest possible costs.

As far as the physical infrastructure is concerned, Dutch government action can be expected with regard to planning (promotion of mainport function, streamlining physical planning procedures) and finance (reshuffling the government budget in favour of infrastructural investments). Business companies are expected to react by increasing the concentration around mainports, through further specialization in logistics and telematic operations, and implementation of energy conservation in transport.

Major changes in energy supply and demand are not expected to occur in the near future. For demand this depends, of course, on more efficient use of energy and increased distribution of energy supplies, both of which are major policy goals in the Netherlands. Oil and natural gas will remain the two most important fuels. With regard to supply, the Netherlands will probably not opt for nuclear energy. The Dutch Government must decide in the very near future whether it is necessary to expand the current level of electricity production and, if so, which technology and which fuel source will be selected.

Although a European Energy Charter would be useful, it would not really alter the Dutch energy system. Some type of energy tax will probably be introduced in the near future in order to reduce energy consumption.

Business will continue efforts aimed at conserving energy, placing more emphasis on combined heat and power generation. As a result of the single market, large-scale consumers will opt for a supply of electricity from external sources, because of lower prices. This will create more competitive conditions in energy supply, which could mean lower costs and changes in the energy mix.

Table 14.1 Location, Resources & Infrastructure -
Business Prospects Until 2010

- Further specialization in logistics
- Further concentration around mainports
- Increase in container transport by rail
- More telematic operations
- Research into and development of road pricing systems
- Energy conservation; cheaper energy from external sources
- Cooperation with government on environmental safeguards

THE PUBLIC SECTOR

The twentieth century has been an age of strong belief in man's ability to change the natural and social environments. This has resulted in a major expansion of government budgets and civil servant employment, and in the creation of an ever increasing array of laws, rules and regulations. Even though certain doubts have arisen about the government's role, it is still considered a major actor in this process of change. Policies and goals concerning the future of the public sector are therefore very important. This section deals with future relations between the public sector and business environment.

Key Features

the Netherlands is a constitutional monarchy with a parliamentary system. The country has many political parties in parliament. As a result, the government is always a coalition and government policies are based on compromises, to a larger extent than in two- or three-party political systems. Coalitions are, however, not the best basis for governments to pursue resolute entrepreneurial policies.

The Netherlands has a public sector corresponding to a welfare system, which provides generous benefits and supports a high proportion of the population. Moreover, the government budget is still experiencing the repercussions caused by the economic crisis of the early eighties. Public expenditure in 1991 amounted to 51.2% of GDP; 29 percentage points concerned income transfers (excluding subsidies and interests). The Netherlands had a budgetary deficit of 3.5% of GDP and government investment was 2.3% of GDP. This percentage is still declining.

The proportion of Dutch government consumption, including expenditures on wages and salaries, is lower than in other industrialized countries. On the other hand, transfer expenditure is much higher. Consequently, taxes and social security contributions exceed those in other industrialized countries, resulting in a high tax burden for both employers and exployees. The relatively low proportion of government investment is a major disadvantage for Dutch competitiveness.

Thus, a key issue in the public sector will be the continuous reform of public finance. A reduction in the share of transfer incomes in favour of public investments would make a significant contribution towards the creation of a more competitive business environment. Another major contributing factor for the future business environment is the success or failure of efforts aimed at improving the efficiency of the political and administrative sector. The outcome will substantially determine the level of Dutch competitiveness, as well as the ability to attract foreign investment.

Recent Trends

During the eighties, exercises in privatization, deregulation and decentralization were conducted to create smaller and more effective public administrations. The results until now have not been impressive. Employment of civil servants continued to rise, both in persons as well as in labour years, although at a declining rate. Nevertheless, some success has been achieved, for instance in the decentralization of social services, the privatization of the PTT, diminished interventions in wages and prices, and the tripartition of the Employment Services.

Another development in this area is regionalization. There are regions emerging in the European landscape which serve as new administrative actors. This is the result of Europe's regional policy to support developing regions, on the one hand. On the other hand, it is a question of economic and political development. Regional-economic specialization is linked to specific infrastructural provisions. Administrative cooperation on a regional scale is a powerful instrument in the process of policy competition, especially with regard to investments in infrastructure. In many respects, the regional level is more relevant for decision-making than the city or the national state.

So far, the Dutch Government has been rather slow in transferring responsibilities from the national level towards lower levels. The new circumstances, however, have stimulated several regions to reinforce their position so as to be better equipped to cope with the new situation. Two such *Euregions* are emerging within the Netherlands, in addition to the Randstad. The Euregion between Rotterdam and Antwerp is slowly emerging. Another main Euregion is the area encompassing Maastricht, Aachen (Germany), Hasselt and Liège (both Belgium).

Policies

Policy competition generated by the need for national states to optimize comparative advantages on a single European market results in a dual task for the Dutch Government: (a) to reduce the high level of government expenditure, mainly by reducing social security costs, and (b) to reshuffle the government budget in favour of public investments in the physical, technical, scientific and educational infrastructure required for a competitive business environment. The introduction of an EMU will force the Dutch Government, as well as other European governments, to pursue low inflation and interest rates and budgetary deficits of less than 3% of GDP. The process of European integration will probably give rise to further fiscal harmonization.

Notwithstanding actual government efforts to maintain the present structure of the Dutch Welfare State, a return to core activities may become necessary during the nineties in the fields of social security, health care, social services and housing. In these areas the Government's core activity might become restricted to providing guarantees for merely minimum subsistence, albeit at a civilized level. Additional social security and social provisions could be obtained via private insurance.

Market forces will probably be (re-)introduced in many areas, for instance in labour market and training facilities, and in the further development and administration of the physical, educational, scientific and technical infrastructures. Competition among public and private suppliers of further training will enhance the quality of *life-time education.* Public-private partnerships may enlarge the financial capacity for investments in infrastructure. Private execution of public policies could reduce costs and enlarge the flexibility of the public sector. As a result, the provision of public goods will increase its share in total government activity, at the expense of the provision of merit goods and executive and administrative functions.

The manner in which devolution of powers will enable urban regions in the Netherlands to attract investments is of particular significance. There are two incentives which might provide opportunities for local authorities in the Netherlands to further develop competitive regions. The first is more scope for administrative manoeuvring, which includes more far-reaching jurisdiction in imposing local taxes. Public-private partnerships are a second potential means of overcoming financial restrictions. A necessary condition is that all public and private actors are prepared to consider economic-geographical regions as primary instruments in international competition.

Prospects

EC reactions to increasing policy competition can be expected in the following areas: EMU, EPU, fiscal harmonization, European urbanization policies and emphasis on Euregions. As far as Dutch public finance is concerned, more can be expected than just a reduction in the proportion of transfer incomes, and increase in the proportion of public investments. Related policies such as decentralization, deregulation and privatization will continue and be supplemented with efforts to shorten planning procedures and establish public-private partnerships.

In so far as the Dutch Government will concentrate on core activities, the scope for private business will grow, for example, in the area of insurance (health care, pensions), training and retraining and services. The construction and building industry as well as (European) investment bankers, business consultancies and R&D institutes will benefit from the increasing importance of infrastructure.

Table 14.2   Public sector business prospects until 2010

- Growth of public-private partnerships
- Expansion of construction and building industry on a European scale
- Expansion of private insurance companies (health care, pensions, etc.)
- Improved linkages between business and education
- Participation of industry in (urban) development schemes
- Growth of international (European) business consultancies

SOCIO-ECONOMIC RELATIONS

Socio-economic institutions deeply affect the business environment. They produce both formal (laws, public and private regulations, etc.) and informal rules (cultures of decision-making, norms, habits, etc.). These institutions reduce the level of uncertainty, facilitating economic contacts and contracts. They display a considerable degree of tenacity. Although institutions can be changed, this neither occurs all at once, nor completely according to a master plan. It is a combined result of global and national shaping forces, actions and reactions by actors in the socio-economic field, and past strategic choices.

Key Features

A striking element of the Dutch system of industrial relations is the dominant role played by central government within labour relations. The centralistic nature of decision-making in the socio-economic sphere and in collective bargaining is closely related to this. A third point concerns the high level of trust placed in tripartite consultation. Neo-corporatist decision-making is at the heart of the Dutch mixed economy. Additional characteristics include the labour force's high level of contentment, the way participation is firmly grounded in legislation and the weak position held by the trade union movement within companies and institutions. Dutch industrial relations are generally of a non-conflictual nature (the number of days lost to strikes in the Netherlands is the lowest in Europe).

Dutch neo-corporatism has strong support among political parties, unions, employers' federations and academics. This support is based on a belief in its potential for promoting economic growth along non-conflictual lines. There is, however, also criticism: Dutch neo-corporatism could hinder the functioning of the market. One aspect currently under attack is that the Minister of Social Services and Employment declares the main results of collective bargaining generally binding for all firms within a given branch of industry.

Another striking feature of prevailing socio-economic relations in the Netherlands is the low level of participation in paid employment. Measured in persons, the Dutch participation rate equals the European level, but there is a major difference when the participation rate is calculated in labour years. This is related to the high proportion of part-time employment. Unemployment notwithstanding, there are shortages in certain sectors of the labour market, including the supply of unskilled labour. Viewed from a perspective of policy competition, the low rate of labour participation is a reason for concern. An effort to raise the employment rate could provide a major shaping factor for the business environment in decades to come.

Recent Trends

There has been a tendency towards decentralization in industrial relations since 1982. Since then the National Government has refrained from direct intervention in wage developments in the market sector. During the eighties socio-economic matters became more the concern of government, management and labour unions. Collective agreements began granting more freedom to individual enterprises and institutions in filling out the details as they wished. With respect to the business climate, this means that the employment situation within a firm can become more tailor-made than previously.

In the nineties, the business environment will have to reckon with a growing supply of male and especially female labour. The growth in the labour force might be 755,000 persons (11%) during the 1990-2000 period; the female labour force is expected to increase by 473,000 (17%) and the male labour force by 282,000 (4%). The proportion of young workers will decrease and there will be a steep increase in the number of older workers. The average educational level will also continue to rise. On the other hand, continuing immigration will result in a growing segment of the (potential) labour supply with a low educational level. Participation in paid employment by people from the lowest educational level will be mainly determined by institutional conditions (for example labour market provisions, conditions for obtaining social security and minimum wage).

Policies

The improvement of labour participation, which has been a goal of successive Dutch Governments, could be improved by the following measures:

- Implementation of a labour-market policy activating the long-term unemployed.
- More temporary employment and agency employment.
- Institutionalization of a system of vocational education on a recurring basis. Technical, market-economic and demographic developments (ageing) will necessitate the (further) development of a competitive training infrastructure for those in, as well as those seeking, paid employment.
- Continuing wage restraints (while Dutch net wages are relatively low, total labour costs are high, in comparison with competing countries).
- Increased differentiation in labour costs (wages in the Netherlands are based on high basic wage level, due to the level of the statutory minimum wage).
- Encouragement of women to participate in the labour process, particularly through incentives (gradual abolishment of the system of tax transfers for non-working partners), as well as through providing facilities for the combination of parenthood and paid employment (by means of childcare, parental leave, etc.).
- Prevention of premature retirement on the part of older employees.
- Prevention of inability to work, and reintegration of the long-term sick and disabled in as far as they are able to work.

Efforts to gear the Welfare State towards more incentives for entering paid labour do, however, meet with considerable resistance from both the supply and demand sides of the labour market. Such efforts focus on the heart of the political debate, and *acquired rights* or conditions so perceived can only be modified with considerable political and social turmoil. This should be kept in mind when examining the prospects for development in this area.

Prospects

The combination of a low employment rate and a well-educated population constitutes a primary shaping factor for the future Dutch business environment.   Institutional conditions and policies are factors which directly affect the supply of labour and, consequently, indirectly affect the demand side of the labour market.

The Dutch Government will have to pursue participation policies in order to maintain the quality of the Dutch Welfare State. Neo-corporatist resistance may emerge as a barrier to stressing work above income (redistribution) in socio-economic policies.

Business can be expected to react positively in removing institutional obstacles to increased participation in paid employment.   Examples include longer production hours, more employment opportunities for women, dual-labour market tendencies (increased investments in training as well as growth in low(er)-paid jobs).   The degree to which business internationalizes is expected to be reflected in industrial relations: trade unions in Europe will seek cooperation and employers' federations will have no choice but to react.

Any future economic performance will rely heavily on the quality of the labour force. A high average educational level is a necessary requirement for a high quality labour force.   The Netherlands scores well in this respect. Additional requirements are linkages between education and business, as well as continued training.

A major competitive advantage could be realized through the further institutionalization of linkages such as industrial training, partnerships between schools and businesses, partnerships between educational sectors and branches of industry and the further introduction of dual systems in vocational education.   Existing neo-corporatist structures could be useful in this respect.   The institutionalization of a business-oriented *permanent education programme* is another relevant strategy for improving the quality of the business environment.

Table 14.3   Socio-economic business prospects until 2010

- Longer production hours
- More employment opportunities for women
- Increased investments in training
- Differentiated pay structures; more low-paid jobs
- Strong dual-labour-market tendencies
- Flexible retirement
- European cooperation of employers' federations

SOCIO-CULTURAL RELATIONS

Socio-cultural relations are a major determinant of the business environment. It is difficult to be precise about the impact of values, norms and attitudes. Some are reflected in what is referred to as *typically Dutch*. They certainly shape the business environment, but it is hard to measure exactly how and to what extent this occurs. It is easier to grasp the impact of processes such as decompartmentalization, demographic developments, individualization and migration. These developments will change the terms for business in general, as well as for specific branches of industry. Furthermore, the development of socio-cultural sectors such as health, education, housing and social security will affect the business environment either directly or indirectly. In turn, the socio-cultural field will be a main arena in the process of policy competition.

Key Features

In the past, religion was a dominant factor in society. The compartmentalization of Dutch society meant a peaceful coexistence in political and social life of organizations with similar goals, but different denominational bases (including religiously neutral organizations). Because many political and socio-economic conflicts were regulated inside and between the compartments, the class structure in Dutch society has never been very marked. Secularization, as well as the development of the Welfare State, the decline of manufacturing and (potential) class conflict, individualization and the information and telecommunication revolution have eroded the foundation of compartmentalization.

The Netherlands has an excellent system of health care which, in principle, is available to everyone. Financial solidarity is the basis of the system. The Dutch do not tolerate great differences in health care. The two-tier system of statutory and private insurance (depending on income) is rather exceptional within Europe. About 8.4% of GDP is spent on health care. The supply side consists largely of private institutions. During the 1990-2000 period, costs will rise by roughly 10%, merely as a result of the expected demographic changes. By 2010 those changes will raise the cost index to almost 120 (1990 = 100). As in other countries, advances in medicine and technology will stimulate further increases in expenditure.

Furthermore, the Netherlands has an extensive statutory system of social security, providing citizens with financial aid in virtually all contingencies, from child support and benefits for widows, widowers and orphans, to unemployment, sickness, disablement or old age. Additional provisions are provided by means of collective bargaining (for example supplementary pensions, pre-retirement schemes).

The Dutch social security system is generous and thus expensive. Spending on health and disablement, in particular, is high. Given the relative youth of the population, expenditure on old age is also high. Most Dutch people consider the system a major achievement.

According to an OECD review, the quality of the educational system is both an economic and a social asset to Dutch society. The educational level has risen considerably during the past decades. A weak point in the Dutch system - in comparison with other countries of Northern Europe - is the neglect of continued adult education. Another problem is the isolated nature of lower vocational education. This type of school produces an alarming number of pupils who finish school without any prospects on the labour market.

The proportion of immigrants is rather low in the Netherlands, compared with other EC countries. Including those with Dutch nationality, it amounts to 5.1% (1989). The Dutch, multi-ethnic society is not without its problems, though. The main ones are massive unemployment among certain groups of immigrants, the lack of success on the part of children from minority groups in the educational system, and the lack of socio-cultural integration. Inter-racial tensions do, however, seem less severe than in surrounding countries. This is probably due to the social taboo on racial discrimination and a tradition of openness and (relative) tolerance. Social security and other welfare arrangements also play a part.

Recent Trends

In general the demographic development in the Netherlands does not differ much from other industrialized countries, in the sense that the birth-rate has become rather low and that the overall population will reach a maximum in the first half of the next century. Until the seventies the population grew relatively rapidly in the Netherlands because mortality decreased and the (high) birth-rate only started declining after 1965. Around 1990 the relative decline in number of young people came to an end. At the moment, life expectancy at birth in the Netherlands is among the highest in the world. The result for the decades to come is an ageing population, with a high proportion of the age-group that was born in the first decade after the Second World War.

Another trend is individualization. Individuals become less dependent on their immediate social environment (family, neighbourhood and community) and more on distant and often more anonymous links (friends, sports clubs, school, company and state). This development has a demographic and a socio-cultural component. The demographic aspect is reflected in the trend towards smaller households and longer lifetimes. The average number of children has declined and so has the period in which parents have their children living at home.

Individualization is also a socio-cultural process. Socio-cultural changes manifest themselves partly in the number of couples refraining from or postponing marriage. A wide variety of primary relationships have emerged, such as *living apart together* and short-term relationships (*serial monogamy*). At the same time, young people tend to leave home at an earlier age, and more often while still single (this trend seems, however, to be reversing during the last couple of years). Whereas in the past, there was a large group of women who never thought of going to work, now many (also married) women want to put their education and training to good use by earning money. Partner dependence is therefore making way for economic independence. This change is not only occurring among the younger generations at a fast rate, but also among the better educated age groups who were in their teens and twenties around 1968. Consequently, all kinds of breadwinner arrangements are losing ground (for example, in social security and taxation).

With regard to maintaining law and order, the Dutch still score relatively high. A vigorous effort is needed, however, if this situation is to continue, especially in the cities. The number of recorded crimes per year has increased since the Second World War by nearly tenfold, whereas the percentage of crimes solved was halved.   Another sign of growing criminality is the increasing length of prison sentences.   Deregulation, as well as prevention, may help promote a climate of law maintenance which serves as a positive contributing factor for a competitive business environment.

Policies

Starting in 1992, a new insurance system for health care will be introduced, gradually providing a statutory basic insurance for everyone. Public institutions, as well as private insurance companies, will provide this basic insurance.   The new system is aimed at controlling the growth in public expenditure on health care.   This is done by separating the demand for health care into public (basic needs) and (additional) private flows.   Market principles, such as competition among suppliers of medical care, will be introduced into the new system.   Furthermore, more attention will be paid to preventive care, which is mainly the responsibility of municipal and regional health services, industrial and school medical services and childcare clinics.   It is not yet clear how responsibilities will be redistributed and where, in practice, the borderline between public and private responsibilities will run.

Social solidarity will undoubtedly be severely tested in the future.   The effects of rising welfare state costs on competitiveness will force the Netherlands to make a strategic choice.   Thus, social security may develop from a system providing income-related benefits to the unemployed, sick and disabled to a system guaranteeing minimum subsistence only.   Additional insurance might become a private responsibility (via collective bargaining or individual insurance).   A basic problem in this scenario would be how to transform the present system into such a *mini-system* in an acceptable way.   An alternative, or additional, route towards economizing on the social security system might be via the privatization of social security administration.   At the moment, employers' federations and unions play an important role in this administration.   Employers and unions have excessively abused the Disablement Benefit Act as a justification for the premature exit of less productive employees.

With respect to the educational system, the main objectives in the Netherlands during the nineties will be:

- Improvement of the linkages between education and business by introducing a dual system of vocational education and their equivalents.
- The introduction of apprenticeships for dropouts.
- The extension of continued education and training for employees.
- Active labour-market policies for the unemployed and for women re-entering the labour market.
- The extension of basic education (including courses in the Dutch language) and other educational facilities for immigrants and other ethnic minorities.

A successful implementation of these objectives will prove to be an important stimulus for a competitive business environment.

A policy for the integration of ethnic minorities, providing more and better opportunities for educating and training young and adult immigrants is necessary for several reasons. Apart from considerations of social justice, there are also economic arguments. Present and expected shortages on the labour market, an inadequate future supply of labour and the rising costs of welfare facilities all point towards the need for including these groups in the labour-market process. Whether or not integration succeeds will probably also affect the Dutch business environment in the decades to come. For investors, the relative absence of major ethnic conflicts and of related problems such as social disintegration, manifest discrimination, (severe) poverty and ethnically related crime, would certainly be an asset.

Prospects

Further desecularization, individualization, immigration, and increasing crime are clear shaping factors in the socio-cultural arena. Long-term dependency on social security, poverty traps and the growing gap between costs and technical possibilities in health care are policy-related shaping factors. A common denominator might be the resulting growing heterogeneity of the Dutch population.

Policy reactions will be as diverse as the various shaping factors. At the EC level, there is a clear need for a European immigration policy, as well as cooperation in maintaining the law and a social policy guaranteeing minimum levels of social security. At the national level, policies reflecting socio-cultural heterogeneity are expected, that is, policy shifts favouring the demands of singles, the elderly and double-income families.

In social security and health care a shift towards providing basic security, supplemented by private insurance, may result from pressures placed on the Welfare State. In the labour market more differentiation in pay seems both inevitable and desirable in order to provide incentives. The Dutch attitude favouring social equality may help prevent the emergence of a permanent (ethnic) underclass. Business will also reflect the growing heterogeneity. Expectations include production shifts to meet new demands (housing, health care, food, sports, leisure), more low-paid jobs, more employment opportunities for women and migrants, increased rewards for the successful, more scope for private health care, insurance and pension schemes, growth of a security industry and cooperation between businesses and government concerning environmental safeguards.

Table 14.4   Socio-cultural business prospects until 2010

- Production shifts to meet new demands   (housing, health care, food, sports, leisure)   - More employment opportunities for women   - Increased rewards for the successful   - More low-paid jobs   - Development of voluntary health care, insurance and pension schemes   - Growth of security industry

TECHNOLOGY

Technological progress is increasingly becoming an important determining factor in the international competitiveness of firms. New products, new production processes, new materials, new logistic concepts and renewal in every possible way are all necessary in order to supply the market with high-quality, attractively priced products. This section addresses the way Dutch firms and the Dutch Government deal with the developments in the technological area.

Key Features

The relationships between science, technology and business seem to have improved during the last decade. The Dutch private sector is inclined to support technological innovation more than in the past. Private R&D in the Netherlands is concentrated in five very large, multinational concerns (Philips, Shell, Unilever, AKZO and DSM). Consequently, strong private research positions are held in chemicals, electro-technicals, foodstuffs and agriculture. Weak positions are held in machinery, transport and services.

The R&D input position of the Netherlands lags slightly behind that of the larger OECD economies, but this position is relatively good, compared with medium-sized OECD economies. With respect to R&D output, the Netherlands scores rather low on patents, although its gap with the EC has closed during the last decade. A high score is, however, realized in scientific publications. The Netherlands has a low share in high-tech products; the shares are higher and ratios more positive for medium- and low-tech products. With process innovations the Netherlands scores above average, while with product innovations the score is slightly below average.

A serious deficit has been signalled for the Netherlands in the number of scientists and people with scientific backgrounds in the years to come. This deficit is caused by a decline in the proportion of young people and by the low participation of women in these subdisciplines. Compared to other countries, the number of technically educated people is low. A considerable increase in the number of science graduates is needed in order to prevent serious deficits on the labour market. Continued technical education becomes increasingly necessary during a professional career.

Recent Trends

Two important characteristics of the current technological situation are acceleration and interdependency. Technological developments occur faster than in the past. Product life cycles are tending to become shorter and shorter. R&D efforts become costlier. Whereas firms once could gain a strong lead through innovation, they now must reckon with imitations of their successful products within a few months. Innovations in the past were mainly the result of mono-disciplinary research. Now technological areas and scientific disciplines are increasingly interdependent, which results in *crossed technologies*. Mechatronics and telematics are good examples of this trend.

All these trends have made it more difficult for smaller firms to remain independent. This is especially relevant for countries like the Netherlands with a small domestic market. The recent discussions about the position of firms like Nedcar, Fokker and DAF have made it very clear that the cost of continuing the technology race requires a bigger base than these firms could provide on their own.

Policies

Technological development cannot be left to the private sector exclusively. Technological advancement needs an inspiring social and political climate. The Government must create the right conditions for the regulation of demand and supply of technological knowledge. Towards this end it is significant that the Government has established so-called Innovation Centres aimed at pooling existing knowledge and stimulating its diffusion for small- and medium-sized firms. Lack of information about the technological state of the art is a serious handicap for most small- and medium-sized firms. These Innovation Centres seem a promising way of achieving the quick and relatively cheap diffusion of technological knowledge required by small- and medium-sized firms in order to hold their own in the single market.

With regard to the scientific community (universities and research institutes), the Government is trying to influence research efforts by means of channelling available funds. There is a preference for more applied research and a stronger scientific orientation. The Government has also demonstrated a willingness to grant more freedom in this type of research.

The education sector should be continuously adapted through more competition, also from abroad, in order to be able to supply the required flow of knowledge. The number of scientifically educated people will have to increase so as to be able to establish a chain of knowledge, from design to final use. Recently new initiatives have been taken aimed at improving the gearing between (technical) education and business. One objective is to provide more scope for dual systems (combinations of learning and working).

Prospects

The Netherlands has realized a growth in its R&D efforts during the last decade, which is similar to that of its main competitors. Its level is close to the top rank but it has not managed to bridge the gap completely. Increasing labour market tensions for technically qualified people, expected shortages of technological research personnel and the relative neglect of natural sciences are all indications of future challenges.

Yet, there are fewer problems with the creation of fundamental knowledge than with the conversion of such knowledge into commercial applications. A more innovative attitude here could have very positive economic returns. This is not only true of high-tech sectors such as biotechnology, but also of traditional, low-tech ones. In addition, Dutch firms should involve themselves in EC technology programmes, more so than is currently the case. This will not only enable them to make use of the available subsidies, but also help them to achieve closer contacts with other European firms with regard to, for instance, technological developments. R&D costs have increased in certain sectors so much that national firms, even in the larger EC countries, are no longer able to finance them on their own. International cooperation seems the only method to remain competitive with firms from the United States or Japan. Partnerships are also sought with universities and other research institutes. Being part of *the right network* is considered very important for economic survival.

The same applies for the technology policy area. As national governments become less and less able to pursue their own technology policies, some of these responsibilities must be assumed at the EC level. It is extremely important at that level that the EC attempts to establish a proper balance between costs and returns of technology expenditures, and between legitimate cooperation of firms on the one hand, and sufficient competition among those firms, on the other hand.

Table 14.5 Technology business prospects until 2010

- Increase in R&D efforts
- Mergers and take-overs for gaining access to technology
- Concentration on core activities and niches
- Increased *networking*
- Cooperation with universities and research institutes
- Development of technology bases

ENVIRONMENT

As a small and densely populated country, the Netherlands must shoulder the heaviest environmental burden per square kilometre in the OECD area. Its population density is one of the highest, its room for waste disposal very limited, and the number of motor vehicles per square kilometre amounts to five times the OECD European average. Due to its geographic location, the country is also exposed to serious air and water pollution originating in neighbouring countries. As a result, the Netherlands displays a great deal of interest in environmental issues, and is, perhaps more than other EC countries, prepared to sacrifice growth for environmental purposes.

Key Features

Global environmental problems receive a great deal of attention in the Netherlands, although the national contribution towards solving them can never be more than minimal. In the Netherlands, the use of CFCs, thought to damage the ozone layer, has declined considerably in recent years and should approach zero in the short term. Potential climatic change is of more than academic interest to a country, more than half of which lies below sea level. Dutch policies with regard to this global problem are directed towards a sharp national decline in CO_2 emissions. Realizing that this problem can only be solved at the global level, the Dutch Government thus tries to give a good example to the international community. 'Environmental diplomacy' aimed at convincing other countries of the need to tackle the main global environmental problems is the primary instrument for Dutch efforts at this level.

Cross-border air pollution resulting in deposition of sulphur dioxide and nitrogen oxide is one of the most important problems on the continental level. Although the Dutch have made some progress in reducing sulphur dioxide and nitrogen oxide discharges from indigenous sources, these reductions are less than assumed in the National Environmental Policy Plan (NEPP). This is mainly due to a growth of traffic which exceeded expectations but also to the international nature of these problems (much of this pollution originates in Central and Eastern Europe). The same holds for the water pollution of the Rhine and Meuse.

At the regional level, the declining quality of soil and groundwater caused by pollution within a limited area pose a problem. Waste disposal is, however, the principal regional problem.

Recent Trends

Official expectations about the future environmental situation in the Netherlands are based upon the following assumptions:

- A gradual reduction in population growth, followed by a decline after 2020; the number of households will, however, increase during the next decades.
- Economic growth will continue at a yearly average rate of 2.5%; sectoral changes will result in an increasing share for services, and declining shares for agriculture and manufacturing; intensive livestock farming will stagnate, but environmentally sensitive sectors such as chemicals and basic-metal are expected to increase more than proportionally; the consumption pattern shows above-average growth rates for transport, heating, and recreation.
- Transport by private automobile will increase further, although at a diminishing rate; public transport will develop more rapidly; internationally, air traffic will show the highest growth rates.
- Energy consumption is expected to increase only moderately in the next decades, due to energy-saving measures and dematerialization in production processes.

Policies

In 1989 the Dutch Government published a National Environmental Policy Plan (NEPP). It contained the following policy lines:

- Promotion of structural source-oriented measures.
- Speedy implementation of measures combating acidification and manuring, and promoting the removal of existing pollution.
- Development of policy instruments aimed at realizing structural changes in production and consumption.
- Incentives to heighten the environmental awareness of both firms and citizens.
- Development of technologies aimed at reducing pollution, for instance through higher standards of production.
- Contributions to environmental policies within the EC.

One year later, a new Cabinet (tending towards centre-left) amended this plan, calling it a National Environmental Policy Plan *Plus*. It was felt that the original measures were not sufficient to bring about the necessary structural changes.

In spite of these positive moves towards bringing about necessary improvements in the environment, the actual outcome of measures imposed so far is less effective than was assumed. The structural changes in production and consumption envisaged in the NEPP are still to come. For example, both firms and citizens have not yet shown the *internalization* of environmentally sound behaviour that is required to bring about a decisive change.

In the NEPP-Plus Programme, proposals were presented for an *energy tax*, aimed at reducing CO_2 emissions through energy conservation. Recent elaborations of this idea have shown that substantial energy savings can indeed be realized this way, with relatively minor economic consequences, as long as the tax is introduced at the OECD level. If the tax were restricted to the Netherlands, however, significant negative economic consequences are expected. Should such a unilateral tax be levied on the *small-scale* part of the Dutch economy (that is, those consumers who are unable to avoid it by moving abroad such as small firms and households), the economic consequences would be less harmful. Although such a tax would still cover half the energy consumption in the Netherlands, the environmental benefits will consequently be proportionally smaller. Such a measure has, however, met with strong resistance from the employers' federations, which view this as the thin end of a wedge and fear damage to their competitiveness on the single market. Industry has therefore let it be known that if there must be an energy tax, then it favours one at the EC level, or preferably at the global level. The Government has not yet made up its mind.

Prospects

The Netherlands would like the EC to play a more stimulating role in global environmental talks. The potential damage to the ozone layer, potential change of climate, and deforestation in the lesser-developed countries are global, not regional, problems. It is essential that useful and workable solutions be found in the near future. At conferences such as the United Nations Conference on Environmental Development (UNCED), the EC could try to bridge the gap between the rich and poor countries in finding such solutions.

Furthermore, the Dutch Government encourages the EC to take full responsibility for the European environment and when necessary, *go it alone*, even if this weakens the competitiveness of the Community as a whole *vis-à-vis* its American and Japanese competitors. The struggle about a European eco tax shows that this is not an easy road to follow.

As far as national measures are concerned, further restrictions on industrial production that damages the environment are to be expected.

There will be less emphasis placed on rules and regulations. Instead, measures conforming with market principles will be preferred, an approach which is also in line with EC policies.

This could help to placate fears in industry about distortions of the Dutch competitive position. Covenants with industry creating a greater potential for mutual control and stimulating process-integrated environmental solutions, might also lead to environmental improvements. If national measures contribute to a cleaner (production) environment, they will help develop an asset in policy competition among EC countries.

Table 14.6   Environment business prospects until 2010

- Active role on the part of employers' federations towards *Brussels*
- Cooperation with government in development of standards
- Generally cleaner production
- Drive towards less-polluting agriculture
- Growth of pollution-abatement sector
- Market opportunities for treating soil, river- and seabeds

THE PRIVATE SECTOR

The preceding sections of this report discussed many highly significant elements for the private sector of the Dutch economy. This section will address the private sector itself. Three structural characteristics can be distinguished here: the structure of production and employment, the interdependence of the Dutch economy with the rest of the world, and the level of competitiveness and market performance.

Key Features

Traditionally, the Dutch economy is an open one. Dutch enthusiasm for economic integration and the removal of trade barriers is therefore not surprising. At the same time, however, this openness makes the Dutch economy sensitive to the economic climate abroad.

Traditionally Dutch firms hold strong positions in:

- Agriculture and food processing.
- Chemicals and oil-refining activities.
- Metal-electrotechnical activities.
- Distributive and business services.

Investments are the medium through which production capacities can be expanded, new technologies introduced, changes realized and infrastructural demands met. In real terms, private investment in the Netherlands is at about the same level as in 1968. Government investment has in recent years dropped to an all-time low. Since government investment in infrastructure, education, and research and development facilities, etc. is crucial to the country's competitiveness, it is clear that a considerable volte-face must be realized if the new requirements of international competition are to be met.

Important international relations exist in the area of direct foreign investment. In 1991 Dutch firms invested Dfl 21 billion abroad, about 16% of their total investment volume. The United States, Belgium and the UK are the most popular destinations. In connection with these investments abroad, the Netherlands is the country of origin for a remarkable number of significant transnational firms. Firms such as Shell, Unilever, Philips, AKZO and DSM are all prominent in their particular sectors. The small domestic market is, of course, an important reason for these firms to invest abroad. In banking and insurance, AMRO/ABN, RABO and ING (Internationale Nederlanden Groep) all enjoy a strong position. ABP is one of the largest pension funds in the world (also due to the peculiar Dutch pension system).

The inward flow of foreign direct investment has been smaller than the outward flow. In 1992 it amounted to Dfl 7 billion. Main countries of origin were again Belgium/Luxembourg, the United States and the United Kingdom.

Recent Trends

Compared with the overall EC export pattern, Dutch manufactured exports are relatively resource-intensive and knowledge-extensive. Both business and government have become aware of this situation. More attention is currently being paid to technology, design, quality, etc., in order to get a better foothold on new, technology-oriented markets. Upgrading the production structure both inside firms and sectors and among sectors is seen as essential for a prosperous development of the Dutch manufacturing sector.

The negative balance on the foreign direct investment account, observed above, could be interpreted as an indication of the Netherlands' relative inability to attract investments. The current situation does, however, seem more encouraging. Recent research indicates an increased attractiveness for foreign investment, especially for distributive activities and holdings. The creation of a fully integrated market seems to have swept away the disadvantages of a small domestic market. As *Gateway to Europe*, the Netherlands seems to have sufficient appeal to firms from Japan and the United States looking for a European distribution and/or assembly plant. Its international orientation, trade facilities, stable socio-political climate, educated labour force and knowledge of foreign languages are all important positive factors. The Netherlands has also deregulated faster and more radically than many other EC countries in several service sectors such as financial services, freight transport and air passenger traffic. Experience with increased competition on the domestic market has given some cause for optimism with respect to winning shares in other markets.

A good example of this is the transport and transhipment sector. The increasing value-added, growing specialization and geographical spreading out of economic activities are all pointing towards fast, flexible modes of transport, for which information technology and logistics are key factors. Dutch firms would seem able to maintain their strong position, especially if the Government were to realize its planned investments in infrastructure and mainports.

Policies

Sufficient dynamism is a precondition for acquiring new markets, for successful competition with firms from abroad on both the domestic and foreign markets for products and services, for a change towards a more knowledge-intensive manufacturing sector, and for government to create excellent conditions for achieving high levels of employment and growth. It seems that the Dutch economy has become less dynamic, due to a wide array of rigid elements on different markets. The relatively low knowledge intensity in manufacturing, the existence of cartels and entry barriers, and the resistance to amending laws and other regulations curtailing competition can all be considered factors that contribute to this lack of dynamism.

Such rigidities have recently been tackled in a more determined way. The expectation of tougher competition among both firms and governments in a fully integrated European market results in a greater focus on economic dynamism as an asset for the future business climate. Firms are aware that they must prepare for increased competition.

Governments are becoming equally aware that they will have to create a more dynamic, cost-conscious and productive environment, in order to keep their country as competitive as possible.

In order to raise the overall competitive position of the Dutch economy, the Government has proposed a number of measures in the white paper *Economy with Open Borders* (1990). These are aimed at improving the functioning of the labour market as well as the relationship it has with education, improving the infrastructure and fiscal climate, creating competitive energy prices, restoring the environment and diminishing the burden of regulations. As so often is the case, this is easier said than done. In any case, implementing these measures is sure to be slow, due to resistance on the part of various pressure groups. Again, this is a more or less common phenomenon in EC countries.

Prospects

The business community will be facing increased competition as a consequence of the single market. Marginal improvements to the existing line of products, for instance, through increases in productivity are no longer sufficient. The realization of the single market presents Dutch firms with an excellent challenge to create new opportunities. The prospects are promising in certain sectors, partly due to the abolition of government regulation in other EC countries. Certain service sectors such as transport and financial services, are in a better position to face the increased competition than their counterparts. The expectations for greenhouse horticulture and other agricultural activities with high value-added, are also very positive. The expected increase in competition will force the business community to re-evaluate all existing arrangements. This concerns both the various markets on which the companies operate, and their internal organization and functioning.

Table 14.6   Private sector business prospects until 2010

- Further internationalization (for example by mergers, take-overs)
- Upgrading manufactured products
- Expansion of services on EC market
- Entry of small- and medium-sized businesses on EC markets
- More entrepreneurial behaviour, for example, establishing new firms

CONCLUSIONS

The preceding paragraphs have outlined the main developments that are of importance for the competitiveness of the Netherlands. Old values, structures, institutions, products and habits will have to change, if the Netherlands wants to meet the new requirements. The EC will have a strong influence on Dutch society. For instance, the single market will force companies to improve their competitiveness if they are to survive and will at the same time offer companies fewer opportunities to hide behind national barriers and institutional arrangements.

As a consequence of the single market, governments will increasingly have to further their national aims in Brussels, both through joint determination of Community policies and by taking advantage of current and new opportunities in the single market. Governments, like companies, will have to reconsider many assumptions on which their present policies are based. Those who do so and then act upon their findings will be rewarded with success. These facts, which are only now gradually dawning on policy-makers in the Netherlands, form the *leitmotif* for this analysis.

Taking into account the European perspective, this report has attempted to identify the shaping factors relevant for business in the Netherlands. What will then be *the primary shaping factor* for the business environment in the next two decades? The answer is that there will be no single shaping factor. The business environment will be shaped by a multitude of *objective* factors in different areas, reactions by the EC and other actors on the global scene, by national governments and other public authorities, and by businesses themselves. When trying to detect main factors which will shape the future business environment, it is, however, difficult to differentiate between more or less *objective* circumstances or developments, and *subjective* public and private actions and reactions. Social circumstances and developments are by definition man-made, although in many cases their existence is not intended to be so. *Objective* shaping factors refer to the outcome of chains of subjective actions and reactions leading to results no one originally intended. The resulting *objective* developments and circumstances generate *subjective* public and private reactions, which in turn, become relevant shaping factors.

From the seven key areas discussed in the preceding sections, the following can be determined as primary *objective* shaping factors for the future Dutch business environment:

- The rise of the EC as a global player.
- The relevance of a competitive infrastructure.
- The need to reshuffle the Dutch Government budget.
- The openness of the Dutch economy (which might be an asset).
- The low employment rate (which certainly is a liability).
- Education and training.
- Socio-cultural heterogeneity (which might be an asset).
- The Welfare State as an asset.
- A mixed picture in the field of technology.
- A heavy environmental burden.

These are all factors which, at the very least, must be taken into account in the preparation of tomorrow's policies. Most of these factors would have been listed, even if there had not been an EC. They determine a country's ability to compete on world markets. The developments in the EC, with the single market, and probably at some stage the EMU and EPU, have increased the necessity to meet the related challenges. At the same time, these developments offer opportunities for both business and government to influence their future business environment. Adequate action now determines tomorrow's competitiveness.

15. Portugal: Shaping Factors*

INTRODUCTION

Very dependent on exchanges (economic, technological, cultural, etc.) with the Community, Portugal will necessarily be affected by the effects of most of the key factors acting on a global level.   But although apparently very open (external trade, emigration, media, etc.), Portuguese society and economy remain still quite closed in terms of behaviour and active relations with the exterior: the one paradigm of some Portuguese firms is that, as far as their export markets are concerned, they know only the purchasers' agents, who visit them regularly.   It is in this sense that one can say that the real stake for Portugal in the period considered will be the passage from a closed society to a society which is more open to the outside.

In the following pages, three types of factors are examined: socio-economic, cultural and historical, political.

SECTION 1: SOCIO-ECONOMIC ISSUES

Macroeconomic Framework: Process of *Convergence*

Portuguese economic development in the next few years will depend on the process of convergence arising from the goals agreed at Maastricht. In this sphere, the fundamental question raised relates to the reduction in the rate of inflation.

Where inflation is concerned, the goal of Maastricht implies rapid deceleration, given that the growth rate of prices in Portugal is about six points higher than that of the best-placed countries in the Community.

There are not many tools which can be used to obtain a significant reduction in the rate of inflation.   Where monetary policy is concerned,

---

*   Prof. J. M. Gago, J. Aguiar, J. F. de Almeida, J. F. do Amaral, L. Fernandes, E. Lopes, C. Noéme and J. M. Pereira.

the fight against inflation has begun with the maintenance of a very high interest rate (a real interest rate of around 10% on current deals) as a result of a restrictive monetary policy and controls of capital inflows. Although it is clear that a policy of this kind will no longer be possible after total liberalization of capital movements (which will happen within a few years), the fact is that the results obtained have not yet been sufficiently clear-cut to justify the costs of this policy.

Another tool used has been exchange rate policy, which has in practice maintained the parity of the escudo with that of other European currencies. The recent entry into the discipline of the European Monetary System will strengthen this maintenance of parity in the future. It is clear that this has meant (and will continue to mean) a real revaluation of the escudo, which, although having undeniable beneficial effects on internal inflation, constitutes on the other hand a negative factor for Portuguese exports.

Finally, a third tool has been incomes policy, by means of social dialogue agreements, the aim of which is to moderate income growth. The success of these agreements has been limited, since for many categories of incomes real increases have been greater than nominal awards due to the relatively favourable situation on the labour market.

In the future, the difficulties which will arise for the economy from the pursuit of an anti-inflation policy will increase. In fact, the restrictive monetary policy has been the cause of a significant reduction in private investment, and its continuation (so long as it is possible to have an independent monetary policy) will cause serious harm to the modern-ization of the structure of Portuguese production.

The policy of stabilizing the escudo will still cause a loss of competitiveness for Portuguese exports although it may promote structural change in the export sector, by directing it towards activities in more advanced technology.

But the most difficult obstacle will be the one resulting from the great difference in wages between Portugal and the average in the European States (a ratio of about 1 to 4). There will certainly at some time be a movement in the direction of approximation of wage levels (helped by the free movement of workers), which will obviously make convergence of inflation rates very problematic.

The process of convergence will therefore create problems for Portuguese firms once, for different reasons (restrictive monetary policy and wage convergence), the two factors of production, capital and labour, become more expensive.

These special problems which the Portuguese economy will meet throughout the process of convergence may be attenuated after the achievement of the third phase of the Single European Market (or even some little time before that).

The achievement of the SEM will give Portugal the opportunity to change its growth pattern quickly, moving from a structure of production very much centred on undifferentiated labour sectors and not very costly in European terms to an economy with qualified manpower of a higher level. This change will require a high level of investment however, and also a rapid process of manpower training. As for investment, one has already seen that the process of convergence will create in the next few years conditions which are not very favourable due to the high interest rates. It should be noted, however, that, even at this stage, these conditions will improve if the cost of capital is reduced through an increase in aid to private investment, which will probably be the case if Community financial support increases as provided for in *Delors package II.*

After the freeing of capital movements (which should come into force towards the end of 1995), there will be an accentuated fall in interest rates, and this will create more favourable conditions for investment. As it is probable that wages will increase, approximating to European levels, there will be a fall in the relative cost of capital as compared with that of labour, and this will be a decisive factor for the move towards a more advanced growth pattern, more capital-intensive and more intensive in skilled manpower.

It is possible however that the timing of these changes may produce dangerous imbalances, particularly in foreign trade, since the conjunction of exchange rate stability, wage increases and liberalization of trade for certain traditional products (within the framework of the Uruguay Round) will mean that traditional Portuguese industry will lose competitiveness which can only be very gradually replaced by more advanced sectors.

These difficulties reveal the non-existence of a policy of redistribution at Community level, unlike what happens in most federal States. If this policy of redistribution is implemented in the future, it will make it possible to establish minimum standards for the whole Community in certain spheres such as education, research or social security. It is only under these circumstances that the least developed regions can achieve these *standards*, having recourse to the means made available by global redistribution policy. This scenario would have very important effects on the competitiveness of Portuguese firms, especially if one takes account of the fact that Portugal will be one of the EC regions where achievement of the SEM will lead most clearly to rapid modernization of the growth pattern, in the direction of more highly qualified human capital and technological progress.

Structural Problems

Three problems are central for Portugal: agriculture, industrial specialization, services, education and science.

The agricultural sector in Portugal has contributed to the lack of adjustment of the Portuguese economy in the last few decades.

The agricultural policy pursued has enabled the development of a bipolar strategy in the sector, favouring the creation of dual structures, from the technological, land, institutional and market points of view.

The North of the country has mainly small or very small farms, usually with poor economic efficiency, while the Algarve (in the South) and, more particularly, the Ribatejo-Oeste region (in the Centre) has a medium-sized land-holding structure, well-equipped from the technological point of view, which shows a certain capacity for internal and external competitiveness.

The development pattern pursued in Portugal has protected inefficient agriculture, the 1980s being marked by two major facts:

(i)   Greater opening up to the outside has made it possible to accelerate the assimilation of the American and North European patterns of consumption/production.

(ii)   The entry of Portugal into the EC, which enabled an important change in the conditions of production of the agricultural sector.

However, as the CAP is above all intended for the countries of Northern Europe, based on cereal production, expansion towards the countries of the South has not made it possible to develop economies of scale competitive with the producer countries of Northern Europe.

Underlying the CAP was the attempt by the EC to adopt a pattern of production characterized mainly by large farms, by low use of manpower and by intensive use of mechanization: these aims can be achieved for specific products (such as cereals) and under particular physical conditions.

The application of the CAP to Portuguese agriculture has strengthened two negative components:

- Productive specialization in cereals with large investments (resulting in a considerable increase in output, in particular of maize), followed by the best-sized farms, whose cost structure is reasonable only because of the price policy adopted. In parallel and as a consequence, there has also been the development of a pattern of intensive animal production.
- A lack of encouragement for vegetable and fruit production where Portuguese agriculture has some comparative advantages.

Portuguese agriculture has not experienced significant changes since the 1970s, but there have also been sociological reasons for resistance to the adoption of a production-oriented pattern:

- Diversification of family incomes, with a high rate of multiple activity.
- Great rigidity in the land ownership system, without significant changes except in the South of the country.
- A high proportion of self-sufficiency production, in particular of small farms.

In the Community and with the exception of Ireland, the group of countries in the EC most suited to Mediterranean production (including Portugal) is the one with the lowest outputs and where the importance of agricultural added value is greatest. These characteristics of Mediterranean output (more intensive labour) coincide with indicators of weaker economic development.

In foreign trade, Europe remains in deficit in products (fruit and horticultural products) from the countries of the Mediterranean basin which have negotiated preferential contracts with the EC.

The reform of CAP would therefore be an opportunity to reorientate the agricultural and agro-food sector, if it enabled further specialization of production in a process of integration within the European area, as a consequence of structural adjustments.

The small size of Portuguese agriculture, its low productivity (of both labour and land), and the ageing of a large part of the agricultural population may be factors which will be beneficial for the agricultural sector in the short term; either by means of supportive measures or by inducement to conservationist agriculture, with an increase in the area of afforestation. The challenge is in the medium/long term and, in particular for agricultural firms with a technological structure closer to European standards.

For these producers, only a new CAP which would favour a strategy of natural integration, exploiting comparative advantage in an expanded economic area, could lead to profitable agriculture:

- Through extensification of agricultural output and stock-rearing, favouring the development of quality breeds.
- By intensification of fruit and vegetable crops which have comparative seasonal advantages: it is possible to produce earlier or even later.
- Through the development of a brand image for specific products where external competitiveness is already guaranteed: wine, olive oil and regional cheese.

In general, Mediterranean products have greater price and income elasticity, with possibilities of a certain growth of the market. However, the market for food products of this type tends to be segmented, putting a premium on differentiation.

We can summarize the factors which determine the future development of Portuguese agriculture at three levels:

(i) The new CAP may affect the North and South of Europe differently. In the North, it will probably be less interventionist; in the South it will tend to take account of specific features of production and the advantages of integrated development. In the countries of Southern Europe, the new CAP could strengthen rural tourism at the expense of investment.

(ii) One may expect the extension of current trends of consumers with higher incomes in favour of quality and differentiation, with a strong boost to market *segments*.

(iii) The development and application of new technologies (e.g. biotechnologies) and easier access to a larger market will probably be factors promoting an increase in trade but also a new social division of labour (through increasing mobility of the workforce). Finally, we will note that the development of agro-food production in Southern Europe will very probably be linked to the development of the agriculture of North African countries, particularly Morocco. Their large-scale production could help the take-off of agro-industries in the South of Europe (particularly in

Portugal) because of technological advantages, services, and transport.

The current international specialization of Portuguese industry makes it particularly vulnerable to liberalizing trends in the world economy. Because of the extent to which the Portuguese economy is open is already quite large, the problem will not be so much the rate of penetration for new foreign products on the internal market, but rather the characteristics of the exporting sectors. Among the latter, particularly noticeable are those which developed during the 1960s, with competitiveness based on low incomes and work mainly as subcontractors, thus without any control over (or even knowledge of) trading channels.

These sectors are today subject to dual pressures. On the one hand there is competition from developed countries which have introduced flexible automation technologies, and adapted to markets which are increasingly segmented. On the other hand, there is the increased competition from other low-wage economies, with increasingly easier access to European markets, as a (predictable) result of the GATT agreements, the end of the Multifibre agreement and the gradual and inevitable opening up to exports from the *new economies* of Central and Eastern Europe.

Many years of escudo devaluation policies have made it possible to maintain many firms' competitiveness artificially. But changes in the macroeconomic framework have put an end to this situation which, moreover, had the effect of *sparing* firms the effort of technological modernization to which they would otherwise have had to agree.

Both the inflows of Community funds and the influx of foreign capital (direct investment) have withdrawn from the centre of concerns of economic policy the problems of the balance of payments, and at the same time have reduced the power of the export sectors to exert pressure. Finally, the steps needed to prepare the economy for monetary Europe led to the abandonment of the policies of devaluation, to the benefit of the struggle against inflation. In particular a policy of very high real interest rates, with Stock Exchange controls, makes investment in modernization or in diversification towards new products particularly unattractive.

The supports of PEDIP have not only been inadequate to promote modernization of the traditional sectors, but have failed as inducers of investment in diversification. In fact, it appears to be indisputable that to a large extent they have operated as partial compensation for high interest rates for bank credit (which favoured high profitability of the banking sector and made privatization operations more attractive). Foreign investment is seen more and more as an irreplaceable factor for diversification of Portuguese industry towards less vulnerable activities. Its strong growth in the past few years is not however free from some grounds for concern:

- The emergence of new alternative destinations, which increases the costs of the policies for attracting capital (that may become quite serious with the long-term stabilization of the countries of Central and Eastern Europe).
- The small proportion of investment from non-EC countries: this may have the dual consequence of devaluation of Portugal as an *extreme frontier of the Community* and the structuring of the Portuguese economy by Community investments within the framework of a regional sub-area, which would underline the already strong trend towards integration in an *Iberian economy*.
- The concentration of foreign investment within the services sector (banking, property, distribution, tourism) to the detriment of industry.
- The (political) favour which large external investments enjoy may create new situations of vulnerability.

The dynamism of the service sector in the past few years might suggest confirmation of certain theses on the Portuguese vocation for provision of services rather than for manufacturing activities. A more careful analysis may however identify some constraints and weak points which may call the sustained development of the sector into question in the near future.

The modernization of retail trade with the rapid penetration of hypermarket networks had not caused significant reactions until recently because losses of market shares by traditional traders were compensated for by the growth in private consumption. At the same time, the retail trade was modernizing through the creation of cooperative purchasing centres. But signs of reaction from traditional commerce (which has significant social importance in Portugal) can already be detected. In effect, considering the existing hypermarkets and those which are in the course of construction, they will supply approximately 7% of final consumption, according to a recent study. This rate of penetration, achieved within a few years, already corresponds to nearly half the rate in France, a country which has one of the strongest presences of large shops in Europe.

The dynamism of the financial sector conceals some artificial factors. The maintenance of highly abnormal bank intermediation margins has enabled rapid recovery of some banks which were in a difficult position, and thus made attractive the privatization of the nationalized banks, generating considerable income for the State.

The liberalization of capital movements, once the privatization process is over, will very probably lead to a re-organization of the sector with mergers, strong investment in computerization and staff reductions, postponed to date by the very favourable situation of the sector in the past few years.

The property sector has gone through a period of *overheating* due to the entry of operators from European countries ready to pay much higher prices who have seen an opportunity for property diversification of great potential in the Portuguese market. The increase in supply which followed the increase in prices is not however being followed by demand, as a clear downward trend in prices can be seen, both for housing and for offices.

The initial boom in demand for premises for tertiary activities appears not to correspond today to initial expectations. Two types of reason are probable:

-   Strong initial growth founded on new phenomena, which will find it difficult to maintain similar rates of growth in the future: training, engineering, research, advisory, evaluation services, etc., created directly by the application of structural funds. It is not at all sure that this demand can be maintained at the same level when current subsidies will fall or disappear.
-   Financial services *inflated* by the speculative boom on the Stock Exchange, by the new legal framework for these activities and by the privatization process.
-   A clear trend towards *relocation* of the most highly developed tertiary sectors to large Spanish cities. Given the disappearance of intra-peninsular frontiers, the multinationals are reorganizing their logistical arrangements in the Peninsula, generally choosing sites for central management services and trading infrastructures in Spain, particularly in Madrid. This phenomenon may still have induced effects on the location of the tertiary sector of services to businesses (advertising, marketing, auditing, etc.).

Portugal's vocation as a developer of international services seems to be confirmed only in the development of tourism, which has benefited in the past few years from a very favourable conjuncture.

Other initiatives to use Portugal as a platform for provision of international services have not succeeded to date, at least at sufficient levels of continuity and content. Two examples are: the production of cinema/video, profiting from the climate and competitiveness of specific services; support services for intercontinental trade, profiting from the advantages of Portugal's geographical position and the natural conditions of some of its ports. The persistent inability to make the sea ports internationally competitive has made unviable the development of this type of service which would put into practice a strategy of specialization known as *Portugal, the gateway to Europe*.

Science and Education

Portuguese scientific development is among the lowest in Europe. With Greece and Ireland, Portugal is very far below Community averages in terms of scientific and technological development.

Some indicators can illustrate this point.

Total Portuguese expenditure on R&D is 0.5% as a percentage of GNP, against 2.5% in France or 1.5% in Denmark, but 1% in Ireland and 0.4% in Greece. The number of research workers (in full-time equivalent) in Portugal is 1.1 per thousand working persons, against a Community average four times as high. The number of scientific authors from Portuguese institutions reported by *Current Contents* was 131 per million inhabitants in 1990, against 327 in Greece, 595 in Ireland and 1,133 in France. This deficit in research workers is expressed in scientific output measured by the number of scientific publications with Portuguese participation, as 800 in 1990, according to the Science Citation Index.

The impact of Portuguese scientific output considered globally is also clearly lower than the Community average: 3.05 citations per article in 1980-89, against 6.22 in Denmark or 5.05 in France.

Although these overall figures show the dimension of the scientific difference between Portugal and the EC as a whole, they nonetheless conceal the activity of several recognized centres of excellence. In general these Portuguese centres of excellence are strongly linked to international networks. Expenditure on R&D, for example, rose from 0.28% of GNP in 1964 to 0.32% in 1978 and 0.50% in 1988. The number of research workers rose from 2,000 in 1978 to 5,000 in 1988. Scientific output in 1990 was twice that in 1985.

The main source of progress has been the reduction in the country's cultural, scientific and technological isolation. Entry into the EC strongly contributed to the acceleration of these processes, the scale of which remains limited however (of the large international scientific organizations, Portugal is a member only of CERN, since 1985/86, and of JET, as a result of becoming a member of the EC in 1986).

The increasing inflow of students into higher education has also contributed to the revival of the universities and the expansion of teaching posts (about two-thirds of current research workers are in fact university teachers).

This expansion will probably continue over the next decade, in the light of the current education indices which show 14.3% illiterates over the age of 18 years, 50% school attendance corresponding to nine years at school, 38% of the age group in secondary education (tenthth to twelfth years of schooling) and 22% of young people between 18 and 24 years of age in higher education in 1990.

The profile of specialization in Portuguese industry, strongly marked by the importance of labour-intensive or low-technology sectors, explains the enormous deficit in the technological balance of payments: Portugal remains a country which imports patents and technology and exports products with a low incorporation of technology (the conversion rate of the technological balance of payments was, according to the last statistics available, those of 1985, 0.11).

The proportion of firms in the whole national R&D capacity is therefore low: 25% of national expenditure and 9.5% of the number of research workers. The growth of public investment in R&D and in education, particularly perceptible after joining the Common Market, has not changed this state of affairs, the number of research workers in firms and their level of expenditure on R&D having changed little.

Moreover, the State laboratory sector (public works, agriculture, industry, etc.) has considerable weight in public expenditure on R&D as a whole (about 40% in 1991), while its role is being increasingly questioned.

Our questioning on the foreseeable evolution of Portuguese scientific and technological development - the current outlines of which we have just sketched - is strongly linked to the hazards of European policy in the direction of the less well-developed regions.

In principle, the increasing application of structural funds to the development of the educational and scientific base of these regions should make possible greater participation in the common scientific effort of the human resources potentially available in Europe.

However, and in our opinion, the experience of the last few years shows that this objective of *convergence* does not result automatically from the structural funds. In particular, increased participation by the European scientific communities in the definition of Community scientific policies appears to us to be essential, scientific backwardness going hand in hand with isolation and peripheralism.

The deliberate intervention of the EC in the development of the educational and scientific base of the least developed regions is therefore, in our view, desirable, since the Nation States have only exceptionally the appropriate motivation, ability or instruments in these spheres.

Community policy should therefore assert itself as soon as possible as a federal policy in scientific and educational spheres, particularly on the basis of the positive definition of objectives of genuine convergence.

The definition of a broad band of convergence in science and access to education, established around European averages of certain indicators (public expenditure on R&D/GNP), number of research workers in relation to the active population, percentage access to different levels of education, etc.) might constitute a powerful political weapon.

Finally we consider that it is natural to conceive, on the Community scale of an integrated Europe, partial *delocalization* of regional scientific resources in respect of the siting of the most exacting industries where technological innovation is concerned. The predictable extension of this phenomenon will, of course, require new redistribution mechanisms.

Iberian and *African* Factors

Perhaps the most important visible effect of simultaneous incorporation of the two Iberian countries into the Community was the explosive growth of intra-Iberian trade. Whereas this trade (export + import) accounted for 6% of Portugal's foreign trade in 1984, it accounted for 14% in 1990, Spain having become our second trading partner (first supplier, third customer). The most recent figures show that Spain may become our first customer.

Although Portuguese exports have increased much more rapidly than the converse flow, the trade deficit is still substantial: the rate of coverage of imports by exports is still of the order of 60%.

Does that show an awareness on the part of Portuguese firms that modernization involves accelerated internationalization?   Unfortunately, an analysis of the structure of Portuguese exports to Spain does not leave us optimistic.   According to our estimates, about 70-75% of exports are from the textile sector (17-18%) or from foreign firms settled in Portugal (Renault, GM, St Gobain, Bertraind, Faure, Grundig, Merloni, etc.) or induced by them (sub-contractors of the latter) achieving 35-37%, or of large national firms (iron and steel, pulp for paper, paper, electrical equipment, etc.) with 18-20%.   That means that the great bulk of Portuguese small- and medium-sized firms will not have exceeded 25-30% of exports to Spain, which is disappointing if one considers that, among this group, there will certainly be many firms with experience in exporting.

Quite a few experts think that this step, still a timid one, of *conquest* of market shares in Spain (including, after that, the creation of distribution networks, even perhaps local means of production) will be decisive for change in Portuguese industry.   Some even talk of Spain as a real *training camp* (before approaching more exacting and difficult Northern European markets).   Others call on the industrials to *push the frontier of the national market as far as the Pyrenees*.   This is the hypothesis of Iberian economic integration as a condition for European integration.

Another important aspect of this process is obviously the change in the investment of each country in the other.   From this point of view, Portuguese investment in Spain is still insignificant.   Spanish investment in Portugal, on the other hand, which was practically nil in 1985, was multiplied by 17 (in US dollars) between 1986 and 1990.   Spain is now the third foreign investor in Portugal, and in 1989, for the first time, Portugal was the first destination country for its foreign investment.

As far as economics are concerned, some people feel that the long-term will reserve for Portugal the role of another region of the *great Iberian market*.   Even today, some international groups are delegating to their Spanish subsidiaries commercial or investment decisions on the Portuguese market (e.g. Saint Gobain).

On a cultural level, exchanges between the two countries have never been so numerous, especially in the spheres of literature, plastic arts or the theatre, and everything suggests that they will continue to develop further in the future.   On a political level, despite some disagreements on specific questions (fishing, nuclear waste), relationships between the States appear to be stable, with Iberian summits taking place each year.   Although the two countries' views on Europe went through a less convergent period due to Portugal's alignment with British positions, there is indeed a natural *southern* solidarity which is gaining ground when it is a matter of the structural support framework or *social cohesion*. It seems clear, moreover, that Portuguese positions have become closer to those of the Mediterranean countries. Today there is nothing to suggest that, in the medium or even in the long term, serious problems might arise which could lead to a resurgence of the old *reservations* or even any hostility between the two Iberian neighbours. But it is undeniable, given the inevitable sub-regional economic integration, that true European integration for Portugal will require a margin of political autonomy in the face of the main Community questions.

In any case, although Spain may represent a centripetal force for a Portugal which is more modern and more integrated into Europe, the effect of a strengthening of the links between Portugal and its ex-colonies in Africa (which have become *African countries with Portuguese as the official language*) is not so clear.

During the last years of colonization (1973) these markets absorbed nearly 15% of Portuguese exports, against 3.4% today. But if one takes account of the enormous growth in total exports, this 3.4% in 1990 is equivalent in volume and value to three-quarters of the exports sent to these countries 20 years ago.

Without political stability, it is very unlikely that this threshold could be exceeded. But if, within a more or less short space of time, stability returns to Angola and to Mozambique, then this could create new conditions in their relationships with Portugal.

The *reconstruction effect* will have obvious implications with regard to imports of capital goods and intermediate products, and on that of contracts for international constructors. The movement of quite a large number of technicians is to be expected and this will increase demand for consumer goods.

But there will be a more lasting *immigration effect* of a different kind: this also (in this scenario) will be the arrival (or return) of those who will want to settle in these countries to develop their own businesses (agriculture, industry, trade and services).

These processes will result in considerable growth in Portuguese exports, particularly if Portuguese firms engaged in reconstruction are numerous and if Portuguese emigrants who have decided to settle in these countries are numerous. We estimate that, depending on circumstances, current exports could be multiplied by two or even three in the next five or ten years (in any case, their level would certainly be less than 10% of exports to Europe).

Where investment is concerned, a recent survey showed that, among 800 Portuguese entrepreneurs who decided to invest abroad, 400 hoped to do so in Angola, against 40 in Spain.

Given the needs of these markets and the possibilities for Portuguese supply, the sectors most involved in this movement will probably be those of the traditional consumer goods industries and the least well developed segments of the metallurgy, engineering and chemical industries.

The *African* factor might therefore breathe new life into industries which, subjected to European competition only (and increasingly to Asian competition) would have had to modernize or disappear. This process may spread over time (therefore attenuate) the costs, particularly the social ones, of Portuguese modernization, but not really contribute to modernization itself.

Demography and Employment

In addition to the problems of ageing of the population (at the peak and at the base) other demographic factors will act in a complex way.

An increase in the unemployed population is possible as a consequence of three phenomena: European integration of Portuguese agriculture; the foreseeable crisis in the traditional industrial sectors; the possible arrival of refugees from South Africa (about 600,000 Portuguese live there) or emigrants from North Africa - in parallel with a net creation of new jobs foreseeable only in the service sectors of the economy.

It is certain that a proportion of agricultural workers will be absorbed by the *rural environment* or will be retired (between 1985 and 1989 the number of retired agricultural workers rose by 100,000 without any radical transformations in this sector).

However, such a set of circumstances could, on the most unfavourable hypothesis, create an additional obstacle to modernization of the economy (in addition to other social and political effects) if contrary demographic movements do not occur: possibly a new wave of Portuguese emigration to the rest of Europe (Spain, France, Switzerland, etc.) and a significant emigration movement towards Angola and Mozambique.

We accept that the size and timing of these demographic movements - the scale of which will depend more particularly on factors outside Portugal - may become key factors for the Portuguese economy.

Finally, the interplay of all these factors will have a positive result only in so far as a change in Portuguese economic agents occurs from a perspective of *cost competitiveness* to one of *global competitiveness* based on quality, in a rather unfavourable context of structural adjustment and technological dependence.

SECTION 2: CULTURAL AND HISTORICAL ISSUES

Values, Attitudes, Behaviour

In addition to territorial redistribution in the form of increased dispersal to the coastal region, the Portuguese population is also undergoing a profound social change, which has become increasingly clear since the 1960s.

Two sectors which are part of the urban middle classes have grown quite appreciably. These are, on the one hand, the technical and managerial classes, which include scientific and intellectual management, technicians and intermediate management; on the other hand, the executive class, which includes executives and administrative staff from trade, services and public administration.

In 1981, these two sections already represented 57% of the urban working population and 34% of the total Portuguese working population on the Continent. A plausible hypothesis is that the urban middle classes, and in particular the two sections mentioned above are an essential sample for the analysis of social values, understood in the sense of the structured preferences of individuals.

In effect they continue to grow in numbers and in social status. Concentrated in them - especially the managerial class - are important educational and cultural resources. Finally, they are highly visible, which tends to confer on them the status of a reference point for other sectors of society. One may then expect that the change in values linked with these partially new protagonists is partly due to their ability to symbolize the reception, production, adaptation and diffusion of these values.

An international study in the 1970s gave the Portuguese a high score for *uncertainty avoidance*, that is to say of the risk of competition, conflicting opinions, and also a high score for an ethic of *sociability* as opposed to that of *personal assertion.*

More recent empirical evidence suggests that there are several trends in values.

On the one hand, there is clear placing of emphasis on personal assertion and achievement. From several examples of this explicit priority, one can cite the very strong preference given to the symmetrical model of family organization, the one which considers occupational activity for the woman desirable, and also a very strong placing of value on the intrinsic content of the work which one is doing or which one wants to do. It must be said, in any case, that this emphasizing of personal achievement is not necessarily incompatible with forms of social participation and with relational ethics, that is to say that it does not necessarily combine with the more narcissistic connotations of individualism.

One also finds in Portugal increasing scepticism in relation to systemic objectives, final and closed models of social organization. There is a move towards more visible, closer, and more consensual objectives. Collective action and participation appear, in any case, to be looking for new formulae, while moving away from the traditional modes of political commitment.

It seems also that there is a readier exchange of different models and values and that a certain tolerance and easing of rules are gradually appearing. Even the traditionally more rigid and intransigent values - ethical, political and religious - are showing some flexibility. They are also spread more widely across groups whose positions were formerly very different.

A final trend concerns the new claim to and practice of combining freely elements drawn from great ideologies which were formerly coherent and separate blocks. Individuals and groups mix and manage these elements in specific combinations, whilst avoiding old rigidities and predictability. The religious or political *catalogues* tend to lose their capacity to identify values and behaviour, because off-the-shelf thoughts are being increasingly abandoned in favour of the crafting of ideas.

One should not, in any case, lose sight of the very varied set of factors able to influence trends in values, able to hinder or reverse them. For example, one should remember the very powerful effects of contagion which come to us from neighbouring cultural areas including the areas of Europe, in a context in which ideas travel further and faster than ever before.

Among these counter-trends may be the effects of nationalism, parochialism, particularism, virtually the opposite of the dynamics of globalization being pursued in Europe. Or again, the manifestations of xenophobia and racism, linked generally to mass immigration and the threat of unemployment and economic crisis.

Even if neither parochialism nor racism is important in Portugal at the moment, the situation cannot be assumed to be immutable. A possible scenario of fragmentation of the European framework might have considerable consequences internally. It might be impossible to maintain satisfactory levels for employment, to vanquish the heritage of very marked regional inequalities, to get rid gradually of the factors of social exclusion within a dualist, tight society, with an *internal third world* of old and new poverty, without hope of mobility or reintegration. The prevalence of counter-trends would then be inevitable.

Atlanticism Versus Europe

Throughout history, in particular since the fifteenth century, the periods where the Portuguese ruling classes have preferred to resort to external resources have been much more frequent and prolonged than those in which ways were sought to develop European Portugal's own resources. These two options - the first of which a political thinker has called *the politics of migration* and the second *the politics of staying put* - could have been complementary, as was the case in many other countries. In Portugal, in fact, they constituted the basis for two opposing visions of the *national destiny*.

On a basis of almost constant hostility with Spain, the *politics of migration* was synonymous with a country turned exclusively towards the sea: trade with the East, colonization of Brazil, mass emigration in periodic waves (until today). Men went away and sent back spices, rare woods, gold, and more recently simply money. Even ten years ago more than 90% of Portuguese overseas trade was by sea.

These are the roots of the *Atlanticism* which informs the ideology of those who see in the maritime tradition a prominent factor of the national identity itself. In practice, Atlanticism has represented the dominance of trade over industry (or over the *wish to industrialize*), of *unequal trade* over development and modernization. The Atlanticist positions cover more or less those which are characterized by the *preservation of the traditional values of a closed society*.

The British alliance (six centuries old, but *economically active* only since the beginning of the eighteenth century, with successive trade agreements very favourable to the British, which inspired Ricardo in his theory of international trade), uniting Portugal with the dominant industrial and maritime power, contributed to the strengthening of the Portuguese trade sector, and to the failures of the timid efforts at industrialization. Finally as a politically, militarily and financially protected country, this led to a political attitude of dependence which was very marked during the period of nineteenth century up to the Second World War.

Somewhat paradoxically, it was at a time when Britain was already in decline as a world power that this privileged link led Portugal, with little industry, towards the opening provided by membership of EFTA in 1959, in the same way as, a dozen years later, Ireland joined the EC.

The particular circumstances of the 1960s created conditions for practical confrontation between *Atlanticists* and *modernizers* the latter very clearly identified this time with pro-European positions. The traditionalists, represented by the dictatorial government of the day, undertook an intransigent defence of *multicontinental and multiracial Portugal*, waging war for thirteen years in the African colonies, supported by most of the big economic groups, whose interests in Africa were vast and diversified; the modernizers at the same time, asserted themselves economically, with unprecedented growth in industry and in trade with Europe.

Democratization and decolonization, after 1974, appeared to withdraw any basis for the Atlanticist positions for good. The road to Europe was presented as being *without a serious alternative*. One of the new political leaders could say in an interview in 1978: *If Europe closes the door on us, what can I offer the Portuguese?*

There are reasons, however, for feeling that this debate is not yet quite closed:

-       The emphasis placed by political leaders and by the media on flows of money from Brussels sometimes suggests an attitude not too different from an *Atlanticist variant*; this time, the wealth does not come by sea, but the country's salvation is due once again not to the efforts and creativity of the Portuguese, but to external financial resources.

-       Some political analysts and *specialists in geo-strategy* have shifted the debate towards questions of defence, pronouncing in favour of more marked identification with American positions and for enhancing the role of NATO (and particularly on that of the US in the defence of Europe) while, at the Community level, they looked for alignment with British ideas.

-       If present conditions are maintained, none of these factors appears sufficient to reinforce the *Atlanticist* positions significantly.

It is not however impossible to imagine some medium-term scenarios which could help refloat them.   The conjunction of a *return to Africa* (trade, investment, people) helped by political stabilization in the ex-colonies, a recession in Europe and internal problems on a social level (e.g. growing unemployment) due to the efforts of *nominal convergence* in an unfavourable external economic climate - this conjuncture would give arguments to those who consider that it is not in the *national interest* to stake everything on the European card.   It is not at all probable that this would lead to a powerful *separatist* current, but Portugal's European policy could eventually become more *reticent* where Political Union is concerned.

SECTION 3: POLICY ISSUES

From the point of view of political institutions, democratic evolution in Portugal has led to a bipartite structure: on some large questions (particularly European integration or macroeconomic management) the two main parties which tussle for power only differ in detail.   At the same time there is a growing lack of interest in *politics*.   This would not be disturbing if a strong, creative and participative civil society existed, as happens in most modern democracies.

A major political crisis, as a result of the *social costs of modernization*, able to shake investors' confidence or the more or less cooperative attitude of the trade unions, is not likely.   But that is linked to the availability of resources to mitigate, in a planned manner, the more serious and localized consequences, as well as any destabilizing effects of the demographic factor or of an unfavourable situation in Europe.

The social dialogue, through the multiplicity of the participants, the nature of the social forces which dominate it, and the interplay of concurrent factors, is a point of convergence of complex economic, social and political dynamic forces.   We do not have a sufficient basis from which to try to trace a prospective scenario in this sphere.

It will be useful, however, to recall briefly the recent history, *speeded up* and full of tribulations, of the Portuguese trade union movement.

In the 1960s and at the beginning of the 1970s, Portuguese trade unionism was closely supervised and controlled.   During the phase of the revolution (1974), the trade union movement was dominated by politics; this was the time of the first confrontations between two politico-trade-union lines.

In the post-revolutionary period, defensive positions predominated and relations between the two main unions (CGTP and UGT) began to be normal.

At the moment, trade union activity has stabilized as has its visibility and its public acceptability.[1]

Submissions still have a defensive character but they no longer concern exclusively wage levels or job protection. They express concerns about quality, training and modernization. The trade unions' role in the social partnership seems to be growing. We can see more flexible positions in regard to problems such as wage levels or regional diversity, in parallel with attempts at more effective intervention in the definition of economic policies themselves. Finally, they are more open to links and coordinating strategies within Europe.

If we were to risk a differential prognosis on the subject of availability for social dialogue in the next few years, we would perhaps say that this availability is potentially greater on the part of the unions than of the business leaders and representatives. The latter appear to be more fragmented, divided by contradictory stances and they reveal clear difficulties of representation.

CONCLUSION: ARTICULATION OF GLOBAL AND SPECIFIC FACTORS IN THE CASE OF PORTUGAL

The analysis and evaluation of the global and specific determining factors between now and the year 2010 require, for the case of Portugal, that one considers its strict articulation, to the extent that the global factors here exert a powerful effect of rationalization and strategic orientation for decisions respecting specific national factors.

Portugal in the European Political Framework

In all the Member States of the European Community there will be particular features which are typical of its path to membership, its ways of understanding the possibilities for change and its strategic interests as a function of different possible future paths.

---

[1] We wish to thank most particularly the leaders of the two Portuguese trade union confederations who agreed to take part in working meetings with the team responsible for this study.

In the case of Portugal, this particular feature has its own form which results from the existence of a marked political split between positions with reference to outside forces (modernizers, liberals, hoping to integrate Portuguese society into the European evolution) and positions oriented towards the preservation of the traditional values of a closed society (protectionists, nationalists, conservatives and authoritarians).

This political split, essential in distinguishing between groups and divisions in the managerial and social elites had, historically, not inconsiderable repercussions on the other social strata. The ascending middle class were divided (distinguishing between groups dependent on internal allocations and groups with skills which enable them to join in international competitiveness) and the lower classes (distinguishing between emigrant groups - which emigrate to Brazil, to Africa, and to Europe - and groups which have no mobility and which depend on the distributive relations ordered by internal political forces).

The importance of this long-lasting political split is independent of the national question, and, especially, of the historical mode in which national independence has been guaranteed within the Iberian context. The traditional mode of response to this question resides in the establishment of protective alliances (with the Vatican, with Britain, with France, and with the United States) which the modernizing elite groups, with the support of other social strata with greater occupational and social mobility, seek to use as a factor for the acceleration of development.

This historical line of Portugal's evolution assumes considerable strategic importance in the context of Portugal's membership of the European Community. Within the general framework of the consolidation of the democracies of Southern Europe (Greece, Spain and Portugal), membership has, for Portugal, the essential characteristic of settling the previous political and economic instability which followed the change of political regime in 1974. It also brought compensation for the loss of a colonial empire (which, in addition to being a time of important migratory flows - constituting, at the time of the return in 1975, about 8% of the total population) was also a factor of complementarity between the metropolitan economy and the colonial economies.

The Community project was a break with the dominant political tradition in Portugal. The Community idea offered Portuguese society, within a short space of time, levels of opportunities for development and levels of strategic complexity to which it did not directly have access, with its own resources and with its own natural speed of modernization.

The European Community cannot be thought of today as a way of resolving the historical accidents of the States which joined it, since these accidents are part of their own singular features. However, it will not be possible to work out coherent and meaningful Community strategies if specific circumstances of this kind are forgotten.

In the case of Portugal, this specific character is reflected in the close connection between the global factors which determine the European Community's possibilities for development and the specific factors which mark out the conditions for Portugal's inclusion in these possibilities. This close connection of global factors and specific factors which determine the future is the result of the effect of strategic rationalization which the European Community produces in the internal decision-making system, whether on the national question, or on the question of economic modernization, or on that of security or that of cultural assertion.

For Portugal and, primarily, for all its strategic decision-makers, this role of a rationalizing factor played by the European Community is vital for a proper interpretation of the framework of possibilities for the evolution of the Community. Portugal's lack of importance in the Community institutions does not enable it to aspire to influence this evolution decisively; on the other hand, an error in evaluation of the trajectory of this evolution means that internal decisions, programmes and projects may not be viable because of a lack of financial and human resources.

In this sense, it will be understood that it is on a basis of evaluation of the global determining factors that the evaluation of the positive and negative effects of the specific national factors will be made so that, on the basis of this articulation, attempts can be made to establish which strategic decisions will determine the main trends in the period under consideration.

16. Spain: Shaping Factors*

INTRODUCTION

In order to understand the characteristics peculiar to the Spanish economy and Spanish society, three crucial elements which set it apart from other EC countries have to be taken into consideration.

The Spanish industrialization process began in the fifties under an autarchic, dictatorial regime, isolated from international competition, and the important growth of the sixties took place within a framework of strong interventionism and protection of the Spanish economy.

This fact is of fundamental importance to explain the relative weaknesses of the productive structures in the Spanish economy. It was a small country with scant levels of income and savings, with no access to the most advanced technologies that were incorporated within the capital goods that were being used in other countries, and a country in which there was a great shortage of natural and energy resources. Furthermore, its scarce levels of corporate capital had been severely weakened throughout a long Civil War and it was a country which could only sustain an inefficient productive level by maintaining autarchic conditions.

This productive structure, the origin of Spanish industrialization, was characterized by the following factors:

- Short production series which meant small firms and the inability to take advantage of economies of scale and scope.
- The use of obsolete technologies.
- Hypertrophy of basic industrial sectors in relation to intermediate inputs and consumption goods sectors.
- A domestic market which was reserved for national producers regardless of prices and costs.
- An economy with an anti-export bias, as in any model of import substitution.

---

* Prof. J. Segura Sánchez.

400

Between 1959 and 1964 the Spanish economy was opened up to foreign competition but, after that, interventionism and internal protection prevailed again.

The result of all this was a legacy of a very deficient productive structure, with low levels of productivity and a long tradition of attempts at upgrading competitiveness through devaluation and not through control of domestic monetary levels of wages and profits.

The second element which sets Spain apart is the fact that the economic crisis of the seventies coincided with an internal political crisis, the transition from a dictatorship to democracy which, though there can be no doubt as to its merits, delayed the Spanish economic adjustment to the crisis and increased the costs of surmounting it.

On the whole, the crisis did not affect the Spanish economy any more than it generally did the rest of the EC (for example, the relative destruction of industrial employment was less than in Belgium and the UK but on a par with Germany and greater than France, Italy and Denmark). The essential difference lay in the time and length of the crisis, because Spain did not begin to react until 1977, which therefore linked the crises of 1973 and 1979 without interruption. The beginning of the recovery was delayed a few years and began in 1986.

In addition to the time lag pointed out, which shifted the evolution of the Spanish economic cycle with respect to the rest of the developed economies, the gradualism with which the adjustment to the crisis took place also implied further costs. On the one hand, it meant greater public deficits; on the other a slower reduction of the rate of inflation; finally industrial reconversion was conceived as an operation aimed at reducing personnel and financial reorganization rather than as a process of overall improvement in competitiveness.

The third and final aspect that has to be pointed out is the weakness of the public sector between the forties and the seventies.

It would suffice to point out that in 1972 public expenditure represented almost 50% of GNP in the UK, between 34 and 38% in Germany, Italy and the US, and that in Spain it represented just about 21%. When Spanish public expenditure did start to register considerable growth it did so in a context of crisis in which a great portion of spending was devoted to unemployment payments and the universalization of public health services. The crucial fact about the entire process is that, while developed economies made a great effort to invest in civil infrastructure (in the fifties and sixties), Spain did not, and, even worse, the importance of capital expenditure in the public budget fell from 25% in 1960 to 18% in 1970 and 10% in 1980.

The result is a woeful lack of infrastructure (communications, hydraulic resources, R&D, transport, etc.) which is a very negative factor for the development of productive activity and competitiveness.

In the following pages, we shall successively consider the main Spanish socio-economic shaping factors, the cultural and historical factors, and the socio-political factors.

SECTION 1: SOCIO-ECONOMIC FACTORS

Competitiveness

The factor which best summarizes the fundamental problem of the Spanish economy is its low level of competitiveness. The objective of an economy such as Spain's, whose level of per capita income in about 80% of the EC average, can only be the maintenance of a steady rate of growth about 1 to 1.5 points per year higher than the EC, and that depends on its capacity to generate internal savings and exports. The level of domestic savings in Spain is quite low, therefore the capacity for potential growth depends essentially on its export capacity, on its international competitiveness.

In spite of the high growth rate registered by the Spanish economy between 1986 and 1990, there are still obvious imbalances. Costs, prices and profitability perform best in high demand sectors, but the increase in employment is concentrated in those sectors of low demand. This would seem to indicate that improvements in competitiveness are occurring in those activities in which there is a significant penetration of foreign capital, and that such entries of capital bring with them up-to-date technologies, commercial networks and elements of competitiveness which do not require new employment and impact differently on the price level. On the contrary, in traditional sectors where outside competition is not strong or where there are market openings for Spanish firms, these firms have expanded production and employment without having to upgrade their level of competitiveness, which throws serious doubts on how long the increase in employment will go on for.

The analysis of the relative Spanish position in the 40 sensitive industrial sectors shows that the behaviour of Spanish exports is specially weak in activities characterized by a strong growth in demand, strong capital/product ratios, important technological content and with significant importance of distribution economies. The list of sectors with good prospects (ceramics, shoes, toys, textile, wine, automobile and shipbuilding) as well as bad prospects (chemical industries, tools and machinery, and electronic machines) is significant enough.

For its own part, the vibrant levels of direct foreign investment, which has covered big Spain's foreign deficits, seem attributable to the fact that the Spanish economy is seen as a point of entry for multinational firms outside of the EC, thanks to the existence of the most liberal legislation in the EC regarding foreign capital, to the existence of relative advantages of labour costs, to the fact that the domestic market is growing, and to the expected reductions of intermediate input costs as a result of the definite elimination of intra-Community tariffs at the beginning of 1993. All of which are advantages characteristic of a weak country within the EC.

In a very synthetized diagnosis, in which only the factors attributable to firms' practices have been pointed out, it is worth examining five fundamental points in any attempt at improving the competitiveness of the Spanish economy.

(i)   The relatively small scale of firms, which makes it difficult, if not impossible, to reap economies of scale and experience which are characteristic of new technologies and the internationalization of markets.

(ii) An inadequate level of technology, which is noted in very low spending on R&D and the deficit of the technological balance of payments which makes it difficult to pursue strategic activities and to have access to technological capital which, for the moment, are the most important source of reduction in production costs.

(iii) A low level of internationalization, with the virtual non-existence of multinational firms, which makes it impossible to penetrate certain markets and weakens the negotiating position of firms in many world markets.

(iv) A low level of self-financing and inadequate debt structure, which is reflected in the frequency with which fixed capital elements are financed by short-term bank credits facilities, which gives rise to high financial costs per unit of product and makes the industry overdependent on banks.

(v)   The exertion of market power by certain services' firms which are protected from foreign competition (repairs, insurance, transport, non-university training and services to firms) which is the source of the Spanish inflationary differential with respect to the EC average, and which in turn contribute to the increase in firms' costs.

There are obviously other factors which affect the level of competitiveness of the Spanish economy. Of these factors, the inadequacies of the system of education and of science/technology, as well as the infrastructural shortcomings already discussed, or the inefficient way in which the labour market functions, stand out. Some of these issues are explored below.

Experts and social agents agree on the importance of the question of competitiveness and the relative low level of competitiveness of the Spanish economy, but differ on the steps that should be taken to correct this. Relevant positions are as follows:

(a)   The Government and most experts maintain that the variables crucial to improving the level of competitiveness are the rate of growth of monetary wages, which is seen as the major cause of the underlying inflation in the Spanish economy (which stands at around 5.5-6% per year) and the public deficit. This is an essentially macroeconomic view of the problem of competitiveness, which is based only on the production costs aspect, which in turn allows the Government to associate an improvement in competitiveness with two of the objectives of the Treaty of Maastricht (inflation and public deficit).

(b)   Employers agree with the Government but at the same time argue that the quotas to be paid by firms to Social Security should be reduced. They also feel that taxes on corporate profits and savings should be reduced, and that there should be greater flexibility in the labour market (reducing firing costs).

(c)   The unions are of the view that wages have no bearing on the level of competitiveness, and that the Spanish real wages are among the lowest in the EC (which is true in terms of wages per hour worked, but not in terms of salary costs per unit produced). They maintain that productivity depends on the level of training of labour and the extent to which social necessities are covered. They feel that the responsibility lies with entrepreneurs and managers who do not run their firms properly.

In summary, there does not seem to be any social agreement as to the key variables for the improvement of competitiveness. At present, for the unions there is simply no question of negotiating any kind of moderation in the growth of wages or cuts in public transference spending.

The Efficiency of the Public Sector

The Spanish public sector has certain shortcomings which are largely the result of its history.

With regard to public income, Spain did not have a modern tax system until very recently: the progressive income tax dates from the fiscal reform of 1977; the harmonization of indirect taxes and the introduction of VAT date from 1986, the year of Spain's adhesion to the EC. Furthermore, there is hardly any fiscal consciousness among citizens. Proof of it is not only the high level of fiscal fraud, but also facts revealed by certain surveys, which indicate that Spaniards hardly think it an offence not to pay taxes.

On the expenditure side, as has already been pointed out, the level of public spending in Spain was relatively low until very recently (it now stands at around 40% of the GNP), and shows a pronounced bias in favour of spending on transfers as against public investment.

The general result is a deficit which in 1991 stood at 4.4% of GDP. Such a deficit can pose severe problems in terms of Spain's possibilities of meeting convergence conditions established at Maastricht. But, more than their inherent value, two factors are particularly unsatisfactory.

The first is that the real budget has little relation with the budget approved in Parliament. For instance, in 1991, the approved deficit was 2.5% of GDP, but the real one was in the order of 4.5%. This indicates the incapacity of Spanish authorities to control public spending, not to mention major errors in budgetary planning. In this sense, two aspects of public expenditure are of crucial importance. Expenditures on unemployment benefits and health and pharmaceutical services on the one hand, which, year after year, are underestimated in the elaboration of the Budget, and whose rate of growth cannot be tolerated even in the short run. On the other hand, there is the growing tendency towards deficit in the Autonomous and Local Administrations, which is only partially offset by the relatively more disciplined control of deficit of the Central Administration.

The second aspect is a relative ignorance as to the real efficiency of public expenditure. There hardly exist cost-benefit analyses per expenditure programme; studies on alternative means of sources of financing for determined services are still only at their beginning; the coordination of ongoing investment projects leaves a lot to be desired.

On the subject of efficiency of the Spanish public sector, public enterprise is worthy of special mention. The general theme of the efficiency of public enterprise has been sufficiently analysed to enable us to identify the problems, which are not too dissimilar to those that affect big organizations (protection from competition, principal-agent relationships, little sensitivity of owners with respect to the profitability of capital, etc.), but there are some aspects which should be highlighted in the Spanish case.

The first is that, for historical reasons, Spanish industrialization during the fifties was built around public initiative (Instituto Nacional de Industria, INI). Throughout the sixties and specially between 1977 and 1982 many private firms which were experiencing difficulties became part of the INI, in a process known as *the socialization of losses*. The INI's concentration on mature sectors (mining, iron and steel, and shipbuilding) and, as already mentioned, the transfer of private firms meant that the INI began to incur serious losses by the end of the seventies, and, until 1985, it was the object of a process of intense industrial reconversion, which was very costly to the taxpayer (the total cost of public and private reconversion has been estimated in the region of 1.5 to 2 thousand billion pesetas).

After this reconversion, a group of non-profitable industrial firms still exist. For political or other reasons the public sector still maintains them and new plans for entrepreneurial reconversion geared towards the drastic reduction of their capacity, or, in some cases their complete disappearance in the future, are being formulated.

The viability of this industrial reorganization, which will allow for the remodelling of the public industrial sector around a nucleus of firms which are - or could be - profitably and efficiently run, depends to a large extent on the trade unions, whose position is very clearly one of confrontation. The trade unions consider that non-profitable public firms should be maintained as a compensation for something they define as a social debt the country has with workers (e.g. in the mining and steel sectors).

The problem is more important than it may seem given the relative weight of trade unions in public enterprises (partly because of their size, partly because of the sectors to which they belong) and their presence in areas of strong political influence (Asturias and the Basque Country). Although the trade unions have, apparently, begun recently to be slightly more flexible, and consider that public enterprise is not a world that is different from private enterprise, their corporate positions on the issue make this the main problem to be dealt with in the reorganization of the industrial public sector in order to maintain a mixed corporation which would imply a strong concentration of industrial capital to improve the level of competitiveness.

Once again, experts and social agents agree on the desirability of an efficient public sector, but differ strongly as to the way in which this should be achieved. Their positions are as follows:

(a)   For the Government it is a greater priority to reduce public deficit for the purposes of macroeconomic policy and EC convergence than to achieve an efficient public sector. In other words, it holds the opinion that a necessary condition for efficiency is the reduction of the deficit.   This implies that the greatest efforts towards rationalization of management and efficiency will be concentrated in those activities that imply greatest costs (e.g. health, unemployment benefits).

(b)   Employers' organizations attribute inefficiency to the public character of their activities, and maintain that the State is not capable of providing any efficient service or running productive activities with any degree of efficiency. Consequently, they hold the view that efficiency depends on the privatization of all the activities that may be profitably run by the private sector: health, teaching, postal services, industrial activities, energy-related activities, transport, etc.

(c)   The Unions consider that, on the contrary, the public sector is not plagued by any specific kind of inefficiency, that its offer of social services should be broadened, that public enterprise can be a useful instrument of industrial policy, and that this type of activity should be run with the greater participation of the workers.   They even maintain that the present deficit, or a deficit of around 3% of GDP, is perfectly compatible with macroequilibria and will have no negative effects on the economy.

Again, there does not seem to be much agreement, so it would appear that there is little hope of broad social agreement on this question, although the need to tackle the problems that stem from public deficit will call for important decisions to be taken, something which has already begun to happen, throughout 1992.

The Labour Market

The Spanish economy did not have a labour market which was assimilable with those of other developed countries until the end of the seventies. During the Franco era, trade unions were prohibited and collective bargaining was only ever established within the official *trade unions* (which were made up of employers and workers) and in which the Government carefully monitored all activity and resolved any conflict. In addition, every productive activity has its own regulation (*Ordenanza* of the sector) in which professional categories, working conditions, holidays, etc. were carefully set out.

With such a trade union structure, the Governments of the Franco regime chose, until the beginning of the seventies, to maintain wages at low levels in exchange for the maintenance of stability in employment (there were very few legal possibilities of firing, the cost of which was very high). When money wages started to rise at sharp rates, between 1971 and 1977, the rigidity of the labour market became a burden for firms. The democratic transition tackled this problem initially in the Statute of Workers (1980) and, shortly afterwards, the reform of conditions which governed the hiring of labour (1984).

In certain aspects, the Spanish labour market still functions in an unsatisfactory manner, which, apart from not benefiting either side, is actually quite harmful to both. Four questions merit further analysis:

The first question deals with the costs of firing. The empirical studies at our disposal show that the compensation that firms have to pay for firing a worker in Spain are about the EC average, but the costs of going through all the necessary steps this usually involves (lawyers, wages, judiciary procedure and time) are indeed very high. These costs do not rebound to the benefit of either party and are derived from the non-existence of systems of conciliation between parties, which then make it necessary to revert to judicial channels. And the mechanisms of legal conciliation which exist are only a way of getting worker and firm to present a dismissal by mutual agreement as an inappropriate dismissal in order that the worker might receive full unemployment benefits and that the firm would not have to pay any part of the compensation, which then falls back on to the public sector.

The second problem concerns temporary contracts not derived from technical motives or the seasonal nature of the activity in question, which came into effect in 1984. The vast majority of new contracts offered between 1986 and 1990 were temporary, to such an extent that they represented some 31% of all contracts by the middle of 1991. This percentage is excessive and is partly due to the deficiencies inherent in such contracts, which can be used indefinitely with the same person, as long as its content is conveniently redefined. This has posed two types of problems. On the one hand, a percentage of non-causal temporal contracts which is more than twice the EC average can cause a dualization of the workforce: 70% with stable contracts and 30% who would be obliged to alternate, indefinitely, periods of employment with periods of subsidized unemployment, which allows them little possibility of improving training and bettering their qualifications. On the other hand, since the six-months temporary contract which holds at present is outlined in such a way that the worker is entitled to receive unemployment insurance benefits (not subsidy) for a further three months, public expenditure on unemployment has rocketed, giving rise to a situation which cannot be sustained even in the short term. A paradoxical situation results in which the more employment generated the greater the payments for unemployment which are derived from a growing rate of coverage - which at present is about 63% - as well as from the high rate of rotation in the labour market that stems from temporary contracts and the unemployment benefits which accompany them.

Thirdly, the system of incentives for training leaves a lot to be desired. There are two types of contracts (training and practices) which involve subsidies and/or allowances in the quotas paid to Social Security by firms if they involve persons of certain age groups (young people) who receive training within the firm. Since very few Spanish firms have departments or activities aimed at meaningful internal training, and given that it is difficult to measure training received outside, these contracts have been abundantly used in an effort to keep down the cost of employing young people, though not to improve their qualifications. This is very clear especially in the light of the fact that this type of contract is used extensively in agriculture, construction and by small firms.

Finally, there still exists a complex legal framework as far as labour is concerned. This can be seen in the continued use of many of the old *Ordenanzas* of the Franco era, which make geographical and functional mobility of labour quite difficult. It also makes the internal assignment of tasks inside firms and the adaptation to changing conditions of the market equally difficult for firms.

As was to be expected, the positions of experts and agents regarding this question differ drastically. Generally speaking, experts are in favour of solving the problems we have been discussing, employers' organizations consider that firing costs are very high, that labour market should be deregulated and that the contracting of labour must become more individualized, while the unions think that temporary contracts are unacceptable and that the firing costs are untouchable.

The System of Education and Professional Training

The inadequacies which are to be found in the training of labour in Spain are one of the major difficulties concerned with the matching of demand and supply of labour, and are a source of problems in the market. To discuss the question of training in Spain we need to distinguish between several different aspects: training carried out within a firm, and regulated training had before entering the labour market.

The first aspect is very important because global trends seem to be heading in the direction of contracting people with sufficient basic knowledge and then offering them specialized training programmes within the firm. This is not the case in Spain, because the problems of qualification were only recently detected by firms (as they have to face stiffer competition) and because the processes of training at work can only be efficiently carried out by firms if they are of a certain size.

The second problem mainly affects the system of public education, especially with regard to professional training and university education. As far as professional training is concerned, everyone seems to think that degrees and diplomas are often obsolete, that the training processes are not very efficient in relation both to the time spent and the type of knowledge gained. As far as occupational training is concerned, which is aimed at the unemployed, if it is true that the quantity has increased in the last few years (at present there are some 400,000 people in such training programmes) it is also true that it is of poor quality, which results in the loss of human capital of long-term unemployed people.

As far as university studies are concerned, the main problem is the inability of the system to offer short graduate programmes which are acceptable to the labour market. Something is only now being achieved, with the reduction of the duration of certain degree courses from five to four years, and with the greater flexibility and specialization of certain degrees, which are geared to serve, more directly, the needs of firms. But it is still early to assess the effect of such measures.

The opinions of experts and social agents coincide on the importance of this question as well as the means of resolving it, although teachers, who consider that a process of reform can affect their status, are somewhat reluctant to make certain modifications to the system of professional and university training.

Convergence and Economic and Monetary Union

The agreements reached at Maastricht and the consequent drawing up of a Spanish plan of convergence aimed at the fulfilment by 1997 of the conditions necessary for convergence, have brought about a great political and social upheaval. This question is being discussed here under the hypothesis that no Spanish government - whatever its political inclination - can pay the political costs that not being among the top EC countries in 1997 would signify. Therefore, with the exception of certain very minority positions the great national debate focuses on the efforts and sacrifices that will have to be made and how they are to be shared by social agents. This does not necessarily mean that the success of convergence is guaranteed even if certain sacrifices are made, nor that the process would not encounter difficulties if there is a change in government after the 1994 elections (which might eventually bring about a coalition government between the Socialists and Catalan regional parties) but it does mean that all political and economic debate will, from now on in Spain, be centred around the conditions of convergence.

On this subject the opinions of the trade unions and the Government differ radically

The trade unions consider that the conditions for convergence regarding the third phase of Economic and Monetary Union approved at Maastricht exclusively imply nominal convergence, but the actual issue is real convergence. What do the trade unions mean by real convergence? To bring real wage levels, social protection, training, equality in income distribution, pensions, unemployment rate and infrastructures to the average levels of the EC. To achieve this, they do not think it necessary to make an effort or, if it is necessary to do so, it should not be at the expense of the workers, but of the rest of society.

Achieving convergence for the third phase of Economic and Monetary Union is, without doubt, the biggest challenge facing Spanish society at the moment. Achieving it will put Spain on course to becoming a member of the group of the most advanced EC countries and will justify, socially, the costs and benefits of belonging to such a group. Not achieving it will be a very negative step because it will mean not only that the society is incapable of reaching agreement, but it might also give rise to greater anti-EC, autarchic and protectionist positions, which are always lurking beneath the surface of Spanish society. Whether one agrees with the Government or not, what is beyond doubt is that the most important part of the process of modernization of the Spanish economy and Spanish society is the fact of its membership of the EC, which explains why the Government of a country like Spain has maintained positions so favourable to the acceleration of Economic and Monetary Union even if it has meant a slower rate of construction of a social Europe. Not to achieve convergence will not only be a political failure which will significantly alter the electoral map and the internal cohesion of political forces, but will also mean the loss of the major dynamizing factor of social and economic change in Spain for many a year.

SECTION 2: CULTURAL AND HISTORICAL FACTORS

The Autonomous Governments and the Organization of the State

From the end of the fifteenth century when the Spanish State was created, it has always been organized in a very centralized way, along the lines of the French administrative model after the end of the nineteenth century. In spite of this, Spain's internal cultural pluralism has been very great, with the existence of two territories that have their own languages which are widely used, as well as an abundant written culture (Catalonia and Galicia), as well as another territory with its own local language which is mainly spoken in the inner agricultural regions, though not so much in the cities, and with little written culture (the Basque Country).

The Second Spanish Republic (1931-39) laid down very advanced statutes of autonomy to these historic territories just a few days before the Civil War began. These statutes were later discarded by Franco's dictatorship, which carried out a policy of very intense cultural repression in Catalonia, Galicia and the Basque Country. In the Constitution of 1978, Title VIII recognized the existence of Autonomous Communities (ACs), made provision for administration at three levels (Central State Administration, Autonomous Administration and Municipal Councils), normalized the situation of the use of local languages, stipulated two ways (fast and slow) of arriving at the creation of ACs and regulated the functions of the Autonomous Governments and the Central State Administration as well as how they are to be shared.

The first Spanish governments of the democratic era opted for a model of development of the ACs which tended clearly towards the homogenization of the seventeen ACs that existed in a double attempt not to distinguish among them, and to play down, as far as was possible, the political revindications of the three historic autonomies, so that the entire autonomous government system would be little more than mere administrative decentralization. At present, after a decade, we might say that more than 80% of the functions and responsibilities of the Central State Administration that could be transferred to the ACs has been effectively transferred to them.

The process has not taken place without problems. On the one hand, there have been problems related to the speed of transfers, which the ACs have always maintained has been too slow, as well as conflicts related to functions which have to be delegated. For example, transfers such as the administering of unemployment insurance, certain aspects of economic policy (concerning energy and industry) and certain natural resources, are still a point of controversy between ACs and the Central Government. On the other hand, disparities between ACs are very sharp and the richer ones are hardly interested in promoting the so-called Interterritorial Compensation Fund. For example, the question of the transfer of the administering of income tax divides the rich ACs (who wish to administer this on their own) and the poorer ones who want it to remain centralized in their belief that territorial solidarity should also encompass budgetary matters. Finally, the fact that half of the ACs are not governed by the Socialist Party since the last general elections, has increased the demands of autonomies run by conservative governments in spite of the centralist and anti-autonomous government tradition of the Spanish right.

Among the economic costs of this process, we have to recall the strong and growing deficits that the ACs have accumulated, which makes it more difficult to achieve the objective of convergence as defined at Maastricht. For example, the civil service has hardly been rationalized and the duplication of functions has increased: there are Ministries in the Central Government which almost have no *raison d'être* because their functions have been almost completely transferred and which, however, still have the same amount of staff as ten years ago. And the intense bureaucratization of the ACs is not justifiable either from a functional point of view (other motives, related to influence, political power or political interests are a different question).

It is quite possible that support for more independent ACs is increasing although the greatest political allies of the Spanish Government in the State Parliament are the Catalan and present Basque minorities. However, in the case of Catalonia, there has been a political increase in pro-independence positions (held by a 10% minority) which will probably force the Catalan Government (one of moderate nationalism) to radicalize its positions. In the case of the Basques, the fight against terrorism has allowed for coalition governments between conservative nationalists and socialists, and although the pro-independence positions are electorally stronger than in Catalonia it probably poses, in the medium term, a less important problem than the course of events that might take place in Catalonia.

Links with Latin America and the North of Africa

For historical, political and geographical reasons in the case of North Africa, and additional linguistic reasons in the case of Latin America, Spain has special links with both these regions, although they are of a different nature.

In the case of North Africa, Spain had an important colonial presence there until the beginning of the twentieth century. This has now been reduced to two specific enclaves in Morocco territory (Ceuta and Melilla) after Spain lost the Rif War and, more recently, the abandonment of the Spanish Sahara and the former Spanish Guinea. Furthermore, the existence of the Canary Islands, which are closer to the West coast of Africa than to the Iberian peninsular, raises further problems. The source of this factor is historical and cultural, though it has a large socio-political dimension since it introduces a very significant level of instability to Spain's international political relationships. The demands of Morocco over Ceuta and Melilla are used by Rabat as a levering force to gain political and economic aid. At the same time, an important part of the Spanish fishing fleet depends on work in Moroccan fishing grounds. The problem is further complicated if we take into account that Spain is the entrance point for North African citizens to Europe and that immigration from these countries, with Spain as the final or intermediate destiny, is very important. This last factor implies not only the existence of strong demographic pressures on the Spanish economy, but also the need for Spain to be the country to put into practice the decisions, which, in this case would be restrictive, with respect to North African emigration towards EC countries.

This combination of problems makes the zone potentially the most destabilizing area of all Spain's international relationships, which could eventually lead to a crisis which would be difficult to solve diplomatically, with possible implications for Spain's military allies.

Latin America is important to Spain for other reasons, fundamentally in economic and diplomatic terms. Spain not only has had, and still has, strong trade relationships with Latin America but also, in the last few years, the diplomatic and political activity of the Spanish Government in the region has made it a crucial mediator in regional conflicts as well as the key to Latin America's relations with the EC. Furthermore, many Spanish firms, private as well as public, have begun their process of internationalization by participating in joint projects with Latin American institutions and firms (e.g. air transport, supply of petroleum, building of electrical plants, roads and dams, urban transport and shipbuilding) and the share of Spanish exports to those countries has increased in the last few years.

In view of all these factors, it is very important for Spain to maintain not only strong diplomatic activity in the area, but also that those countries achieve a stable rate of growth of income which would allow a consolidation of these markets and a more stable political situation in both regions.

The Feeling of *Europeanness* within Spanish Society

The last factor that has to be pointed out is the extent to which Spanish society has assumed its *Europeanness*. In spite of its long experience of an autarchic regime and its relatively economic - and, most of all, political - isolation from the rest of Europe until not too long ago, surveys carried out about the acceptance of the idea of a European Community and the citizens' feeling of *Europeanness* reveal that Spain ranks among the top pro-EC countries in the Community. This should not surprise anyone because during the years of dictatorship, Spaniards identified Europe with democratic liberties, tolerance and social and economic welfare.

However, this acceptance of the idea of *Europeanness* loses sight of the short-term sacrifices, the discipline and the limits to national sovereignty that this involves. It is significant that in spite of all pro-European declarations coming from all sides of the Spanish political spectrum and despite the unanimity with which the Treaty for adhesion was approved in Parliament, there is almost no political party or social agent that does not demand, in one way or another, the renegotiation of this Treaty, although they know that this is almost impossible.

The loss or reduction of the feeling of *Europeanness* would be negative for Spanish society, a society in which there still exist (although they are not as robust today) strong autarchic traditions rooted in reactionary and even anti-democratic political positions which would probably become stronger if there is a new economic crisis. For example, the trade unions have already begun to point out in one way or another that if the EC demands sacrifices for workers today, with promises of future benefits, or if the EC is not *a Europe for workers*, the Community project will not suit them. And within the Conservative Party it is not uncommon to hear arguments which, although they depart from a formal declaration of Europeanism, demand special treatment for Spain as a condition for acceptance of Community projects.

It is quite possible that part of these messages are motivated by a certain amount of electoral opportunism, especially since the Spanish Government has voiced a strong commitment to face the necessary costs of fulfilling the conditions for convergence defined at Maastricht, or in the wake of the general elections which must take place no later than October 1993. But the element of risk is a source of concern because Spain's strong bid to modernize its society after its return to democracy is based on its adherence to the EC and a more significant international presence.

For all these reasons, it is very important that in the process of the construction of Economic and Monetary Union, Spain should not have to make important net sacrifices - although it may have to assume certain costs - and the same can be said of all the less well-off countries of the EC. And, for this reason, the existence of compensatory mechanisms to offset the initial, short termed, negative effects of Economic and Monetary Union, as well as important degrees of solidarity within the EC, is an absolutely necessary condition in order for the Community project to be taken on in a satisfactory manner by all its partners.

SECTION 3: SOCIO-POLITICAL FACTORS

The Construction of a Social Europe

For a country like Spain it is clear that the elements of solidarity in EC activities are going to be fundamental. For two reasons. The first is political, because a real EC calls not only for a single market and foreign policy based on common defence, but also action aimed at reducing social differences between citizens. The second reason is economic, because a country whose per capita income is 80% of the EC average is a potential net beneficiary of any common policy or programme. In great measure, as has already been pointed out, the level of acceptance that the EC manages to maintain among Spaniards will depend on the extent to which the efforts and discipline that it demands of our society can lead, not only in the long run, to an improvement in the standard of living.

The delay in the construction of Social Europe, which only exists, for the moment, in the form of an outline of intentions which have not even been ratified by all members of the EC, gives some cause for concern. However, it is possible that the Social Charter is not the essential element for the beginning of the construction of Social Europe, and that this depends in far greater measure on the policies for infrastructure, training, regional development, etc., that the EC is able to implement. A single market with competition rules which are widely accepted, is an indispensable base for improving the efficiency of resource allocation which is a necessary condition for the improvement of the potential well-being of all concerned. But the latter often requires, as well, redistribution mechanisms which are not very well developed within the EC.

Expectations in this field are not positive either, due to the problems that stem from the size of the EC Budget and the very nature of the EC's Agricultural Policy. And also probably because the institutional organization of the EC in aspects such as the role of Parliament and the Commission is not conducive to the introduction of active policies of solidarity. Advances in the field of Monetary Union, liberalization of productive factor markets, the achievement of a single monetary authority, deregulation of public procurements, etc. are all crucial elements in the construction of a fully integrated economic area. But when a single currency, single market and single monetary authority (as well as a single foreign and defence policies) exist, a single public budget and single social legislation will most certainly exist as well, which will allow for the implementation of policies designed to achieve objectives which are not derived from single individual preferences.

To recognize that in addition to the objectives of efficiency the EC has to pursue objectives of equity, is only to recognize that there is a desire to construct a real community of nations. And, in any case, the political viability of the EC will depend on its capacity to allow its lesser developed members to reap certain benefits during the process of the construction of the EC, and to prevent the development of a Europe of two different speeds with a group of countries confined forever to the back of the queue.

As is obvious, this question hinges not only on the internal EC variables already pointed out, but also on the prospects for the world economy and the way in which the future process of enlargement of the EC is carried out.

The Enlargement of the EC

The political and economic aspects of this question are viewed somewhat differently by different political groups and social agents.

From the political perspective there is almost general agreement that the EC should include all European countries, or tend towards this, because this would mean a stronger community which would be able to negotiate on equal terms with the US and Japan. However, it must be recognized that the capacity to absorb new members, especially the group of less advanced countries, is limited (the problem of the former Federal Republic of Germany with East Germany is irrefutable proof of this) especially in the middle of a process of internal consolidation of Economic and Monetary Union; and also because the entry of any new member, whoever it might be, is not without political significance.

In spite of these precautions, from a political point of view, there is a general attitude of tolerance, in the same sense that there is a willingness to admit the requests of all those countries that fulfil the internal political requirements.

From an economic standpoint, the position is somewhat different, because the effects of the entry of new members on the interests of a country like Spain are different. Briefly put, the entry of economies whose situation is above the EC average will not pose problems to adaptation nor cause any delay in achieving the objective of greater economic unity. Their entry would improve the average level of income of the EC and would allow for greater margins for the implementation of solidarity policies; but it will also result in the greater influence of what is called Europe of the North, shifting even more the centre of EC gravity to the German and Nordic zone. The entry of countries whose economies are below the EC average would probably strengthen positions in favour of solidarity and the construction of a Social Europe, but will make it much more difficult to advance in that direction.

This ambivalent position, which in one way or another is probably widespread in many EC countries, is even more extreme in the case of Spain because the Spanish economy is neither strong enough to be as influential as Central EC economies, nor weak enough to benefit from important compensation, especially if new countries, with weaker economies than Spain's, enter the EC.

Constitutional Change and Political Stability

A question which affects Spain more than other EC countries is the need to introduce constitutional modifications to bring certain features of the Spanish judicial and political system into line with the rest of the EC. This is because the Spanish Constitution is more recent and was the product of a complex political agreement among very varied forces - from the Communist Party to the remnants of Franco's regime - and even *de facto* powers such as the church and the Spanish army.

This political balance gave birth to a constitutional text which was technically excellent (the date at which it was elaborated meant that it could draw on a lot of experience and international doctrine). It was very extensive and at the same time very open, which allowed for very varied interpretations of many of its central points. In particular, Title VIII (Autonomies) was drawn up in such a way that the model for the final organization of the State was left open (see earlier) and the economic aspects are so flexible that they admit options as diverse as a strong centralized economy, with powerful planning instruments, and a system with hardly any public sector intervention.

It is quite probable that this flexibility inherent in the Constitution was necessary in 1978 and its great merit was that it allowed all Spaniards to live together in mutual agreement for the first time in 40 years, though not without some costs. The Constitution is such that more than seventy important issues (from electoral norms to the financing of the ACs, from freedom of education and the financing of it to the Economic and Social Council) hinge on a subsequent Law, which has increased the conflictive interpretations among institutions (among parties of different ideologies, between the ACs and the Central Government, between private institutions and public ones) and has meant that the Constitutional Court has become a veritable *Third Chamber* for the approval or rejection of some important laws.

The approval of a law of constitutional development requires a qualified majority of Parliament, which lends a desirable amount of stability to the law, although, at the same time, it makes approval difficult. But frequent appeals to the Constitutional Court by those who do not think that their partisan positions are reflected in the law, and the Constitution's great ambiguity on some essential points has meant that in the last few years there has been a growing tendency towards constitutional change, which has been reflected in certain electoral programmes.

In spite of this factor, there is a certain generalized fear on the part of all political parties as to what any change in the Constitution could mean, not so much for the change in itself as for the wave of demands for further changes that this could spark off, which, at worst, could lead to a break in the consensus that exists with respect to the basic value of the Constitution. In so far as the present Constitution is admitted - tolerated, at any rate - by all quarters as a rather complex equilibrium, the modification of any part of it can be viewed as an alteration of that general consensus.

A greater degree of legal harmonization in the EC, as well as common legislation on new matters, might possibly force the modification of some part of the Constitution (for example, the electoral question). The general feeling at present is that there should be as little change as possible, the view being held that the very flexibility of the Constitution would allow the inclusion of possible new interpretations since no provision within it excludes them. This question is at present being resolved in judicial and constitutional circles, but in any case it will be appropriate that if such modifications are to be made, they should entail the introduction only of aspects relating to questions not treated in the Constitution. Any modification to its present content should be avoided. If there is any modification, there is likely to be intense pressure to change other aspects of the Constitution - which do not have to be made because of adherence to the EC - in questions relating to the ACs, the institutional framework of the intervention of the State in the economy and even issues related to the educational system. This could probably lead to a lesser degree of general agreement with respect to the Constitution and a certain element of political instability.

The Position of the Trade Unions

Trade unions have been legal in Spain since 1978. They have a long tradition of political struggle and a history of revindications which went beyond the world of trade unionism during the Franco era. In the early years of the new democratic era, until the mid-eighties, the two majority unions (*Comisiones Obreras* and *Union General de Trabajadores*) had very close ties with the two left-wing parties (Communist and Socialist, respectively) so much so that party militants were almost necessarily members of the appropriate union.

There are certain implications to these characteristics of the union movement, among them the relative lack of experience in the field of collective negotiation and the strong political slant to many positions adopted. Furthermore, union membership, even today, is very low and applies mainly to the big firms, especially those that are public. With this background, the apparently contradictory double tendency in both unions is hardly surprising: on the one hand, there is the propensity to override the authority of their *own* political parties if the latter do not fully support their demands; the other is the tendency to adopt strongly corporate positions.

Between 1977 and 1985, there was only a year in which the majority of Spanish unions did not maintain global negotiating positions which led to different social agreements on national issues, either with Employers' Organizations or with Employers' Organizations and the Government. They were agreements which allowed for the establishment of parameters for variations in monetary wages in accordance with the expected rate of inflation, or which secured certain compensations beyond wage increases. However, over the last six years, after the Spanish economy had overcome the crisis which began in the seventies, there has not been another agreement. Good relations between the party in power (the PSOE) and the main majority union (the UGT) no longer exist, and the unions have begun to take positions which have led to increasingly sharp confrontation with the Government (cf. the general strike at the end of 1989), to such an extent that government-union relationships have almost completely broken down.

This radicalization of the union positions hinges on certain political factors which will not be analysed here and now, factors such as the historical ties between the PSOE and the UGT, and which have a lot to do with the conviction on the part of the latter that a socialist government must accept all the positions of a socialist union. Furthermore, the unions feel that workers have made many sacrifices in order to overcome the crisis and that the Government is adopting increasingly conservative measures on economic issues, which work against their interests.

However right the unions may be in their general positions, their present strategy is one of confrontation which can be seen in the following ways:

- Their objective to increase the purchasing power of wages by increases in monetary salaries, rather than supporting policies to control inflation.
- The refusal of any kind of wage limitation, a position they support with the argument that wages do not affect either employment,

inflation, or the level of competitiveness, and that Spanish real wages are among the lowest in the EC.

- Demands for elimination of any kind of temporary work contracts which do not derive from the seasonal nature of the firms' activities.
- Demands for increases in the level of unemployment coverage as well as the quantity and length of time during which unemployment benefits are received.
- The refusal to accept the firing of workers or the regulation of employment in uneconomic public firms.
- The systematic use of pressurizing tactics, which culminated in a general strike for half a day during the month of May, and a projected complete general strike in October of 1992. This action is prompted by the Government's proposal to modify unemployment benefits.
- Radical opposition to any regulation of strikes that is not determined by the unions themselves (in spite of the fact that time after time, minimum services have not been provided, and in spite of chain strikes in public services).

Apart from political tensions and instability, such positions have other negative effects. Among them:

- A dualization in the labour market due to the fact that wage adjustments are made for the benefit of workers with fixed employment (69% of the market), but if collective bargaining results in excessive wage rises for firms, adjustments of employment only occur for those workers who have temporary jobs (31%), whose redundancy costs are lower.
- The appearance of radical, independent unions in certain sectors, who are after improvements only for their own members, and use their power to paralyse certain fundamental services.
- A general critical attitude towards government economic policy without any kind of reserve or exception. When inflation increases it is because government economic policy is bad; when it goes down it is insufficient and only goes to show that wage increases do not affect prices. When unemployment rises it is an indication of the Government's lack of employment policy; when it goes down, it is only seasonal, or it has not gone down sufficiently, or it just

goes to show that employment can be created even when monetary wages go up higher than the government intends.

- The appearance of strong opposition to the conditions of convergence agreed at Maastricht, since such convergence is nominal and what really counts is real convergence.

All this is indicative of the radical opposition of the unions to any convergence plan as well as any reduction in public transference expenditure, and to any further deregulation of the labour market. It is also perhaps the factor which contributes most to negative expectations for the Spanish economy in the near future.

17. UK: Shaping Factors*

INTRODUCTION

Some shaping factors are specific to the United Kingdom in the sense that they are essentially *internal* in their origins and impact. In varying forms and degrees, however, several of them are present also in a number of other European Community countries.

Six shaping factors can be identified as likely to be of particular importance for the future of Britain over the coming two decades: an ageing population, environmental problems, use of new technologies, changing employment patterns, becoming a mature economy and the social dimensions. Each of them has a number of implications for business strategies and several of them may be expected to affect or be affected by the European Community.

SECTION 1: AGEING POPULATION

Change in Total Population

The total UK population is forecast to rise by 4.5% (2.6 million) from 57.4 million in 1990 to 60.0 million in 2010. This increase is more than the 3.3% increase in the previous two decades, but will take place mainly in the first decade of the period and is expected to be followed by a slowing down of the rate of increase in the 2000-10 decade, and by a levelling off and then a slight decline in the subsequent decades. Thus, in common with most other countries in Western Europe, the period of rising population is expected shortly to come to an end.

While population forecasts two decades ahead tend to be more reliable than most other kinds of forecasts over such a period, there is inevitably some uncertainty about future changes in each of the three main elements in population change: mortality rates, fertility rates and net migration

---

*   W. Daniel, J. Northcott and I. Christie.

rates. Forecasts based on alternative higher and lower assumptions for these suggest that by 2010 the change in total population is likely to be within the range of a high variant of an 8.2% increase to 62.1 million and a low variant of no increase at all.

Mortality rates are expected to continue their slow gradual decline as a result of medical advances and, more importantly, general improvements in living conditions, particularly in sanitation, housing, heating and nutrition. Mortality rates could improve at a faster rate than expected because of greater interest in health care and concern to adopt a healthy lifestyle, or they could improve at a slower rate because of less healthy living patterns with more obesity, alcoholism, stress and lack of exercise. One new factor which could prove to be important is AIDS, which initially was predominantly a disease suffered by homosexuals, haemophiliacs and drug addicts, but which has recently been spreading in the general heterosexual population - the numbers of cases are still small, but are rising at a high rate. Information on sexual behaviour patterns and on the current level of HIV infection is at present too limited for it to be possible to make accurate predictions of likely future incidence of the disease, and it is also uncertain how soon vaccines for prevention or drugs for cure will be developed. However, at present it is not foreseen that deaths from AIDS will be sufficiently numerous to make a significant difference to overall mortality rates in Britain by 2010.

Birth-rates are more prone than death-rates to sudden shifts, particularly in response to changes in social conditions such as income prospects, child-care provisions and employment opportunities for women. Recently birth-rates have been tending to fall for women in their 20s, but to rise for women in their 30s, as more women, particularly those in professional occupations, marry later and defer starting families until they have established themselves in a career. Average completed family size for women born in 1975 is expected to be 2.0 children, just below the 2.1 needed for replacement.

In recent years the main migration flows, both in and out, have been to and from the United States, Australia, New Zealand and the other countries in the European Community, and these are expected to continue. There have also been predominantly inward flows from Commonwealth countries in South Asia and Africa, but these are likely to be reduced in the years immediately ahead as a result of more severe restrictions on immigration.

As with other countries in Western Europe, there is the possibility of substantial new migration flows from Eastern Europe and the republics of the former Soviet Union; or from countries in the Third World with problems of rising population, poverty and political upheaval; and there is also the possibility of a sudden inflow from Hong Kong around the time of reunion with China in 1997. The sharp rise in numbers seeking asylum from 4,000 in 1988 to 34,000 in the first nine months of 1991 may be an indicator of things to come. These possibilities are not allowed for in the official forecasts.

Changes in Age Structure

While the relatively small changes in total population expected should present no serious problems, the changes in age structure associated with it will be more important in their effects.

Between 1990 and 2010 the number of children under 15 is forecast to remain about the same (fewer infants but more older children), and the number of teenagers (15-19), which has recently been falling sharply, is forecast to fall a little further, but then return to slightly above the present level by 2010.

The number of young adults (20-34), which rose by 2 million between 1970 and 1990, is forecast to fall by 2.4 million (nearly one-fifth) between 1990 and 2010. This decline will be rather more than offset by an increase in numbers in the 35-59 age groups, and there will also be an increase of 0.6 million people in the 60-64 age group.

The number of older people in the 65-79 age groups is not forecast to change greatly, but there are expected to be increases of over 100,000 (9%) in the number of very old people aged 80-84 and of nearly half a million (52%) in the number aged 85 and over.

Dependency Ratio

The number of people in the most active working age groups (20-59) is forecast to rise by only about half a million, while the number under 20 is forecast to rise by 0.7 million and those over 60 by 1.3 million. Consequently the share of the total population accounted for by those in the most active working age groups will fall from 53.4% of the total in 1990 to 52.1% in 2010.

This will be an adverse shift in the sense that it means an increase of 5% in the numbers in the dependent age groups for every 100 people in the most active working age groups, and therefore implies that the latter will have to contribute more of their earnings than otherwise to support the others, or that pensions will need to be lower than otherwise, or that more people will need to carry on working over the age of 60 for longer.

However, it should be noted that in 2010 the dependency ratio will still be more favourable than in 1970, when only 50.6% of the population was in the 20-59 age groups.

Fewer Young Adults, More Old People

The decline in the number of young adults will mean fewer young single people with income available for fashion goods, entertainment and other discretionary expenditure, and with potential mobility in employment, and also fewer people setting up home and starting families.

The increase in the number of older people will also have implications. In 1990 there were 10.5 million people above the present national insurance retirement age (65 for men and 60 for women), and the number will not increase greatly by 2010; but by 2030 the number will have increased by nearly 40% to about 14.5 million, and the consequent problems for national insurance contribution levels, pension levels and retirement ages will need to be addressed well before then.

The increase in the number of very old people over 80 will give rise to problems far sooner. When people get very old their health tends to deteriorate and the cost of providing health care increases sharply - people over 85 cost the National Health Service, on average, more than 13 times as much as people aged 5-64; the increase in numbers of very old people may therefore be expected to result in higher demands on public health expenditure.

Also, very old people, even when in good health, often need help from other people to look after them. Traditionally, this care has most often been provided by families and friends, particularly daughters. However, with better job opportunities and different attitudes from the generation before, it is likely that fewer women will in the future be prepared to look after their ageing relatives than before. So increasing numbers needing care, and fewer numbers prepared to provide it informally, is likely to place increasing burdens on residential institutions and other public services providing care for old people.

Changing Family Patterns

In addition to changes in population age structure there will also be changes in household structures and family patterns. Britain has the second highest marriage rate in the European Community, but also the second highest divorce rate. The number of divorces has risen six fold since 1961 and it has been calculated that four out of ten marriages in 1987 are likely to end in divorce. However, most divorced people remarry and in 1989 in one-third of all marriages one or both partners had previously divorced.

Cohabiting before marriage has become more common, with 50% of women marrying in 1987 having previously cohabited with their future husbands. Births outside marriage have risen from 5% of the total in 1960 to 28% in 1990, and the number of abortions for single women has risen from 44,000 in 1971 to 116,000 in 1990. With more divorces and separations and more births outside marriage, the number of lone parent families has risen and the proportion of all children who are in lone parent families has gone up from 8% in 1972 to 15% in 1990.

It can be calculated that, if recent trends continued, by 2010 most couples would cohabit before marriage; the majority of marriages would end in divorce, followed by remarriage; and all births would be outside marriage. However, it is most unlikely that all these trends will continue indefinitely - the rise in divorces appears already to be levelling off. Also, the changes do not necessarily mean the breakdown of all responsible relationships - for example, the great majority of the increase in births outside marriage were registered by both parents at the same address, implying a joint home for the child even without marriage, and lone parenthood is most commonly a temporary condition following separation or divorce, followed later by remarriage and renewal of two-parent status.

What has been happening is changes in attitudes and relationships following a more permissive view of premarital sex, improved contraception and availability of abortion and, in particular, greater equality and independence of women leading to aspirations towards a more *symmetrical* style of marriage with both partners working and more shared activities and interests than in a *traditional* marriage, with fixed and separate roles. It appears that this aim for marriage is more demanding and more often leads to breakdown and an attempt to start again with someone else. The result has been that the previous norm of lifetime unions is being superseded by a more varied pattern, with many partnerships lasting less than a lifetime. The new pattern of greater diversity and change implies a need to modify arrangements for housing, education, child care and social security which were designed on the assumption that the traditional life long nuclear family was the form that embraced the overwhelming majority.

SECTION 2: ENVIRONMENTAL PROBLEMS

One of the characteristics of the past decade in Britain has been increasingly widespread concern over a very broad range of environmental issues. There is often a lag between public awareness of a problem and willingness to accept the costs or restrictions on freedom of action involved in dealing with it; and a further lag between acceptance of the need for action and putting into place the arrangements for giving effect to it. Even so, there seems little doubt that stronger environmental concern will be an important shaping factor in Britain over the coming two decades and give rise to new kinds of policy measures to deal with a wide range of interlocking problems.

Countryside

One area which has been attracting increasing attention is the preservation of the countryside, both the habitats of endangered species and the natural beauty which attracts deeply-held affection.

Although the size of the expected increase in the total population of Britain is not seen as presenting a serious problem, there are a number of problems associated with its spatial distribution. England is already the most densely populated country in Western Europe, and over a number of years problems of congestion in some areas have been increased by a tendency for people to move towards the South-Eastern parts of the country, with population increases of more than 30% expected in the last 15 years of this century in the six most popular counties.

At the same time there has been a movement of people out of the bigger cities into small towns and country areas, sometimes following jobs which have moved away from the more congested and expensive centres, sometimes seeking better living conditions in rural areas, either for long-distance commuting to existing jobs, or for retirement, or for one followed by the other. This population movement has been accompanied by more intensive agricultural practices, which have brought higher output, but also involved the destruction of hedgerows and woodlands and brought water pollution from excessive use of chemicals.   At the same time rising prosperity and increasing leisure have brought an increase in car-based tourism and outdoor recreational activities.   The result of these developments has been to push up house prices, bring traffic congestion to rural areas and change the physical appearance of the countryside.

In the next two decades it seems likely that further increases in affluence will result in more people wanting to live in rural areas and more people wanting to spend their leisure time in the countryside, leading to increased pressures on space.   At the same time, changed agricultural policies, with emphasis on *set-aside* and promotion of tourism, will release more land for development.   Hence there are likely to be difficult policy problems because of shortage of building land for houses in the crowded urban areas and the inherent difficulty that the kinds of development which make country areas more accessible to enjoy tend also to bring in large numbers of people and destroy the peace and beauty which attracted people to them in the first place.

Towns and Traffic

There have also been increasing environmental problems in the towns, particularly London and the major conurbations.   Industry has for a long time been moving out of congested inner city areas to more spacious sites in the suburbs and, more recently, to small country towns and to new estates outside the towns.   Offices, too, have increasingly been moving out to suburban and new *park* sites.   And shopping, too, has been moving away from the city centres to new hypermarkets on the periphery of towns and to great new regional shopping and recreation centres on greenfield sites serving sub-regional catchment areas.   All three developments have in common the characteristic that the new locations are not served well, if at all, by public transport, and access is by car.

At the same time there has been a sustained expansion in car ownership and use.   In 1951 six households in seven had no car; now only one in three has no car, and one household in five has two or more cars.   In the course of two decades the total number of cars has increased by three-quarters and so has the average annual car mileage per person.   Total annual car mileage doubled between 1960 and 1970 and doubled again between 1970 and 1990; and it is forecast by the Department of Transport to grow by a further 45-76% by 2010.   On average, people now travel about 10,000 km a year by car, more than twelve times as far as they travel by rail or by bus and coach.   Cars account for more than five-sixths of all household expenditure on transport and more than one-eighth of total household expenditure.

However, the dispersal of the cities has resulted in the decline of many existing city centres and the older inner residential areas around them; and the increase in car traffic has led to increasingly serious congestion. In London, for instance, despite a succession of road improvement and traffic management schemes, traffic congestion has spread over wider areas and longer hours and average speeds have dropped to barely 19 km an hour - only 6 km an hour more than with horses and carriages a century ago. This has delayed ambulances and fire engines, extended passenger journey times, and increased stress, fuel costs, air pollution and generation of greenhouse gases.

The private car is a means of freedom and symbol of affluence of sufficient power to make politicians most reluctant to contemplate restraint of car use in pursuit of environmental policy goals. However, the growing congestion in British towns and cities, the contribution of car emissions to acid rain and the greenhouse effect, and the growing resistance to new road projects all point to increasing pressures for changes in policy.

It seems increasingly likely that in the coming two decades there will be a reversal of past policies, with the emphasis in future placed on:

-    Renewal of city centres and restrictions on development of out-of-town facilities.
-    Improvement of public transport systems and introduction of cheaper fares (at present fares in London are the highest in Europe and double the average in European Community capitals).
-    Withdrawal of remaining tax subsidies on company cars (which in recent years have cost six times as much as the subsidies to British Rail).
-    Raising the tax on petrol, introduction of charges for use of city road space and more priority bus lanes.
-    Establishment of more traffic-free precincts and facilities for pedestrians and cyclists.

Water and Waste

In recent years there have been increasing problems of contamination of groundwater, rivers and coastal waters and beaches. Groundwater has been polluted by leaching through the soil of nitrates from excessive use of fertilizers and from spillage of animal slurry and liquor from silage, and also from toxic chemicals through careless use of pesticides, herbicides and industrial solvents.   Drinking water has also been contaminated by carcinogens shed from coal tar linings in water mains, and from lead from the domestic water pipes in older houses.   There have also been problems from discharge of industrial chemicals and untreated sewage into rivers and coastal waters, and concerns over disposal of toxic and hazardous solid waste and storage of nuclear waste.

These problems have already led to many failures to meet standards, adverse reports, and prosecutions.   Over the coming two decades these problems may be expected to lead to major investments in water and sewage treatment plants, tighter restrictions on use of farm chemicals, and closer control over the disposal of toxic and hazardous solid wastes.

Energy, Air Pollution and Greenhouse Gases

Increasing car traffic has resulted in increasing emissions of nitrous oxides and sulphur dioxide (which cause smog, ozone depletion and acid rain), hydrocarbons (which can be carcinogenic), lead (which can cause brain damage), and carbon monoxide (which is toxic in confined spaces.)   The introduction of a small tax differential lifted the sales of unleaded petrol from under 5% of the total in March 1989 to 40% in May 1991; and the requirement for all new cars made after October 1990 to be capable of using unleaded petrol and for all those from 1993 to be fitted with catalytic converters, suggest that the lead problem will be largely dealt with in a few years' time and the larger problem of nitrous oxides from vehicles will be greatly reduced over a rather longer period.

Coal and oil-fuelled power stations are the largest source of sulphur dioxide emissions, and the second largest source (after vehicles) of nitrous oxides.   Plans have been made to fit desulphurization plants to clean up the emissions from some of the largest power stations in order to meet internationally agreed targets for reducing flue gas emissions.   However, the equipment is extremely expensive and the newly privatized power companies are hoping to reduce the cost of meeting the targets by increasing their use of imported coal (which is cheaper and has a lower sulphur content) and building new power stations fuelled by natural gas (which is cleaner.)   But higher imports would further weaken the balance of overseas payments, and both proposals would involve speeding up the already rapid decline of the domestic coal industry, bringing social costs and incurring higher unemployment payments for the government, so it is likely that the power companies will have to rely mainly on the installation of cleaning equipment.

A much bigger problem is the response to global warming. The announcement of a conditional target of reducing carbon dioxide emissions to 1990 levels by 2005 has not yet been followed by the introduction of policies to ensure that even this modest target is met - indeed, expenditure on energy saving has been falling and energy saving equipment continues to be subject to VAT, while sales of gas and electricity are exempt from it. Despite recession and depressed industrial output Britain's carbon dioxide and sulphur emissions rose further in 1991.

However, with growing domestic and international pressure, it is likely that policies will change in the coming years, with taxes, subsidies, investment, research, regulations and information to promote the development of new energy sources and encourage greater economy in energy use. In the medium term there is likely to be a substantial shift from coal and petroleum to natural gas for power and heat generation, and in the longer term an expansion of non-fossil fuel-based energy sources. Further development of nuclear power is unlikely, partly because of safety concerns and partly because in Britain nuclear power has involved very high capital construction costs and produced power twice as expensive as other sources. However, Britain has particularly large potential for wave power and also opportunities for wind and tidal power, and it is likely that renewables (development of which was halted in the past ten years) will become much more important by 2010.

It must be remembered, however, that at present nuclear power accounts for only about 17% of electricity in Britain and electricity accounts for less than one-third of primary energy consumption. It follows, therefore, that even if there is a considerable expansion in energy *generation* from non-fossil fuel sources, the main weight of measures to reduce carbon dioxide emissions will need to fall on reducing energy *consumption*. Fortunately, there is considerable scope for this, for example: in better insulation of buildings and refrigerators, more efficient boilers, more economical lighting systems, lean-burn engines in vehicles, shifts to rail and water transport, and more recycling of waste materials. There is also scope for changes in behaviour patterns which have the effect of using less energy, for example: more use of walking and cycling instead of cars, more use of telecommunications instead of mail or personal travel, more home-working and living nearer to jobs, and more home entertainment and active leisure activities in place of car-based recreations.

Policy Implications

There are a number of policy implications which stand out from the various environmental issues that are emerging. The first is that there is growing public concern over a wide range of issues, from localized pollution to international problems such as ozone depletion and global warming; and this coupled with gradually increasing willingness to pay the costs of achieving better environmental quality.

The second is that environmental aspects involve externalities which are not dealt with automatically by the free play of market forces. The issues are complex and interdependent and not likely to be addressed satisfactorily without the introduction of new kinds of government policies, properly co-ordinated - a reversal, in this area, of the trend of the past decade towards diminishing government intervention.

Third, while some of what is needed will involve costs, many of the changes will be economically worthwhile on their own account - for example measures to economize on energy use will often show a high economic return.   Specifically, studies have shown that the changes necessary to achieve current carbon dioxide reduction targets will involve major shifts but probably not any significant overall reduction in economic growth. In Britain, this would probably apply even if the changes were made unilaterally, since the loss of export earnings from energy-intensive products would be offset by higher earnings from exports of North Sea oil to countries not making similar cuts in energy use.

But fourth, while the changes needed to meet current global warming targets should be relatively easy to achieve in the coming decade or two, thereafter the IPCC's recommendation of much greater cuts needed eventually implies much more radical and difficult changes in the longer term.

SECTION 3: USE OF NEW TECHNOLOGIES

The consequences would be very far-reaching if there were major *breakthroughs* in fields such as superconductivity at ambient temperatures, energy from nuclear fusion, voice recognition systems, or computers with human characteristics. But such breakthroughs are very unlikely in the course of the next two decades.

What *will* be a very important shaping factor is the *cumulative* effects of a wide range of *incremental* developments in a number of different technologies - particularly the core enabling ones: information technology, biotechnology and new materials. Their impact will of course depend on the extent to which their potential is actually exploited in the many different possible areas of application.

Information Technology

Advances in microchip technology have been doubling the power of chips every two years. For example, the power of microprocessor chips has increased from 29,000 transistors in *Intel's* 1979 *8088* chip, to more than 1 million in current models and more than 50 million expected by 2000. Similarly with memory chips, capacity has increased from 0.25 megabits in 1985 to 64 megabit chips planned to be in production very soon. New production technologies and the use of new materials such as gallium arsenide promise even greater increases in power in the future.

There are also important developments which are increasing the effective power of chips: RISC (Reduced Instruction Set) chips which make more economical use of a chip's power; ASIC (Applied Specific Integrated Circuit) chips which can be tailor-made for specific applications without undue extra cost; transputer chips which contain their own processors and memories; and self-testing chips which remove the need for expensive testing of complex chips on the assembly line. There is also the possibility, although probably not until after 2010, of more power still by using opto-electronic (light operated) switches, superconducting materials, or organic materials.

The spectacular improvements in chip performance have made possible corresponding improvements in the performance of computers. They have become smaller, lighter, more versatile much more powerful - and very much cheaper. In parallel with improvements in microprocessors there have been improvements in design (for example the use of parallel processing), in storage (digital paper, optical compact disks and memory chips) and in displays. There have also been great advances in software, with programs for an increasingly wide range of applications. Further development is likely to concentrate on devising *expert systems* for suitable areas of application and on making systems easier to use without lengthy training. Considerable efforts are also likely to go into techniques for voice recognition, machine translation and systems to enable robots to perform in a more human way; but because of the complex problems involved it is doubtful whether any of these technologies will reach a state where they have much impact by 2010.

There will be continuing major advances in telecommunications, with the adoption of *Open Systems* standards for universal compatibility and the conversion of the public telephone system to ISDN (Integrated Services Digital Network) which will provide improved transmission facilities for computer data, fax, text and pictures as well as telephone calls. And existing telecommunications systems will be enhanced or supplemented by use of fibre optic cable for higher carrying capacity to make possible a wider range of services, use of data compression techniques to improve the effective capacity of existing cables, use of direct broadcasting by satellite and microwave systems to distribute additional television channels, and use of cellular radio and zone phones to extend the use of the telephone system.

Other New Technologies

While information technology will continue to be the most widely pervasive, important developments are likely also in a number of other technologies.

Biotechnology

Biotechnology is a cluster of technologies based on developments in microbiology, biochemistry, genetics and fermentation technology. It includes genetic engineering, enzyme technology and a number of processing technologies in which important developments are likely in the course of the coming two decades. Many of the potential applications involve ethical problems and arouse public anxieties which mean that regulatory and legal constraints have to be surmounted as well as complex scientific and technical problems. Accordingly, there is much uncertainty about the likely extent of future advances and of the impact of applications.

New materials

Further developments in new materials promise scope for applications in many different areas. For example, new ceramics have properties of lightness, hardness, stiffness, compression strength, thermal stability, electrical resistance and corrosion resistance which are of value in engines and electrical equipment. New engineering plastics and polymers, reinforced by carbon fibres, combine strength with lightness. New kinds of laminated wood are three times as strong as ordinary timber. And there are new alloys and special steels which have useful engineering applications. Work is also proceeding on *functionally gradient* materials which change their composition and properties between one surface and the other.

Superconductors

Some substances have the property of conducting electricity without resistance - but only at very low temperatures. There will be important applications if the phenomenon can be produced at less low temperatures, and even more important ones if it can be produced at ambient temperatures. The application that is likely to come first (although probably not until after 2010) is in super-fast computers (where small size makes cooling less of a problem.) Another potential development is in magnetic levitation for frictionless movement by high-speed trains. The most dramatic (but also probably very remote) development is its use to cut electric power costs with more efficient generators, loss-free transmission and high density storage to reduce peak generating capacity needs.

Energy

Important developments are likely in improving the efficiency of gas and other fossil fuel power stations, and of nuclear power stations, and also in improving the economics of renewable energy sources such as waves, tides, wind, solar, biomass and geothermal. There are also likely to be important advances in the technologies involved in the use of energy, for example in improving efficiency of insulation, lighting, electric motors and vehicle engines. However, fast breeder nuclear reactors and nuclear fusion reactors are still at an early stage of development and are not likely to be commercially viable by 2010.

Applications

Important applications of the new technologies are likely in a very wide range of areas of activity.

Agriculture

Information technology will be more widely used in farm management, but biotechnology is likely to be the technology with the most important uses, with new biological pesticides and fungicides, new vaccines and animal care products, hormones to get faster livestock growth, and genetic engineering to produce new varieties of plants and livestock with more commercially valuable combinations of properties.

Manufacturing

The use of microelectronics in products and processes in manufacturing industry increased in a single decade from under 5% of factories in Britain in 1977 to 63% in 1987 - a much faster rate of diffusion than previous new technologies and a much wider spread across industry sectors than other current new technologies such as new materials (11% of all factories in 1987) or biotechnology (3%).

There has also been increasing use of various kinds of automation: CAD (Computer Aided Design), automated storage and transport, quality control and inspection systems, robotics, CIM (Computer Integrated Manufacturing) and FMS (Flexible Manufacturing Systems.) They have been found worthwhile and profitable, increasing productivity, reducing costs, improving quality, increasing flexibility of operation, and expanding sales. There is no doubt that new technology will be used further to extend automation in the future.

Use of new materials will also be of growing importance in some industries such as vehicles, aircraft and sports goods. Biotechnology will also have increasing applications in some industries, particularly food, drinks, pharmaceuticals and agricultural chemicals.

Offices

In the past two decades there has been increasingly widespread adoption of IT equipment and systems in offices: copiers, personal computers, laptop computers, work stations, word processors, desktop publishing, electronic mail, fax, automated telephone exchanges and cellular phones.

Increasing use has been associated with the increasing performance, versatility and reliability of the equipment available, and with the steep fall in costs. Future developments in technology seem sure to result in considerable further improvements in performance and falls in costs, and hence in a steadily extending range of applications. However, the arrival of the all-electronic, paperless office does not seem near - so far the new systems appear to have resulted in the use of *more* paper, not less.

Shops, banks

The financial sector is already one of the most IT-intensive in Britain, with electronic data exchange, document storage and automatic teller systems, and there is considerable use of computer-based systems in insurance, estate agency and financial, tax and legal services also. Shops are increasingly using computer-based systems for sales monitoring and stock management and bar code scanners for faster check-outs. EFT/POS (Electronic Funds Transfer at the Point of Sale), after many false starts, is now becoming more widely used.

Substantial investment is planned to increase use of all these kinds of automation, and there is the possibility of other applications for new technologies. Smart cards (credit-card sized pieces of plastic with microchips embedded in them) or laser cards (working on the same principle as compact disks), which can hold and process large amounts of information in a very small space may come into increasing use for holding personal financial records and handling a wide range of transactions, and also for keeping a variety of personal, household, professional and business information.

Home banking may be more widely used, and also home shopping, although the former will be limited by its inability to deliver cash to the home and the latter by its inability to deliver goods.

Despite all these innovations, it is likely that cash will still be used for the great majority of small purchases.

Health

There are many important applications for new technologies in health care: computer-based systems for hospital management, medical statistics, and patients' records in general practice; expert systems to help in diagnosis; use of genetic engineering in new drugs and in techniques for diagnosing or treating genetic disorders; use of lasers in eye surgery and dental treatment; and use of fibre optics, magnetic, acoustic and computer technologies for a range of diagnostic and high-tech surgery systems.

Environment

New technologies will have a range of important applications in environmental protection and improvement, for example: waste recycling, pollution monitoring, energy efficiency, gas emission control and climate change research. There are also likely to be environmentally motivated applications in transport, for example in vehicle engine design, traffic control and new transport systems. Of particular importance will be the development of new sources of vehicle fuel to replace petrol and diesel oil. Ethanol and methanol fuels and hybrid petroleum/electric vehicles may be in limited use in the early 2000s, but vehicles powered by hydrogen seem unlikely to be available until later.

Domestic

Many, perhaps most, homes are likely to be equipped by 2010 with substantially extended information and entertainment facilities, including HDTV (High Definition Television), and many other microelectronically controlled products, but it is unlikely that more than a minority of enthusiasts will go to the trouble and expense of installing fully integrated computer systems controlling security, heating, and a full range of appliances.

Teleworking from home, at least for part of the working week, will become more common in the limited range of occupations for which it is practicable, but domestic robots to do all the housework are likely to remain an unrealized dream - the unpredictable circumstances of most homes make them one of the most difficult of all environments to program for safe and efficient operation of robots.

Factors in Adoption

The important thing about new technologies is that they are only of value if they not only have a practical application, but if they are actually adopted. For this, new applications must be capable of being produced on a commercial scale, must serve a useful function, and must do it better than alternatives and at a cost which is competitive. Beyond that, some applications must get past other specific constraints. In industry adoption depends on firms having enough people with the right specialist expertise to use them and enough financial resources to develop the applications and install them - both often serious constraints in smaller enterprises. In offices adoption also depends on the availability of suitable skills and funding - although these are becoming less of a constraint as equipment gets cheaper and easier to use. In food and agriculture there are constraints on some applications arising from public concerns over safe food, maltreatment of animals and environmental damage. In medicine there are sometimes ethical or legal difficulties, particularly in the use of genetic engineering techniques. In medicine, education and social services there are often constraints imposed by costs - for example the expense of new drugs or high-tech surgery. All these considerations will tend to slow down the pace of adoption of new technologies and reduce their impact - although not sufficiently to prevent the cumulative effect of two decades of incremental developments being very considerable.

A further factor underlying the pace of adoption is the institutional, social and technical infrastructure. Britain has a reputation for being very strong in invention, but very weak in exploitation, and it is frequently argued that this may be connected with the scale and direction of R&D. Total government expenditure on R&D is a smaller percentage of GDP in Britain than in Germany, France or the United States (although higher than in Japan). Almost half of it goes on defence, compared with a third in France, an eighth in Germany and less in Japan and most other industrial countries (except the United States.); and only 9% of it goes on industry - far less than in most other industrial countries. And R&D spending by industry itself represents a far lower percentage of GDP than in Germany and Japan.

At the same time, higher education and training in most of the new technologies is generally reckoned to be behind most other comparable countries; engineers and scientists are less well paid, relative to people with a financial background, than in other countries, and less often promoted to top positions; and the ablest students tend to seek courses in arts rather than sciences and careers in the professions rather than in industry.

Finally, in some areas the pace of adoption has been slowed down by lack of investment in technical infrastructure - for example, wider spread of home informatics has been impeded by the slow spread of broad band cable networks and the exploitation of renewable energy resources has been held up by lack of basic development work.

The deficit in trade in electronics has worsened from 400 mECUs in 1980 to more than 3,500 mECUs in 1988. There are accordingly grounds for concern that, unless higher priority is given to exploiting new technologies, Britain may not get the full potential benefit from them in the coming two decades.

SECTION 4: CHANGING EMPLOYMENT PATTERNS

The main shaping factors which will determine the prospects of achieving future full employment with good jobs and rising incomes are: demographic changes affecting the size of the potential future labour force; changes in occupational patterns and future skills needs; changes in the labour market and their effects on wage inflation; and the form and speed of economic growth and its effects on future job creation.

Employment and Unemployment

The most striking change in the pattern of employment over the past two decades has been the growth in unemployment, which has risen from 1-2% in the early post-war years to an average of 10% in the 1980s and heading for this figure again. Whereas previously the number unemployed was no greater than the number of unfilled job vacancies, currently it is more than 14 times as great. The total number unemployed rose to a peak of more than 3 million in 1986 and, after falling back in later years, is rising towards 3 million again in the current recession; and the numbers would be higher still were it not that the method of counting has been changed more than 30 times in the past few years.

The social costs of a return to pre-war levels of unemployment is high, not least because the basic level of national insurance unemployment benefit is little more than a quarter of previous earnings, compared with more than 50% in most other countries in Western Europe. The cost to the government is considerable, with each extra million unemployed costing an extra 3.7 bn ECUs a year in benefits and a further 7.9 bn ECUs a year in lost tax and national insurance receipts and increased administrative costs. The cost to the economy as a whole in lost output is much greater still.

This damaging increase in unemployment can be explained in terms of a number of interconnected causes: demographic changes have increased the potential labour force seeking work; slow economic growth has not created many additional jobs (in the current recession and the one in the early 1980s one-third of jobs in manufacturing were lost, and increased employment in the service sector has only marginally more than offset this); and slow economic growth has been partly the result of macroeconomic policies which in turn have been partly conditioned by deficiencies in the working of the labour market and in the provision of education and training for skills.

Future Labour Force

As a result of demographic change the total population in the most active age groups (20-59) is expected between 1990 and 2010 to rise by only about half a million, with a decline in the younger age groups more than offset by increases in the older ones. This compares with an increase of about 2 million in other age groups.

Activity rates for men in Britain are the highest in the countries of the European Community, and rates for women are the second highest after Denmark. Rates for married women have risen until they are almost as high as for non-married women. It seems unlikely that there will be substantial further increases in age-specific rates for either men or women, and this will limit the size of the likely increase in the potential labour force.

Changes in Occupations and Skills

Between 1951 and 1971, non-manual jobs rose from one-quarter to nearly one-third of total employment in Britain and they have since increased further. There seems to be a tendency in all advanced industrial countries for the share of non-manual jobs to rise to between one-third and one-half of the total.

Also, within non-manual employment, there has been a tendency for an increasing proportion to be in the higher-level occupations - professional, scientific, technical, managerial, administrative and entrepreneurial. And within the manual occupations, there has been a shift from the unskilled to the skilled. And at all levels there has been a tendency towards increasing quality requirements, with a steady rise both in the formal qualifications and the general knowledge and abilities expected.

At the same time, *unemployment* has been increasingly concentrated in the groups without the required skills. Youth unemployment in Britain has been mainly among school leavers with low educational qualifications, or none at all; and, once unemployed, those with the least qualifications have had most difficulty in getting back to work. The most authoritative forecasts of occupational changes in the 1990s and after suggest a strong continuing increase in the numbers in scientific, engineering, technical, managerial, entrepreneurial and professional occupations; smaller increase in office and personal services and in skilled manual occupations; but continuing decline in the numbers of manual and low-skilled jobs.

These changes will be driven by a number of powerful forces:

Technology

The increasing importance of making effective use of new technologies is putting an increasing premium on people with the special skills to use them.   For example, surveys have shown that lack of people with specialist new technology expertise has been the most important single factor impeding the use of microelectronics in British industry, and that use of microelectronics resulted in losses of unskilled jobs, but *increases* in skilled manual and white-collar ones.

Quality

Rising competition in industrial markets has led to an increasing emphasis on product and process quality, and to greater use of new technology and higher grade labour for achieving it.   Similarly, in construction and much of the service sector there has been a tendency to move up-market with greater emphasis on quality of service and greater need for people with higher skills and qualifications to provide it.

Single European Market

The establishment of the Single European Market, together with the increasing integration of the global economy, will lead to intensified competition and the need for higher quality standards and effective use of new technologies for success - again implying greater reliance on more highly trained people.

Structural change

The structure of the economy has been changing, with the greatest sectoral increases in business and professional services. These increases are expected to continue in the future, giving rise to increasing requirements for more highly qualified people.

A key factor in future employment changes will be the extent to which skill levels can be improved to meet the higher requirements expected. At present, managers in Britain tend to be less qualified than in other countries; the number of engineers trained is far less than in other leading countries; and natural scientists tend to be used disproportionately in the defence industries.

Even more important than the supply of graduates is the level of education and training achieved by the rest of the population. Only about half of young people stay in education or full-time vocational training after the minimum school leaving age of 16. This is less than in Spain, Italy and Germany and compares with more than 75% in France, Belgium and Denmark, and more than 90% in the Netherlands, Sweden, Canada, the United States and Japan.

Improvements in the numbers staying in education and training, and in the numbers going on to higher and further education, and also an expansion of retraining for older workers, will be essential for avoiding increasing numbers of people becoming unemployed for lack of the necessary skills. This need has long been identified, but not remedied by effective action to increase private sector investment in training or improve staying-on rates in education; it seems likely that in the course of the next two decades, however, some of the necessary changes will be undertaken.

Changes in the Labour Market

A further factor in employment prospects is the operation of the labour market. Some countries (for example Austria and the Nordic countries) have established central regulating and planning mechanisms which achieve a useful degree of cooperation between government, business and trade unions to keep wage increases broadly within what can be afforded as a result of productivity increases. In some countries (for example Japan, Switzerland and the United States) there is less unionization and less government intervention, but wages tend to be kept within the limits of what can be afforded through the operation of free market forces. But a third group of countries, which includes Britain, are in an intermediate position, without the central regulation of the first group or the flexibility of the second group.

The consequence has been that wage increases have frequently tended to exceed productivity increases, pushing up costs and prices and reducing international competitiveness. Earlier attempts to introduce statutory incomes policies, after a while, broke down. More recently, legal changes, together with high unemployment, have weakened the trade unions and greatly reduced the number of strikes. However, they have not stopped the tendency for wages to rise faster than productivity, particularly for the more skilled groups of workers.

In the past this has led to higher inflation than in some competing countries, and this in turn resulted in depreciation of the foreign exchange rate. However, the Government's previous aim of keeping sterling within fixed bands, following entry into the Exchange Rate Mechanism, and, even more, the adoption of a single European currency envisaged later, will mean that this option is no longer available. Hence it will be imperative for wage inflation to be ended, or at least brought down to average Community levels, in order to avoid chronic depression and associated high levels of unemployment.

There are some signs that wage claims are being moderated, although it is too early to know whether this will continue after the current recession is ended, or whether structural changes will be undertaken in the coming years to enable the labour market to operate in a less inflationary way.

Economic Growth

For a combination of reasons (considered in the next section) economic growth in Britain is not expected to be very rapid over the coming two decades, and this will tend to limit the total increase in jobs available, even if Britain's long-standing problems of inadequate investment in training and inflationary wage bargaining processes are satisfactorily addressed.

Future Employment

The balance of probability is that the combined effect of the shaping factors will result in the number of jobs available growing rather more rapidly than the number of people wanting jobs, and hence a tendency towards lower rates of unemployment than have been experienced recently.

Recent sectoral changes are likely to continue. Employment in agriculture and mining will continue to decline, and also employment in manufacturing (although higher productivity will bring substantial increases in output.) There will be further falls in the numbers employed in transport, and increases in communications. There will be increases in employment in services, particularly in business and professional services.

There will be continuing increases in the proportion of total employment accounted for by the higher-level occupations and continuing increases in skill levels and qualification requirements in almost all occupations and economic sectors. Unemployment, particularly long-term unemployment, will be concentrated even more than now among those with the least skills and qualifications.

SECTION 5: *MATURE* ECONOMY

Britain's economy has become 'mature' in the sense that over a long period its share of world output has been falling, it has performed poorly compared with other West European countries, and the rate of growth of GDP has been slow and tending to get slower still. There are serious underlying weaknesses, but also some actual and potential strengths. Average annual growth over the next two decades seems unlikely to exceed 2-2.5%, and this constraint will be an important shaping factor in relation to potential developments in many other areas.

Performance

Britain was the first country to have an industrial revolution, and was for a period the world's leading industrial economy. Since then, however, over a period of more than a hundred years, its position has been slipping, accounting year after year for a diminishing proportion of world output and trade. This was inevitable as other countries also industrialized. What has given cause for persistent concern is the way that over the past four decades the British economy has grown more slowly than others in Western Europe, giving rise to a decline in relative living standards, worsening trade balances and doubts about future prospects.

OECD figures show that, over the period 1960-73, GDP in the 'Group of Seven' countries rose by an average of 5.5% a year; but Britain's economy grew more slowly than any of the others, at little more than half the average rate. In the 1973-79 period, when the world economy was disrupted by the oil price rise shocks, the *Group of Seven* economies grew only half as fast; but again Britain's economy grew much more slowly than any of the others, at half the average rate. In the 1979-88 period Britain's economy performed somewhat better, but still grew more slowly than the average. Since then, however, there has been a recession in Britain which started earlier, went deeper and lasted longer than in most other industrial countries, and has turned out to be the longest and deepest since the Second World War, with GDP falling in five out of the six quarters since mid-1990.

The performance since 1979 is particularly disappointing, because in that year a new government introduced radical changes in economic policy which were intended to remedy long-standing structural weaknesses and secure significantly faster and sustained growth. While the initial effect was to produce a severe recession, in the mid-1980s growth rates were faster, averaging 4% a year between 1984 and 1988, and giving rise to claims that a British *economic miracle* had been achieved, with a breakthrough to permanently faster growth.

However, the rapid growth was based largely on an expansion of credit, which caused consumption to rise much faster than output and imports much faster than exports. It was therefore not sustainable, with the result that the growth in GDP fell from 4.7% in 1988 to -2.5% in 1991.

Altogether, over the whole period 1979-92, GDP growth averaged 1.7% a year. This was somewhat *better* than the average of 1.4% a year in the 1973-79 post-oil-shock period, but far *worse* than the average of 3.0% over the whole 1950-73 period. Moreover, there are many indications that important weaknesses remain to impede the achievement of better performance in the future.

Weaknesses

The poor economic performance in recent years would matter less if it had been associated with the laying of foundations for greater success in the future. Unfortunately, there are a number of ways in which the UK economy appears to have been getting, not stronger, but weaker.

Manufacturing output

Manufacturing output has risen by a total of only 6% over the 1979-92 period - less than in any other OECD country and only about one-sixth of the OECD average. Output is currently only about 3% above the level achieved in 1973.

Manufacturing investment

It is unlikely that the shakeout of two recessions has left industry *leaner and fitter*, because gross investment in manufacturing has been lower than in 1979 in 9 out of the 12 subsequent years; and in some years *net* investment has actually been negative at a time when other countries were increasing their investment in manufacturing. Over the whole period since 1979 average gross investment in manufacturing has been *less* than in either the 1974-79 or the 1960-74 periods.

New technology

Investment in non-military R&D to make best use of new technologies has also been below the levels of other countries.

Training

Investment in vocational education and training has continued to be inadequate, resulting in a labour force with lower levels of skills than in other countries Britain must compete with. It remains to be seen whether the setting up of local Training and Enterprise Councils led by senior business figures will improve this situation.

Productivity

Productivity in manufacturing has risen by more than 50% since 1979. This is a higher annual rate of increase than in 1973-79, but no better than the long-term average rate of increase between 1951 and 1973. And whereas in most other manufacturing countries higher productivity has been associated with higher output, in Britain the rise in productivity since 1979 has instead been associated with a drop of one-third in employment in manufacturing industry and a corresponding increase in the numbers unemployed. Higher productivity in manufacturing has not been matched by similar increases in other sectors and since 1979 annual increases in productivity per head for the economy as a whole have been substantially *less* than the long-term average between 1951 and 1979.

Unemployment

Unemployment rose from 1.2 million in 1979 to 3.3 million in 1986. It fell back to 1.7 million in 1990, but has since been rising steadily again and is expected to go above 3 million before starting to fall again. It continues to involve heavy economic cost in terms of government expenditure and loss of potential output.

Trade balance

Since 1970 the volume of imports has been rising three times as fast as the volume of exports, and the volume of imports of finished manufactures five times as fast. Trade in manufactures, which used to be in substantial surplus to pay for necessary imports of food and raw materials, has in recent years been in substantial deficit.

Oil

During the early 1980s the deterioration in trade in manufactures was more than offset by the sharp rise in earnings from North Sea oil. Later in the decade, however, oil prices fell and output declined a little, greatly reducing the net surplus.

Invisibles

Later in the 1980s the deficit in manufacturing was offset by rising net receipts from invisibles - in particular higher earnings from financial services and from increased overseas investments following removal of controls on financial movements in 1979.

However, net earnings from invisibles subsequently fell back by more than a half between 1986 and 1989, and have not recovered since.

Current balance

With the rising deficit in manufactures and the fall back in earnings from oil and invisibles, the overseas balance on current account went into record levels of deficit : -28 bn ECUs in 1989 and -21 bn ECUs in 1990. Even in the midst of the current recession, imports have been exceeding exports, bringing a current account deficit of 8 bn ECUs in 1991; and if recovery takes the form of a consumption-led boom higher deficits may be expected in future years.

Possible Explanations

Many explanations have been advanced for the generally poor performance of the UK economy. Among the recent ones have been criticisms of the Government for maintaining too high an exchange rate for sterling, making exports difficult to sell and imports cheap to buy

- popular with consumers but damaging to industrial competitiveness - and requiring the maintenance of higher real interest rates than other countries in order to support sterling by attracting hot money to London (nearly 120 bn ECUs in 1991), again putting industry at a disadvantage. There have been criticisms of other government policies, such as inadequate encouragement for investment in manufacturing, concentration of R&D support on military applications, insufficient support for industrial training, and misjudgements of macroeconomic policy.

Likewise there have been criticisms of the economic policies of previous governments. Unfortunately, the record of each government's economic policies, in terms of growth of GDP, has been worse than that of the one before:

Period	Government	Average Annual % Growth in GDP
1951-1964	Conservative	3.0
1964-1970	Labour	2.7
1970-1974	Conservative	2.6
1974-1979	Labour	2.0
1979-1992	Conservative	1.7

Among other explanations offered for the relatively poor performance of Britain's economy have been: slowness in giving up the Empire and the Sterling Area; higher levels of defence spending than in most competitor countries; obstructive trade unions; incompetent management; class divisions; a capital market structure which forces industry to plan for short-term results; too much interference in the free working of the market; inadequate intervention to deal with externalities not provided for by the market; high taxes and public spending; neglect of the social and industrial infrastructure; an education system geared to arts and humanities rather than science and engineering; a culture encouraging bright people to go into the professions rather than industry; too many accountants and not enough engineers in industry; political institutions which are old-fashioned and adversarial, involving excessive secrecy, too little devolution and sharp changes in government policies; and a number of others.

There is some element of validity in most of these explanations, even those which appear to be in opposition to each other. The failure of successive governments to achieve lasting improvements in economic performance may be in part because the weaknesses are deep-seated and their causes complex. However, there are also a number of actual and potential strengths.

Strengths

Among the factors which may be expected to strengthen the British economy and improve its prospects are:

North Sea oil

North Sea oil and gas production has passed its peak and continued long-term decline must be expected. However, the experience in almost all other oilfields has been that the reserves eventually discovered turn out greatly to exceed the proved reserves in the early years of development; and the proportion of reserves which are commercially worth exploiting rises continually as techniques improve, particularly in areas like the North Sea where the technologies used are new and still being further developed. There is also the consideration that the marginal costs of further exploration and development are reduced by the availability of the platforms, pipelines and other facilities already constructed. And any future rises in price will further increase the reserves worth exploiting. Thus production is likely to decline gradually, not to fall sharply.

Earnings from North Sea oil and gas are far below their peak because of lower prices, but they are still considerable, amounting to more than 12 bn ECUs in 1991. While the net surplus has become relatively small, the saving in the cost of the imports that would otherwise be necessary is likely to remain an important advantage for the British economy well into the twenty-first century.

Renewables

Britain is exceptionally well endowed with potential wave-power energy sources, and also has a number of suitable sites for windpower and tidal energy schemes. It will take time for development work to improve the economics, and it will require considerable investment to exploit the potential. It is likely, however, that as North Sea oil declines, and concern to reduce greenhouse gas emissions increases, these so far untapped resources will prove to be an important asset.

Industry

While manufacturing in general has been in relative decline, there are still some strong sectors, and strong companies in weak sectors, which have good potential to expand in the future.

Inward investment

For a long time Britain has proved to be an attractive location for inward investment from a number of countries, particularly the United States, and, more recently Japan, which has seen manufacturing in Britain as a way of getting past obstacles to selling in the European Community - for example, 90% of the output of the new Nissan car plant is intended eventually for export to other countries in the European Community. This inward investment has gone some way to offset the inadequacies of indigenous industrial investment and, as well as providing jobs, exports and tax revenue, it has in some cases brought in new technologies and stimulated the diffusion of innovative management practices, notably in quality assurance. On the other hand, the intention of recently arrived Japanese companies to achieve a high percentage of local sourcing has not in the main been fulfilled, and in time it may be expected that there will be an increasing outflow of repatriated profits. Moreover, little product research, design and development capacity has come to Britain from Japanese inward investors. This may change as the Single European Market develops, but Britain's advantages as a location may in time be seen to be offset by disadvantages stemming from relative lack of investment in education, training, technology diffusion and infrastructure.

Financial services

Despite the end of the Empire and the Sterling Area, London is still a major world financial centre, and banking, insurance and other financial services, and also other business services such as advertising and management consultancy, provide an important source of overseas earnings. While London's position relative to other centres is far from secure, reflecting the pound's weakness relative to the Deutschmark and uncertainties about British commitment to an eventual single European currency, the City's financial services are likely to continue to make a useful contribution to overseas earnings.

Entertainment

Although experiencing relative decline in manufacturing, Britain has been more successful in television, film, popular music and other cultural, information and entertainment services which are becoming increasingly important in world trade.

Language

Britain has been a beneficiary of the fact that English is the first language of the United States, Canada and Australia, and is the first foreign language in Japan and many other countries, particularly in Western Europe. This advantage seems likely to be of continuing importance in the course of the next two decades. However, the spread of English as a second language in competitor countries, especially in Western Europe, may erode this advantage in terms of attracting inward investment from the United States and the Far East.

Forecasts

In view of past trends, current weaknesses and strengths, and likely developments in Britain, the European Community and elsewhere, it seems unrealistic to expect a dramatic improvement in Britain's economic performance over the coming two decades, but also reasonable not to expect a disastrous deterioration. The most likely outcome is of continued growth in the economy, but only at moderate rates - probably averaging about 2-2.5% a year.

However, even growth at this annual rate will result in a total increase of slightly more than 50% in GDP by 2010, with investment up by about a half, consumers' expenditure up by slightly less than a half, and government consumption up by about one-third. Imports may be expected to go up about twice as much as output, with a total increase of nearly 100% by 2010, and exports by about 120% to remove the present deficit and pay for the higher imports.

In the course of the two decades between 1990 and 2010, output is expected to increase (in real terms) in all the main sectors, but with particularly large increases in manufacturing, communications and business services. Within the manufacturing sector the most spectacular increase is expected again to be in the electronics industry, the output of which rose from 8 bn ECUs in 1970 (in terms of 1985 prices) to 28 bn ECUs in 1990, and is forecast to increase further to about 70 bn ECUs in 2010, when it will be the largest of all the manufacturing industries in terms of value of gross output. Other disproportionate increases in output are forecast in vehicles, paper and printing, and rubber and plastics.

Changes in the British economy may be expected as a result of reductions in defence expenditure and measures to reduce emissions of greenhouse gases. However, they are likely to be mainly changes in the distribution of growth rather than changes in the overall rate of growth.

SECTION 6: SOCIAL DIVISIONS

Widening gaps between higher and lower earnings, social benefits frozen in real terms and tax cuts favouring mostly the higher incomes, have greatly increased income inequalities in the 1980s.

This, together with persistent mass unemployment, is creating an *underclass* which is not sharing in the benefits of increasing national prosperity; if it continues it is likely to lead to increasingly serious social divisions and tension.

Earnings

Between 1886, when records were first kept, and 1979, wages and salaries rose greatly, but the differential between higher and lower earnings did not change much, with the bottom decile of earnings about 60-65% of the median in most years and the top decile about 140-150%. Between 1979 and 1991 the bottom decile of incomes rose by 24% and the top decile by 64%. It can be calculated that if the earnings of the top decile continued to increase at more than two and a half times the rate of the bottom decile, by 2010 the gap between them would be double what it was in 1979 and about double what it was in Victorian times.

Such a sharp widening of differentials over the course of only three decades would be more acceptable to the lower earners if it were a necessary part of an economic upsurge bringing a faster rise in even the lowest incomes than they would have got with slower growth and a more equal distribution. However, since 1979 economic growth has been *slower* than in earlier periods, so that low earners have not had the compensation of greater absolute increases in earnings for themselves, or the consolation of better performance for the economy as a whole, to make up for the widening of the gap. Hence if the combination of widening differentials and diminishing growth continues it may be expected to give rise to increasing opposition.

Social Benefits

Most social benefits used to be indexed to rise automatically in line with prices or average earnings, whichever was the greater, in order to ensure that those dependent on benefits were not only protected against inflation but also enabled to take their share of rising national prosperity. After 1979, however, most benefits were indexed only for inflation. This meant that their value was frozen in real terms, while earnings continued to rise. Consequently, year by year they have come to represent declining proportions of average earnings, and the gap between the (mostly poor) people dependent on social benefits and the (mostly less poor) people with earnings has widened. At the same time some benefits have been reduced - for example by replacement of grants by loans - and conditions of eligibility have been tightened - for example by removing young people from entitlement altogether. This has further widened the gap between earners and those dependent on benefits.

There have also been increasing problems with the operation of the social security system. Policy has had the dual aims of reducing the number of people in a *dependency culture* reliant on social benefits, and of cutting the cost of benefit payments, and has sought to achieve both aims by as far as possible *targeting* benefits on those considered to be in greatest need. However, this has given rise to three problems: first, because of the stigma and difficulties of making claims, many people have not taken the benefits they are entitled to; second, levels of benefit have been kept low so as to hold them below wage levels and leave people with an incentive to seek paid employment; and third, despite this, the loss of eligibility for benefits when people get work means that taking a job can cost them loss of benefits equivalent to most of their prospective earnings, so that they face a marginal rate of *tax* far higher than used to be faced by people on the very highest incomes.

Consequently, many people have been caught in a *poverty trap* from which it is difficult to escape to significantly higher living standards, and have remained permanently dependent on social benefits. If the trend towards a wider spread of earnings, with a relative fall at the bottom, were to continue, it would present an increasingly difficult policy dilemma: either benefits would have to be set at levels so low that those dependent on them would suffer great hardship and the health of children and elderly people would be put at risk; or else benefits would rise into the range of lower earnings, in which case many people would no longer derive any financial benefit from getting a job. Hence if the spread of earnings widened further it would increase the incompatibility between removing people from dependency on benefits and targeting benefits only on those in greatest need, and would increase pressures to abandon the targeting policy in favour of putting more emphasis on universally provided benefits which have no adverse effects on incentives to work or save.

Taxation

Changes in income tax have mostly taken the form of reductions in the standard rate, which benefits middle and upper incomes, and in the abolition of the top rates, which benefits only those on top incomes. The cost of tax reliefs on mortgages for houses, which do not help people on low incomes, has quadrupled since 1979, and changes in the taxation of capital gains and inheritance have favoured the wealthy. At the same time there have been increases in VAT, which tends to bear more heavily on below-average incomes, while the finance of local government by rates on property was for a period replaced by a flat rate poll tax. Thus while the total burden of taxation has increased slightly from 35.5% in 1979 to 36.7% in 1991, there has been a redistribution of its incidence which has been strikingly favourable to those on top incomes. The net effect of the changes has therefore been to widen the gap in after-tax incomes.

Income Distribution

The growing spread in earnings, the freezing of social benefit levels and the regressive effects of tax changes have together resulted in a marked widening of inequalities in incomes. Between 1979 and 1989 the average of all incomes grew by 23.7%; but while the average of the upper half of incomes increased by 26.9%, the average of the lower half increased by only 5.3%; and while the average of the top tenth of incomes increased by 43.8%, the average of the bottom tenth increased by only 2.0%. Thus over this period the upper half of incomes has been rising five times as fast as the lower half, and the top tenth of incomes 22 times as fast as the bottom tenth.

It can be calculated that, if this trend continued, between 1979 and 2010 the upper half of incomes would more than double, while the lower half of incomes would increase by only 17%; and the top tenth of incomes would more than treble, while the bottom tenth would increase by only 6%. Such an unprecedented widening of the spread of incomes would be likely to bring increasing social tensions and resistance. It is therefore unlikely that it will be allowed to happen.

One consequence of the widening inequality of incomes which has taken place already has been an increase in poverty, despite rising national prosperity. Between 1979 and 1987 the number of adults with incomes below half the national average has doubled, and so also has the number of children. One quarter of all children are now in households dependent on incomes below half the national average.

Social Divisions

The persistence of mass unemployment has been bringing large numbers of people into poverty over long periods. The means tested benefits which form the basis of the social security system have been locking increasingly many unemployed people into a *poverty trap*, making it difficult for them to get back into employment. The widening spread of incomes levels means that increasingly many people in employment are also in poverty because their very low incomes are insufficient for supporting their families. And the increasing number of lone parent families are mostly also in poverty because of the low level of benefits and the way the tax and benefit systems make it difficult to take up employment, even when suitable opportunities are available. Thus the combined effects of changes in society, developments in the labour market and the way the social security system works, are resulting in a steady rise in the numbers in poverty, despite improvements in the living standards of the rest of the population.

The increase in the numbers in poverty is particularly great with children - they are themselves among the main explanations for poverty. Thus there is the prospect of a cycle of deprivation, with parents who have fallen into poverty and face very circumscribed life prospects bringing up children in deprived conditions likely to result in their growing up into an adulthood of poverty also. In particular, their difficult family background will often impair their chances of doing well at school and acquiring the qualifications for good jobs, so that, like their parents, they in turn are more likely to become unemployed for lack of the necessary skills.

Thus there has been an increasing number of people living in poverty, overlapping with an increasing number of people dependent on state benefits, comprised disproportionately of long-term unemployed, ethnic minorities and residents of deprived inner city areas. There is the danger that this growing *underclass* will be subject to increasing hardship and deprivation, with a permanence extending to further generations, and that this will lead to increasing bitterness and alienation from the rest of the community - including a withdrawal from involvement in democratic political processes if these are seen as offering little hope of bringing an improvement in their life prospects.

At the same time there is the danger that the rest of the community, in their increasingly middle-class economic and social life, will come to resent the *underclass* on account of their diverging attitudes and behaviour and the mounting burden of social welfare benefits.

In these differences lie the prospect of widening social divisions and the possibility of tensions and conflict. They also imply a heavy economic cost, with a substantial part of the population making little contribution to output of goods and services.

While there can be no certainty about it, it may be hoped that awareness of the dangers will lead to the adoption of timely measures to avert them by reducing unemployment, checking the growth of income inequalities and modifying the basis of the benefits system.

CONCLUSIONS: CONVERGENCES AND DIVERGENCES OF OPINION ON POLICIES

In general, there is a fairly strong convergence of informed opinion about the importance of the UK-specific shaping factors and the nature of the problems they present, but a wide divergence of opinion both about the particular policy responses required by them and about the likelihood of their being adopted.

These differences tend to be largely along party political lines.

Ageing Population

There is general agreement about the facts of likely future population change and about the need for higher spending on health and care for the very old; also on the need for a review of pensions policies - but not on what changes should be adopted.

Family Pattern

There is a mixed reaction to recent changes in family patterns and a wide range of views on how far current trends will continue. There are also differences in policy response between those who accept the changes and want policies to provide for them, and those who hope to discourage further changes by *not* providing for them.

Environment

There is fairly general agreement that environmental issues are becoming increasingly important, and on some of the measures needed in response to them - for example, investment to improve standards of water supply, installation of flue gas cleaning plants, and use of catalytic converters on vehicle exhausts. However, with other policy measures, such as improvements in public transport, restrictions on car use, discouragement of out-of-town shopping centres, and the introduction of a carbon tax, there is far more disagreement on what needs to be done, how much of it, and how soon.

New Technologies

There is general agreement on the importance of using new technologies to best effect, but sharp differences of opinion on whether government intervention is needed in order to secure this and, if so, in what form, and how much.

Employment

There is universal dislike of the high level of unemployment and widespread recognition of the need for improvements in vocational education and training. However, there are crucial disagreements on the relative priority to be given to reducing unemployment as opposed to other policy objectives such as reducing inflation, and there are differing views on the best way to improve training and, in particular, on the need for government involvement.

Economy

There has for a long time been wide recognition that the performance of Britain's economy has been poor, and there is increasing recognition that this poor performance has continued even in recent years. There are, however, fundamental disagreements over the principal causes and, even more, over the merits and faults of particular government policies. Accordingly, there is no agreement on the policies best calculated to secure better performance in the future.

Social Divisions

The effects of widening gaps in earnings, frozen social benefits and tax cuts favouring upper incomes are widely noted in the outward signs of poverty visible on the streets. However, the full extent of the spread of inequality of incomes is not yet widely appreciated, and neither are the implications of growing social divisions. Accordingly, appropriate policy responses have not yet received much attention; when they do, there are likely to be sharp divergences of opinion.

Institutions

The importance of the changes in institutions made in the course of the past decade is not in dispute. However, there is the fiercest controversy, on party political lines, between those who approve of the changes and wish to see them extended, and those who disapprove of them and wish to see them halted or, as far as possible, reversed.

Constitution

Similarly there are sharp differences, also mainly on party lines, between those who see major constitutional changes as very important and are urgently concerned to bring them about, and those who see them as unimportant, unnecessary or undesirable and are concerned to prevent them being introduced.

Index